Napoleon Lajoie

Napoleon Lajoie

King of Ballplayers

David L. Fleitz

McFarland & Company, Inc., Publishers

Jefferson, North Carolina, and London

LIBRARY OF CONGRESS CATALOGUING-IN-PUBLICATION DATA

Fleitz, David L., 1955–
Napoleon Lajoie, king of ballplayers / David L. Fleitz.
p.   cm.
Includes bibliographical references and index.

ISBN 978-0-7864-6879-9

softcover : acid free paper ∞

1. Lajoie, Napoleon, 1874–1959.   2. Baseball players—
United States—Biography.   I. Title.
GV865.L29F54   2013   796.357092—dc23   [B]   2013022704

BRITISH LIBRARY CATALOGUING DATA ARE AVAILABLE

On the cover: Napolon Nap Lajoie posing with a silver dollar horseshoe
at Cleveland's League Park on June 4, 1912
(National Baseball Hall of Fame Library, Cooperstown, New York)

Manufactured in the United States of America

*McFarland & Company, Inc., Publishers
Box 611, Jefferson, North Carolina 28640
www.mcfarlandpub.com*

For Deborah

Table of Contents

Acknowledgments

I would like to thank a few people and organizations that helped make this book possible.

The availability of information on the Internet has boomed in recent years, especially as it relates to baseball. One can easily find individual statistics for all players dating back to the beginning of professional baseball in 1871, while a terrific website called Baseball Reference (http://www.baseball-reference.com) provides player game logs, box scores, and, for games of recent decades, play by play descriptions. Sean Forman and his team deserve a great deal of credit for developing this constantly expanding trove of information, and this book would have been much more difficult to write without it. Project Retrosheet (http:/www.retrosheet.org) is also full of useful information and is highly recommended as well.

Other helpful websites display digitized, searchable copies of newspaper and magazine pages, saving the researcher from hours of poring through microfilm. One is called Paper of Record, a historical newspaper search engine that features images of *The Sporting News* beginning with its inaugural issue in 1886. The Brooklyn Public Library has digitized the *Brooklyn Eagle* from the years 1841 to 1902, and the LA84 Foundation, endowed with funds left over from the 1984 Olympic Games in Los Angeles, maintains a digital archive of *Sporting Life* and *Baseball Magazine* for the 1885 to 1920 period.

In recent years, Google (http://www.google.com) has entered the digitizing market with Google Books and Google News. These archives are free, and extremely useful to any sports researcher. The Society for American Baseball Research (SABR), also maintains a site called BioProject (http://bioproj.sabr.org), to which I have contributed several articles. BioProject has posted more than 1,400 biographies of major league players of the past and the present, and the information found there has been highly useful as well.

Though no book-length biography of Napoleon Lajoie has ever been published, SABR celebrated Lajoie's career in a 77-page issue of its magazine *The National Pastime* in 1988. It was written entirely by James M. Murphy, a newspaperman who worked as a writer and editor for 35 years in Rhode Island, Lajoie's home state. Murphy's work was an invaluable source of information on the ballplayer's minor league career, as well as his early, pre-baseball life.

The Eugene C. Murdock and Charles W. Mears collections of baseball books and materials at the Cleveland Public Library were, as always, invaluable. The library in downtown Cleveland has recently opened a center for baseball research, called the Sports Research Center, which is a welcome development to anyone who loves baseball. As usual, I received fine assistance from the knowledgeable staff members at the National Baseball Hall of Fame Library in Cooperstown, New York. I also conducted research at the University of Michigan in Ann Arbor, which houses a fine collection of newspaper microfilm, at the Toronto Public Library, and at Bowling Green State University in Ohio.

Introduction

In 1985, a writer and researcher named Charles F. Faber published a book titled *Baseball Ratings: The All-Time Best Players at Each Position*. In this work, Faber outlined his "Faber System," a series of statistical formulae that gave numerical ratings, for both offensive and defensive skills, to stars of both the recent and distant past. Using these ratings, Faber proposed to identify the greatest performers of every era and at every position. Toward the end of the book, Faber presented his final list of the greatest players of all time, and to the surprise of many (possibly including Faber himself) the number one player in baseball history was not Ty Cobb, nor Babe Ruth, nor Willie Mays.

The greatest baseball player who ever lived, according to Faber's rating system, was Napoleon Lajoie. In addition, Lajoie, according to Faber, was the second-greatest defensive player of all time, with only Pittsburgh second baseman Bill Mazeroski ranking ahead of him, and his 1901 campaign, in which he hit .426 and drove in 145 runs for the Philadelphia Athletics, was the greatest individual season in the history of the game.

In 1989, baseball historians and statisticians Pete Palmer and John Thorn published the first edition of their massive work, *Total Baseball*. Palmer and Thorn devised their own formula, which they called Total Player Rating, and used it to create their own lists of greatest performers. According to their calculations, Napoleon Lajoie was the third greatest player of all time, behind only Babe Ruth and Ted Williams, and finished ahead of Mazeroski as the greatest fielder who ever lived. In the second edition of the book, which appeared in 1991, Thorn and Palmer moved Lajoie past Williams into the second slot on their Total Player Rating list, with Ruth in the top position.

Though some may find fault with any rating system that puts Napoleon Lajoie ahead of Willie Mays, Ted Williams, and others, no one can deny that Lajoie, who played major league baseball from 1896 to 1916, was one of the greatest stars in the history of the game. Newspapers of the era referred to him as "King of Ballplayers," and it is not an exaggeration to say that his arrival in Cleveland in 1902 saved American League baseball in the city. He was so popular in Cleveland that in 1903, when a local newspaper held a contest to find a new nickname for the club, the fans voted to call the team the Napoleons, quickly shortened to Naps. The Cleveland Naps they were until Lajoie left the team after the 1914 season, after which the club became the Indians, the name by which it is known to this day.

Lajoie's accomplishments were many. He was the sixth player, and the first second baseman, elected to the Baseball Hall of Fame in Cooperstown, New York. He was the third player (after Cap Anson and Honus Wagner) to accumulate 3,000 hits during his career, and at the time of his retirement in 1916, his total of 657 doubles was the highest in major league history. His lifetime batting average was .338, and he won three batting titles (or four, or five, depending upon the source). He was the undisputed "king of ballplayers" during the first several years of the twentieth century, and his decision to jump from the National League to the upstart American League in 1901 gave viability to the new organization, and may well have assured its eventual success.

Why, then, has such a titan of the game's history been almost forgotten? Though baseball historians and researchers have produced many biographies of Ty Cobb, Babe Ruth, and Ted Williams, no full-length account of the life of Napoleon Lajoie has ever appeared on the nation's bookshelves (though in 1988 the Society for American Baseball Research devoted an entire 77-page issue of its publication *The National Pastime* to him). In the present day, his name only pops up when a major league hitter joins him in the 3,000-hit club, as Derek Jeter of the Yankees did in 2011. Once widely regarded by fans and sportswriters as the greatest second baseman of all time, Lajoie fares less well these days. Many today put Joe Morgan, the Cincinnati Reds star of the 1970s, in that position, with Lajoie demoted to third or fourth place, or lower, on the list.

There may be a few reasons for this outstanding ballplayer's apparent obscurity. For one, Napoleon Lajoie did not have a poetic nickname. He was not the "Georgia Peach" nor the "Iron Horse" nor the "Sultan of Swat." Instead, people called him "the big Frenchman," a descriptive, but hardly musical, moniker. In person, he was "Larry," a nickname awarded by an early teammate who found his given name too difficult to pronounce. Willie Mays "The Say Hey Kid" and Honus Wagner ("The Flying Dutchman") were only two of the many great players in history whose nicknames proved more colorful, and more enduring, than "Larry" or the "big Frenchman."

Lajoie, who spent his entire career with teams in Philadelphia and Cleveland, played in an era when sportswriters lionized New York stars. He missed out on the mythmaking that elevated the reputations of Babe Ruth, Lou Gehrig, and other New York icons. Though he could be a friendly, easygoing man, Lajoie guarded his privacy, and while he no doubt enjoyed the adulation that came his way, he did not seek it. As the legendary baseball writer Grantland Rice wrote in 1952, Lajoie "never cared for the crowd or the mob. He never asked for popularity. Or wanted it." He was proud of his accomplishments, but after he retired from professional baseball, he preferred to remain out of the spotlight during the last four decades of his life. He also has one important item missing from his baseball resume. Like other greats such as Ernie Banks, Ken Griffey, Jr., and Rod Carew, Lajoie never played on a pennant winner, and never had the opportunity to perform on the grand stage of the World Series.

In 2011, when Jim Thome made a triumphant return to his original team, the Indians, after hitting his 600th career home run as a Minnesota Twin, some media personalities hailed the veteran slugger as the greatest position player in Cleveland history. They must have forgotten about the man who played for the franchise a century before and performed in such a spectacular fashion that the fans chose to name the team itself after him. Jim Thome, Lou Boudreau, and Rocky Colavito were popular Cleveland players, but no one called the team the Jims, the Lous, or the Rockys. For 12 seasons, the Cleveland ballclub was called the Naps as a tribute to the first superstar of the American League, a man who deserves, at long last, to have his story told in its entirety. This is Napoleon Lajoie's story.

1

Woonsocket

Next to Senator [Nelson W.] Aldrich, [Napoleon Lajoie] is the most important
personage in American history born in Rhode Island since the Revolution.—
Alfred H. Spink, *The National Game*, 1910[1]

The story of Napoleon Lajoie, one of the greatest stars of the American national pastime, begins in rural Canada among people who spoke French, not English, in their daily
lives. The ballplayer's parents, Jean-Baptiste Lajoie and the former Celina Guertin, were
descended from the hardy people who emigrated from France in the seventeenth and eigh-
teenth centuries and sought to build better lives in the New World. Lajoie, pronounced
"la-ZWAH," means "the joyful one" or "the happy one," and was often given as a surname
to people who were outgoing and vivacious. The sons of large French families often adopted
such surnames with the *dit* appellation (*dit* meaning "called") to differentiate themselves
from their parents, and because Lajoie is a common name, it is difficult to pinpoint where
the ballplayer's ancestors came from. However, we know that one Pierre Addenin dit Lajoie,
who may have been the ballplayer's great-grandfather, left the town of Auxerre in north-
central France in 1770 and made the trek to Canada. Eight decades later, Jean-Baptiste
Lajoie and Celina Guertin married in St. Pie-sur-Bagot, Quebec, in 1852 and settled on a
farm near the town of St. Hyacinthe, about 30 miles east of Montreal. Jeremie, their first-
born, arrived in 1853, and was soon followed by daughter Cleothe and sons Albini and Prospere.

Farm life was difficult in the economically depressed Canadian province of Quebec.
The Lajoies, like most French-speaking families in rural Quebec, struggled to feed their
growing brood, fighting the severe winters and poor soil. Most farmers grew potatoes and
raised chickens to provide everything their families ate, bartering for necessities with other
poor farm families with whatever surplus they could scratch together. Wheat was the only
crop grown in Quebec with the potential for export, but the climate was not particularly
suited for its cultivation; in addition, the poverty of the province prevented the development
of infrastructure, including roads that would have aided in transporting a harvest to market
in the larger cities. For these and other reasons, agriculture stagnated in Quebec, and food
production could not hope to meet the needs of the growing population. Hunger, and even
starvation, were everpresent threats to the inhabitants of one of Canada's poorest provinces.

During the late 1860s, word reached the rural poor of Quebec that prosperity, as well
as a less hostile climate, reigned a few hundred miles to the south. The United States was

the fastest-growing country in the world, its incredible expansion interrupted, but not halted, by a bloody civil war that began in the spring of 1861. Four years later, the war ended with the nation once again united. Peace brought waves of immigrants from all corners of the world to a nation with the room, and the resources, to take all of them in and more. Farmers in the plains states, ranchers in the southwest, and factory owners in the east clamored for workers. There appeared to be limitless opportunities available for those who were willing to work hard, and the farmers of Quebec, who were used to arduous labor, took notice. During the next several decades, a wave of French Canadians fled Quebec, with fully one-third of the population of the province moving south to seek better lives in a new land.

Jean-Baptiste and Celina Lajoie decided, as did so many of their countrymen, that the United States offered the promise of a more successful existence for themselves and their children. Accordingly, they left their farm in St. Hyacinthe (no one knows if they sold it or, like many other Quebec families, simply abandoned it) and made their way south. Jean-Baptiste and Celina, who was in the late stages of pregnancy, crossed the border with their three sons and one daughter in tow, but quickly returned to Canada when their latest child, Joseph, made his appearance ahead of schedule. Shortly afterward, they left their native land for good and settled first in Rutland, Vermont, a town of sawmills and marble quarries, where they remained for a few years and produced another daughter. Jean-Baptiste, who Americanized his name to John, found work in Rutland, as did oldest son Jeremie, now in his middle teens. The other Lajoie boys would, in turn, leave school and take paying jobs during the next few years.

Life in Rutland was an improvement over rural Quebec, but before long, news reached the Lajoie family of an even more prosperous section of their adopted country. New England had become the center of textile manufacturing for the nation, with woolen mills and cloth manufacturing plants popping up wherever a rushing river could be harnessed as a power source. There were many such rivers in Massachusetts, Connecticut, and Rhode Island, and businessmen constructed textile mills with huge water wheels attached to provide the power. Tens of thousands of Canadians had already moved to New England, creating huge French-speaking enclaves in the cities and towns around the mills. This opportunity proved too appealing to resist, so in 1870 the Lajoie clan picked up and moved again, this time to Woonsocket, Rhode Island. There two more Lajoie sons were born: David, in 1871, and Napoléon, the last of the brood, on September 5, 1874.

Woonsocket, a town that straddles the Blackstone River on the northern border of the state, was then a collection of six smaller communities, one that boasted several mills and the other five of which were each centered on a single huge textile plant. Globe Village, where the Lajoies set up housekeeping, was located south of Woonsocket Falls between Front Street and the river. The Globe Mill was a magnificent five-story stone structure powered by three water wheels and a Corliss steam engine. It housed more than 40,000 spindles and 900 looms, and employed about 500 people. Thousands of French-speaking Canadian émigrés found work in the Globe and other mills of Woonsocket, and so many families settled there that by 1900 Woonsocket was the most French city in the United States, with about 60 percent of its population claiming French-Canadian descent.

These former Canadians brought their devout Catholicism with them to Rhode Island, and as in their native country, the local church was the center of community life. The Lajoies and most other immigrant families joined Woonsocket's French-speaking house of worship, the Church of the Precious Blood, located in Globe Village not far from the giant mill. It was the first French Catholic church in Woonsocket, and during the next three decades, the local diocese, based in Providence, would be obliged to build five more Catholic churches in town to serve the waves of immigrants from Quebec. The Lajoies, however, remained at Precious Blood, where their descendants appear on the church rolls to this day.

Napoleon Lajoie (who had no middle name, and eventually dropped the *accent aigu* over the "e" in his first name) was fully 21 years younger than his oldest sibling, and was born when his mother was just over 40 years old and his father 45 or so. Like his older brothers, Napoleon, whose friends called him "Poli," was a strongly built and ruggedly handsome boy who, the family hoped, could be counted on to go to work after only a few years of schooling. In 1880, when a canvasser for the decennial United States census recorded the "Lagoie" family in his tally sheets, the five-year-old Napoleon and the nine-year-old David were the only Lajoie boys not yet working. Jeremie had left the mill and taken a job as a hack driver, while Albini (called Ben), Prospere, and Joseph toiled as cleaners and spinners.

John, the former Jean-Baptiste, was not employed in 1880. The head of the Lajoie family, who had worked hard all his life, suffered from lung congestion and chronic bronchitis that proved so debilitating that he was, by the age of 50, an invalid. No longer able to work, he remained in bed at home, cared for by his wife and younger children until March 13, 1881, when he died at age 51. Buried in the cemetery of the Church of the Precious Blood, he was the first of many Lajoies to be interred there during the subsequent decades. Napoleon, the youngest, was only six years old when he lost his father.

John Lajoie's death left Celina with eight children, and though the two oldest were grown and on their own, the other six were not yet ready to be independent. By 1885, when Napoleon was ten years old, he had already abandoned school for a job in the mill as a sweeper and cleaner. He had also started a nomadic life with different family members in the Globe Village section of Woonsocket, living at one time or another with married brothers and sisters between brief stints under his mother's roof on Sayles Street. The Woonsocket city directories of the period list Napoleon Lajoie at several different addresses, none for any length of time. Still, he was working and helping to support his mother, as any good son would be expected to do.

The only friction that existed between Napoleon and his mother centered on the sport for which she had no use and which her youngest son could not live without. Napoleon, like many other sons of immigrant families, had discovered baseball when he was about ten years old. Boys in the Globe Village neighborhood played ball in the street, running the improvised bases and chasing the ball down the dirt road while dodging the horse-drawn wagons that lumbered by. Napoleon, strong and tall for his age, was a natural at this pastime and was usually the first player picked when his neighborhood pals chose up sides. Celina Lajoie, however, disdained her son's interest in the game, decrying it as a waste of time and a distraction from work. Neither mother nor son would budge from their positions, and the more Celina criticized baseball, the more Napoleon seemed to love it.

Napoleon's friends came up with a plan to hide

Celina Lajoie, the ballplayer's mother (author's collection).

his participation in their games from his mother. Celina Lajoie spoke no English and understood only a few English words, but knew that her son was playing ball on the streets of Globe Village when she heard his friends call out "Napoleon" or "Poli" in the excitement of play. Therefore, Napoleon's friends decided to call him "Sandy." The nickname seemed ridiculous, as Napoleon's hair was jet black, but the very inappropriateness of the new moniker kept his identity hidden. Mrs. Lajoie, by all accounts, did not know that Sandy, the best ballplayer in town, was her own son, and Napoleon's baseball exploits continued unabated. (Another brother, probably David, was called "Dick" for the same reason.) Recalled brother Jeremie long afterward, "Mother never suspected anything when she heard the kids calling for 'Sandy' and 'Dick,' and the boys would sneak out of the house to go and play."[2] Years later, long after the ball playing boys of the 1880s had become men in the twentieth century, Napoleon's old playmates still addressed him as Sandy.

Napoleon was not the only Lajoie to play ball, but the others were too busy working to spend much time at the sport. Years later, after the youngest of the Lajoies had become famous, brother Joseph recalled his own experiences for writer F. C. Lane. Napoleon, said Joseph, "was the baby of the family and had a little better chance than the rest of us. Whether or not any of the other brothers could have made a success at ball-playing I cannot say, but they never had a chance. They had to work as soon as they were able. Most of them married young and had families to support. There is not much chance for a laboring man under such conditions. I don't know whether or not I should ever have been a player. I used to play ball a little on spare occasions, usually what they called town ball. But I had to go to work, married early, and that was the end of playing baseball for me."[3]

In later years, Napoleon Lajoie often told interviewers that his father was dead set against his ballplaying, and that the head of the household "shouted that ballplayers were bums and that nobody respected them."[4] Since John Lajoie died when Napoleon was six years old, it is highly unlikely that the future baseball star was the object of the elder Lajoie's ire. The older boys played ball, however, and were in their twenties or late teens when John was still alive. Perhaps John directed his remarks at them, and perhaps they did not pursue the sport because of their father's opposition.

All of the Lajoie boys were strapping youngsters, six feet tall or more, stronger and taller than most of their fellows in town. All the Lajoies, in turn, eventually abandoned the textile mill for more physically demanding, and better paying, jobs as teamsters and hack drivers. Jeremie Lajoie, the oldest, had done so while his father was still alive, and before long the others followed in his footsteps, as they usually did. Napoleon left the mill during the 1890s and, according to the 1893 Woonsocket city directory, found employment as a clerk in C. F. Hixon's new and used furniture store on Main Street. Perhaps toiling behind a counter and unloading wagons full of furniture did not appeal to the young man, for he approached his brother Joseph, who worked in a lumberyard, and asked to be taken on. The yard owner agreed, and Napoleon went to work at City Lumber as a teamster. He later recalled that he earned $7.50 per week, a good salary for a young man in Globe Village.

For the next few years Napoleon, who celebrated his 20th birthday in the fall of 1894, drove a team of horses around Woonsocket, making deliveries and picking up loads of lumber. Still dissatisfied with his employment, he went to work for a neighbor, Narcisse Patinaude, at Combination Livery Stable. There, he not only delivered goods such as straw, hay, and coal, but often dressed up in a suit and top hat to drive people to weddings, funerals, and other important functions. This job gave Napoleon a trove of stories to relate in later years; in one, he told of a man with an English accent who promised to pay five dollars for a ride into town. When Napoleon's hack arrived in Woonsocket, the man was gone, having left a decaying fish on the seat of the buggy. "What the [blank] am I going to do with that [blank] fish there?" the young driver demanded of his supervisor. The supervisor thought for a moment and replied, "Why, you keep it for seven days, and then if nobody calls for it, it's yours."[5]

The money was good, but Napoleon earned even more in another line of work, one that he embraced with great enthusiasm. Napoleon Lajoie, the hack driver, was also a fine semipro baseball player. "I first heard of the major leagues," he recalled many years later, "when they used to post the scores on a big board in front of a pool hall in my home town. I still remember the magic names they used to put on those boards — Con Daily, King Kelly, Old Hoss Radbourn, John Clarkson, and

Napoleon Lajoie at age 18 (author's collection).

John Montgomery Ward."[6] Most of these players starred for the Boston Beaneaters, the closest National League team to Woonsocket and a perennial pennant contender. While Napoleon toiled for a few dollars a week in his hometown, the Beaneaters ruled major league baseball, winning the league championship in 1891, 1892, and 1893. Napoleon, who loved playing ball, dreamed of performing on the highest level and leaving the workaday world behind. He later recalled:

> I had found that there wasn't much future in the woolen mill. Joe got me a job in the lumber yard which paid better, and I took it. But I had already begun to pick up more money on the side as a ball player. I began as a semipro when I was about seventeen, and the first game or two was paid two dollars for my work. That seemed like easy money to me, and it looked all the more easy when the amount rose to five and even ten dollars. I know Joe used to think I was very lucky when I was working in the lumber yard for two dollars a day, to be able to go out and make ten dollars on a Saturday afternoon. And I suppose I was lucky.[7]

By his later teenage years, Napoleon had reached his full adult height. He stood six feet and one inch tall and tipped the scales at about 175 pounds, making him one of largest and strongest competitors in any game he played. After a stint with a neighborhood team called the Globe Stars, Napoleon, who batted and threw right-handed, was invited to join the Woonsockets, a collection of the best players in town, in 1893. The Woonsockets traveled to games in Connecticut and Massachusetts as well as Rhode Island, with only fair success, and their 1893 season was cut short by money and personnel troubles. The team was launched again in 1894 and found more success on the field, largely due to its young French-Canadian star, Napoleon Lajoie.

Napoleon, who was still Sandy to his ballplaying mates, spent time at second base and in the outfield, but mostly served as the catcher for the Woonsockets. He was fearless behind the plate, catching the fastest deliveries of the Woonsocket pitchers without complaint despite the rudimentary protective gear then available. He was also the team's best hitter, batting in the cleanup spot and already displaying the style that would carry him to the major leagues. Then, as later, he was a bad ball hitter, eschewing the possibility of a walk in favor of belting any pitch he could reach with his bat. The box scores and game accounts that appeared in the local newspapers described many long hits and game-winning plays by the young star, but few walks.

The competition was stiff, and he did not star in every game; in one contest against the rival St. Anne's club, according to the local paper, Napoleon went hitless in five trips to the plate and committed three errors in a 13–10 loss. In late June, in a contest against the squad from Manville, Massachusetts, Napoleon produced only one hit, a long home run that helped the Woonsockets to a 17–10 win in a bitterly fought game. The two teams played twice more that season, with each side winning once, and in the last contest Napoleon, the hard-hitting catcher, drove in four runs in an 8–6 win, though five Manville runners stole bases against him that day.

Napoleon was beginning to draw favorable notice, and late in 1894 an item appeared in the local paper, the *Evening Reporter*, to the effect that young Lajoie would soon join the team at the College of the Holy Cross in Worcester, Massachusetts. Holy Cross, a New England baseball powerhouse that sent several players on to successful careers in major league ball, was a Catholic institution that might have been too academically challenging for Napoleon, who left elementary school after only a few years of the most rudimentary education. Nothing ever came of it, and in 1895 Napoleon, now 20 years old, returned to the Woonsockets.

On July 4 of that year he suffered through one of the most trying games of his semipro career. The Woonsockets had developed a rivalry with a team from Franklin, Massachusetts, called the Carters, and the two teams scheduled a Fourth of July match at Agricultural Park in Woonsocket. Unfortunately, Napoleon Tessier, star pitcher and member of the "Napoleon battery" (Tessier and Lajoie) did not appear for the game, and the club was forced to start a substitute in his place. That pitcher hurt himself running the bases, and because Woonsocket now had only eight players, the Carters lent them a benchwarmer to complete their lineup. It didn't matter much anyway, because the Carter pitcher was Fred Woodcock, a former Brown University standout who played for the Pittsburgh Pirates of the National League in 1891 and 1892. Woodcock shut down the Woonsockets on one hit, while Napoleon Lajoie, the catcher and batting star, failed to hit safely in four times at bat. The Carters also stole five bases against Lajoie in their 11–4 win, which was called after seven innings when a sudden downpour drenched the field.

Small-town semipro baseball was often a catch-as-catch-can proposition, and the Woonsockets endured their share of difficulties. On one occasion, the team's star hurler, Napoleon Tessier, failed to appear for a game because he was sleeping off a bender in a jail cell. Early in 1895, Holy Cross sent a team of college boys to play in Woonsocket, but the local fans, more than 1,200 of them, became irate when they discovered that all the best Crusaders players, save one, had stayed home. The only Holy Cross star to make the trip was Louis Sockalexis, a hard-hitting outfielder from the Penobscot reservation in Maine. Two years later, Napoleon Lajoie would play against Sockalexis, the first recognized Native American major leaguer, in the National League. On this day, the Woonsockets held Sockalexis hitless while Lajoie smacked two long doubles in a 12–0 win.

As the season wore on, Woonsocket players came and went, and by August, the team had trouble keeping a regular cast of players together. Napoleon Lajoie, however, proved to be a steady, reliable performer. His batting average, from the available box scores in the local papers, remained well over the .300 mark all season long. He could play anywhere, seeing most of his action as a catcher but also playing second base and shortstop, and could have filled in well in the outfield if needed. Though the box scores reveal that Lajoie, as a catcher, allowed a large number of stolen bases, his hitting more than made up for his throwing. He was the hardest hitter in the local semipro ranks, and he kept the fans entertained with his home runs and triples.

The Woonsockets, due to personnel and scheduling troubles, were often idle on Saturdays, so Lajoie earned extra money by loaning himself out to other teams. One story, told by a newspaperman named Mickey Landry, described a game between two small-town Massachusetts teams that probably took place in 1895.

> I didn't see Lajoie play, but I heard the story many, many times from my father. He saw the game. Uxbridge was playing Whittinsville. They were bitter rivals. Just as the game was about to start, [Napoleon] rolled onto the field driving his horse vehicle to the Hecla (Uxbridge) bench. He tossed aside his stove pipe hat and peeled off a long black coat, under which he was wearing a baseball shirt. He wore sneakers and carried a glove that looked as if it had been through a war. Lajoie had a real good day for Hecla, both at bat and in the field. At the end of the game, he was paid $2, jumped into his team, and headed back to Woonsocket.[8]

The city of Fall River, Massachusetts, located about 30 miles southeast of Woonsocket, hosted a team in the New England League. The Fall River Indians were highly successful, having won the league pennant in 1893, 1894, and 1895, but the manager and several key players had moved on to other teams at season's end. The new field leader, a veteran minor league manager named Charlie Marston, needed to fill the holes in his lineup, so he traveled around New England, chatting up friends and associates in his quest for ballplayers. In January 1896, while visiting Boston, he stopped in for a visit to the sports desk of a local newspaper. There he encountered Boston Beaneaters manager Frank Selee and Fred Woodcock, the former major league pitcher who, as a member of the Carters, had faced the Woonsocket nine several times during the previous few years.

As Marston related the story, he asked Woodcock if he knew any good players who might be available to strengthen the Fall River nine, and the pitcher answered in the affirmative. "I know of a good batter," said Woodcock. "I don't know his name, but he is a big Frenchman who lives down at Woonsocket. I call myself a pretty fair pitcher, but I haven't anything that he cannot hit all over the field. I can't get the ball past the plate."[9]

Woodcock, who was also interviewed by sportswriters after Lajoie ascended to major league stardom, told the story differently. The pitcher said that he had not mentioned Lajoie's name to Marston because he hoped to get the hack driver turned ballplayer into a Carters uniform for the 1896 season. As Woodcock told it, he sent a telegram to Lajoie, asking if the young man would consider playing another season in semipro ball. Lajoie, said Woodcock, was a frugal sort and sent a penny postcard in reply. The postcard contained a six-word message. "I am out for the stuff,"[10] it said, or so Woodcock liked to claim in later years. Woodcock took this answer to mean that Lajoie was ready to leave the semipro ranks and graduate to a professional player's salary. It was only then that the pitcher contacted Marston and tipped him off to the Woonsocket star.

Selee was rebuilding his Beaneaters after a disappointing finish in 1895, but showed no interest in Woodcock's scouting report. Marston, however, was intrigued enough to travel to Woonsocket and ask around town for a "big Frenchman" who could hit the ball a mile. After a few false starts, someone pointed the manager to the Consolidated Livery stable, where Napoleon Lajoie worked. As Napoleon recalled it, "One day I was sitting in the office when Marston came in and said, 'Can you tell me where I can find that big French kid called Sandy?' 'You must mean me,' I said."[11]

The two men held a brief conversation, and Marston, satisfied with the young man's bearing and attitude, signed him to a contract that day. Marston had not brought a contract form, but wrote out the terms on the back of a stray envelope. Napoleon, who earned about $7.50 a week as a hack driver, agreed to play for $100 per month for a five-month season and signed the envelope to seal the deal. Napoleon Lajoie was now, officially, a professional baseball player. As he once said, "That $100 looked like all the money in the world."[12]

"I asked him where he wanted to play," said Marston later, "and he said he wanted to play second. As I already had a good second baseman, however, I told him there was no chance, and he replied that he could play any place except pitcher."[13] That was fine with Napoleon, who was instructed to report for spring practice in Fall River on April 1, eight weeks hence. He bid the manager goodbye and went back to work. He continued to drive his hack for the remainder of the winter and early spring months, waiting impatiently for his professional baseball career to commence.

2

Fall River

Manager Marston has signed Napoleon Lajoie, of Woonsocket, an excellent general player and a fine hitter, who may be tried at first base. Lajoie is a six footer, and weighs about 170 pounds. Fred Woodcock highly recommends him. —Sporting Life, February 15, 1896. This was the first reference to Lajoie in a national publication.

The Fall River Indians had won three New England League pennants in a row, but the team, like the rest of the clubs in the circuit, struggled financially. Due to inconsistent attendance and bad summer weather, the ballclub had reportedly lost $350 in 1895 despite its championship performance. The deficit would have been much greater had the club not sold its best player, third baseman Joe Harrington, to the Boston Beaneaters of the National League at season's end. Minor league teams made money not only from ticket sales and concessions, but also from developing young stars and selling them to higher-level clubs. Napoleon Lajoie, the semipro slugger, was exactly the sort of raw talent that Charlie Marston hoped to groom in Fall River and peddle to the National League when the time was right.

The New England League featured three teams from Massachusetts (Fall River, Brockton, and New Bedford), one from Rhode Island (Pawtucket), and four from Maine (Lewiston, Augusta, Portland, and Bangor). Its president was Tim Murnane, who had played for the pennant-winning Boston National League clubs during the 1870s and then switched to newspaper writing, serving as sports editor of the *Boston Globe* while also administering the league. Murnane's position on the *Globe*, and the popular daily column he produced, gave the New England League a certain amount of much-needed publicity. However, attendance suffered badly around the circuit in 1895 because Fall River ran away with the pennant race early on, and travel costs for long train trips to and from Maine ate away at every team's bottom line. Fall River appeared to be in good financial shape, but other New England League clubs were fighting for survival; indeed, two of the eight teams failed to finish their schedules in 1896.

Though the 21-year-old from Woonsocket was new to the professional game, he drew attention right away. In mid–April, the *Boston Globe* analyzed the Fall River roster and singled out Lajoie as a man to watch. Said the paper, "Lajoie is a Woonsocket boy, who has made his mark in semiprofessional clubs in this vicinity. He is a big fellow, and when his bat connects with the ball it means trouble for the fielders. The position he is slated for is center field, and he is said to cover a great deal of territory."[1]

The Fall River club conducted training camp at its home park, squeezing in as much practice as possible in the rainy, and sometimes snowy, New England spring weather. After a slew of April exhibition games, including one against the Boston Beaneaters in which Lajoie went hitless, Fall River opened its season at home on Friday, May 1, with a 7–6 win against Lewiston in front of a few hundred fans. Lajoie, who batted seventh and played center field in his first professional game, singled in four trips to the plate. On the following afternoon, before a weekend crowd of 1,600, the newcomer smacked a triple and a single in a 6–3 victory over Portland.

Fall River played its first seven games at home, winning all but the last contest as Napoleon Lajoie quickly found his footing in the professional game. Though the pitchers in the New England League, some of whom had played National League ball, were much more talented than the semipro hurlers he had previously faced, Lajoie was not intimidated by the faster competition. He drilled four hits in a 10–7 victory over Lewiston, and in a 21–4 rout of Bangor, he contributed two more safeties. He went hitless the next two days, but snapped out of his short slump with two doubles and two stolen bases in a 25–5 stomping of Lewiston, the first game of a long road trip to Maine. He hit his first professional home run on May 14 in Portland, one of five hits he struck that day. In late May, before his professional career was one month old, league president Tim Murnane singled out Lajoie as a good bet to climb the baseball ladder before long.

Napoleon Lajoie was one of two position players on the Fall River Indians who displayed promise of eventual major league success. The other was Phil Geier, two years younger than Lajoie, who had played in the Virginia League in 1895. Geier, an outfielder who also caught a few times when needed, was a small (five feet and seven inches), scrappy hustler with speed. He, like Lajoie, produced a number of multi-hit games for Fall River as his average hovered near the .400 mark. The pitching ace of the team, left-hander Fred Klobedanz, was another Indian who drew interest from the major leagues; he suffered from bouts of wildness, but had won 28 games for Fall River in 1895 and was building another fine record in 1896. He, too, had National League managers inquiring about his availability. The rest of the team was a hodgepodge of characters, from teenaged prospects to veterans like 42-year-old catcher Mike (Doc) Kennedy, who had played five seasons of National League ball beginning in 1879, then bounced around the minors for 13 years before landing in Fall River. In all, 11 men on the Fall River club had either played in the majors or would do so in the future.

Phil Geier, the 19-year-old right fielder who started the season in the fourth slot of the lineup, nearly kept pace with Napoleon Lajoie and established himself as another good bet to advance to the majors. Still, despite Geier's impressive hitting and fielding, Napoleon stood out. He made circus catches in center field, piled up the multi-hit games, and stole bases with abandon. In late May, Charlie Marston shifted him to the cleanup slot and pushed Geier down to fifth, a move that energized the offense and helped Fall River to grab first place by Decoration Day.

Napoleon showed his versatility in June, when Marston moved him to second base, then to first, as needed. Later that season, he also caught several games, displaying to the major league scouts that the valuable first-year pro could play any non-pitching position on the field. He might have made a success on the mound as well with his strong, accurate throwing arm, but he hit and fielded so well that there was no reason to try him out as a hurler. Napoleon's skill at multiple positions was one of his major selling points, though Frank Selee of the Boston Beaneaters reportedly did not believe the glowing reports on the young man from Fall River. To Selee, Napoleon was primarily a center fielder, and because Boston employed Billy Hamilton, one of the best in the game, at that position, the Beaneaters showed little interest in him.

Though the Boston papers were mostly concerned with news of the Beaneaters and the National League, they had taken note of the hard-hitting Lajoie by mid-season. On June 2, he enjoyed one of his best games as a professional, spearheading a 13–9 home victory over Portland with three hits, two of which were homers. This earned him a measure of praise in the *Globe*, which recounted the contest and stated that "Lajoie's batting was the feature, his second home run hit being the longest ever made on the grounds."[2] On the next afternoon, Napoleon demolished Portland once again, going four-for-six with a single, a double, and two triples in a 17–11 Fall River win. The Indians moved briskly into first place, a few games ahead of Pawtucket, largely due to the hitting and fielding exploits of the former hack driver from Woonsocket.

The local fans, casting about for a suitable nickname to give the young phenomenon, called him the "Slugging Cabby," while some game write-ups in the local papers referred to the free-swinging Lajoie as "Old Slashaway." The latter moniker was apt, because he had already impressed onlookers with his utter refusal to take a walk. Napoleon Lajoie was a bad-ball hitter from the beginning of his professional career, and his disdain for the base on balls was the most distinctive feature of his batting style. With his long arms and long bat, he could, and often did, step across the plate (which was legal then) and drive pitches far outside the strike zone into the deepest parts of the outfield. He even perfected a one-handed swing for such occasions. As he explained to an interviewer years later, "I go to the plate with the idea of hitting the first good ball sent up, as I believe in working on the aggressive."[3] This approach worked, as Lajoie's batting average stood at a league-leading .425 after 27 games.

He also showed a competitive streak, a welcome trait in 1890s-style baseball, though the budding star let his emotions boil over on more than one occasion. In Augusta, an umpire named Charlie Brady made a call that went against the Fall River club and pinned a loss on the league-leading Indians. Lajoie, still seething about the game hours afterward, saw Brady at the team's hotel after the game and had to be physically restrained by his teammates from assaulting the arbiter. Another umpire who felt Lajoie's sharp temper was Tommy Connolly, a quick-witted immigrant with Irish parentage (though he was born in England). Connolly, who worked many of Fall River's games, would follow Napoleon Lajoie to the major leagues, where he called games for more than 30 years and eventually gained induction into the Baseball Hall of Fame. In 1896, however, Connolly was just another hard-working minor league arbiter, forced to deal with the indignities of low-level ball. Years later, Lajoie hailed Connolly as "probably the best umpire of all time," but admitted, "I used to try and kick him in the shins once in a while just like anyone else."[4]

Games with double-digit scores were not unusual in the New England League, a circuit with small, hitter-friendly ballparks. Perhaps the wildest game of the season was played on August 1 at Pawtucket, where the outfield fences stood almost comically close to the infield. Fall River lost to the Pawtucket nine that day by a score of 32–22, with Lajoie belting three of Fall River's 19 hits. Nine days earlier, Fall River traveled to Augusta and defeated the home team, 29–3, as Lajoie walloped two homers and two singles. The "Slugging Cabby" kept hammering the ball as the season wore on, and his average remained well above the .400 mark. Phil Geier, who held second place in the batting race, was more than 40 points behind his teammate. Napoleon Lajoie was unstoppable, and in mid–July the *Boston Globe* was moved to call him "the most promising player in America" and "the batting phenomenon of the season."[5]

Lajoie gave his best performance on July 2, in the tiny Pawtucket ballpark. The "Slugging Cabby" lived up to his new nickname that day, smacking six hits in seven trips as Fall River demolished the outmanned Pawtucket squad, 31–5. Every man in the Fall River lineup belted at least three hits that day as the team raked the Rhode Islanders for 33 safeties. This contest was the last of a four-game series, all of which Fall River won as Lajoie pounded out 15 hits in 22 trips to the plate. On the next afternoon in Brockton, Lajoie chipped in with four more hits, including a game-winning homer in the tenth inning. The Fall River fans turned out to cheer their newest star, and in his first professional season, Napoleon Lajoie became the biggest celebrity in town since Lizzie Borden, a local woman who had been acquitted of murdering her parents in a sensational trial three years before.

Lajoie provided the fireworks on the Fourth of July. Fall River played a home-and-home doubleheader against New Bedford that day, and in the opener, played at New Bedford, Lajoie walloped another tenth-inning walk-off homer to give Fall River a 5–4 win. The hit was an arching fly ball that carried over the fence in the deepest part of the outfield; the *Globe's* headline the next day proclaimed, "Over Center Field Fence It Sailed Gaily."[6] The two teams then traveled to Fall River for the second game, in which Lajoie belted two doubles and a triple in a 16–1 win before the contest was called after eight innings due to darkness. Minor league pitchers could not contain the young man from Woonsocket, and the *Globe* remarked, "The fact is slowly sifting through the wool of the New England League that it doesn't pay to give Lajoie a chance to hit the ball when there is anything depending on the result."[7]

Charlie Marston was determined to sell Lajoie, Geier, and pitcher Fred Klobedanz to National League clubs before October 1, when any higher-level team was allowed to draft a minor league player for $500. All three of the Fall River stars could be expected to command more than that on the open market, though some big league teams appeared to be happy to wait until October and scoop up any player who had not been sold. Lajoie, then hitting about .430, could reasonably fetch $1,000, a good price for a New England League player at the time, while a tandem of Lajoie and Geier could set a team back by $1,500. Marston, who began receiving inquiries by telegram from major league clubs in July, let it be known that $1,500 was his price for the pair.

Timing, however, was of the essence. Fall River held a six-game lead over second-place Pawtucket in late July, but if Marston sold off his stars too soon, the Indians would have a fight on their hands to hold the lead. If he held onto them too long, National League teams would turn elsewhere for help, or lose interest as their pennant chances faded in late summer. Marston was assured of receiving $500 for Lajoie in October (or perhaps immediately, because the Pittsburgh Pirates reportedly offered to pay that sum in July), but by playing National League teams against each other, he could bid up the price for the "Slugging Cabby" and command a good payout for Phil Geier as well.

Though the Boston papers raved about the hard-hitting outfielder in nearby Fall River, Beaneaters manager Frank Selee was not interested in paying the price Marston set for his young slugger. The year before, Selee had bought another Fall River star, third baseman Joe Harrington, intending to groom him as the successor to the aging Billy Nash (whom Selee traded to Philadelphia that fall) in the Boston infield. Harrington's minor league stardom did not transfer to the National League as the newcomer batted only .201 for the Beaneaters in 1896. In August of that year, Selee released Harrington to Syracuse of the Eastern

League, and the youngster never again played in the majors. With Harrington's example fresh in his mind, Selee turned down the opportunity to purchase Lajoie, and instead entered negotiations with Marston for the services of left-hander Fred Klobedanz. Marston asked $1,200 for his ace pitcher, but in mid–August, he agreed to sell Klobedanz to the Beaneaters for $1,000.

While the Boston club turned its attention elsewhere, the Philadelphia Phillies followed the progress of both of Fall River's hitting stars. Philadelphia manager Billy Nash, who had taken a leave of absence from the Phillies and gone on a scouting mission to New England, was originally interested in Phil Geier and traveled to Maine to see the young right fielder in action. While there, he was impressed with Geier, but recognized that Napoleon Lajoie was an even better prospect. Nash spoke briefly to Lajoie, liked what he heard, and decided to enter the bidding for both men. The Phillies were going nowhere in the National League race, so Nash followed the Fall River club back to Massachusetts for further inspection.

Nash may have attended the game between Fall River and Augusta on July 23 in which Lajoie slammed two homers and two singles, and probably saw a contest at Brockton five days later when Lajoie went three-for-five with a long home run. On July 31, with Nash, Frank Selee, and an Eastern League manager, Billy Murray of the Providence Grays, in the stands, Lajoie suffered through a rare bad game, striking out three times and producing a single in five trips. This performance may have dissuaded Selee from signing the "Slugging Cabby," but perhaps it made no difference by this time. Nash wanted both Geier and Lajoie, and opened negotiations with Charlie Marston.

The New York Giants were also interested in Lajoie. Arthur Irwin, the manager of the floundering New York club, was ready to seal a deal with Fall River to buy Lajoie and Geier for $1,500, but the mercurial Giants owner, Andrew Freedman, put the brakes on the transaction. Reportedly, Freedman objected to the deal on ethnic grounds. "I want no Frenchmen or Dutchmen on my team," declared the owner, as reported in a New York paper. "Get me a couple of Irishmen."[8] Other reports said that Freedman objected to paying inflated prices for minor league phenoms, too many of whom had failed in the National League. The Giants passed, while the Pittsburgh Pirates inquired about both players but were put off by the price tag. The Brooklyn and Chicago clubs also showed interest.

Though many people discounted statistics compiled in the New England League as a product of poor pitching and small ballparks, National League teams could not help but be impressed with Napoleon Lajoie's .400-plus batting average, fielding versatility (he played mostly center field, but caught seven games and appeared on the infield too), and game-winning hits. The local papers were full of speculation, with Lajoie and Geier reportedly headed, as a pair or separately, to Chicago, Louisville, or any number of other cities, but the Philadelphia Phillies moved to close a deal with Fall River. By August 5, the parameters of the transaction had fallen into place, with the Phillies agreeing to buy both players for Marston's set price of $1,500. "I was rather anxious to see Boston get Lajoie," admitted Marston a few days later, "as the Boston club is well patronized by Fall River people, but I sold the men to the club who paid the price."[9]

Three days later, Geier and Lajoie were still wearing Fall River uniforms. Marston, no doubt wishing to squeeze every possible inning out of his star performers, had not yet seen a check from the Phillies, and explained to the local reporters that neither man would leave Fall River until the club received its payment. On Saturday, August 8, Napoleon Lajoie belted a single, double, and triple in an 18–3 win against Pawtucket. This proved to be his last contest with Fall River, for Charlie Marston had finally received his promised $1,500 from the Philadelphia ballclub. Lajoie and Geier left Fall River the following morning on a train bound for Philadelphia, while Charlie Marston assured the Phillies that they were getting a bargain. "You are paying me $1500 for a man who you would not sell for $10,000 after he plays out the season with you,"[10] he boasted to Billy Nash after the transaction was finalized.

Fall River slumped badly after Lajoie and Geier left, but held on to win the New England League flag by two and a half games over Bangor. The Fall River club made a small profit on the season due to the sales of Lajoie, Geier, and Klobedanz, while other teams in the circuit were not so fortunate (Augusta and Portland failed to complete their schedules). On an individual level, Napoleon Lajoie finished with an average of .429 to win the New England League batting title, with Phil Geier in second place at .381.

The Philadelphia ballclub was pleased with its new acquisition, and the national sporting press took notice of the latest addition to the Phillies roster. *The Sporting News*, the St. Louis–based weekly paper that had made a name for itself as the go-to source for baseball information, was impressed with the Fall River star.

> Lajoie is a big, lusty fellow, six feet high and a ball player all. You can tell that the first time you look at him. Some men you can't size up in one game. You can, this man. Philadelphia nabbed him because it was the only club that would put up the price — $1,500 for a $5,000 man — for if he is not worth the latter price after he has been in the league one season, many will lose their guess. He gives promise of being a larger and a better man than Bill Lange without the love for soubrettes.[11]

Lange was the Chicago outfielder whose off-the-field adventures made headlines in the papers and caused headaches for his manager, Cap Anson. Lange, though largely forgotten

The 1896 Fall River Indians, champions of the New England League (1897 Spalding Guide).

today, was one of baseball's biggest stars during the 1890s, though his behavioral problems sometimes overshadowed his talent. Napoleon Lajoie, who struck many observers as a younger version of the immensely talented Lange, possessed more than enough ability to succeed in major league ball. If he could avoid the pitfalls of sudden fame and success, he stood a fine chance to become a star for many years to come.

3

Off to Philadelphia

Lajoie, of Fall River, is not a fancy grand stand player. He can hit like a battering ram, however, can field and run, and has a good, strong throwing arm.—Sporting Life, August 8, 1896

Charlie Marston gained fame as the discoverer of Napoleon Lajoie, and in future years he enjoyed telling the story of his greatest find with a certain amount of embellishment. Because of Marston, the tale gained currency that the Philadelphia ballclub considered Phil Geier the real prize acquisition, and that Napoleon Lajoie was a mere throw-in on the deal that sent them both to the major leagues. Lajoie himself, in later years, treated this description of events as true. However, a look at the New England League statistics for 1896 dispels this myth. Lajoie was the most dangerous hitter in the circuit, winning the batting title with a .429 average while whacking 15 home runs, a large total for any league in nineteenth-century baseball. His fielding was, if possible, even more impressive. Lajoie played most of his games as an outfielder, but also did top-notch work behind the plate and at second base, and the Phillies recognized that they could place the Rhode Islander almost anywhere on the field with good results. The Fall River club would never have included a player as valuable as Lajoie as an afterthought on any deal, not when he could have been sold for a good price all by himself. Geier, who stood only five feet, seven inches tall, was a good player, but Lajoie was clearly a better one, as most observers no doubt recognized.

Geier held one advantage over Lajoie in that he was two years younger, not one as most people believed at the time. For some reason, Lajoie gave his birth year as 1875, not 1874, leading everyone to believe that the newest Phillie was 20 years old, not 21. Athletes, then as now, often shaved a year or two (or more) off their ages when they signed their first professional contracts, and perhaps Lajoie was merely one of a long line of players who did so. Or maybe Lajoie actually thought that he was born in 1875. He claimed so all his life, and most baseball records, and even his tombstone, show his birth year as 1875. However, his baptismal certificate, on file at the Woonsocket city hall, tells the real story. When Lajoie joined the Phillies, he was less than one month shy of his 22nd birthday. As a major league rookie, he was older than many other superstars of the game's history, such as Babe Ruth, Ty Cobb, and Mickey Mantle, all of whom were teenagers when they made their debuts.[1]

Though Lajoie had played mostly in the outfield at Fall River, the Phillies considered putting him at first base, which had posed a problem for the team for several seasons. Jack Boyle, a former catcher, manned the sack in 1894 and 1895, but his .253 average in the latter year was one of the lowest in the league among regular players at any position. In December of 1895 the Phillies bought the 37-year-old Dan Brouthers, a five-time batting champion who was once the most feared slugger in the game, from Louisville and gave him the first base job. "Big Dan," unfortunately, was on the downslide of a distinguished career and fading fast. Brouthers batted .344 in 1896, but he was so slow in the field that he could not even play the least demanding position on the diamond in a passable manner. In July Philadelphia management handed Brouthers his ten-day notice of release and moved outfielder Ed Delahanty to first base.

Delahanty was a good fielder, but hated playing on the infield and had spent nearly a month lobbying Philadelphia manager Billy Nash for a move back to his favored position by the time Napoleon Lajoie joined the club. When the newcomer first appeared in the Philadelphia clubhouse, Delahanty confronted him. "You're a first baseman," he said. "You tell the boss that you're a hell of a first baseman and you and me are goin' to be pals."[2] Lajoie did as instructed, earning Delahanty's friendship along with his gratitude when Nash put Lajoie on first base and moved "The Only Del," as the papers called him, back to left field.

Delahanty, seven years older than Lajoie, was the best player on the team and the most dangerous hitter in the National League. He was also a disciplinary nightmare for his managers. As historian Robert Smith described him,

> Men who met Ed Delahanty had to admit he was a handsome fellow, although there was an air about him that indicated he was a roughneck at heart and no man to temper with. He had that wide-eyed, half-smiling, ready-for-anything look that is characteristic of a certain type of Irishman. He had a towering impatience, too, and a taste for liquor and excitement. He created plenty of excitement for opponents and spectators when he laid his tremendous bat against a pitch.[3]

Ed Delahanty (author's collection).

Delahanty, the Cleveland-born son of Irish immigrants, and Lajoie, the French-Canadian from Woonsocket, became fast friends and, before long, roommates on the road.

Delahanty, who like Lajoie was a right-handed batter and thrower, was a hard-drinking carouser who often found trouble away from the ballpark, a trait he shared with many of his Philadelphia teammates. He introduced his new friend to his favorite bars and taverns around the league, and Lajoie, who was not long removed from driving a team of horses through the streets of Woonsocket, Rhode Island, could not help but be impressed. Despite his love of the high life, Delahanty was still the most feared hitter in the league, having batted over .400 in a season twice and having led the National League several times in runs batted in, home runs, and slugging average. Lajoie saw that Delahanty could enjoy himself off the field and still produce at the highest level on it, and accepted the veteran slugger not only as a friend, but as something of a role model.

The team's other hitting star, right fielder Sam Thompson, had a personality that was almost the opposite of Delahanty's. A clean-living, serious-minded 36-year-old, Thompson had starred for the pennant-winning 1887 Detroit Wolverines (with Dan Brouthers) before coming to Philadelphia in 1889. He had driven in 165 runs in 1895, one short of his own major league record that Babe Ruth broke nearly three decades later, though "Big Sam" started to slow down a bit in 1896. While Delahanty was a noted spendthrift, Thompson was so famous for saving his money that the sportswriters made him the butt of jokes in their columns about his frugality. Managers never had to worry about Thompson's behavior, though the same claim could not be made about many of the other Phillies. Team discipline was an annual problem for the ballclub, and the club owners were often forced to deal with behavioral episodes both on and off the field.

Most of the major league magnates in that era were wealthy, imperious, and autocratic individuals, and the main owner of the Philadelphia ballclub was no exception. John I. Rogers, called Colonel Rogers after attaining that rank in the state National Guard, was a prominent attorney and one-time Democratic state legislator who had been involved in the business end of the game since the 1870s. He and Al Reach, a prominent player of the 1860s and 1870s who built a prosperous sporting goods business after his playing days, assembled and financed an independent team in Philadelphia in 1880. That team, originally called the Quakers, entered the National League in 1883 and by the end of the decade became known as the Phillies. Though Al Reach was better known in the baseball world, Colonel Rogers eventually gained majority ownership of the club. By the time Napoleon Lajoie joined the Phillies in 1896, the Colonel held almost total power over the team's affairs.

During his tenure at the head of the club, Colonel Rogers beat back challenges from three rival leagues. The Union Association placed a team in Philadelphia in 1884 but collapsed after only one season of play, while the Athletics of the American Association lasted a bit longer, going under after the 1891 campaign. The most serious threat to the Phillies came in 1890, when most of the National League's top players seceded from the circuit and set up their own Players League. Rogers, however, held on to most of his stars, and the Players League passed from the scene after only one year. To fight off the competition, the Colonel, a skilled lobbyist, convinced the National League to let him lower his ticket price to 25 cents (rather than the 50-cent admission required of other clubs in the circuit). The Athletics, who also charged a quarter per ticket, lost the financial war and disbanded a year later, leaving the Phillies as the only game in town. Still, Colonel Rogers fought hard to keep his 25-cent ticket price, though other National League teams were still required to charge 50 cents. This concession by the league, and the Colonel's constant battle to retain it, earned Rogers and his club the enmity of his fellow owners.

His players also found little to admire in their boss. Their salaries took a nosedive after the Athletics went out of business, and the frugal Rogers drew much resentment from his charges for his penny-pinching methods. Even Sam Thompson, the stoic slugger, was moved to complain about the poor quality of the team's travel accommodations and meals on the road. "I shall not play again in Philadelphia," declared Thompson in October 1893, "and I told [manager] Harry Wright it would be a waste of time for him to write me about signing. The cheese-paring methods of the management, together with the fact that for five years I have had to face the sun in right field, have been the causes leading to my resolution.... The management [has] made a barrel of money, but they grind the players into the dirt."[4] Thompson, however, could not play for anyone but the Phillies due to the reserve clause in the standard player contract, which bound a player to the same team from one year to the next, forever if the team so chose. This clause, which professional baseball magnates fought to protect for more than eight decades, was a contract feature that Rogers, as the attorney for the National League, had worked to strengthen.

The Phillies played their home games at the Huntingdon Street Grounds, constructed by Reach and Rogers in 1887 and rebuilt after a devastating fire seven years later. Also known as National League Park, this structure housed the team until 1938 and was later called the Baker Bowl. Entirely contained within a single city block, the right field area was tiny, with the fence standing only 272 feet from home plate. Left-handed sluggers, particularly the veteran Sam Thompson, found the right field stands an inviting target; Thompson, who joined the Phillies in 1889, wound up hitting more home runs in National League play than any other nineteenth-century batter, with most of his round-trippers coming at home.[5] The rest of the outfield, however, was much larger, with a distance of 341 feet down the line in left and 408 feet in center. Right-handed sluggers like Delahanty made a living pounding doubles and triples, and the occasional inside-the-park homer, to the left side of the diamond. The park rewarded players who could hit to all fields, especially left and center, and appeared to be a perfect hitting environment for the free-swinging rookie from Fall River.

Indeed, the Phillies, aided by the dimensions of their ballpark, were the hardest-hitting team in baseball in that, or perhaps in any, era. In 1894 the club batted a record .349 as a team and placed all four of its outfielders—Delahanty, Thompson, Billy Hamilton, and substitute Tuck Turner—in the .400 class. Veteran catcher Jack Clements, the longest-serving member of the Phillies (having joined the club in 1884, its second year of play in the National League) batted .394 in 1895, the highest mark ever recorded by a major league catcher in a full season. The Philadelphia park was a hitter's paradise and a nightmare for pitchers, and high-scoring games were the rule rather than the exception, as Napoleon Lajoie would quickly discover.

The Phillies had finished third in 1895 under manager Arthur Irwin, but Colonel Rogers was not satisfied with Irwin's leadership. Rogers had long been enamored of third baseman Billy Nash, the captain of the Boston club that had won three National League pennants in a row from 1891 to 1893, and believed that Nash possessed the qualities to push the Phillies to the top of the league. Accordingly, on November 15, 1895, Rogers executed perhaps the most disastrous trade in Philadelphia baseball history. On that date, Rogers sent center fielder and leadoff man Billy Hamilton to Boston for Nash, who succeeded Irwin as manager of the club.

Though sluggers like Sam Thompson and Ed Delahanty attracted most of the attention, "Sliding Billy" Hamilton was the key to Philadelphia's offensive juggernaut. He was the leading base stealer in the National League, perhaps the fastest man on spikes in that era, and a high-average hitter who won two batting titles. In 1894, Hamilton had scored 192 runs, the highest one-season total of all time. He crossed the plate 166 more times in 1895 as the Phillies led the league in scoring with 8.3 runs per game. However, some teammates and opponents regarded Hamilton as a "record player," interested more in his stolen base totals and batting average than in team success. He and manager Irwin had clashed repeatedly over Hamilton's aggressive baserunning, and though his tactics produced results—he is one of only three men in major league history to average more than one run scored per game—the Phillies, inexplicably, deemed him expendable. Sliding Billy took his talents to Boston, where he helped the Beaneaters win two pennants and was praised by the highly respected ballplayer-turned-sportswriter Tim Murnane of the *Boston Globe* as "the most valuable center fielder, all things considered, in the game today."[6]

Philadelphia's main weakness, as virtually everyone recognized, lay in its pitching. In both 1894 and 1895, the Phillies posted the highest team batting average in the league (with their .349 mark in 1894 the highest in history), but only two teams in each season compiled a worse earned run average. The hitter-friendly home ballpark was partly to blame, but so was management's failure to develop and nurture young hurlers, too many of whom (such as Willie McGill and "Brewery Jack" Taylor) wound up drinking themselves out of the National League. Another problem was posed by the presence of Jack Clements, the veteran left-handed catcher who had been a fixture in the Philadelphia lineup for more than a decade. Clements, who grew cranky as his career approached its end, reportedly despised young pitchers and would humiliate them on the field, catching their fastballs with his bare hands and returning the ball by firing it at their feet and forcing his hurlers to run after the sphere.[7]

The Phillies' pitching difficulties were illustrated clearly one July afternoon in Chicago, where the team played Cap Anson's Colts about a month before Lajoie joined the club. In that contest, Ed Delahanty walloped four home runs, two of which cleared the outfield walls while the other two were inside-the-park shots to the deepest part of center field. Delahanty also singled to complete a five-for-five day with seven runs batted in, but the Phillies pitchers could not hold the Colts in check, and the Phillies lost the game by a 9 to 8 score. Not until 1986 would another major league player smack four homers in a game that his team lost.

Injuries also derailed the Phillies that season. In May, Billy Nash, the third baseman and manager, was hit in the head by a pitch from Tom Smith in Louisville. Bothered by headaches and dizziness, he sat out more than half the team's games and hit poorly when he played, leaving the Phillies without much to show for the trade of Billy Hamilton. Shortly after Nash returned to the lineup, he broke a finger while catching a pop-up and took to the sidelines again. Sam Thompson, at 38, was slowing down due to back pain and abdominal problems; the mustachioed slugger batted under .300 in 1896 for the first time in his career and barely reached 100 runs batted in after driving home 165 the year before. Ed Delahanty sat out for a while with a sore shoulder, and a Baltimore batter broke pitcher Al Orth's thumb with a line drive. The team also suffered from weak play at shortstop, where rookie Bill Hulen, the last left-handed thrower to play the position on a regular basis in the major leagues, committed 51 errors in 73 games.

The Phillies were so far out of contention by the time Lajoie joined the team that manager Nash, still bothered by the effects of his May beaning, left the club for weeks at a time on scouting missions. The team had spent the previous month bouncing between seventh and eighth place, belatedly realizing that Billy Hamilton's contributions could not be replaced by Nash, who batted only .247 in 65 games while Hamilton stole 110 bases and scored 153 runs for Boston. The 1896 edition of the Phillies scored nearly 200 fewer runs than the 1895 club, putting Nash's job in jeopardy before he had completed his first season at the helm. Colonel Rogers was an impatient man and had no qualms about cutting his losses and hiring someone else at season's end.

Napoleon Lajoie made his first appearance in a Philadelphia uniform on August 11, 1896, in a Tuesday exhibition game against a minor league team in Atlantic City, New Jersey. He made a good impression on his new employers, driving out two singles and a double. On the following afternoon, he played his first major league game in Philadelphia against the Washington Senators, one of the league's perennial sad-sack teams. Lajoie played first base and batted fifth in the lineup, belting a single in the fourth inning that drove Ed

Delahanty in from third with his team's first run. He scored later in the inning, and wound up the day with one hit in five trips to the plate against Washington hurler Win Mercer. He also handled an assist and nine putouts without an error. The Phillies won the game 9 to 0, and the *Philadelphia Evening Reporter* remarked, "The way [Lajoie] did his work yesterday impressed the 2600 spectators as being all right.... Unless all signs fail, he promises to be a valuable addition to the team." In a sidebar on the same page, the paper summed up the new man with the statement, "Lajoie will do."[8]

Francis C. Richter, however, saw the new man differently. Richter, the Philadelphia correspondent for *Sporting Life*, was always quick to criticize the Phillies and their management, and was never shy about allowing his frustration with the team to color his writing. After Lajoie had played with the Phillies for only a week, Richter evaluated the newcomers and proclaimed Lajoie, who started out slowly with the bat, "the biggest disappointment of all." Continued Richter,

> He is big and heavy and totally lacking in action, both in fielding and in batting. His first base play is accurate enough, but machine-like in action, and crude in execution, due, probably, to lack of experience at the position. The latter defect may be remedied by practice, but the inertness is doubtless natural and therefore ineradicable.... [He] doesn't swing properly at the ball, and seems unable to gauge a drop or a slow ball.[9]

Just as Richter's scathing criticism hit the newsstands, Lajoie's bat came alive. He hit his first major league home run, an inside-the-park blow, on August 20 in a 4–3 win over Louisville in the second game of a doubleheader, though the homer was his only hit of the day. On the following afternoon, the Phillies were involved in another close game with Louisville when they broke the contest open with eight runs in the ninth inning, sealing a 13–3 win. Lajoie hit a double and two singles for his first three-hit game, and followed it up with a four-for-five performance against the Colonels the next day. He put together several multi-hit games during the next few weeks as his batting average climbed out of the .100s and approached the .300 level.

The 21-year-old minor league star gained a nickname shortly after joining the Phillies. The team's ace pitcher was "Brewery Jack" Taylor, a hard-drinking right-hander from Staten Island, New York, who, for whatever reason, found the name Napoleon Lajoie too difficult to pronounce. Taylor regarded both "Napoleon" and "Lajoie" as insurmountable tongue-twisters, so after a while the pitcher simply gave up and addressed the newest Phillie as "Larry." Taylor's teammates followed his example, and from that day on, the newcomer was known as Larry Lajoie. He answered to that name for the rest of his life.[10] It did not take long for his last name to undergo a metamorphosis as well; instead of "la-ZWAH," the French pronunciation of the name, people tended to accent the first syllable, and his name came out as "LA-zho-way." The newly-named Larry did not object to this pronunciation, and though his family and fellow Francophones in Woonsocket said the name in the French style, the ballplayer became LA-zho-way to his teammates and the public.

His second home run of the season was his most dramatic. The Phillies and the Cincinnati Reds went into extra innings on September 1 in Philadelphia, and with two out in the top of the tenth inning (the Phillies chose to bat first that day, which the home team was allowed to do at the time), Lajoie came to the plate with two men on and the score tied at six. Frank "Blinky" Dwyer, who later became an umpire, was the pitcher for the Reds, a cagey ten-year veteran who won 24 games that season. The rookie was not intimidated. Lajoie found a pitch he liked and drilled it into the deepest part of center field. He scampered around the bases for a three-run inside-the-park homer, which proved the winning margin in a 9–6 Phillies win.

Phil Geier rode the bench in September, but Larry Lajoie became the regular first baseman for the club and impressed players and sportswriters with his play. Many were surprised that a big man like Lajoie could be so graceful in the field. Said W. H. Koelsch, the New York correspondent for *Sporting Life*, "Lajoie is certainly a good man, and although he looks like a big clumsy fellow he puts the ball on a man faster than any player seen on the Polo Grounds this year. He is also a good batter, and Nash has secured a prize, at least that is the verdict of the local critics."[11]

Tommy McCarthy, the former Boston Beaneaters star who spent 1896 with Brooklyn, joined the chorus of praise for the young Phillie. "I caught a couple of balls on the banking off him in Philadelphia," said McCarthy, "that would have been home runs in Boston. Had Lajoie been a member of the Boston team he would have had a record of 18 or 20 home runs."[12] Even Francis Richter lightened up on his criticism, allowing that Lajoie "fills the bill" and "does not wait for bases on balls. He can hit anything and 'goes right at 'em.' Up to yesterday he had hit safely 39 times and has made seven two-baggers, eight three-baggers and two home runs. He can't bunt, though."[13]

In his first major league campaign, Napoleon (now called Larry) Lajoie played in 39 games, all at first base, and closed the season with a rush, boosting his batting average to .326 and his slugging percentage to .543, a mark that would have been the fourth best in the league had Lajoie compiled it over the entire season. Colonel Rogers was pleased with Lajoie, but not with his manager, Billy Nash. The Phillies had too much talent to have finished in eighth place, 28½ games out of first, so in November, Rogers announced that Nash would return to the playing ranks in 1897. In his place, Rogers appointed a man who had played only briefly in the major leagues and had never managed a team on baseball's highest level. The new manager of the Phillies was an intense, demanding disciplinarian named George Stallings.

4

Crossroads

I do not think there is a position on a ball team that Lajoie could not fill better than almost any other man now playing the game. Pitching would require most effort on Larry's part to develop himself, but I am confident he would with practice make a winning pitcher. He is a splendid catcher: everybody knows how well he can cover first base, and he can do equally as well at any infield position, while the outfield is easy for him. — George Stallings, Philadelphia manager, March 1898[1]

George Stallings, who had led the Detroit Tigers of the Western League to a fourth-place finish in 1896, was a 29-year-old Georgian who had reportedly studied to be a surgeon before devoting his life to baseball. A well-traveled catcher and outfielder, he had played in the majors only briefly, appearing in four games for Brooklyn in 1890 when the new Players League created a raft of roster openings. He stroked only two hits in 20 trips to the plate, and when the Players League ended, so did Stallings' hopes of top-level success as a player. He returned to the minors and started his managerial career a few years later. His Nashville team won the Southern League pennant in 1895 and brought Stallings a reputation as an up-and-coming talent. Because he was still an active player for Detroit, the Phillies acquired his services by drafting him off the minor-league roster.

Off the field, George Stallings was the model of a graceful Southern gentleman, but his demeanor on the bench was something else. Stallings was as highly competitive and fiery as any field leader in the game's history, regularly blowing up at umpires and berating his players for mistakes and bad plays. Stallings, whose expletive-laden tirades became the stuff of legend, was the kind of man who "could fly into a schizophrenic rage at the drop of a pop fly," as New York writer Tom Meany described him. "Sputtering with a fury that invited apoplexy, Stallings told off ball players as they haven't been told off since."[2] He turned sarcastic and belittling when things did not go well, and many of his players, while admiring his baseball knowledge, grew to despise the man personally. However, he had compiled a fine record in the minors, and Colonel Rogers apparently believed that the Phillies, a team prone to misbehavior off the field, needed a strong dose of discipline and that Stallings was the man to provide it. The new manager was also a highly intelligent man, and had impressed Al Reach, the Philadelphia co-owner, with his knowledge of the game. Reach, who interviewed Stallings at length, was the man who convinced Rogers to hire him.

The new manager had his work cut out for him, as far as team discipline was concerned.

The Phillies were a hard-drinking bunch who had made life miserable for Billy Nash, whose attempts to establish order were often frustrated by Colonel Rogers; as Sam Thompson put it in an interview with a reporter in his hometown of Detroit, "as soon as the players realized that the manager was helpless and that he was not the boss, they commenced to make life a burden for him. There are some men on this team that would drive a saint to drink. Nash took orders every day from Colonel Rogers. He was a non-entity."[3] Thompson disavowed the statement a few weeks later, claiming that the quote came from a friend of his, but the sentiments expressed therein were held by many.

Though team business manager Billy Shettsline publicly fretted about the cost of a preseason training trip to the South, Stallings set up a spring camp in Atlanta in his home state of Georgia. There he introduced several activities that would not only get his Phillies in shape, but keep them interested and out of trouble. One innovation was the late-night, long-distance bicycle ride, which the players enjoyed despite the bruises and bumps incurred when they fell off, which was often. Ed Delahanty, a novice rider, avoided serious injury one day when he lost control of his bike, fell to the pavement, and was immediately run over by the equally inexperienced Napoleon Lajoie.

Most of the National League teams played their first games on April 22, but the Boston and Philadelphia clubs met at Boston on Monday, April 19, for the season opener in front of 14,500 fans. In that game, Lajoie's first Opening Day, the Phillies roughed up Kid Nichols, the Beaneaters ace, for three runs in the first eight innings, while Al Orth (the Curveless Wonder, people called him) threw shutout ball. In the top of the ninth, the Phillies had two men on when Lajoie came to bat with two out. He jumped on an inside fastball from Nichols and drilled a liner over the left field fence for the first National League home run of the season, giving the Phillies a 6–0 lead. In the bottom of the inning, the Beaneaters made it interesting, scoring five times against a suddenly ineffective Orth, but the Phillies retired the side in time to complete a 6–5 win.[4]

The Phillies won eight of their first nine games, with an offensive explosion sparked by Ed Delahanty and Larry Lajoie. On April 24 in Philadelphia, Lajoie belted five hits, with two singles, a double, and two triples keying a 12–4 win over the Giants. "His hardest hit," said Francis Richter in *Sporting Life*, "was a double, which rebounded from the left field wall like a shot out of a gun."[5] The Phillies first baseman did, however, commit three errors. Delahanty, who had closed the 1896 season with a 13-game hitting streak, hit safely in the first nine contests of 1897, with 17 hits in his first 34 trips to the plate. Lajoie suffered a split finger on April 27 at Boston, knocking him out of a few games, but the Phillies kept winning, and on May 1 they occupied first place by half a game over the defending champion Orioles. Lajoie, with hits in 11 of his first 22 times at bat, hit safely in every game until May 4, when Boston held him off the board in a 5–2 Beaneaters win.

Meanwhile, Sam Thompson struggled. His kidney and back problems flared up, and he played in only three games before taking to the bench. He was in so much pain that he left the team in May and sought relief at the spas in Mount Clemens, Michigan, not far from his home in Detroit. He did not return to the Phillies in 1897, and except for an aborted comeback bid the following year, his career in Philadelphia was over. Thompson's departure coincided with a return to their usual inconsistent form for the Phillies, who began May with five losses to Boston and Baltimore, then went on the road and won five consecutive games against weaker competition in St. Louis and Louisville. The rest of their May road trip was a disaster, with nine losses in a row at Cincinnati, Pittsburgh, and Cleveland. They lost their tenth straight at Chicago before closing the trip with two wins against

Lajoie bats against the New York Giants in 1897 (*Frank Leslie's Illustrated Newspaper*, September 16, 1897).

the Colts. The Phillies, who had begun the month in first place, ended it buried in eighth position.

Injuries mounted as the losses piled up. Billy Nash, still on the mend from the serious beaning he suffered the year before, split a finger and was forced to the bench, while Delahanty played on a painfully sprained, heavily taped ankle. Stallings juggled the lineup madly, even putting Lajoie in the leadoff spot on May 24 against the Spiders in Cleveland. Larry, who played right field that day, banged out two hits and stole a base, though the Phillies lost a 9–8 slugfest to Cleveland pitching ace Cy Young. The next day, center fielder Duff (Dick) Cooley batted leadoff, with Larry, restored to first base, in the second slot. Larry and the latest Phillies right fielder, Phil Geier, contributed three hits apiece as the Phillies scored seven times in the eighth inning to take a 9–6 lead, but the Spiders answered with four in the ninth for a 10–9 win.

The manager's mood turned sour as the season slipped away, and many observers were stunned when they heard Stallings blasting his own players to reporters on the road. He also freely criticized other teams, especially the defending champion Baltimore club, despite the fact that the Phillies had not defeated the Orioles in almost two years, going 0–12 against them in 1896 and losing their first five matchups in 1897. As Cincinnati reporter F. C. Baldwin said of Stallings, "He is hurting himself and club by talking too much. On numerous occasions here Stallings was not a bit backward in stating that his players did not know a sacrifice hit or stolen base from Egyptian hieroglyphic, and showed other signs of contempt. Stallings talks too much about other teams as well as his own.... Stallings should be made to use more diplomacy, and not show his newness so much."[6]

The players could not believe Stallings' attitude. The manager regularly harangued his players in full view and hearing of opponents and fans, and once loudly berated his men to the reporters as "mentally drunk" and "the dumbest team coming down the pike."[7] Some baseball writers, including longtime Hall of Fame historian Lee Allen, have credited Stallings with coining the term "bonehead," which he used to describe his charges. Tongue-lashing was "an art with him,"[8] said Hank Gowdy, his catcher on his later Boston Braves team, and at no time in his career was Stallings' penchant for verbal fireworks more apparent than in 1897. Not even veteran stars like Delahanty and former skipper Nash were immune to the torrents of abuse. "There are no stars in any team I handle." said Stallings. "All men are the same level to me."[9] If Colonel Rogers expected Stallings to shake up the Phillies, he succeeded. The local papers praised Stallings for his uncompromising leadership style, though the ballplayers grumbled among themselves as the weeks wore on.

Lajoie, the team's budding star, came in for a severe dressing down on May 20 in Pittsburgh, when his attention wandered in the field and a ball skipped by him at first base. The miscue led to a four-run rally that sealed a victory for the Pirates. Stallings, who donned a uniform and played right field that day, yelled at Lajoie that the ball was coming his way, but Lajoie did not react until the ball was out of the infield. The next day, Stallings, still fuming, took to the bench and inserted Jack Boyle at first base. He exiled Lajoie to right field, where he remained for the next several games.

Stallings, in his first major league managerial post, overreacted to the losing and shifted players around the field and up and down the lineup with wild abandon, though the absence of Thompson and injuries to Geier, Nash, and others played a part in the constant changes. Lajoie played mostly at first base but saw time in right field, while the second base, third base, and center field positions were unsettled all year long. The increasingly frustrated Stallings saved his most venomous tirades for second baseman Bill Hallman, the popular team captain who had been a fixture in Philadelphia since 1888, and became enraged when most of the players took Hallman's side in their many disputes. By late May, the drinking and other off-the-field problems that had marred previous seasons returned, with many Phillies breaking curfew in defiance of their manager.

All the while, Napoleon Lajoie staked a claim as the best young hitter in the National League. He and Ed Delahanty provided the Phillies with a powerful one-two punch in the third and fourth slots in the lineup, though with Stallings' constant shuffling, they could never be certain where they would bat each day until they looked at the lineup card before the game. Lajoie, like Delahanty, was a high-average hitter with extra-base power, and opposing players marveled at the hard shots that rocketed off his bat. Already, third basemen around the National League had learned to play deep against Lajoie, and some observers believed that if Lajoie worked on his bunting, he might beat out singles hitters like Willie Keeler and Jesse Burkett for the batting title.

Stallings was determined to tighten his control of the team, and on June 1 he took action against some of his problem players. He traded Bill Hallman and outfielder Dick Harley to the St. Louis Browns for infielder Tommy Dowd, then sent pitcher Kid Carsey and backup catcher Mike Grady to the same club for catcher Ed McFarland. Carsey had won 20 games for the Phillies a few years earlier, while Hallman and Grady were .300 hitters. McFarland was slated to spell the oft-injured and aging Jack Clements behind the plate, while Dowd, a veteran infielder who had been fired as manager of the woeful Browns, was acquired to take Hallman's place at second.

With these two trades, Stallings sent a message to the remaining Phillies. St. Louis was baseball's Siberia during the 1890s; though the Mound City, then the fourth most populous city in the nation, was a great baseball town, the Browns remained at the bottom of the standings each year due to inept management and cash-poor ownership. Tommy Dowd was the last of five men who managed the Browns in 1896, and the first of four who held the post in 1897. George Stallings no doubt hoped that the remaining troublemakers on his ballclub would take note and improve their behavior, lest they be sent west to the land of intense heat, high humidity, and the occasional bounced paycheck.

The Phillies limped along at the .500 mark for a while after the trade, and on June 12 a 5–0 win against Cleveland boosted them to fourth place in the tightly bunched league standings. However, a six-game losing skid dropped the Phillies back to eighth, and another 12-game slide in August pushed them down to ninth, 25½ games behind the leaders. The Phillies had tuned out their abusive manager. They stayed out late at night, gave little effort at Stallings' morning practices, and resisted his suggestions for improvement. The fans, disgusted by their team's performance, stayed away, and attendance at the Huntingdon Street Grounds dropped as the summer wore on. At least the Phillies succeeded in defeating the Orioles in Baltimore on August 3. This 5–3 win, which featured two hits by Lajoie and three by pitcher Al Orth, broke Philadelphia's embarrassing 22-game, two-year losing streak against the three-time National League champs.

By mid-season, the national sporting papers were filled with criticism of the Phillies and their apparent indifference. Tommy Dowd, who had grown to despise Stallings in a matter of weeks after his arrival from St. Louis, fell victim to the hidden ball trick in the first game of a three-game set at home against Washington, and in the third game his error let in the winning runs in a 3–1 loss. The Phillies lost all three contests to the Senators and then traveled to Brooklyn, where Dowd let a ball get between his legs at second base. Lajoie, in right field, made no effort to back up the play, and batter Billy Shindle dashed around the bases and scored. Ed Delahanty misplayed a liner by Gene DeMontreville into a home run against Washington, and did the same for Mike Griffin a few days later against Brooklyn. At least Delahanty had an excuse, as he was playing on a bad ankle that had been sore for weeks. Stallings raged, but his players paid little attention. They gave so little effort that they were guilty of "somnambulism," as Ernest Lanigan of *The Sporting News* charged in mid-season.

The Phillies' antipathy for their manager was no secret around the league, and during the disastrous Washington series, Colonel Rogers drew up a statement of support for Stallings and ordered all the players to sign it. The document stated that the Phillies were not, in fact, trying to "throw down" Stallings, and pledged their full support for his leadership. All the Phillies affixed their signatures, but the gesture fooled no one. The players were certainly at fault, but Stallings drew his share of criticism as well; as *The Sporting News* put it, "'The Staggering Stallingites' is the latest title bestowed upon that Quaker aggregation so woefully mismanaged by the gentleman whose mouth is always in a state of volcanic eruption."[10]

The season continued to deteriorate. Catcher Jack Clements, who had suffered from painful hemorrhoids and a sore back during the previous few seasons, hit poorly and became the target of Philadelphia's notoriously impatient fans, who sent boos raining down upon the veteran whenever he appeared at bat. Tommy Dowd, who had traded one poisonous situation in St. Louis for another in Philadelphia, joined Clements, Jack Taylor, and others in conspiring against Stallings. Frank Hough, baseball reporter for the *Philadelphia Inquirer*, blasted the team regularly, and in late August called the Phillies "the biggest set of ingrates and leg pullers that ever came down the baseball pike" and added that Stallings should be wary of "jolliers, who, like gift-bearing Greeks will throw hobosh into him whenever it suits their purpose."[11]

Discipline problems had been brewing for some time. On a western trip in June, the manager had levied several hundred dollars in fines against his men for their behavioral infractions, but the Phillies apparently believed that, as usual, the money would be restored to them if they played well. When their next payday arrived, the players discovered that Stallings had no intention of refunding their money. Instead of shocking the Phillies into mending their ways, the manager's decision angered his charges and increased the sniping and backbiting to poisonous levels. More than a few of his men regarded Stallings as a minor leaguer who had been promoted out of his depth, and by August, some of the less inhibited Phillies were openly second-guessing, and even mocking, their manager on the bench during the games.

Ed Delahanty, who had cut a wide behavioral swath during his career, was not one of the troublemakers on the 1897 edition of the Phillies. He was the undisputed star of the team, especially after Thompson's abrupt departure in May, and "the only Del" took the honor seriously and kept his drinking under control that year. However, he was not a forceful leader and did not care to deal with the festering problems that ate at the heart of the team. He concentrated on his playing and produced his usual outstanding season, ending the year with a .377 average and 109 runs scored. Only an early ankle injury and a late-season slump kept him from challenging Baltimore's Willie Keeler for the batting title. Still, Stallings could not resist lashing out at his best player, complaining that the hobbled Delahanty covered as much ground as "a sewer manhole lid."[12] Given Delahanty's popularity with his teammates, such undeserved criticism only increased the animosity of the Phillies toward their manager.

Napoleon Lajoie, in his first full major league season, carried an average above the .360

mark, led the league in total bases, and impressed onlookers with his skillful play at first base. He did all this despite a growing antipathy toward Stallings, which displayed itself in increasingly immature and irresponsible behavior. Lajoie was 22 years old during the summer of 1897, and despite his push to stardom, was still one of the younger Phillies. Only a year and a half removed from driving a team of horses through the streets of Woonsocket, Rhode Island, Lajoie was impressionable enough to adopt the behavioral attitudes of his older, more worldly teammates. In August, with the Phillies hopelessly buried in the second division, Napoleon Lajoie reached a crossroads in his young career. He had developed a taste for the high life and had fallen in with the hard-drinking element of the Philadelphia club.

In mid–August the Phillies went on the road to Washington, the city that had been the scene of many of their off-the-field problems. Center fielder Dick Cooley, while playing for the Browns a few years before, had found a bar in the nation's capital that sold beer for five cents a bottle. Cooley, thrilled with this discovery, spent lots of time at the establishment with several of his St. Louis teammates, who dubbed themselves the "five cent gang." Cooley and Lajoie had become fast friends, and the two became steady patrons of Cooley's favorite bar, as did "Brewery Jack" Taylor, the talented but unpredictable pitcher. The three men formed a Phillies version of the five cent gang, a group that sometimes expanded to include their hard-drinking teammates. Lajoie was a big, strongly built man, but even he could become unsteady with too much beer in his system, as George Stallings would soon find out.

On Wednesday, August 11, the most serious situation of the season unfolded in Washington. After a long night, and probably a morning, of hell-raising, Lajoie, Cooley, and Taylor arrived at the ballpark in such an intoxicated condition that the three could barely stand up, much less play a game of baseball that day. Taylor was so drunk that Stallings put him on a train back to Philadelphia, dispatching a groundskeeper to carry the inebriated man's baggage. Lajoie and Cooley napped the afternoon away on the bench; then, while boarding the omnibus for the ride back to the team hotel, Larry argued with a heckler on the street and struck the man in a rage. A nearby patrolman arrested Lajoie and escorted him to the local police station, where the ballplayer remained until he posted a $15 bond. Stallings fined him another $50 for the incident.

One would think that the arrest of a teammate would have an effect on the other Phillies, but the behavioral issues became even worse as the weeks dragged on. Two unnamed Phillies were arrested after a nighttime spree a few days later, and shortly afterward three more Philadelphia ballplayers spent a night in jail for disorderly conduct. The club dropped all the way to tenth place in the 12-team National League, and many of the players blamed their manager. One player complained, "Stallings has wrecked the team by letting some of the best men go in foolish trades, and he has publicly rebuked the rest of us because we cannot win. No man knows what position he will be asked to play tomorrow, and we are all disgusted with the way things have been run this year."[13]

Lajoie's behavioral problems came to a head on Friday, August 27. The Phillies played at home against Pittsburgh that afternoon, and Lajoie arrived at the ballpark in a noticeably intoxicated state. The enraged Stallings did not take his star first baseman out of the lineup; instead, the manager ordered Lajoie to take the field, where he committed an egregious error that allowed two Pirates to score in the top of the first inning. The young star then made the situation much worse by directing a stream of vile language at the fans behind the Philadelphia bench, who were riding him mercilessly about his obvious impairment. Satisfied that Lajoie had sufficiently embarrassed himself in front of the home fans, Stallings then pulled the youngster from the game, inserting Phil Geier in left field and moving Ed Delahanty to first. Lajoie was immediately suspended without pay, and sat in the clubhouse as the Pirates came from behind in the late innings and pulled out a 6–5 win.

Lajoie's punishment left the Phillies in a quandary, as Delahanty left the team at game's end and returned to Cleveland, his hometown, after receiving word that his 18-year-old sister was critically ill. On Saturday, August 28, Stallings, with no better options, donned a uniform and put himself in the lineup at first base, though he had played in only one major league game in seven years. He performed well, belting a single and a double, though the Pirates won their second in a row against the Phillies, this time by a score of 6 to 4.

Despite the seriousness of Lajoie's offense, his suspension lasted only four days, and the Saturday contest was the only full game that the young first baseman missed. There was no Sunday baseball in Philadelphia, and Monday's game against Louisville was rained out. By Tuesday, Lajoie had sobered up and apologized for his behavior, at which point Stallings returned his star slugger to the lineup.

Stallings' decision may have been motivated by his own desire to return to the bench, and with Delahanty absent — the slugger's sister passed away on Saturday, and he did not return to the team for a week — the temptation to restore one of the team's two stars to the lineup must have been overwhelming. Besides, Stallings greatly, and publicly, admired Lajoie's talent, if not his behavior. "Lajoie has shown me he is the most natural ball player ever born," wrote the manager in a letter to *Sporting Life* the previous April. "His hitting and his playing are perfectly natural in every respect. He makes hard chances look easy by the simple way he handles himself. He is a jewel of the first water and is bound to be heard from this year."[14] Stallings, who hoped to put together a semipro football team to play at the Huntingdon Street Grounds during the fall months, had even suggested to the papers that the strongly-built Lajoie would make a fine football player.

Francis Richter, the Phillies correspondent for *Sporting Life*, recounted the embarrassing episode in the magazine's September 4 issue, and delivered a public plea to the young player to mend his ways. Wrote Richter:

> Napoleon Lajoie, in his first full season in the League is acting in a manner that bodes ill for his future unless he at once calls a halt on himself. He has had several lapses from sobriety this season which have cost him heavily, and on Friday last he capped the climax by appearing on the field in such a condition that he disgraced himself, and had to be taken out after the first inning after he had lost the Phillies the game. Subsequently he was laid off indefinitely without pay. This brought him to a realizing sense of his position. He was very contrite, and after much persuasion and many solemn promises he was reinstated yesterday. I think that the lesson will prove beneficial, and that henceforth the club will have no reason to complain of him. He is a strong and valuable player, who should by strict attention to business be able within a year to command the limit [in salary] and to secure it for many years to come. Indeed, the probability is that he would have secured it next season from the Philadelphia Club owners, who are quick to appreciate fidelity and capacity, but for his bad breaks this season.
>
> The pity of the thing is that Lajoie has been simply a victim of good nature. He is a big, wholesome fellow with no vicious traits, but lacking in experience. This and his susceptibility to certain deleterious influences in the team and a foolish idea of being a "good fellow" have led to his downfall. I sincerely hope that he will learn, and learn quickly, before he injures his ability and popularity beyond redemption, that better than being a "good fellow" is being a "just fellow" just to himself, to his employers and to the public. That sort of fellowship will carry him a long way in his chosen profession. The other sort will drag him into the path strewn with wrecks of other "good fellows," in their time just as promising as Lajoie.[15]

Lajoie, chastened by the incident, resumed his place in the lineup and caused no more problems during the rest of the season. It remained to be seen if the young man from Woonsocket would learn from his mistakes, or, like many other players, fall victim to high living and behavioral carelessness. Though major league professional baseball was barely two decades old in 1897, the sport had already seen more than its share of broken-down old ballplayers whose lives had been ruined, and sometimes ended, by their inability to deal with success and public adulation. Napoleon Lajoie was as talented as any of them; despite alcohol-related problems and clashes with his manager, he finished the year with a .361 batting average and led the league in slugging percentage (.569) and total bases (310). He had a bright future ahead of him, if only he could develop a sense of maturity to match his undeniable talent.

Lajoie was one of three promising young stars who played their first full campaigns in the National League in 1897. In Louisville, a bowlegged 23-year-old infielder and outfielder named John (Honus) Wagner made his debut in June and batted .338 in 61 games, giving hope to one of the league's worst teams. Wagner, like Lajoie, could play almost any position, and though he looked ungainly and awkward in the field, he made all the plays despite his lack of grace. Meanwhile, the Cleveland Spiders signed a 25-year-old named Louis Sockalexis, a college football and baseball star from Holy Cross who made headlines with long hits and fancy catches in the early months of the season. Sockalexis, a member of the Penobscot Indian tribe in Maine, was the first recognized minority player of any kind in National League history, and his fine play caused the Cleveland writers to discard the name Spiders and, for the first time, refer to the club as the Indians in his honor.

The league, however, was embarrassed when two of these three potential superstars came to grief in 1897 due to off-the-field issues. Lajoie's problems, as previously detailed, were difficult enough for the Phillies to handle, but the newly-named Indians found even more trouble with Sockalexis. After a few months of stellar play, the Native American outfielder began drinking to excess and injured his ankle during the July 4 weekend with a drunken tumble out of a second-story window. After several more similar escapades, the Cleveland team suspended its newest star without pay. He, like Lajoie, apologized profusely and returned to the team, but his future, which once looked so promising, was in doubt as the 1897 season drew to a close.

Honus Wagner, the son of German immigrants, liked to drink beer, but controlled it well enough to escape the troubles that ensnared his two fellow first-year stars. The most scathing criticism of Wagner in 1897 came from columnists who complained about his filthy uniform; the Louisville rookie, they suggested, would do well to have his baseball togs laundered a bit more often. Perhaps Wagner knew how to handle the baseball lifestyle more successfully because his older brother Albert had already played in the National League, or perhaps he was simply more mature than Lajoie or Sockalexis. At any rate, all three men had proven that they possessed more than enough talent to succeed in the national game. Their task, as the 1898 season unfolded, was to harness it in a positive way.

5

Turning the Corner

[Lajoie] is the one batter in the League who compels pitchers to keep their eyes open and to be ready to jump at any time. Apparently he does not swing hard at the ball, his swing being more of a jerk. He lets go his bat with one hand just as it meets the ball. Some day one of his hard hits will break some fielder's hand or arm or crush in a rib or two. They certainly have the power. — Amos Rusie, New York Giants pitcher, 1898[1]

Though George Stallings appeared to fly into a theatrical rage at the slightest provocation, his belligerent manner was part of his overall managerial strategy. He regarded himself as a master psychologist, and he treated the players under his command differently depending upon their personalities. "Stallings handles men very skillfully," said second baseman Johnny Evers, who served as captain on the Georgian's world champion Boston Braves team of 1914.

> First he sizes up a player, and if he thinks he is of the type that will have his spirit broken by "riding," he encourages him, jollies him along, and does little scolding. But with the other type of player he is different. If a man is inclined to take things too easy or be careless, [Stallings] can give him one of the best tongue lashings I have ever heard, and I have listened to a good many. He gets these men so that they will go out and fight to the finish, fearful lest they may do something which will displease their boss.[2]

Stallings was a colorful character, and some of the stories concerning his behavior became part of baseball lore. He was so fidgety on the bench that he wore out four or five pairs of suit pants each season, and he was so finicky about keeping the ground around the bench area free from litter that opposing players would scatter bits of paper in his dugout just to watch his frenzied reaction. While managing the Braves, Stallings once called on Hank Gowdy to pinch-hit. "Now, you bonehead," boomed the manager, "get up there with a bat and see if you can hit the ball." So many Braves were used to being called "bonehead" that seven players got up and stepped toward the bat rack.[3]

However, Stallings' leadership style was an utter failure with Napoleon Lajoie. A proud man, Lajoie had no use for the sarcasm, arrogance, and all-around bullying behavior of his manager, no matter how skilled Stallings claimed to be as a leader of men. Even when Lajoie himself was not the target of a Stallings verbal assault, he resented seeing his fellow Phillies subjected to such treatment. He was loyal to his teammates, and though his star was on the rise, Lajoie disliked Stallings as much as any player. On several occasions during his career,

Lajoie rebelled against what he perceived as random, pointless expressions of authority by those in positions of power. His later disputes with his managers, and especially with umpires, fit such a pattern. Secure in his talent and proud of his accomplishments, Napoleon Lajoie wanted nothing more than to play his game without the distraction of an abusive, and possibly insecure, authority figure.

Colonel Rogers could have fired Stallings after a disaster-filled 1897, but the sharp-tongued manager kept his job for another season. To prepare for the upcoming campaign, Stallings made another trade with the St. Louis Browns in an attempt to remove some more troublemakers from his roster. In November 1897, at the winter meetings in Philadelphia, Stallings announced a blockbuster deal. He sent catcher Jack Clements, infielder Tommy Dowd (who had come from St. Louis only six months before), pitcher "Brewery Jack" Taylor, infielder Lave Cross, and $1,000 to the Browns for pitcher Red Donahue and infielders Bill (Klondike) Douglass and Monte Cross. Lave Cross, no relation to Monte, was the only Phillie whose departure Stallings regretted, while the other three were free to go as far as the manager was concerned. This transaction was one of the biggest trades of the 1890s, and proved to the baseball world that Stallings would fight to impose his will on the Philadelphia club. Stallings also bought a house near the ballpark, signaling to all that he planned to remain the boss of the Phillies for the long term.

This deal had implications for Napoleon Lajoie, the 23-year-old budding star of the ballclub. With second baseman Lave Cross gone and first sacker Klondike Douglass joining the team, Stallings proposed to move Lajoie to second base. That was fine with Lajoie, who had often described the second sack as his favorite position on the field.

His contract for 1898, however, was another matter. After he batted .361 and led the National League in slugging percentage and total bases the season before, the Phillies made him a "limit man," granting him the league-mandated maximum salary of $2,400. However, Rogers demanded that each Phillie sign a contract that contained a temperance clause, requiring the player to abstain from liquor during the season. In Lajoie's case, the team proposed to hold back $300 of his salary and make it payable at season's end if he could get through the campaign without an alcohol-related incident. Lajoie rebelled at this proposal and indicated his displeasure by refusing to report to spring training at Cape May, New Jersey, unless the clause was removed from the agreement. Training camp opened without Lajoie on March 15, but because all of the other Phillies signed their contracts with a minimum of grumbling, the team's new second baseman found himself alone in his opposition. He tarried at home in Woonsocket for about a week, then traveled to Cape May on March 22 and signed the contract, with the temperance clause intact.

Lajoie had stayed in shape by playing handball in Woonsocket all winter, and onlookers remarked that Larry, who was warmly greeted by his teammates, looked to be in excellent

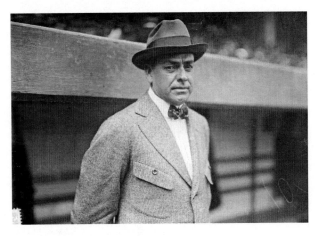

George Stallings, who managed the Phillies in 1897 and 1898, shown here in 1914, as manager of the Miracle Braves (Bain Collection, Library of Congress).

physical condition. Stallings was happy to see the young star, despite the turmoil of the previous year, and expressed confidence that Larry could handle his new position.

> Lajoie is a natural-born ball player, and one of the fastest in the country. If we had not secured Monte Cross I most surely would have played Larry at shortstop. He is too good an infielder for third base, since there is not room for him to show his best skill. At second base Lajoie will have a chance to make a name for himself. He is sure on ground hits and thrown balls, and will eat up those little pop flies back of second base. The base runner who can intimidate him does not live. His size will be an advantage to him in making double plays, since he can throw over the head of almost any man who would try to block him. He is the fastest man on his feet on the team, and I will stake my reputation that he makes a success as a second baseman.[4]

The training sessions unfolded peacefully, and the Phillies appeared to build a spirit of togetherness in Cape May (which was most likely selected as a training site because Colonel Rogers owned a summer home there) that had been absent the previous summer. Lajoie excelled at second base, as expected, and Sam Thompson reported that his back pain was gone, enabling him to swing the bat freely again. The three additions from St. Louis fit in well, as did a newcomer from Bedford, Ohio, named Elmer Flick, who had batted .396 at Dayton in 1897. Swinging a bat that he made himself on a lathe, the 22-year-old Flick fought for a position as an extra outfielder, though he had also played the infield in the minors. Only five feet, eight inches tall, the left-handed hitter belted line drives that were almost as scorching as those produced by Delahanty and Lajoie. Francis Richter was impressed by the young man and told his readers, "Flick is going to make the outfielders hustle to hold their positions. He is the fastest and most promising youngster the Phillies have ever had, and appears to be equally at home in the infield as well as outfield. As a batter he is just what the doctor ordered."[5]

Ed Delahanty did not want the responsibility of the captaincy, and, according to the local papers, Napoleon Lajoie was not a candidate for the position due to his behavioral problems of the year before. Instead, Stallings, after giving the job to the veteran Monte Cross during the exhibition season, appointed center fielder Dick Cooley to the position when the season began. The new captain was only a year and a half older than Lajoie, but had already completed five seasons in the majors and had batted .329 in 1897. He, like Lajoie, had angered his manager with his alcohol-related escapades the year before, but Stallings accepted Cooley's apologies as sincere. Besides, Cooley was popular with his teammates, and with some of the previous year's bad apples now plying their trade in St. Louis, Stallings believed that Cooley would mature into a reliable leader.

Pre-season optimism was tempered, in Philadelphia and other cities, by off-the-field matters. For several years, a dispute had raged between the United States and Spain over Spanish rule in Cuba, an island 90 miles south of Florida. Tensions, fanned by sensational news reports from the island, grew during the first few months of the new year, and after the battleship USS *Maine* exploded in Havana harbor on February 15, 1898, killing more than 250 American sailors, war between the two countries was inevitable. Congress, at the request of President William McKinley, declared war against Spain in April, driving baseball news from the front pages just as the season was set to begin. The country's attention was riveted on the war, not on baseball, as shown by the disappointing attendance figures at National League ballparks in April and May.

The optimistic spirit of Cape May did not last long. The Phillies won four of their first five games, then lost six of seven and plunged into the second division before the 1898 season was two weeks old. On May 17, they closed a short homestand with an embarrassing 17–2 loss to the defending champion Orioles from Baltimore, then went on the road and displayed their inconsistency, following up a seven-game losing skid with six wins in a row. The Phillies, despite their many personnel changes, were as frustrating as ever, and in early June a 3–10 slide, capped by a 16–4 loss at the Polo Grounds in New York, left the Phillies in eighth place, too far behind the leaders to hope for a second-half revival. The Philadelphia ballclub had reverted to form, as did George Stallings, whose sarcasm and verbal abuse returned in full force.

Lajoie, after hitting .361 the year before, struggled to keep his average slightly above the .300 mark in the early going. He took some criticism in the papers for "bullheadedness" in trying for extra-base hits and, as usual, refusing to take walks, but he was still a serious threat to opposing pitchers. Ed Delahanty, on the other hand, started poorly and did not reach .300 until late May. While fighting to bring their averages up, the two Phillies sluggers argued strategy with manager Stallings, a devotee of "small ball" who demanded plenty of bunting and sacrificing. Both Delahanty and Lajoie believed that swinging away would, for them, be much more valuable to the team than deliberately making an out merely to move a runner up one base. They may have been right, but Stallings brooked no dissent, and tension between the Phillies stars and their manager appeared before the season was a month old.

Batting averages around the league dipped in 1898, and not only for Lajoie and Delahanty. The cumulative league average dropped from .292 to .271 as almost everyone found it harder to scratch out the base hits. Baltimore's Willie Keeler, the 1897 batting champ, lost 53 points off his average and still won his second consecutive batting title. The offensive explosion that occurred after the league moved the pitching distance to its present 60 feet and six inches in 1893 had abated, probably due to improved fielding and the fact that the pitchers had adjusted to the new diamond geometry after five seasons. Players also complained about poor quality, "punky" baseballs that seemed deader than the ones used previously. Elmer Flick, however, bucked the prevailing tide in April and May of his rookie season, batting above the .380 mark in limited action.

As the Phillies struggled, Sam Thompson was the first to bail on the faltering ballclub. The aging veteran, who had played in only three games the year before, started well in 1898, hitting the ball at a .349 clip. However, his back and kidney pain returned, and by mid-May he could no longer swing a bat without severe discomfort. Frustrated by his physical problems and unwilling to put up with his acerbic manager, the 38-year-old slugger boarded a train for his home in Detroit on May 13 and quit the team, though he did not bother to notify the Phillies of his retirement until after his arrival in Michigan. So insulted was Colonel Rogers by Thompson's attitude that a year later, when the ballplayer asked for his release to the Detroit Tigers of the Western League, Rogers bluntly refused to give it. The club kept Thompson from seeking another playing position in organized ball, and carried his name on its reserve list until 1901, by which time the veteran was 41 years old.

Fortunately for the Phillies, they had a ready replacement for Thompson. Elmer Flick had caddied for the injured star during April and early May, and when Thompson quit the team for good, Flick stepped into the lineup and hit the ball with authority. His fielding was erratic, but in time he would learn to handle balls hit off the short right field fence in Philadelphia. However, the infield was again unsettled, especially after the club released the slumping Billy Nash at the end of May. Nash, Stallings' predecessor as manager, had never recovered from his 1896 beaning and was batting only .243 at the time of his release. He was only 33 years old, but never again played major league ball.

Six wins in a row at the end of May relieved the pressure on the players for a brief time, but a 2–5 skid against Pittsburgh and St. Louis at home drove Stallings to deliver his worst outbursts of the season. The manager was particularly galled by the fact that three losses to the woeful Browns came at the hands of pitchers Kid Carsey, Jack Taylor, and Duke Esper, all of whom were former Phillies. The Browns, who lost 111 games that season, had no business beating a far more talented ballclub, but the Philadelphia offense had simply stopped producing. The hardest-hitting team in baseball had fallen into a mass batting slump, losing a doubleheader in Cleveland on May 21 to Cy Young, who pitched a three-hitter, and Jack Powell, who shut out the Phillies on seven hits. Lajoie, Delahanty, Cross, and Nash all went hitless in both games, though the new man, Elmer Flick, had five hits in seven trips.

The pitching staff, with little batting support, also struggled. Starters Al Orth and Red Donahue alternated good games with bad ones, while newcomers like left-hander Wiley Piatt and right-hander Bill Duggleby fought for a place in the rotation. Duggleby, called "Frosty Bill," was one of the few Phillies who hit well. In his first time at bat in the major leagues, on April 21, 1898, Duggleby came up with the bases loaded and walloped a grand-slam homer. The next player to match that feat in his initial plate appearance was Jeremy Hermida of the Florida Marlins in 2005. However, Duggleby's grand slam was the highlight of his short stay in Philadelphia. He went 3–3 before Stallings sent him to Wilkes-Barre of the Eastern League, and "Frosty Bill" did not return to the Phillies until 1901.

The Philadelphia fans, faced with a slumping team and distracted by news of military excursions to Cuba and the Philippines, stayed away from the Huntingdon Street Grounds. The grumbling among the players intensified, threatening to ruin the 1898 season as completely as the 1897 season had been wrecked. George Stallings, ordered by Colonel Rogers to rule the team with an iron hand, refused to let up on the pressure, and his tirades became even more vicious as the losses mounted. Napoleon Lajoie, who harbored a severe disdain for dictatorial managers, grew to dislike Stallings as much as any Phillie. The papers reported that several players, Lajoie and Cooley among them, peppered team business manager Billy Shettsline with complaints, which were certain to reach Colonel Rogers at his summer cottage in Cape May. The manager, who was still regarded by many of his charges as a minor leaguer promoted out of his depth, may not have realized it, but his position was eroding by the day.

By early June, Stallings had so totally alienated the Phillies players that captain Dick Cooley, with the support of most of his teammates, denounced his manager in no uncertain terms in a statement to the local papers. "We are fed up with the way Stallings has been riding us," stated Cooley, "and decided we had enough of him and would regard him as our manager no longer. For weeks, he has been handling us like a lot of cattle. We may not be the best team in the league but we don't intend to put up with Stallings's tactics."[6] This statement was a virtual declaration of war, and as the Phillies sank in the standings, behavioral issues cropped up again. Immediately after Cooley's press release, the Phillies lost three of four in Boston and looked almost helpless in so doing. Cooley, despite his status as captain, was one of the main offenders, as he and Napoleon Lajoie celebrated a rare win in Boston on June 14 by staying out drinking all night and were fined by Stallings the next day.

This punishment did not sit well with the other Phillies, and the team simply stopped performing for their despised manager. Lajoie held up his end at bat and in the field, but the defiantly listless Phillies committed five errors in a 12–0 defeat to the Beaneaters the next afternoon. The club then went to New York and gave its weakest effort of the season against the Giants, committing 14 errors (none by Lajoie) in two games and losing by the scores of 11–3 and 16–4.

The *Philadelphia Evening Journal*, aghast at the prospect of another lost season, ripped into the team after the New York fiasco. "Stallings' misfits are the poorest imitation of base ballists that have appeared on the Harlem meadow in many, many moons," wrote the paper's baseball columnist. "A family of self-respecting Simians would be ashamed to don the Slobtown uniform at this stage of proceedings. Yesterday their error total amounted to only nine.... A dozen or more unscorable blunders increased the respect the spectators didn't have for the pitiable outfit from the town of 'Billy' Penn."[7] The other papers echoed similar sentiments, and it was obvious to all that George Stallings could not continue as manager of the Phillies. After the two embarrassing losses in New York left the Phillies with a 19–27 record, the Philadelphia co-owners, John Rogers and Al Reach, dismissed Stallings on the morning of June 18 and replaced him with Billy Shettsline.

George Stallings would manage again in the major leagues, and though he won one of the most unexpected World Series victories in history as boss of Boston's "Miracle Braves" of 1914, most of his future charges regarded him much as had the Phillies. Stallings "will crab and rave on the bench with any of them," said Johnny Evers, his captain on that 1914 championship club. Evers, however, admired Stallings for his baseball acumen. "Mr. Stallings," said Evers, "knows more base ball than any man with whom I have ever come in contact during my connection with the game."[8] If nothing else, Stallings deserved credit for his foresight in moving Napoleon Lajoie to second base, the position at which the former hack driver from Woonsocket built his Hall of Fame career.

The next manager of the Phillies was as unlike George Stallings as any field leader could be. An overweight man with a jovial disposition, Billy Shettsline had never played professional ball, having joined the Phillies organization in 1885 as a ticket-taker and general office boy. Working his way up the ladder under the patronage of Colonel Rogers, Shettsline became the business manager of the team by the early 1890s. Though Shettsline, unlike Stallings, had no playing or managing credentials at all, Rogers apparently believed that the popular front office figure would reduce the tension surrounding the team and allow the players to perform to their potential. He also no doubt viewed the 35-year-old Shettsline's appointment as a way to save on payroll, as the new manager merely had new responsibilities added to his workload.

Despite Shettsline's total lack of experience, the Phillies responded to his low-pressure leadership style and almost immediately turned their season around. In Shettsline's first game, a home contest against the Giants on June 18, the suddenly lively Phillies eked out a 6–5 win as Lajoie and Cooley, punished by Stallings a few days before, produced three hits apiece. The local papers praised Lajoie's fielding as "remarkable" in their columns the next day. Though Rogers and Reach had characterized Stallings' removal as temporary, mostly because his contract ran for another year and a half, no one believed that the acerbic Georgian would ever return to Philadelphia. The club won seven of its first eight contests under Shettsline, and the general mood of the players appeared to be greatly improved. Before long, the club owners reached a settlement with Stallings, who returned to his previous post as manager of Detroit in the Western League.

The team continued to play inconsistent ball, with a seven-game losing streak (capped by a 15–0 drubbing at the hands of the Orioles) dropping the Phillies back to eighth place in early July. Still, though the pennant was already out of reach, Shettsline's influence was a positive one. He stopped the constant lineup shuffling, and put the starting pitchers to work in a more regular rotation. Wiley Piatt, a rookie lefthander who won only four games for Stallings, compiled a 20–10 record under Shettsline and solidified the pitching staff, which had been a perennial problem for the Phillies. The new manager, who had always been friendly with the players, was such a breath of fresh air that one anonymous Phillie told a Cincinnati reporter, "A player who wouldn't work for Shettsline after the royal way he treats us would be an ingrate of the first water."[9]

Dick Cooley, given more leeway as team captain by Shettsline, drilled the Phillies in bunting technique during morning practices and turned Larry Lajoie into a good bunter. The inability to lay one down had been identified as one of the rare weaknesses in Lajoie's skill set; now, bunting became another weapon in his offensive arsenal. With National League third basemen playing far back due to his scorching line drives down the line, Lajoie found that he could beat out a bunt almost any time one was needed, and even when it wasn't. He was fast in his younger days, with 23 triples and 20 stolen bases in 1897, and his newfound bunting ability gave him another way to get on base.

Despite the turmoil surrounding the team, the biggest story of 1898 was the emergence of Napoleon Lajoie as a star of the first rank. Despite his one problem with curfew near the end of Stallings' managerial tenure, he had kept his batting average in the .300s and assumed the National League lead in doubles and runs batted in. Now permanently established at second base, he caused opponents to wonder how such a big player could handle the position so easily and display such wide range. "He plays so naturally and so easily it looks like lack of effort," observed Connie Mack, who would later manage Lajoie in the American League. "Larry's reach is so long and he's fast as lightning, and to throw to at second base he is ideal. All the catchers who've played with him say he is the easiest man to throw to in the game today. High, low, wide — he is sure of everything."[10]

Tim Hurst, the former umpire who managed the St. Louis Browns in 1898, was most impressed with Larry's hitting. After the Phillies won three of four from the Browns in St. Louis in June, Hurst told *Sporting Life*, "That big Lajoie is a wonder with the willow. He is the most natural ball player I ever saw. Every time he came to the bat in the series here I would hold my breath, and every minute I expected to see him land the ball out of the lot."[11] At age 23, Larry threatened to surpass the still dangerous Ed Delahanty as the best hitter in the National League, and because he was such a gifted fielder, many reporters were already nominating him as the premier player in the game. He committed only one error in a 28-game stretch in mid-season, and as *Sporting Life* asserted in August, "All over the circuit Lajoie is now being accepted as the greatest second baseman in the League as well as the greatest all-round ball player in America."[12]

Not everyone would put Lajoie ahead of "the Only Del," at least not yet. In one game, the Chicago Colts took a one-run lead into the ninth inning against the hard-hitting Phillies. Clark Griffith, the Chicago pitcher, retired two Philadelphia batters, but the Phillies put the tying run on second base with two out. The next batter was Delahanty, with Lajoie waiting on deck. Griffith, after sizing up the situation, elected to walk Delahanty and pitch to the equally menacing Lajoie. The strategy worked, as Larry popped up to end the game. Later, someone asked Griffith why he chose to take his chances with Lajoie.

"I noticed," said Griffith, "that Delahanty was looking at the fences. Lajoie was looking at the infield setup, seeing where he could slash one between 'em. I decided to take the guy with the least ambitious look."[13]

Washington pitcher Gus Weyhing, a former Phillie who had been a fixture on the major league scene for more than a decade, remarked on Lajoie's penchant for chasing bad balls. "He can hit high ones on the inside, that is, so far inside that the ball shaves his jersey. And he can carom a low ball off his socks. But if you get the sphere plumb over the plate, he might not hit it. That's what you call wild or crazy hitting, but some of the great assassins of pitchers were wild-pitch hitters such as Dave Orr, for example."[14] Lajoie, who walked only 21 times in 1898, was not nearly as selective at the plate as Delahanty (77 walks) or the rookie Flick (86 walks), who slumped after his outstanding start and wound up barely clearing the .300 mark at season's end. Still, Lajoie hit the ball harder than anyone and joined with Flick and Delahanty to form a three-man slugging combo that no other National League team could match.

Lajoie also learned to use his size to his advantage. Jake Beckley, the Cincinnati first baseman, was infamous for tripping, spiking, and manhandling opposing base runners, but Lajoie refused to stand for such punishment. On August 27, Beckley planted himself in front of first base as Lajoie ran out a hit. Beckley was a big man, but Lajoie was a bigger one, and the Phillies star simply ran over Beckley, spraining the Cincinnati infielder's wrist and putting him on the shelf for a month. Larry had sent a message to the rest of the league, and although the Phillies lost that game by a 3–2 score, the club followed up with five wins in a row. The Phillies were finally playing to their talent level, and Francis Richter, perhaps a bit giddy with the club's turnaround, proclaimed in August that the Phillies were "inherently the league's strongest team."[15]

Largely due to the hitting of Lajoie and Delahanty (who lifted his average to .334 that year and led the league in stolen bases with 58) and a much improved pitching staff, the Phillies came to life in August and started to climb the standings. Buried in eighth place when Shettsline took over, the Phillies moved up to seventh during the last week of August and set their sights on sixth place, the final slot in the first division of the 12-team league. They battled the New York Giants for the sixth position, and in late September, after splitting a four-game set with the Giants at the Polo Grounds, the Phillies stood only one game from the top half of the league.

The Phillies, like most other clubs, often complained about certain umpires, and one of the least popular arbiters in Philadelphia was a first-year man named Tom Brown. Recently retired from a 17-year career as a player, Brown found rough going as an arbiter, becoming involved in several controversies with the Phillies that increased in vehemence as the year wore on. In September, *Sporting Life* reported that the Phillies had complained about Brown's work in a hard-fought Labor Day doubleheader split against the Orioles, calling the umpire "hot-tempered, indiscreet and, so far as the Phillies were concerned, vindictive."[16] Rogers and Reach asked league president Nick Young not to assign Brown to any more Phillies games, but Young refused to consider their request. With Shettsline's men fighting to finish above the .500 mark, Brown was put in charge of a key series between the Phillies and the league-leading Boston club.

The Phillies lost the first contest, and in the second game of the series, played on Friday, September 30, they howled at a blown call that helped the Beaneaters score four runs in the second inning and, with 30-game-winner Kid Nichols on the mound for Boston, put the contest virtually out of reach. Lajoie was as incensed as any of his teammates, and after the second inning he passed the umpire and made his feelings known. Lajoie claimed later that he said nothing more insulting than, "Tom, I thought it only took three pitches to strike out a man instead of five."[17] Brown flew into a rage and tossed Lajoie from the game, and when the Phillies second baseman loudly denounced the arbiter as "crooked,"

Brown ordered Lajoie from the premises. Because the umpires had recently been empowered to issue suspensions for what the league magnates had called "villainously filthy language," Brown suspended Lajoie for three days.

Without Lajoie, the Phillies lost that game to Boston by a 7–3 score, and on Saturday Boston hurler Fred Klobedanz, his former Fall River teammate, defeated Philadelphia by a 5–2 count. There was no game on Sunday, so with the three-day suspension over, Lajoie re-entered the lineup against the Giants on Monday in New York. He went hitless as the Phillies lost that contest, 3–0, dropping their record to 69–68.

The team needed to close the season with a rush to clear the .500 mark, and Lajoie provided it on October 4 at the Polo Grounds. Amos Rusie, the Giants right-hander, held the Phillies at bay for eight innings and entered the ninth with a 3–0 lead. Rusie, whose once-powerful fastball had slowed perceptibly due to arm and shoulder miseries, faltered in the ninth as Ed McFarland singled and, after he retired Monte Cross, pitcher Wiley Piatt hit a slow bounder to the mound. Rusie's wild throw to first allowed McFarland to score, and after a walk to Dick Cooley, Rusie struck out Klondike Douglass for the second out. Ed Delahanty then singled home Piatt and advanced Cooley to third. The score was now 3 to 2, with two men on and Lajoie at bat.

Delahanty stole second while Rusie concentrated on Lajoie at the plate. "Without question," said Rusie to a reporter a few weeks earlier, "Lajoie hits harder than any batter in the League, and I am always a little leery when I face him for fear one of his hot ones will get me."[18] Lajoie, with the game on line, hung in against the wildness-plagued Rusie, who had hit both Lajoie and Delahanty with pitches earlier in the game. Rusie's best strategy would probably have been to walk the most dangerous hitter in the league, but Lajoie wanted no part of a free pass, intentional or not. Lajoie swung at a fastball and drilled in to the outfield, scoring Cooley and Delahanty and winning the game by a 4–3 score.

The Phillies ended the campaign with seven games against tenth-place Brooklyn, winning four of them to beat out the Giants for sixth place with a game and a half to spare. Colonel Rogers not only awarded the promised payout to the players for finishing in the top half of the league after their poor start, but, as the papers reported, all the Phillies received their temperance bonuses as well. The club, riven by internal strife for several seasons, appeared to have turned the corner, and many observers expected the Phillies not only to challenge for the 1899 pennant, but to win it.

6

"The Best That Ever Happened"

Speaking of Lajoie, he's the best man on second I ever saw. Nothing gets away from him, for he's got a hand as big as two of mine. Zing comes Mr. Ball, out goes the big mitt, and Mr. Ball's flight is through. I tell you, he is a great player. — Bill Bernhard, Philadelphia pitcher, 1899[1]

The Phillies entered the 1899 season with high hopes, but the National League landscape had changed dramatically during the winter months. The 12-team league was too large, and calls to fold up some of the poorly supported, perennial second-division clubs such as Louisville and Washington were being taken seriously in league circles. After much discussion, the magnates decided to leave the 12-team structure intact for the 1899 campaign, but several clubs in the circuit underwent drastic changes.

The Cleveland Spiders had often challenged for pennants during the 1890s, but weak fan support and the lack of Sunday baseball threatened the future of the sport in that northern Ohio city. In 1898, a public boycott of the streetcar lines operated by brothers Frank and Stanley Robison, who also owned the baseball team, caused such a sharp drop in attendance that the Robisons moved most of their games out of Cleveland during the second half of the season. The Spiders spent almost all of August and September on an extended road trip, causing some of the nation's writers to refer to the team, which was dominated by players of Irish descent, as the "Wandering Micks." The Spiders were not the only endangered team. Years of financial mismanagement had finally caught up with St. Louis Browns owner Chris von der Ahe, who was faced with bankruptcy and the sale of his ballclub at a sheriff's auction. A disastrous stadium fire in early 1898, coupled with a losing, dispirited team, threatened the existence of National League baseball in St. Louis.

The Robison brothers, frustrated with the situation in Cleveland, moved to solve their problems with a bold stroke. Through a middle man, they bought the St. Louis Browns at auction, then moved all of Cleveland's star players (including Cy Young, Jesse Burkett, and manager Patsy Tebeau) to the Mound City, instantly creating a club that was not only financially stable but also loaded with talent. Though the Spiders were left with what Lee Allen once called "the sorriest shell of a team ever seen in the major leagues"[2] by the Cleveland–St. Louis merger, the new Browns (renamed the Perfectos by the local papers) had suddenly thrust themselves into pennant contention.

The owners of the Brooklyn Bridegrooms, later called the Dodgers, had looked into buying the Browns, but instead set their sights on Baltimore, where the three-time league champion Orioles drew so poorly that they teetered on the brink of failure. In February 1899, the Baltimore and Brooklyn magnates effected a merger of the two teams, with almost all of Baltimore's stars shifting to Brooklyn to play for the Bridegrooms. Ned Hanlon, the longtime Baltimore manager, also moved north, where he became the field boss of the newly merged club (renamed the Superbas after a popular vaudeville act of the day). John McGraw, Baltimore's gritty third baseman, refused to move to Brooklyn, and was left behind in Baltimore to manage the decimated Orioles. Brooklyn, which had finished a distant tenth in the National League in 1898, was now, like the St. Louis squad, an instant contender.

These moves proved troubling for teams such as the Philadelphia Phillies and the Boston Beaneaters, which had neither the inclination nor the opportunity to strengthen themselves by simply buying out another team and absorbing its best players. The nation's sportswriters decried the advent of what they called "syndicate baseball," but the league allowed the franchise sales and subsequent talent shifts to proceed. In addition, Brooklyn and St. Louis intended to use their junior partners in Baltimore and Cleveland as virtual farm teams. Ned Hanlon, after the Brooklyn-Baltimore merger, became the manager of the Bridegrooms and half-owner of the Orioles simultaneously, and he could, and did, shuttle players between the two clubs as needed with little interference. The St. Louis club did the same with the Cleveland Spiders. These two teams thus enjoyed a competitive advantage that was not available to the Phillies and Beaneaters.

Because of the emergence of "superteams" in Brooklyn and St. Louis, the Phillies found the road to their first National League pennant more challenging than ever. However, they had one asset that neither the Perfectos nor the Superbas could match. Neither of those teams owned a player as talented as Napoleon Lajoie. Lajoie had, by this time, emerged as the best young player in the game, and it was not hard to find knowledgeable observers who considered him the premier performer in the National League, bar none. In May of 1899, *Sporting Life*, the Philadelphia-based weekly paper, put Lajoie's photograph on its cover with the caption, "The League's Greatest Second Baseman, Hardest Hitter and Best General Player."[3]

The Phillies selected Charlotte, North Carolina, as their spring training site, and Lajoie arrived in his usual good spirits and excellent physical condition. Though some of his teammates used their sojourn in Charlotte to lose their excess poundage, Lajoie had no need to drop any weight. He had, as usual, spent the winter months playing handball with his friends in Woonsocket. He merely needed to fine-tune his batting eye and become acquainted with the latest additions to the Philadelphia roster.

One of the new arrivals was Roy Thomas, an outfielder who presented a distinctly different style of batting from what the Phillies were used to. Thomas had graduated from the University of Pennsylvania several years before, had starred in the semipro ranks since then, and was a 25-year-old who specialized in fouling off pitches until he worked the pitcher for a walk. Foul balls were not then counted as strikes, and Thomas displayed such incredible bat control that he once, according to legend, fouled off 27 pitches in a row before drawing a free pass. Thomas had virtually no power (in 1900, 161 of his 168 hits were singles), but scored a lot of runs because he knew how to get on base. Billy Shettsline, intrigued by Thomas' unusual skill set, placed him at first base and penciled his name into the leadoff spot.

Another fresh face belonged to a 28-year-old pitcher named Bill Bernhard, a right-hander who would figure prominently in Napoleon Lajoie's future. Bernhard had been courted by the Phillies in 1898 after pitching well in the New York State League, but when Colonel Rogers failed to offer him enough money, Bernhard turned down the chance to pitch in the majors and played instead for independent teams. Rogers raised his offer in early 1899, so Bernhard signed and reported to the Phillies in Charlotte. The Phillies added him to a mound corps that looked, on paper, much stronger than their pitching staffs of recent years.

Charlotte was unseasonably cold and rainy while the Phillies trained there, forcing the players to conduct many of their workouts indoors in a local gymnasium. There wasn't much to do in Charlotte at night, so captain Dick Cooley entertained his teammates by playing the piano and leading the Phillies in sing-alongs. He also held strategy sessions and bunting drills. Manager Billy Shettsline trusted Cooley and left most of the field leadership to his captain, who appeared to have rehabilitated himself after several alcohol-related incidents during the previous two seasons. The Philadelphia papers referred to the team as "Cooley's men" or "Cooley's Phillies," in recognition of his leadership abilities.

Lajoie in 1899 (Transcendental Graphics/the ruckerarchive.com).

The season began on April 13, and despite the threat of rain on an overcast day, about 12,000 fans came out to see the spectacle of Opening Day. The Phillies boasted new uniforms in white with green trim, a new color scheme that may have been a nod to the Irish ancestry of Delahanty and many of the other Philadelphia players. Napoleon Lajoie brought his new pet, a 45-pound brindle bulldog that he had bought in Woonsocket a few weeks before. With a bright green bow around its neck, the bulldog joined the parade of players in the pregame ceremonies and made itself at home on the Phillie bench during the game. Lajoie, who received a large display of roses from his admirers when he went to bat the first time, singled in five trips to the plate as the Phillies defeated Washington by a 6–5 score.

The Phillies started the season well, and both Delahanty and Lajoie showed their hitting form early. On April 27, Lajoie belted a homer and a triple as the Phillies bombed the Beaneaters, 20–3. Boston pitcher Fred Klobedanz, Lajoie's old Fall River teammate, failed to last through the first inning, and after the Phillies had safely put the game out of reach, Boston manager Frank Selee sent outfielder Chick Stahl in to pitch the last two innings. The defending league champion Beaneaters played ragged ball, issuing 14 walks and committing seven errors, and the lopsided score gave hope to the Philadelphia fans that their team might finally subdue their perennial rivals in their bid for the pennant. Two days later, Lajoie drilled a double and three singles in an 8–5 victory over the Giants. Lajoie and Delahanty both entered the month of May with batting averages well over the .400 mark, putting the Phillies in the thick of the fight for the early league lead.

Delahanty, who batted third in the Philadelphia lineup, and Lajoie, who hit in the cleanup slot, were the hardest-hitting duo in the major leagues, a distinction that became clear to all on May 13, 1899. On that day, in a contest played at the Polo Grounds in New York, Delahanty walloped four doubles off Giants pitcher Tom Colcolough, while Lajoie pounded out two singles, a double, and a triple in a 9–0 Phillies win. Late in the game, after both Delahanty and Lajoie had smashed hits off the brick wall in center field, Giants second baseman Kid Gleason retrieved the baseball and showed it to umpire Ed Swartwood. The ball had been split open and pounded out of shape by the force of Delahanty's and Lajoie's blows. The ball's rubber core was broken completely in two, making the baseball lopsided and causing the yarn around the core to spill out of the torn cover. Swartwood put a new ball in play, but kept the damaged one as a keepsake. "I have never seen a ball knocked to pieces before," said Gleason after the game, "and I guess no ball was ever hit so hard as Delahanty and Lajoie banged that one."[4]

Delahanty and Lajoie, who were roommates on the road, were fast friends as well as rivals for batting supremacy on the team. "I'll bet they look at the batting averages less than any other two players in the league," said infielder Monte Cross during a mid-season series against the Reds.

> Here are two men playing side by side that are the best batters in America, yet they are not the least bit jealous of each other. Delahanty had added quite a number of hits to his string since he came here [to Cincinnati], while Lajoie has not been so fortunate. At the next stand it may be Lajoie who will do the batting and Delahanty have a slump. No matter which way it breaks, they will not worry about it. They are easy-going good fellows who are hustling for team, not their individual records.[5]

The Sporting News gave much of the credit for Lajoie's ascent to his friend Delahanty. "[Delahanty's] hitting has stirred Lajoie's sluggish blood," the paper claimed, "and the Frenchman is lining them out now, while his base running has also made the big second baseman envious."[6]

The Phillies, after winning four straight from the Giants at home, were tied with the resurgent St. Louis Perfectos for the league lead, with the Chicago Orphans (so named after the firing of longtime manager Cap Anson a year before) half a game behind. Lurking one game off the pace was Brooklyn, the other combination team, with a lineup made up mostly of the former stars of the Baltimore Orioles. Most observers expected Brooklyn to challenge for the flag, and in mid–May the Superbas made their move. They defeated the Phillies in three hard-fought games at home on May 15, 16, and 17, in a series marred by constant arguments with the umpires.

The first game of the series was a close one until the eighth inning. With the bases loaded, Brooklyn's Willie Keeler, the high-average singles hitter and bunter extraordinaire, smashed a hard shot past a startled Ed Delahanty in left field and made it around the bases for an inside-the-park, grand slam homer that gave the Superbas an 8–5 win. On the following afternoon, umpires Al Warner and Ed Swartwood angered the Phillies by charging two damaging balks against pitcher Red Donahue and calling several Phillies out on the bases when they appeared to be easily safe. When the Phillies protested one of Warner's out calls, the arbiter allegedly cursed them, then ejected and fined several of them as the Superbas escaped with a 6–5 win. The arguments were even worse the next day, when a bad call by Warner allowed Brooklyn to score the winning run in the ninth. The Phillies, who entered the series in a tie for first place, left it two and a half games behind.

The Phillies were so upset by the umpiring in the series that six players (including Cooley and Elmer Flick, but not Lajoie) signed affidavits attesting to Warner's obscene language and general incompetence and sent them to the league office, after which nothing more was heard about them. The players also petitioned Colonel Rogers to lift the club-imposed automatic $25 fine for any Phillie ejected from a game, insisting that umpires used the rule to punish the Philadelphia players more severely than those on other teams. Rogers expressed his sympathy, but declined to remit the fines. At least the Phillies could take heart in knowing that they were not the only ones who believed that Swartwood and (especially) Warner had cost them two of the three games. Almost all of the papers in Philadelphia and even many in Brooklyn and New York City agreed with them, roasting Warner as "incompetent" and worse.

The Phillies tried to put a positive spin on the triple defeat. Lajoie, while pacing angrily after the third game, fulminated to a reporter, "Well, if it takes two umpires, doing all in their power, helping Brooklyn to down us, it shows that we are just about 50 per cent stronger than that team, and can lick them with fair umpiring in nine out of ten games, and if we can do that to Brooklyn we can do it to pretty nearly all of them."[7] However, the Superbas, managed by Ned Hanlon and built on the core of Hanlon's Baltimore pennant winners, were too strong. They took the lead on a western swing later in May, then compiled a 12-game winning streak and kept control of first place for the rest of the season.

While the Phillies fought to stay in the pennant race, Larry Lajoie continued his rampage against National League pitchers. On June 2, his walk-off solo homer in the bottom of the ninth inning gave the Phillies a win against the Pittsburgh Pirates by a 4–3 count, and on June 19 he destroyed another baseball in a 9–0 win over the Reds. While facing left-hander Ted Breitenstein in Cincinnati, Lajoie belted a hard liner that caromed off the center field wall and bounded back toward the infield as Lajoie legged it out for a triple. The force of the ball's collisions with Lajoie's bat and the wall knocked it lopsided and, as before, broke its rubber core in two.

After the game, Lajoie went out with some Cincinnati friends and gave the bat he used that day to one of his acquaintances as a souvenir. He then went hitless the following day as a local paper, the *Enquirer*, marveled in a headline, "No boards were loosened in the fence, and no balls were knocked lopsided."[8] The Phillies lost to the Reds by a 3–2 score, and Lajoie went hitless again the next day, though he made several fine fielding plays in a 7–6 Philadelphia win. Lajoie was unconcerned about his two-game slump. "I went eight games last year without making a hit," he said to a Cincinnati reporter. "I was hitting hard, but I could not get one safe. Delahanty went seven straight games without sending anything to [league president] Nick Young. When Del got his eye back he rather made up for lost time. The next 14 times up he made safe hits."[9] Actually, Delahanty made ten hits in a row, a record that Lajoie tied several years later. Lajoie broke out of his mini-slump on the 21st with four singles in a 9–5 win that allowed the Phillies to solidify their hold on third place.

Lajoie's performance against the Reds impressed the sports staff of the *Cincinnati Enquirer*.

> Well may it be said of Napoleon Lajoie that he's the best that ever happened. Taking everything into consideration, batting, fielding, and base-running, and the big Frenchman must be rated the best player in the history of the league.... One would think a man of his weight and stature entirely out of his element in such a position where it requires so many quick turn and twists, yet Lajoie "keeps step with procession," and does everything so gracefully that he makes hard plays appear to be easy ones.[10]

A story, probably apocryphal, made the rounds that a hard line drive from Lajoie's bat killed not one, but two, unlucky birds one afternoon. Perhaps that tale was an exaggeration, but if anyone could hit a ball that hard, Lajoie could.

Lajoie displayed so much range at second base that he ran the risk of colliding with the outfielders, particularly right fielder Elmer Flick. On Monday, May 30, Lajoie and Flick slammed into each other while chasing a fly to short right. The collision knocked Flick out of the lineup for three games, while Lajoie continued playing. Lajoie's chest was deeply bruised, however, and after a week of playing in pain he took five days off to let the injury heal. Said Francis Richter in *Sporting Life*, "For this injury the player's doctor has prescribed absolute rest, besides trussing him up like a chicken."[11]

The right field area in the Huntingdon Street Grounds ballpark was so small, and the Phillies second baseman ventured into it so often, that Flick became annoyed at his teammate's forays into the outfield. Flick had a strong throwing arm, which allowed him to throw out runners at first base on what looked like clean hits, so he resented Lajoie's excursions into what he believed was his territory. Twice during the 1899 season, Flick berated Lajoie with such vehemence that the two men nearly came to blows. Though Lajoie's relationship with Delahanty was a strong one, he and Flick did not get along, and their increasingly bitter quarrels would have an important effect on the team in the future.

Despite a spate of poor pitching performances, the Phillies stayed in the top half of the league, mostly due to the prodigious hitting of Delahanty, Lajoie, and Flick. The St. Louis Perfectos had led the league in the early going, but faded as the summer heat and clubhouse tensions between the newly arrived ex–Spiders and the holdovers from the Browns took their toll. The Baltimore Orioles, meanwhile, had managed to keep a few good players away from their Brooklyn masters and, under the direction of first-year manager John McGraw, fought for a spot in the first division. In early July, after the Phillies won four of seven games against league-leading Brooklyn, they held fourth place, five and a half games out of the lead, with the fading Perfectos and surging Orioles right behind. Just ahead of the Phillies were the Beaneaters, who held onto second place despite their aging and injury-riddled roster, and Chicago, a contender for the first time in several seasons.

Though Hanlon's Brooklyn team was the best in the National League, the Phillies might still have mounted a challenge were it not for the most serious injury of Napoleon Lajoie's career so far. On July 14, 1899, in a game at Cincinnati, he slid into second base on a force play and collided with Reds rookie shortstop Harry Steinfeldt at full speed. It appears that Lajoie swerved in mid-slide to avoid spiking Steinfeldt, who fielded a grounder directly in his path. Steinfeldt's head struck Lajoie's knee with great force, knocking the Cincinnati player unconscious for more than five minutes. Lajoie, however, was the more seriously injured of the two, with a severely damaged knee which swelled up immediately. Steinfeldt returned to the lineup the next day, though he complained of headaches for months afterward, but Lajoie's knee had suffered so much trauma that he could not put any weight on it. He remained bedridden for about three weeks, and did not appear at practice again until early September.

While the Phillies carried on in his absence, Lajoie remained at home in bed, with his leg encased in a bandage and tied tightly to a cotton-covered wooden splint. The papers reported that the knee was twice its normal size due to synovitis, commonly called "water on the knee," which caused the skin to swell up painfully both below and above the joint. "Lajoie's injury is a serious one," said the Phillies team physician, Dr. John A. Boger, as quoted in the *Richmond Times*.

> It affects a delicate part — the knee cap — a portion of the body that should be free from injury in a man who must be active, as is required of a base ball player. Lajoie is a good patient. He follows instructions implicitly and I place more than ordinary reliance on him to pull through quickly.
>
> The world little knows of his physical powers. Strong, alert, well preserved, and perfectly developed, he will recover more rapidly than a less powerful man, yet possessing all these

rare physical gifts we can take no chances with him and his treatment must be adhered to if he expects to fill his part in the future as well as in the past. I cannot say definitely when he will be able to enter the game again, but I hope it will be within a few weeks.[12]

On July 27, 13 days after the injury, the doctor reported that the swelling had gone down a bit, and as the *Times* put it, "the nurse and physician were so well pleased that the fourteen runs made by the Pirates against the Phillies on Saturday were forgotten."[13]

Lajoie's injury was a fatal blow to Philadelphia's pennant hopes; as the *Boston Post* remarked, "It is only a fair assumption that, with [Lajoie] on the team, Brooklyn and Philadelphia would be now neck and neck for the lead."[14] Elmer Flick was also lost to the team in early August when he tripped over second base and dislocated his knee. He expected to be out for the rest of the season, but re-entered the lineup on September 4. Unfortunately, he reinjured the knee while chasing a foul fly in his first game back and put himself on the shelf for another three weeks.

The Phillies struggled in Lajoie's absence, with a parade of second base hopefuls (Joe Dolan, Pete Chiles, and Red Owens among them) trying, and failing, to make the grade at the position. Still, the Phillies fought their way into third place, and even passed the Beaneaters for second, largely on the strength of Ed Delahanty's bat. "The Only Del" stepped

The 1899 Philadelphia Phillies. Ed Delahanty is third from left in the middle row, next to manager Billy Shettsline. Lajoie is third from the left in the top row, and Elmer Flick is seated second from left at the bottom (National Baseball Hall of Fame Library, Cooperstown, New York).

up when the club needed him the most, leading the league in hits (234) and doubles (56) and winning his first batting title with an incredible .410 average. Delahanty also compiled a 31-game hitting streak, setting a Phillies team record that stood until Jimmy Rollins broke it in 2006.

Perhaps Delahanty's performance was partially sparked by financial considerations, because Colonel Rogers had publicly promised the players a $5,000 pot to split evenly if they won the pennant, and $2,500 if they finished in second place. The pennant was out of reach by August, but the runner-up spot was a distinct possibility, and the thought of a few hundred dollars of bonus money apiece at the end of the season appealed to the Phillies players.

Lajoie's injury was not the only stumbling block for the Phillies in 1899. On the same day that Lajoie was injured, team captain Dick Cooley was hit by a ball in the mouth during a morning practice session and driven from the lineup. It was the second time in two weeks that the captain had suffered a similar injury, and since Cooley's bat had recently gone cold, fans and reporters speculated that the captain had resumed drinking. He had also exchanged heated words on several occasions with the unruly Philadelphia fans, who were impatient with the team's failure to catch Brooklyn and took it out on the thin-skinned field leader. Cooley angrily denied that he had fallen off the wagon, but Colonel Rogers decided, despite a lack of solid evidence, that Cooley had broken his temperance pledge. Rogers then suspended his captain without pay.

Cooley had played center field for most of his career, but when rookie Roy Thomas impressed one and all with his fielding skill early in the season, Shettsline placed Thomas in center and shifted Cooley to first (rather than move Lajoie or Delahanty there). This arrangement put Cooley much closer to the grandstand, and as Brooklyn pulled away in the pennant chase, the fans turned surly and took out their frustrations on the captain. Rogers, who had gained controlling interest in the club earlier that year, may have been giving the fans what he thought they wanted when he suspended Cooley, but with Lajoie out, the team did not need another open spot in the lineup. Cooley's suspension also forced Delahanty, against his will, to take the captaincy.

Cooley was popular with his fellow Phillies, and the players almost unanimously took his side in his dispute with management, but Rogers was not a man to waver once his mind was made up. Rogers not only suspended Cooley, but refused to trade or sell him to another team, though many other National League clubs would have worked out a deal for him. The incident showed Rogers at his vindictive worst, and illustrated the powerlessness that most National League players felt. Such high-handed treatment of a possibly innocent player was the kind of injustice that had caused the Players League revolt of 1890, and would play a part in the baseball war that was still two years in the future.

The Phillies imported a minor leaguer named Billy Goeckel, who had performed well at Wilkes-Barre in the Atlantic League, to take Cooley's place at first. Goeckel fielded passably but hit poorly, with only four extra-base blows among his 37 hits. The right side of the infield, once a Philadelphia strength, was now the team's biggest weakness. In the meantime, Napoleon Lajoie, distressed by his enforced inaction, chafed on the bench. Buck Freeman of the Senators, interviewed by a *Washington Post* reporter, said that Lajoie told him, "I just want to get back in there and get a swipe at the ball. It will do my bum knee more good than a week of witch hazel baths and massages."[15] His knee healed slowly, and not until September 12, after a three-month layoff, did Lajoie again practice with his teammates.

In the end, the battle for second place (and the promised $2,500 bonus from Colonel Rogers) came down to the last seven games of the 1899 season, in which the Phillies and Beaneaters played three games at Philadelphia followed by four more in Boston. With Lajoie watching from the sidelines, the Phillies won the first two contests by 6–3 and 3–1 scores, pulling back into a tie for second with five games remaining. Then disaster struck the team once again. Roy Thomas, the rookie center fielder who had stepped into Dick Cooley's place and scored 137 runs from the leadoff spot in the lineup, was injured in an unexplained off-field accident. The Phillies players mourned the loss of Thomas, but expected that, with a large amount of money on the line, team management would reinstate the healthy and rested Cooley to fill the hole in the outfield.

Colonel Rogers, however, was in no mood to put Cooley back on the roster, no matter how badly he was needed. To the chagrin of the fans and players, Rogers and Shettsline decided instead to put Larry Lajoie, gimpy knee and all, in center field and move Pete Childs to first base. Larry tried his best, but managed only a single as the Beaneaters defeated the Phillies 6–0 behind Ted (Parson) Lewis' eight-hit shutout. Now it was on to Boston, where the Phillies needed to win three of four to grab the coveted second slot.

Predictably, Rogers refused to budge, Cooley remained on the sidelines, and Lajoie collected only three hits, all singles, in the final four games. Delahanty and Flick, both battling minor injuries and slumping at the worst possible time, failed to solve Boston's curveball expert Vic Willis on Wednesday, October 11, in a 6–0 Beaneaters win. The Phils took a 7–3 win on Thursday, but a three-hit shutout by Kid Nichols on Friday clinched second place for Boston and deprived the Phillies of their hoped-for payday. Philadelphia won the final game to finish third with a 94–58 record, nine games behind pennant-winning Brooklyn and a single game behind Boston.

The 1899 campaign was a mixed bag for Lajoie. He played in only 77 of the 152 scheduled games, and his still-aching knee prevented him from performing at his usual level during the last few games of the season. Still, he scored 70 runs and drove in 70, and his .378 average was his highest yet in the major leagues. At age 25, he had already established himself as the best all-around player in the game, and his prime years lay ahead of him. In addition, he had completed the season without a major behavioral incident, and appeared to be maturing into a reliable team player.

Perhaps the presence of Lajoie in the lineup all season might not have made up the nine-game bulge between the Superbas and the Phillies, but Dick Cooley's rude dismissal and the constant drama caused by Colonel Rogers also contributed to the disappointing finish. Though the Phillies ranked first in the league in attendance (partly due to the 25-cent admission price), the fans were growing increasingly frustrated with the team. Still, hopes remained high for the 1900 campaign as fans looked forward to a healthy Lajoie, continued great hitting from Flick and Delahanty, and improved pitching.

The National League eliminated its four least-profitable clubs after the 1899 season, with Baltimore, Cleveland, Louisville, and Washington disappearing from the baseball map. The Phillies, who went 24–4 against Cleveland and Washington in 1899, could no longer expect to pad their record by beating up on the hopeless tail-enders. The Phillies knew, however, that the other seven remaining National League teams faced the same situation, and the Superbas, who walloped the helpless Cleveland Spiders 14 times without a loss, would be hard-pressed to match their win total in a more competitive eight-team league.

7

A Painful Season

Lajoie in practice the other day demonstrated what a really marvelous all around player he is by curving the ball on a throw to the plate. With a little practice Lajoie might be as great a pitcher as he is an infielder. — Francis C. Richter, April 1900[1]

A competitor to the National League emerged during the last few months of 1899. A group of disgruntled baseball men, including former Baltimore manager John McGraw and longtime Chicago star Cap Anson, challenged the established order with an attempt to revive the old American Association. They spent the winter months lining up capital, scouting locations for ballparks, and battling the established National League in the nation's newspapers. By January the proposed new circuit appeared to have established six reasonably viable franchises, four in the west and two (Boston and a Baltimore entry to be owned by McGraw) in the east. The new Association needed two more eastern clubs to proceed, with Philadelphia and New York its main targets. Philadelphia, supported by *Sporting Life*'s Francis Richter, a longtime National League critic, was the linchpin of the new league. If a solid franchise could be established there, many dissatisfied Phillies, including Ed Delahanty and Napoleon Lajoie, might be persuaded to join up.

National League players were hungry for an alternative to the high-handed treatment they had received at the hands of their bosses since the collapse of the Players League ten years before, and when the new Association held an organizational meeting in Philadelphia in late January of 1900, Delahanty and Lajoie mingled with the would-be magnates, gauging for themselves how stable and viable the new league might be. The papers had reported that in November 1899, an emissary of the proposed Association had traveled to Woonsocket and offered Lajoie a $3,000 contract, along with a healthy signing bonus, to leave the Phillies and throw in his lot with the new circuit. Since no team yet existed in Philadelphia, Lajoie turned down the offer, and Delahanty, despite his attendance at the Association meeting, allowed that he was "not much interested anyway."[2] He said, not too convincingly, that he was there to renew his acquaintances with longtime friends Anson, McGraw, and others.

In the end, the proposed Philadelphia team in the new Association never materialized, and its failure to launch caused the downfall of the would-be competitor to the National League. In mid–February, with the start of the new baseball season mere weeks away, Association president Cap Anson admitted defeat and promised to try again in 1901. In the meantime, the Western League, a Midwestern-based circuit which had long harbored hopes of achieving parity with the National, moved some of its teams into larger cities (including Chicago and Cleveland) and renamed itself the American League. This circuit was still considered a minor league in 1900, but bore watching as a future threat to the established structure of major league baseball.

Lajoie, who spent much of the winter in Philadelphia instead of Woonsocket, and Delahanty were closer friends than ever, united by their similar personalities and by their shared disdain for Phillies management. Each man believed that he was underpaid, though each made the National League maximum salary of $2,400 per year. However, it was no secret around the league that the stars of other teams received higher salaries through creative contract language, easily attainable bonuses, or sometimes through payments under the table. Colonel Rogers, in contrast, held fast to the league-mandated salary cap despite the presence of Delahanty, the 1899 batting champ, and Lajoie, widely acclaimed as the best all-around player in the game. Rogers angered his men by filling his contracts with temperance clauses and penalties for bad behavior, using those restrictions as an excuse to withhold funds until the end of the season. Believing that his stars had no recourse but to accept things the way they were, Rogers expected Lajoie and the other Phillies to sign on the dotted line as usual. Lajoie and Delahanty, however, had other ideas. They decided to hold out for $3,000 apiece, and refused to sign their contracts for 1900 until they received what they wanted.

Several other Phillies followed the lead of the team's two biggest stars and declined to sign their agreements as well. They were angry with Colonel Rogers' meddlesome ways and his one-sided contracts. Some of the players believed that Rogers should have given them the promised $2,500 second-place bonus at the end of the 1899 campaign, though the team had fallen one game short of the mark, because they had fought so hard in the effort. Besides, Rogers' refusal to reinstate Dick Cooley, in their view, kept the team from passing Boston in the battle for second position. Cooley, though his relationship with Rogers had been damaged beyond repair, was still the property of the Phillies. Rogers turned down all offers from other teams for his former captain, deeming them insufficient, and offered Cooley a take-it-or-leave-it contract for $1,200, half his salary of the year before. Rogers' treatment of the still-popular Cooley angered the players and strengthened the holdouts — Flick, McFarland, Piatt, Douglas, and Bernhard among them — in their resolve.

As the 1900 season approached, the holdouts made noises about quitting the game, and some of the local papers took their statements seriously. According to the *Philadelphia Record*,

> This will probably be the last season for four of the best players of the Philadelphia base ball team. Having grown tired of the "iron hand" of base ball club owners, Delahanty, Platt, McFarland and Flick are thinking very seriously of giving up the game to embark in other lines of business. Delahanty will probably open a saloon in this city. Piatt says he will have a saloon in Lexington, Ky., next winter and unless he is treated better will not return to Philadelphia another season. McFarland, the Phillies' crack catcher, says he would rather be at home all year around, and his parents have been trying to persuade him to give up ball playing. He says it is quite likely that he will accept his father's proposition and enter the shoe business in Cleveland. Flick's father is a prosperous chair manufacturer in Cleveland, and next year the business may demand the assistance of Elmer.[3]

The fact that Lajoie's name was not listed in the report is telling. Other players had options; indeed, Billy Lauder, the team's regular third baseman in 1899, decided to forsake the Phillies and enter the business world after a dispute with Colonel Rogers over a promised bonus. First baseman Billy Goeckel, who already owned a degree from Penn, was disillusioned with the game and quit to start a law practice. The league featured several players, such as Philadelphia's Wiley Piatt and Pittsburgh pitcher Sam Leever, who taught school during the winter months, while the ranks of National Leaguers included an increasing number of men (John McGraw among them) with college educations. Lajoie, however, had little schooling and no working experience outside of baseball, other than his brief careers as a mill worker and hack driver. He was an athlete, and although he might have opened a pool room or a saloon, the success of such an endeavor would have depended solely upon his fame as a ballplayer. At the age of 26, his best years lay ahead of him, and it was highly unlikely that he would have walked away from the game, no matter how much he disliked his employers.

Lajoie and the other unsigned Phillies nonetheless made the trip to Charlotte, North Carolina, for spring training. Once again, the weather was cold and rainy, and only rarely were the Phillies able to go outside for proper practice. They spent much of camp playing simulated games in the local YMCA and playing handball in a large meeting room at the City Hall building. With Dick Cooley gone and Roy Thomas firmly in place in center field, Shettsline decided to move Delahanty back to first base, though some of the local writers, noting that the veteran slugger had roundly disliked playing on the infield in the past, recommended that the manager instead move Lajoie to first and find someone else to play second. However, playing first base would make it easier for Delahanty, the captain, to direct the team on the field. Besides, Delahanty would be playing beside his best friend Lajoie, whose outstanding range at second would cut down the area that Delahanty would be required to cover. The veteran slugger took grounders at first without apparent complaint.

Delahanty, as Shettsline's captain for 1900, directed spring training activities despite his lack of a contract. Delahanty was in a difficult position, unwilling as he was to sign an agreement while still bearing responsibility for the on-field performance of the club. He and Lajoie had agreed not to sign their contracts until both men were satisfied, so his status was tied to Lajoie's, and if Lajoie decided to walk out on the team when the season started, Delahanty would almost be required to follow his friend's lead. Their dalliance, minor though it was, with the Association a few months before put both men in an awkward situation, as Colonel Rogers must have been deeply unhappy when he heard that his two superstars were present at the Association meeting and chatting up the organizers of the proposed rival circuit.

While the team battled the elements in Charlotte, Brooklyn manager Ned Hanlon decided to grab some free publicity. The Superbas had won the pennant by an eight-game margin in 1899, but Hanlon proposed to strengthen his club even further with a public offer to the Phillies of $8,000 for either Delahanty or Lajoie.[4] He then, as an alternative, proposed to trade his longtime star shortstop Hugh Jennings for either man. Colonel Rogers and the Philadelphia media had long been infatuated with Jennings, whose leadership abilities were well regarded around the league and who might have been installed as Philadelphia's playing manager. However, Jennings was a sore-armed 31-year-old who could no longer play shortstop and was on the decline as a batter due to repeated beanings. It would have been ludicrous for the Phillies to trade either Delahanty or the much younger Lajoie for a broken-down former star, no matter how good a leader he might have been. Rogers dismissed the proposal as "too ridiculous to even merit consideration,"[5] and also rebuffed New York Giants manager Buck Ewing, who offered to pay $15,000 for both Philadelphia stars.

John McGraw, however, was more attractive to the Phillies. McGraw had managed the Orioles in 1899, only to have his job disappear when the league folded the Baltimore franchise at season's end. Hanlon, who owned half of the Brooklyn-Baltimore consortium, sold McGraw's contract to St. Louis, but McGraw, who had business interests in Baltimore, refused to go west. Though McGraw was heavily involved in the proposed new American Association, the new circuit was a long way from fruition, and perhaps Hanlon would be tempted to offer the longtime Baltimore star to the Phillies for Delahanty or Lajoie. In the end, the Association fell apart before it ever played a game, due to the new circuit's inability to establish a presence in New York and Philadelphia. McGraw, after meeting with St. Louis owner Frank Robison, decided to play in the Mound City after all, and the prospect of a McGraw-Lajoie or a McGraw-Delahanty trade disappeared.

In early April, with Opening Day fast approaching, seven Phillies remained unsigned. Still, despite a spate of offers from other teams for Lajoie and Delahanty, Rogers declared that he would not sell either man, though he would also not let them play more than a few games until they signed. "We only want men on our team who are good, loyal, honest, and honorable," he told the *Philadelphia Press*. "Only when we find they are traitors would we consent to sell them, and we don't believe we have any of this class. Any man who went south at our expense and would strike would be in the position of receiving money under false pretenses."[6]

The tension between management and players mounted as the days passed. Contracts were set to take effect on Monday, April 16, when the Phillies were slated to play the first of two exhibition games against the Montreal Eastern League club in Philadelphia, and it appeared doubtful that any unsigned player would take the field on that date without an agreement. Elmer Flick and Wiley Piatt agreed to terms before the deadline, but five players—Lajoie, Delahanty, Roy Thomas, Klondike Douglass, and Ed McFarland—were not under contract on that date. The Phillies played the first game against Montreal without the remaining holdouts, while the second contest was rained out. Turning up the heat on the Phillies, Lajoie declared that he and Delahanty would not accompany the team to Boston for the National League opener on April 19 if their demands were not met.

Colonel Rogers replied with some pressure of his own.

> The Philadelphia club will not accede to the demands of Delahanty and Lajoie. These men were fined by Manager Shettsline for not playing on Monday, and the fine will be doubled if they do not play tomorrow. Further, they will be suspended without pay unless they leave for Boston with the team on Wednesday evening, and unless they come to terms it is highly probable we will trade them to some other club for other good players. Manager Hanlon of the Brooklyn club was here to see me today, and we can get Jennings tomorrow if we want him.[7]

Lajoie and Delahanty held fast to their demands, and neither management nor players would budge. The team, according to a report in the *Philadelphia Record* on April 18, offered Delahanty a $2,400 contract and a $600 additional sum to serve as captain, but Delahanty "argues that he might not be captain more than a month, and that the club owners would then be able to hold back the captaincy money." "The only Del" had heard rumors that Rogers was still interested in acquiring Hugh Jennings from Hanlon's Superbas to fill the leadership role, so the veteran suggested that he would accept a present of $600, leaving the captaincy out of the equation entirely. As for Lajoie, said the *Record*, "[he] claims that, being heralded as a wonder and having all sorts of fancy offers made for his release, makes him worth $2,800 to the club.... He says men like Jennings, McGraw, and others are getting that amount of money, and he thinks he is worth just as much."[8] If this report is accurate, then Lajoie had, for the first time, reduced his demands, if only slightly, giving hope that the standoff could be resolved in short order.

Though Colonel Rogers appeared willing to continue the salary battle, Al Reach and Billy Shettsline were anxious to find a resolution. League rules stated that an unsigned player could play as many as five games without a contract, so team management had until Tuesday, April 24, to reach an agreement with its four remaining holdouts (Roy Thomas having signed on April 17). Shettsline, however, did not want the discussions to drag out too close to, or past, the deadline. With the number of teams in the National League reduced from 12 to eight, Shettsline knew that each of the remaining clubs would be stronger in 1900, and the Phillies did not need the distraction of a long salary hassle. A fast start to the season was vital to Philadelphia's pennant hopes, so Shettsline moved to break the stalemate.

According to Lajoie's later account, the Philadelphia manager met with both men at Delahanty's home in Philadelphia on Wednesday, April 18, and while Delahanty signed his contract at the house, Lajoie affixed his signature later that afternoon at the ballpark, signing his name on the agreement with a lead pencil. Although both sides were reluctant to talk about the negotiations afterward, both Delahanty and Lajoie were now in the fold, and the crisis was over.

The Philadelphia papers ran rampant with speculation about the agreed-upon terms of the contracts, and several people who were close to the situation — or thought they were — voiced their opinions freely. *Sporting Life*, the Philadelphia-based national sports weekly, quoted an anonymous observer who insisted that he knew the inside story. "A very close friend to Lajoie," stated the paper, "said yesterday that he knew for a fact that the Philadelphia Club had made every concession to Delahanty and Lajoie. 'They are each getting $3,000 [the friend said], Larry's contract calling for $2,400, with an extra $600 contract on the side.'"[9] As it turned out, the unnamed friend was half right. Delahanty received his desired $3,000 in the form of a $2,400 playing contract and a $600 payment for the captaincy, which Billy Shettsline guaranteed whether or not the veteran was replaced as captain during the season. Lajoie, however, signed for $2,600, with $200 of the amount in the form of a bonus.

Why did Lajoie, after his extended holdout, settle for only $200 more than the salary he received in 1899? According to the testimony he gave later when the contract became the subject of a legal dispute, Lajoie believed that he and Delahanty did, in fact, receive the same pay. Delahanty signed first, claimed Lajoie, after which Shettsline told Lajoie that Delahanty had signed for $2,600. Thus satisfied, Lajoie agreed to the same amount. Shettsline later disputed this account, but the fact remains that Lajoie's salary was $400 less than that of his friend Delahanty. Perhaps Shettsline, at Colonel Rogers' direction, told Larry what the ballplayer wanted to hear in order to get his signature on the dotted line and end the holdout.

Not long after the two stars signed their contracts, Lajoie happened to discover the truth about their salaries. In a 1941 interview, Lajoie related that he found out about the deception during a road trip in May, when he and Delahanty returned to their rooms after a game against the Reds in Cincinnati. Said Lajoie, "Delahanty emptied the contents of his pockets on a table and among them was his pay check. I got a sudden hunch that it might be worthwhile to take a look at that check, so I walked over and took a quick peek over his shoulder. A little arithmetic followed and I discovered that he was getting $3,000 per season. By asking a few questions, I learned that Delahanty thought I had signed before him and

Elmer Flick, Lajoie's teammate in Philadelphia and Cleveland (author's collection).

was getting the same amount."[10] By his own later account, Lajoie then stormed into Colonel Rogers' office when the team returned to Philadelphia and demanded an extra $400 to even his pay with Delahanty's. Rogers predictably refused, and Lajoie, who had been dissatisfied with his treatment by team management for several years, now had one more reason to despise his employers.

The wildest game of the season was the first one, in which the Phillies furnished the opposition for Boston in the Beaneaters' home opener on April 19. Boston pitcher Vic Willis could not get his curveball over and had to rely on a mediocre fastball, which the Phillies pounded all over the South Side Grounds, scoring 17 runs in the first eight innings. Napoleon Lajoie belted three singles in his first five trips, while infielder Joe Dolan had three hits and five other players had two. They knocked Willis out of the box and treated his successor, rookie Harvey Bailey, rudely as well, building a 17–8 lead as Boston came to bat in the ninth. Phillies hurler Al Orth then lost his command, allowing the Beaneaters to push nine runs across the plate to tie the score at 17.

In the tenth, after Boston manager Frank Selee sent his ace, Kid Nichols, to the mound, Delahanty opened the inning with a walk. Lajoie also walked, and Flick followed with an infield single, though shortstop Herman Long threw Delahanty out at the plate while Lajoie took third and Flick raced to second. Ed McFarland then singled home both runners to give the Phillies a 19–17 lead. Red Donahue, pressed into service in relief for the Phillies, retired the Beaneaters in the bottom of the tenth, sealing a win for Philadelphia in the highest-scoring Opening Day game in baseball history.

Lajoie was a proud man, and during a May series at the Polo Grounds in New York, according to a report in the *Brooklyn Eagle*, he gained revenge against the Giants for a perceived slight. Larry, so the story goes, had tried to get a friend into the stadium with a pass, but the gatekeeper refused to honor the visiting player's request and made the friend pay the usual 50-cent admission fee. "I'll play even for this," promised Lajoie, and during his first time at bat that day, he deliberately hit seven consecutive foul balls out of the Polo Grounds and onto the elevated train tracks outside the stadium. Each baseball cost Andrew Freedman, the home team owner, a dollar and a quarter, so Larry derived great pleasure in costing the Giants nearly nine dollars for insisting on 50 cents at the gate.[11]

Though both Lajoie and the Phillies started the season well, with the team grabbing first place in early May and Lajoie batting well above the .400 mark, there were tensions just below the surface. Larry's relationship with Elmer Flick had been a contentious one from the start, most likely beginning on the day Flick joined the club at spring training in Cape May, New Jersey, in 1898. Larry, following the lead of the veteran Phillies, enjoyed making life miserable for newcomers, and Flick, a country boy who made his own bats, was an easy target for the big second baseman. Flick's hard hitting, and the sudden retirement of Sam Thompson, earned him a regular spot in the lineup, but he and Larry still clashed on occasion. One bone of contention was Larry's penchant for ranging far into right field to snare popups and short flies, a practice he may have developed to make up for the limited range of Thompson. Flick, Thompson's successor, grew to resent those forays into the outfield and, on at least two occasions, berated his bigger teammate for venturing into his territory.

There may also have been an element of professional jealousy at work. Larry, whom *Sporting Life* had hailed the year before in a Page One article as "the league's greatest second baseman, hardest hitter, and best general player,"[12] took pride in his accomplishments. However, by the end of May, Elmer Flick, not Napoleon Lajoie, led the National League in both batting average and home runs. Perhaps Larry did not mind losing the 1899 batting title to his good friend Ed Delahanty, but battling Elmer Flick for the honors in 1900 may well have been another matter. It is also possible that Larry, who had discovered Delahanty's higher salary only two weeks before, was still fuming about what he regarded as a deception on management's part. Larry never forgot the fact that, as he saw it, the Phillies had lied to him about his salary, and the situation no doubt put the second baseman in a thoroughly foul mood.

On May 31, 1900, the Phillies fans were surprised to see neither Elmer Flick nor Napoleon Lajoie in the lineup. Joe Dolan manned second base and Pete Chiles patrolled right field against Chicago that day, while Billy Shettsline told the local reporters that Lajoie and Flick had been injured in an on-field collision while engaging in horseplay, or "sky-larking," during practice that morning. Each man would be out for a few days, said Shettsline, but the manager, curiously, offered no further details.

The truth, which became public before the day was out, was much more serious. In the clubhouse that morning, Flick and Lajoie became embroiled in an argument; some of the local papers said that the ownership of a bat was the issue that ignited the dispute, but others claimed that the two hard-hitting stars often rode each other over their clothes, behavior, and other matters. Flick, enraged by a vile name uttered by Lajoie in his direction, charged at the second baseman, who punched Flick several times in the face, blackening his eyes. Lajoie, too, took some punishment before captain Ed Delahanty separated the two combatants. Lajoie, however, was not finished, and attacked Flick again. This time Lajoie threw a left-handed haymaker that missed Flick's head and slammed into a wooden wash-stand nearby. The fight ended immediately, because Lajoie's left thumb was broken by the force of the errant punch.

The first-place Phillies club, with two of its three star batters missing, defeated the visitors by a 3–0 score that afternoon, but its pennant chances had been all but destroyed by the pre-game melee. Lajoie's injury kept him out of the lineup until mid–July, while Flick, though less badly hurt in the fracas, declared loudly that he would no longer play for the Phillies as long as Lajoie remained on the team. He complained to the papers that Lajoie "has been picking on him ever since the middle of last season for no reason whatever to his knowledge,"[13] according to a report in *Sporting Life*. Only Billy Shettsline's considerable powers of persuasion convinced Flick to return to the club when his facial injuries healed. Four days later, Flick re-entered the lineup.

Colonel Rogers suspended Lajoie without pay, but the second baseman's reputation sustained an even larger hit than his pocketbook. The bullying behavior that so enraged Flick was now a matter of public record, and the local reporters could not resist rehashing Lajoie's previous escapades, including his suspension for drunkenness in 1897, in their columns. Flick, who impressed the Phillies rooters by battling the much larger man to a draw, was now the darling of the local fans, and drew loud and sustained cheers in his first game back against Pittsburgh on June 4. In contrast, Lajoie was roundly booed when he next appeared on the field and was met with a "storm of hisses and hoots" when he struck out with the bases loaded against Boston on July 17.

More importantly, Lajoie's extended absence cost the Phillies their best chance to win their first National League pennant. Lajoie, hitting .401 at the time of the assault, was replaced by the weak-hitting Joe Dolan, and the club began to sink in the standings. A dis-astrous western road trip in late June and early July brought 13 losses in 18 games and knocked the Philadelphia ballclub from first place to fourth in the tightly competitive eight-team league. Perhaps the low point of the season came on July 12 in Cincinnati, when Reds pitcher Frank (Noodles) Hahn threw a no-hitter, the only such gem of the 1900 season, against the power-hitting club that, despite missing Lajoie, still boasted Delahanty and Flick in its lineup.

Lajoie returned to the field the next day, though his thumb still hurt, and provided an immediate lift. Perhaps no team in baseball history has ever been no-hit one day and erupted for 23 runs the next, but the Phillies performed that feat against the Pirates in

Pittsburgh, with third baseman Harry Wolverton pounding out five hits (three of them triples) while Lajoie, Flick, and catcher Ed McFarland swatted four apiece. The lopsided win ended a 4–15 skid and presaged a good home stand, with the Phillies winning nine of 14 at the Huntingdon Street Grounds. The lift was short-lived, as another poor road trip (ten losses in 12 contests) dropped the club further behind the league leaders. Lajoie and Flick hit well, but the Phillies, preseason favorites to win the championship, struggled to stay in the first division as the summer wore on.

As if the team did not have enough problems, its character and sportsmanship came into question in September. Opposing teams had always grumbled about the Phillies and their penchant for sign-stealing, but perhaps few knew that reserve catcher Morgan Murphy, a light hitter and mediocre fielder, was nonetheless almost as valuable to the club as the sluggers Flick, Delahanty, and Lajoie. Eschewing a seat on the bench, Murphy instead parked himself in the outfield bleachers (or sometimes on a perch outside the ballpark) and trained a pair of binoculars on the opposing team's catcher. Murphy then relayed the catcher's signs to the Philadelphia third base coach by waving a newspaper or by employing some other agreed-upon signal. The coach would then whistle or call out some code word to let the batter know when a fastball was coming.

The Philadelphia sign-stealing operation was nothing new. Both *The Sporting News* and *Sporting Life* had been making remarks about it for several years, and rumor had it that Billy Nash's beaning in 1896 was caused by a misinterpreted stolen signal, as Nash, who was expecting a curveball on the outside of the plate, instead leaned into an inside fastball. Murphy, however, developed the operation into a science, and was brazen enough to steal signs on the road, sometimes renting a room across the street from the ballpark in Boston, Cincinnati, and other cities. Colonel Rogers had carried Murphy on the roster in 1899 at full salary, though the catcher did not appear in a single game that season. Other teams stole signs, but Murphy was the acknowledged master of the art.

On September 17, 1900, the Phillies ballclub proved itself too clever for its own good. It was a rainy afternoon, with puddles forming on the infield and outfield, and Cincinnati Reds shortstop Tommy Corcoran noticed that Pete Chiles, coaching third for the Phillies, kept his left foot in exactly the same spot all game long, even though he had to submerge his shoe in a puddle to do so. The suspicious Corcoran waited for the end of an inning, then made a beeline for the coaching box and began digging in the muddy dirt with his bare hands. He brought up a buzzer attached to a wire, which he and the other Reds tore out of the ground and followed all the way across the outfield to the center field bleachers, as Murphy with his binoculars beat a hasty retreat.

Many around the league had known that Murphy, who was also an expert lip-reader, had been stealing signs for years; indeed, Dick Cooley, the former Phillies captain who played for the Pirates in 1900, had warned his new teammates that Murphy was the key to the operation. Now the information had been made embarrassingly public, and the reaction was swift and harsh. Brooklyn manager Ned Hanlon confronted Shettsline about the matter and fumed to the *New York Sun*, "No wonder opposing pitchers were hammered all over the lot at Philadelphia, while on the road the Philadelphias couldn't hit a balloon."[14] Said Brooklyn club treasurer Frederick Abell, "The Philadelphias have fattened their batting averages and have won many games at home because of this unfair trick, and I should like to know whether the League thinks that these players should rank in the official averages this year.... The League should take some action in this matter and someone should be severely censured."[15]

Indeed, the Phillies had, for several years, performed unusually well at home. In 1900, the Phillies owned the best home record in the league at 45–23, while winning only 30 of their 70 games on the road. Individually, Ed Delahanty appeared to be the main beneficiary of Murphy's assistance, according to figures compiled by Delahanty's biographer Jerrold Casway in 2004. Casway's research reveals that "the only Del" won the batting title in 1899 by hitting .461 in Philadelphia and .366 elsewhere, while in 1900 the big left fielder hit .371 in Philadelphia and a mere .291 on the road. Lajoie, too, enjoyed a boost from his home field, with a .388 home mark and a .313 road log in 1900.[16] Now, the revelation of institutionalized cheating (though there appeared to be no written rule against such shenanigans) brought the hitting accomplishments of both Lajoie and Delahanty into question. Reds manager Bob Allen spoke for many when he proclaimed, "Not one of the batting averages of the Phillies has been made honestly."[17]

How much of an advantage did the Phillies gain from their thievery? One might surmise that Ed Delahanty, a disciplined hitter with a good sense of the strike zone, would find great value in the knowledge that a fastball was on its way to the plate. John McGraw, the former Baltimore manager, suggested as much when he opined that "lay back and swing" batters like Delahanty or Pittsburgh's Honus Wagner would prosper the most from such ill-gotten knowledge. In addition, Delahanty was aging (he was 33 years old in 1900), and had seen his batting average fall from a league-leading .410 in 1899 to a more pedestrian .323 the following year. Perhaps the Phillies veteran realized that his bat was slowing down, and so would have appreciated Morgan Murphy's assistance, questionable though it was. It must have embarrassed him deeply when Corcoran dug up the buzzer and Cincinnati coach Arlie Latham remarked loudly, "Ah, discovered — Delahanty's batting average."[18]

Larry Lajoie, on the other hand, was the king of the bad ball hitters, and often claimed that he did not pay much attention to what a pitcher threw. By all accounts, Larry was the kind of "natural" hitter who could never be accused of over-analyzing the situation. He simply lashed out at the first good delivery he saw, no matter what kind of pitch it was. Though Larry never commented publicly about the sign stealing controversy, the high averages that he compiled after leaving the Phillies indicate that he, for one, probably did not benefit much, if at all, from Murphy's antics.

Casway called 1900 the "hoodoo season" for the Phillies, and it ended with both Delahanty and Lajoie on the bench for the last seven games of the campaign. On October 2 in New York, Delahanty split his finger on a throw to first base, while Lajoie took a fastball to the elbow from Win Mercer of the Giants in what proved to be his last plate appearance in a Phillies uniform. The club slipped into third place, eight games behind the pennant-winning Brooklyn club and four behind the second-place Pittsburgh Pirates. It was a relatively good finish for the Phillies in the National League, but Colonel Rogers was not pleased. With typical candor, he publicly blamed his players for the disappointing season, charging that they were "taking the field like a lot of tired day laborers, tired before the game began."[19] The ballclub, without Delahanty, Lajoie, and Flick, played three postseason exhibition games against minor league clubs in the small Pennsylvania cities of Chester and Norristown, losing two of them in desultory fashion. The Phillies were tired after a hard-fought season and appeared eager to put the 1900 campaign, and their demanding boss, behind them.

Though the baseball season was over, several controversies lingered into the winter months. Pitcher Wiley Piatt, whose season ended when he was hospitalized with a near-fatal case of typhoid fever in early September, was enraged when Rogers docked his salary by $600 due to his absence from the ballclub. Piatt complained that Rogers' unilateral action deprived him of the necessary funds to pay his $240 hospital bill, and that he could not even afford train fare home to Ohio. Rogers, for his part, blamed Piatt's lack of conditioning for his illness and, despite mounting criticism from the local papers, refused to reconsider his stance. The majority owner may have saved $600 in salary, but turned one of his best pitchers, who won 47 games for the club in 1898 and 1899 but fell to nine wins in 1900, into an enemy. Several other players were irked when their final paychecks were short by varying amounts for long-forgotten transgressions that dated back to spring training in Charlotte.

Napoleon Lajoie, too, was unhappy with his employer. Though he got along well with manager Billy Shettsline, even joining a local chapter of the Order of Eagles with the manager and Ed Delahanty during the winter months, Lajoie knew that Shettsline held little decision-making power in the organization. Al Reach, Rogers' longtime partner, was a respected, honest baseball man, but after Rogers acquired majority ownership in the team, Reach had been shunted to the sidelines by the ambitious colonel. Though Lajoie was, by general agreement, the top all-around player in the National League, his career was totally dependent on the whims of one difficult man. Lajoie loved playing in Philadelphia, but his annual battle with management over salary dampened his enjoyment of the sport. "Colonel Rogers was an attorney who loved to argue," said Lajoie years later. "The average player, seeking a raise of $100, had no way of winning his battle with the Colonel.... Rogers would then assume such a crestfallen appearance that the player would slink out of his office ashamed of himself."[20]

For years, Colonel Rogers had exercised near-dictatorial power over his players, and since the failure of the Players League revolt of 1890, the players had no recourse. Now, thanks to a new circuit called the American League, they did. The former Western League looked to expand its reach into the eastern part of the country beginning in 1901, and when the established National League opposed its plans, a new baseball war began. This latest dispute between players and management would set off a bidding war for talent, with Napoleon Lajoie the prize catch.

8

The American League

Lajoie I look upon as a ball playing genius, endowed with more natural talent as a natural ball player than any star we have seen since Charley Ferguson. Lajoie may not have an excess of gray matter floating around in his head. I speak of his great mechanical talent, pure and simple. — Frank Selee, Boston manager, 1899[1]

The American League was the creation of Byron Bancroft (Ban) Johnson, a one-time Cincinnati sportswriter who reanimated a failed minor circuit, the Western League, and became its president in November of 1893. Based in the Midwestern states, Johnson's circuit soon became the top minor league in the nation, with some of its teams outdrawing the bottom-tier National League clubs on a yearly basis. With skilled managers such as Charles Comiskey in St. Paul, Connie Mack in Milwaukee, and former Philadelphia field leader George Stallings in Detroit, the Western League offered a competitive brand of baseball that no other minor league could match. Johnson was determined that the many ills of the National League, especially its brawling style of play and poor treatment of its umpires, would have no place in his organization. He supported his arbiters, suspended the worst of the on-field fighters, and gave the public a product that it could support.

As early as 1896, Johnson voiced his intention of eventually achieving parity with the established National. "The Western League," said Johnson in February of that year, "has passed the stage where it should be considered a minor league.... It is a first-class organization, and should have the consideration that such an organization warrants."[2] In 1900, Johnson changed the name of his circuit to the American League, shifted Charles Comiskey's team from St. Paul, Minnesota, to the south side of Chicago, and placed a franchise in Cleveland, which had been abandoned by the National League when the Spiders disbanded after the 1899 season. The American League was still minor, but well positioned for another leap in status.

After a successful 1900 season, in which Comiskey's Chicago White Sox won the first American League pennant, Johnson was emboldened to take on the National League. Setting his sights on the eastern part of the country, Johnson and his backers awarded franchises to Baltimore (where John McGraw was put in charge) and Washington, both of which had been dropped from the National League roster two years before. The league president then seceded from the National Agreement, the covenant that defined the roles and powers of the major and minor leagues, and declared that the American League was now equal in stature to the National. When the established league rebuffed Johnson's attempts at compromise and refused to consider relaxing its salary limit, not to mention its contract language which bound a player to a team for life (the hated reserve clause), the American League declared war. Johnson placed new teams in the baseball hotbeds of Boston and Philadelphia and set out to sign as many disgruntled National League stars as the new circuit could afford.

Napoleon Lajoie needed little prodding to throw in his lot with Johnson's American League. Like most Phillies players, he had had his fill of Colonel Rogers, one-sided contracts, and the league-mandated salary limit of $2,400. The salary battle that he and Ed Delahanty waged before the preceding season was still fresh in Lajoie's mind, and the more he thought about it, the more convinced he became that Rogers had pulled a fast one on him. Lajoie would jump to the new league in an instant if he could be shown that the management of the new Philadelphia franchise was trustworthy and honest. Fortunately for the new league, Johnson awarded ownership of the new team, called the Athletics, to a group of investors headed by local businessman Benjamin Shibe and former Pittsburgh Pirates manager Connie Mack.

Ben Shibe was a good friend and business partner of Al Reach, the part owner of the Phillies whose relationship with Colonel John Rogers had grown more distant with each passing year. Shibe, who never played the game, had become wealthy by manufacturing and selling baseball equipment. He was an innovator, having designed improved protective gear for catchers and a streamlined method for producing high-quality baseballs. He was well regarded in both baseball and business circles for his honesty and integrity.

Connie Mack, whose given name was Cornelius McGillicuddy, was a former major league catcher who, after an unsuccessful stint as manager of the Pirates during the mid–1890s, had taken over the Milwaukee franchise in the Western League and built it into a strong contender. The patient and soft-spoken Mack was only 38 years old in 1901, but had already established himself as one of the most respected figures in the game. After his Milwaukee Brewers finished a strong second to Comiskey's White Sox in the 1900 pennant chase, Ban Johnson asked him to go to Philadelphia and build a new team to compete head-to-head with the Phillies. Mack agreed, perhaps because he recognized that many of the unhappy Phillies stars, especially Napoleon Lajoie, did not need much inducement to jump to the new league. Mack accepted the challenge, moving his family to Philadelphia and setting to work signing players and building a major league franchise from scratch.

The Athletics needed a place to play, and Colonel Rogers unwittingly provided Mack and Shibe with a prime piece of real estate. In an attempt to halt the planned expansion of Ban Johnson's circuit, the National League embraced another effort to revive the American Association. The Association's Philadelphia backers took an option on a piece of land at 29th Street and Columbia Avenue, which was serviced by railway and streetcar lines and was easily accessible for large numbers of fans. However, Rogers saw the Association as an opportunity to increase business at the Huntingdon Street Grounds, and demanded that the Association's Philadelphia team play its home games in the Phillies' ballpark. The colonel got his way, as usual, and when the Association dropped its option on the land, Shibe and Mack picked it up and built their new park there. Other National League owners bitterly condemned Rogers for his greed and lack of foresight.

The success of the Philadelphia Athletics ballclub, and of the new league as a whole, depended upon its ability to lure major stars into its ranks, and no star was more coveted by Ban Johnson's league than Napoleon Lajoie. On February 14, 1901, Lajoie met with Mack and *Philadelphia Inquirer* sportswriter Frank Hough, a strong supporter of the new league who was keenly interested in breaking Colonel Rogers' monopoly on major league baseball in Philadelphia. Hough acted as an agent for the new organization, advising Mack on the nuances of the local sports scene and making contact with players who could be induced to jump to the American League.

Lajoie drove a hard bargain, and induced Mack to give up virtually everything the 26-year-old star asked for. First, Mack agreed to pay Lajoie a salary of $4,000 a year for two years, and to fully guarantee it even if the league went bust. Lajoie also arranged for Mack to put his entire 1901 salary into a bank account which carried the names of the ballplayer's landlord, a man named Johnson, and Frank Hough. From that account, the two men would draw out a check every two weeks and deliver it to Lajoie.

Because Lajoie was the biggest star not only of the Athletics, but also of the new league itself, Mack named him the captain of the club. This was a risky move, as Lajoie's behavior had often caused problems during his five-year tenure with the Phillies. Lajoie was only three years removed from his embarrassing drunken episode on the field in August of 1897, and his fistfight with teammate Elmer Flick nine months before was still fresh in everyone's minds. Nonetheless, Mack decided to trust his most important acquisition, perhaps reasoning that a more positive atmosphere would bring out Lajoie's leadership qualities.

With Lajoie in the fold (though the Athletics did not officially announce his signing until late March), Connie Mack worked day and night to complete his roster. With players bouncing back and forth from one league to another, the process proved an exercise in frustration. He had signed an outfielder from Tennessee named Al Davis, who had performed for Minneapolis in 1900. Davis accepted a $75 advance from Mack and boarded a northbound train for Philadelphia. However, Davis fell asleep on the train and woke up in New York, where he decided to sign a second contract, this one with Brooklyn of the National League. Davis' defection left Mack short of outfielders, a situation only partly remedied when Larry Lajoie's old Fall River and Phillies teammate, Phil Geier, agreed to terms. Geier was a good fielder, but had never hit much during his five seasons in the National League.

Mack tried to lure Elmer Flick to the American League, and for a while it looked as if Lajoie's Phillies teammate and fellow pugilist would give the Athletics another strong bat. Flick initially agreed to Mack's offer of $3,000, but soon began making demands. He wanted his salary, like Lajoie's, guaranteed, and he demanded legal protection from a National League blacklist should the new circuit fail. After a while, Mack decided that his pursuit of Flick was not worth the trouble and dropped the matter. He then made a play for Sam Crawford, a promising 20-year-old outfielder with the Cincinnati Reds, but Crawford, after agreeing to terms, changed his mind and returned to Cincinnati. Though the new ballclub needed help in the outfield, Mack showed little interest in Ed Delahanty. The veteran slugger was still highly popular with the Philadelphia fans, but because Delahanty had received, and spent, a sizable advance on his 1901 salary from the Phillies, he remained in the National League.

Two other recruits, both pitchers, signed contracts and quickly reneged on them, changing the course of baseball history in the process. One was Vic Willis, the curveball artist who had supplanted Kid Nichols as the ace of the Boston Beaneaters staff. Willis, who earned the league maximum salary of $2,400 in 1900, met with Mack and agreed to a contract for $3,500, with a $450 advance payment to seal the deal. Willis promised to show up for spring workouts in early April, but Mack became suspicious when the pitcher asked permission to report a week late. Sure enough, Willis was still dickering with the Beaneaters.

The Boston club offered the same salary as Mack, so Willis, like Davis, repudiated his deal with the Athletics. He sent the $450 back to Mack and returned to the National League, leaving Mack fuming. "We owe it to the public," said Mack, "to make examples of these venal players and those disreputable club owners who are just as bad if not worse in tempting men to break contracts."[3]

Vic Willis was a fine pitcher who enjoyed a Hall of Fame career, but the second man who burned Connie Mack became one of the greatest hurlers of all time. Christy Mathewson, only 20 years old, was a baseball and football star at Bucknell University in his native Pennsylvania. Signed by the New York Giants in 1900, he pitched three National League games in September of that year, lost them all, and was sent back to Norfolk of the Virginia League. However, most knowledgeable baseball men considered "Matty" a future star, so the Giants worked out an ethically questionable deal in which they convinced the Cincinnati Reds to draft Mathewson off the minor league roster for the standard $100 price. The Giants then traded their sore-armed former pitching star Amos Rusie, who had not played a game in two years, to the Reds to get Mathewson back. While all this wheeling and dealing was going on, Mathewson decided to return to college. He did not sign a contract for 1901, making him, in his estimation, a free agent.

That's when Connie Mack entered the young man's life. Mack, who also saw the vast potential in the right-handed pitcher, offered Mathewson $1,200 to pitch for the Athletics in 1901, but Mathewson proposed instead that he be allowed to finish the college term and report to the Athletics in June. Mack, who always held a special regard for college-educated players, agreed, and in January the youngster signed a contract for $700. Matty's signing was a major coup for the Athletics and for the new league, robbing the National League of one of its brightest young prospects. The satisfied Mack even sent his newest acquisition a check for $50 in March, when Mathewson requested an advance on his salary to buy books for the spring term at Bucknell.

Unfortunately for Mack, New York Giants owner Andrew Freedman was not a man to accept defeat. He called Mathewson to New York and threatened not only to file suit against the young pitcher, but also to have him permanently banned from all of organized baseball. Mathewson was shaken, and on March 25, the *Philadelphia North American* quoted the pitcher as saying, "I have not yet signed with any club, and at present am undecided what to do. I have offers from the Philadelphia American League and New York National League clubs and will accept one or the other."[4] One week later, Mathewson reported to spring training with the Giants. He sent a check for $50 to Mack, who refused to cash it. Though the Athletics had signed contracts with both Mathewson and Willis, neither man suffered any consequences for his actions, though perhaps Mack was secretly pleased when Phillies fans roundly booed Mathewson when the Giants made their first trip to Philadelphia later that year.

As had happened in every previous baseball war, players bounced from one league to another (and, in many cases, back again) during the early months of 1901. Because Ban Johnson wanted to build strong ballclubs in the three cities where his circuit went head-to-head against the established league, the new Boston, Chicago, and Philadelphia franchises attracted the best of the National League defectors. Boston's American League entry decimated the Beaneaters, luring third baseman Jimmy Collins and several other popular Boston stars to the new league and adding Cy Young, late of the St. Louis Perfectos, to its pitching staff. In Chicago, Charlie Comiskey hired star pitcher Clark Griffith of the rival Orphans (later called the Cubs) as his manager, while the Athletics grabbed the biggest prize of all

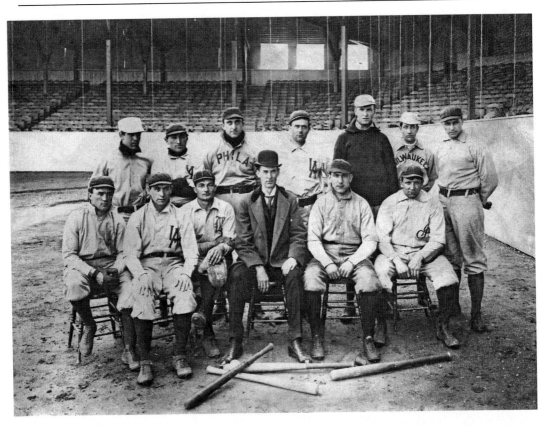

A photograph of the 1901 Athletics taken during spring practice, before the new team's uniforms had arrived. **Top row: Fultz, Geier, Bernhard, Powers, Carr, Ketcham, Fraser. Bottom row: Piatt, McIntyre, Cross, Mack, Lajoie, Seybold** (Charles W. Mears Collection, Cleveland Public Library).

in the person of Napoleon Lajoie. These three teams would win the first six American League pennants, and 16 of the first 19.

Lajoie was not the only Phillie who decamped to the new league, as pitchers Chick Fraser, 15–9 in 1900, and Bill Bernhard (15–10) also made the move. Fraser, a right-hander, had lost 27 games for Louisville as a rookie in 1896, but had learned to control his wildness and had a bright future at the age of 27. Bernhard, who turned 30 before the 1901 season began, had established himself as a solid, dependable member of the Phillies rotation. Left-hander Wiley Piatt, a two-time 20-game winner whose battle with typhoid fever was a factor in his disappointing 9–10 performance in 1900, also signed on with Mack's outfit, giving the Athletics the foundation of a good pitching staff.

However, the latest baseball war was just beginning. After Mack officially announced the signings of Lajoie, Bernhard, and Fraser on March 20, Colonel Rogers and the Phillies responded seven days later by filing an injunction to prevent the trio from playing for the Athletics. The main issue at hand was the presence of the option clause, or reserve clause, in the standard National League contract. This language reserved the services of each player from one year to the next as long as the team wished to exercise it, and because Lajoie and the others had signed contracts that contained that clause, Rogers believed that the trio would be forced by the court to return to the Phillies.

American League attorneys saw the matter differently. The reserve clause, coupled with the infamous "10-day clause" which allowed a team to release a player with only ten days' notice, made the contract so one-sided, in their view, as to be legally unenforceable. Such an agreement bound a player to his team for life, while allowing a National League magnate to shed a contract at any time. Because a player owned no leverage in the relationship, the National League was able to impose its $2,400 salary limit on even its biggest stars. Such an agreement was coercive and lacked "mutuality," said Ban Johnson's legal experts, and the American League expressed confidence that the three judges that were slated to hear the case would see things their way.

While the legal controversy gained steam, Larry Lajoie reported to his first American League camp in top shape after playing handball regularly during the winter months. Several other players were absent or delayed with family or business issues, but the players trickled into camp, which was held at the soon-to-be-completed ballpark on Columbia Avenue. The Athletics slowly began to take shape as April wore on. The new park was on track to be completed by Opening Day, though the grass would take a while to grow in, and fan interest in the team appeared to be high. A pickup game against a team of local athletes drew more than 900 fans on a cold, wet day, while more than 3,000 people attended a match against the Yale University nine a few days later. The Athletics, heartened by these encouraging indicators, plowed ahead with plans for the season.

The Phillies' suit against the new ballclub was due to be heard in a Philadelphia court-room on Saturday, April 20, four days before the start of the 1901 American League campaign. The weeks before the hearing were filled with pretrial motions, consultations with attorneys, and strategy sessions in which Lajoie, the main object of the exercise, was prepared for his appearance on the stand. A team of lawyers assisted him and the other two ballplayers in writing the statements that they were required to submit to the court. In Lajoie's statement, he allowed that he had signed a contract with the Phillies for the 1900 season, but claimed that he was not aware of the presence of the option clause. Had he known that such a clause was part of the agreement, said Lajoie, he would never have signed it. He stated that he was induced to sign the contract by Shettsline's assertion that his pay was the same as Ed Delahanty's, which, Larry insisted, was a lie. Furthermore, in a triumph of legal hair-splitting, Lajoie denied that the Athletics had persuaded him to sign a contract with them for the 1901 campaign, a statement which may have been technically correct (because the team did not incorporate itself until June of that year) but seemed puzzling to those outside the legal world. He did not admit or deny that he had signed with the Athletics, but merely that the team, which did not yet exist as a legal entity, did not convince him to do so.

On the morning of the hearing, which was held in courtroom number 5 of the Court of Common Pleas at the City Hall building in downtown Philadelphia, Napoleon Lajoie, wearing a suit and tie, waited with the attorneys for both the Phillies and the Athletics while presiding judge J. Willis Martin and associate judges Robert Ralston and Maxwell Stevenson dealt with other cases. Finally, at about 11:30, the case of *Philadelphia Ball Club v. Lajoie* was called to order, and after some preliminary motions and statements, Lajoie was called to the stand.

The well-rehearsed ballplayer performed admirably. Attorney John Johnson, representing the Phillies, tried to paint the second baseman as an irreplaceable part of the team, one whose loss would cripple the National League franchise in the city, but Lajoie demurred. He downplayed his talent and accomplishments so skillfully that local writer and humorist Charles Dryden was moved to comment, "[Johnson] wanted to know if Larry wasn't a peach, a jim dandy, a great second baseman, and a sure drawing card. In low tones and with a modest mien that paralyzed the fanatics, Larry said he had never heard of himself."[5]

Johnson's line of questioning then moved to the contract Lajoie had signed with the Phillies in April of 1900, which set his salary at the National League limit of $2,400, plus a bonus of $200. Lajoie insisted that he never received the extra $200 (though when shown a receipt for the amount, Larry stated that he signed it before he received the money). He said that he received a total of $2,121.16 during the 1900 season, having been unfairly docked a day's pay for some unnamed transgression and also having paid for a uniform and a pair of shoes that he never received. The testimony then shifted on the ballplayer's main grievance against the Phillies, his assertion that the club promised, and failed, to pay him the same amount as Delahanty. Lajoie told the court that it was not until he saw Delahanty's paycheck in May of 1900, when the Phillies were in Cincinnati to play the Reds, that he realized that the team had lied to him.

Johnson grilled the ballplayer on that point. "Wasn't Delahanty paid $600 extra for captaining the team — wasn't he captain of the nine?"

"I don't know. He was supposed to be the captain. I heard it said that he was the captain," replied Lajoie.

"Oh, no," said the lawyer, "did Delahanty act as captain?"

"No, he did not."

"Well, who did?"

"Why, Shettsline. He seemed to manage and captain from the bench. He wanted to be the whole thing."[6] This assertion was surprising, to say the least, but Lajoie then made two more unusual statements. He claimed that he knew nothing about the rumor that he was to serve as captain of the Athletics, though he said that he had read speculation in the newspapers on that point. He also said, after attorney James Dale of the Athletics took over the questioning, that he had asked for, but never received, a copy of his 1900 contract from the Phillies.

"Did Mr. Shettsline say anything to you at all about the reserve clause contained in that contract?" asked Dale.

"Don't remember that he said a word."

"What did he say about your salary?"

"Mr. Shettsline said I would get the same amount of money as Delahanty. He asked me to sign for $2,600. He said 'Del' and I were to get the same."

Shettsline then took the stand and was asked if Lajoie was, in fact, a particular star at one position. "Yes, we've played him at second base, but you can't hook him up wrong anywhere," replied the manager.

"He can dodge foul balls as well as questions he don't like," remarked Johnson.

Shettsline testified that the team had made a significant investment in Lajoie, and stood to lose a large amount of money should he be allowed to jump to another ballclub.

"How much have they invested in the grounds?" asked Dale.

"Two hundred thousand dollars," Shettsline replied.

"Now you have spoken about the expert playing of the different men. Can you mention any player of last year's team that was more expert than another?"

"They were all experts."

"No. I mean not so expert as Lajoie."

"Yes, there's Petie Chiles for instance, he was..."

"Expert at the buzzer," cracked one of the attorneys.

"Isn't Joseph Dolan, who is now playing second base for you, an expert?" continued Dale.

"He is a good ball player, but not as good as five or six other second basemen in the League."

"Do you think Lajoie is?"

"Yes, sir, I do. I think he's the best thing that ever happened."

When Dale asked Shettsline if he wanted Lajoie to return to the Phillies, the manager smiled and hesitated a bit before answering in the affirmative. "What made you smile and hesitate?" asked Dale. "Did you think if you got Lajoie back you would fire him on ten days' notice?"

"No, sir. I did not," the manager replied. He stated that Lajoie's broken thumb, sustained in his fight with Elmer Flick in May of 1900, cost the Phillies the pennant. The club was in first place at the time of the injury, said Shettsline, but fell off the pace during the summer months.

Dale asked, "Well, hasn't that been the history of the Philadelphia Club for many years?" Shettsline mumbled a reply, to which the attorney retorted, "Has your club ever won a championship?" The Phillies manager merely smiled and was excused from the stand.[7]

Colonel Rogers then addressed the court and, in a long-winded oration that lasted more than an hour and a half, painted a grim picture of the future of the sport should the Phillies lose their case. Said Rogers:

> If the right of the club to hold its players by reserve rule is abrogated, and the club is not to enjoy the right to the ten days' notice, I prophesy that every dollar of capital now invested in professional base ball will be withdrawn. The ten days' notice is the spur to the player to do his best. When a club takes a player it engages him with the understanding that he must be up to the standard. He knows that, and when he signs a contract he knows what he is signing. If the player were not confronted with the ten days' notice clause he would play poor ball, perhaps become listless. The ten days' notice is the club which compels him to do his best. Considering the time they are engaged in their employment these ball players are paid salaries far in excess of those received by your Honors. Players like Lajoie are the attraction which draws the crowds to the ball grounds. The position of the club in the championship race is due to its players, and if they should play poor ball the people would not support the club.[8]

The proceedings lasted until mid-afternoon, largely due to the Colonel's verbosity ("[Rogers] came to bat and fouled 'em off for a couple of hours,"[9] said Dryden), and because oral arguments were not yet completed, the three judges recessed the hearing until the following Saturday, April 27. This delay meant that the Athletics would begin their season with the status of Lajoie, as well as Bernhard and Fraser, undecided. Though many experts believed that the Phillies' case was weak, Connie Mack knew that one could never predict the outcome of any case with certainty. Besides, even if the Athletics emerged victorious in this particular proceeding, Colonel Rogers would no doubt file an appeal and keep the case active for months, costing the Athletics thousands of dollars in legal fees. Mack, Lajoie, and the other affected players could only wait while the judges decided their futures.

Lajoie and the Athletics turned their attention to the upcoming season. The ballclub, though still shaky at a few positions, was set, and word of mouth around Philadelphia was overwhelmingly positive about the prospects of the new team. The Phillies, who had managed to hold onto hitting stars Ed Delahanty and Elmer Flick, had opened their home campaign on April 18 with 4,500 people in the stands, a number that represented about half of their usual Opening Day turnout. This news boded well for the Athletics, and the most optimistic of team officials privately hoped for an attendance in five figures when the team made its first appearance at home.

Bad weather delayed the opener for two days, but on Friday, April 26, the people of Philadelphia turned out in record numbers. On a cold, overcast day, more than 15,000 fans (10,594 paid) pushed their way into the new ballpark, overwhelming the local police who hastily set up rope barriers in the outfield for the extra patrons to stand behind. Finally, after some semblance of control had been established, the game commenced, though the contest was continually interrupted by the traditional presentations of flowers and gifts to favorite players. When Larry Lajoie came to bat in the first inning, he received the largest floral display of all, a gigantic horseshoe of lilies and roses. He grounded out to the infield in his first trip to the plate in an Athletics uniform, but he soon gave the people what they came to see, pounding out three hits and scoring the team's only run in a 5–1 loss to Washington.

On Saturday morning, the attorneys for the Athletics and Phillies returned to court and completed their arguments, after which the three judges indicated that their decision would be revealed a few weeks hence. That afternoon, the Athletics lost again with 10,000 in the seats, though Lajoie belted three more hits in three trips. Finally, in their third home game on Monday, he led his team to a 2–1 win over visiting Boston with four hits, two of them triples. After his first failed plate appearance three days before, Lajoie had smacked ten hits in a row, tying the major league record held by four players, one of whom was Ed Delahanty. The streak came to an end on Tuesday in a loss to Boston, though he rapped out two more hits to bring his average to .750. The American League agreed with Lajoie, who was off to the fastest start of his career.

The play was often ragged in the early going, and though Larry Lajoie kept belting the ball at an almost unbelievable rate, he could not win games for the Athletics all by himself. The pitching was dangerously thin, and after a 14–1 win on May 1 against Boston, Connie Mack was out of hurlers. Having no better options, he sent a local amateur star named Pete Loos to the mound to face the Americans (who would not become the Red Sox until later in the decade). Boston blasted Loos for nine runs in the second inning and scored ten more in the third after Loos was mercifully removed from the game. Larry did his part, scoring three times and contributing a homer and a double, but the early deficit proved too much to overcome as Boston left town with a 23–12 victory.

Lajoie continued to wallop the ball, and the Athletics also received a strong contribution from a portly outfielder named Ralph "Socks" Seybold, who had starred for the American League's now-defunct Indianapolis franchise after bouncing around the minor leagues for nearly a decade. Seybold's protruding belly drew its share of razzing from fans around the league, but the 31-year-old could hit. He batted behind Lajoie in Connie Mack's batting order, keeping his average in the .300 range and providing protection for the American League's premier hitter. Lave Cross, the veteran infielder who left the Brooklyn Superbas and signed with Mack's outfit, solidified the third base slot and, like Seybold, added some offensive pop. However, the Athletics received little production from the shortstop and first base positions, and Mack worked overtime to fill the remaining holes in his roster.

By mid–May, Mack was so desperate for help at first base that he moved catcher Doc Powers there and signed Morgan Murphy, the sign-stealer extraordinaire, to fill in at catcher while he beat the bushes for a first sacker. He found his man in Harry Davis, a former National Leaguer who had starred for Mack with the Pittsburgh Pirates several years before.

Davis had enjoyed some good seasons for the Pirates and the Giants, but fell out of the majors and toiled for Providence of the Eastern League in 1899 and 1900. Souring on baseball, the college-educated Davis quit the game and took a desk job with the Lehigh Valley Railroad in his native Pennsylvania. He declined Mack's initial offer, but the Athletics manager was a persuasive man. "I need you," said Mack, so Davis, more out of friendship than anything else, quit the railroad and joined the club on May 21. Thus began a new partnership with Connie Mack, one that would last for more than a quarter of a century.

On May 17, good news arrived from the courthouse downtown. Judges Ralston, Stevenson, and Martin released their ruling, in which they denied the injunction sought by Colonel Rogers and declared that the contracts signed with the Phillies by Lajoie, Bernhard, and Fraser were null and void. The judges agreed with the Athletics that the standard National League contract was too one-sided in the favor of the team owners to be enforceable; specifically, it lacked "mutuality." Citing several precedents in English and American law, the court also ruled that the Phillies failed to prove that Lajoie's talents, at the plate and in the field, were so unique that they could not be replaced.[10] The ruling was a major victory for the American League, and though Colonel Rogers and the Phillies promised to appeal the case to the Pennsylvania Supreme Court, the three ballplayers could rest assured that they would remain the property of the Athletics for the remainder of the 1901 season.

"The terrible Lajoie," as *Sporting Life* described him, made history on May 23 in Chicago, though not in a way he wanted. The game that afternoon between the Athletics and the White Sox started out calmly enough, with no runs crossing the plate in the first two innings, but the White Sox scored seven times in the third and knocked left-hander Eddie Plank out of the game. In the bottom of the frame, the Athletics pushed five runs across and forced Chicago's starter Jack Katoll to the sidelines. The White Sox shut down the Athletics for the next five innings, taking an 11–5 lead into the ninth, but Mack's charges rose again, scoring twice and loading the bases with none out. As Lajoie strode to the plate, Chicago manager Clark Griffith ordered his pitcher, Zaza Harvey, to the bench and took over the mound duties himself.

Lajoie was the hottest hitter in baseball, and because the Philadelphia slugger had already belted a long double earlier in the game, Griffith feared that another such blow would bring in three more runs and cut the Chicago lead to one. Griffith decided on an unusual, and seemingly unprecedented, course of action. He calmly threw four pitches wide of the plate, far enough outside that not even the game's most notorious bad-ball hitter could reach them. He had walked Lajoie intentionally with the bases loaded, forcing in a run but keeping the Chicago lead at three runs. Griffith then induced the next three batters, Socks Seybold, Harry Davis, and Morgan Murphy, to ground out, allowing only one more run and ending the game with an 11–9 win.[11]

William H. Phelon, in the *Chicago Daily Journal*, said of Griffith's maneuver, "It was one of the nerviest plays ever turned on a local diamond, and risky enough to scare an elephant."[12] It was also a testament to Lajoie's utter dominance of the American League in 1901. Not even Babe Ruth was ever walked intentionally with the bases full, and no other American Leaguer received a run-scoring free pass on purpose until the Tampa Bay Rays walked Josh Hamilton of the Texas Rangers in a similar situation in 2008. Tampa Bay pitcher Troy Percival's explanation of Hamilton's walk could have described the strategy behind Lajoie's pass as well. "You don't pitch to Superman," said Percival, "when you have Wonder Woman on deck."[13]

While the Athletics struggled with inconsistency and an ever-changing cast of characters, Lajoie's bat proved one of the bright spots for the new ballclub. On a road trip to Milwaukee, Chicago, Detroit, and Cleveland in July, he belted 24 hits in 11 games and capped it off with a single, double, triple, and homer in a 12–6 win at Cleveland on July 30. Lajoie, who scored three runs that day, was the second American Leaguer to hit for the cycle, as teammate Harry Davis had turned the trick against Boston three weeks before. On July 31, in the first game of a homestand, Lajoie drilled another homer in a 13–10 win against Boston. He compiled a 28-game hitting streak, led the league in almost every important category, and fielded in spectacular fashion. Lajoie was the undisputed "King of Ballplayers," and although the Athletics drifted along in fifth and sixth place during the summer months, his exceptional play gave hope that the club would climb into the first division by season's end.

Lajoie hit a brief slump in early September, dropping his batting average under the .400 mark (according to figures kept by *The Sporting News*) and causing a minor behavioral incident in Baltimore on September 13. On that date, the Athletics trailed John McGraw's Orioles by a 12–10 score in the ninth inning when Mack's club put two men on with two out. Larry, the next batter, was seething over another bad day at the plate and, much to his manager's consternation, refused to take his turn at bat. No amount of coaxing could induce the team's best hitter to leave the bench, so Mack sent catcher Doc Powers in to pinch-hit. Powers flied out to end the game.

All was forgotten the next day, when Lajoie burst out of his slump in spectacular style. The Orioles traveled to Philadelphia for a doubleheader on that Saturday afternoon, and in the first contest Larry pounded out four hits in four times at bat, moving his batting average back over .400 and leading the Athletics to a 7–2 win. In Game 2, the Athletics trailed 2–1 in the bottom of the ninth with no one on base and two batters standing between Lajoie and another turn at the bat. With two out, Baltimore right-hander Jack Dunn, who had kept the home team under control all day, finally weakened. Philadelphia's Joe Dolan hit a slow bouncer to Dunn that should have ended the game, but the Oriole hurler threw the ball past first base for an error with Dolan taking second. Harry Davis then singled Dolan home to tie the game and bring Lajoie to the plate.

The crowd, which had started for the exits with Dolan's feeble grounder, came alive as Lajoie set himself in the batter's box. Dunn, no doubt tired from his nine innings of work, put a delivery too close to the plate, and Lajoie whaled away at it with his powerful swing. The ball sailed far into the distance, bounding between the Baltimore fielders and rolling to the far reaches of the outfield. He slid into third with a triple as Davis crossed the plate with the game's final run, handing the Athletics a dramatic 3–2 win. Lajoie's teammates rushed to congratulate their hero, but before they could reach him, the fans surged onto the field. They staged a wild, loud celebration as several of the strongest of their number lifted Lajoie onto their shoulders and carried him off the victors' clubhouse.

This impressive display of fan affection, which local reporters compared to the raucous demonstration that ensued when Lon Knight's game-winning single clinched the city's American Association pennant in 1883, started both Lajoie and the Athletics on a tear that lasted for the remainder of the 1901 season. Lajoie, his bat rejuvenated by the thrilling doubleheader win over the Orioles, closed the campaign with 37 hits in his last 58 times at bat for a .638 average. His slump was over, and though the Athletics did not improve upon their fourth-place standing in the league, the club won 11 of its final 13 contests to finish with a 74–62 record.

Certainly, Larry Lajoie was the Superman of the American League in 1901. At season's end, the statistics showed that Lajoie had not only led the league in almost every category, but had obliterated his nearest competitors in so doing. His batting average, listed at the time as .422 and adjusted by later researchers to .426, is still the highest ever recorded in league history and outpaced his nearest challenger that season, Baltimore's Mike Donlin, by a record margin of 86 points. Lajoie led the circuit in home runs (14), runs batted in (125), runs scored (145), doubles (48), slugging percentage, and every other important category except triples and stolen bases. With 232 hits in 131 games played, he was held hitless only 17 times all year.

Lajoie is recognized as the first Triple Crown winner in American League history, though many historians discount his gaudy statistics as the product of weak pitching in a brand-new major league. Critics also point out that he took advantage of the absence of the foul-strike rule; though the National League had decreed that foul balls would be called as strikes (but not as a third strike) beginning in 1901, the junior circuit would not follow suit for another two years. Still, he belted 42 more hits, scored 25 more runs, and accumulated 71 more total bases than anyone else in the league. Coupled with his defensive excellence at second base (he led the league in putouts and fielding percentage), one could make the case that no player in history, not even Babe Ruth, has ever dominated his league as completely as did Lajoie in 1901.

Despite the presence of the premier player in the game, Connie Mack's Athletics needed

The 1901 All-American team. Top row: Bradley, Lajoie, Waddell, Bernhard, Mercer. Middle row: Sullivan, Cantillon, Fraser, Pickering. Bottom row: Davis, Barrett, Irwin (Charles W. Mears collection, Cleveland Public Library).

a late-season surge to edge into the first division by season's end. Injuries, defections, and other problems left the Philadelphia club scrambling to fill holes and put a quality team on the field for much of the season. One bright spot was the discovery of a left-handed pitcher from Gettysburg, Pennsylvania, named Eddie Plank. He was a gangly 25-year old rookie who had never played minor league ball, having made his reputation in the amateur leagues and with the nine at Gettysburg College. Plank was so raw that in his first major league game on May 18, umpire Tommy Connolly stopped the contest and showed the youngster how to deliver the ball to the plate without committing a balk on every pitch. Plank was a fast learner, winning 17 games and beginning a career that would see him play for Mack for more than a decade and win over 300 games.

Socks Seybold, large stomach and all, batted .334 with 90 runs batted in, and Harry Davis, the ex–Pirate and Giant whom Mack rescued from a railroad desk job, solidified the first base position with a .306 mark and 72 RBI. Lajoie's former Phillies teammates, Chick Fraser (22–16) and Bill Bernhard (17–10), joined with Plank to form a good, if not spectacular, starting rotation. However, the shortstop position remained a problem for the Athletics all season. Joe Dolan batted only .216 and fielded poorly, and in mid-season Mack moved Lajoie to short for 12 games while catcher Doc Powers played the outfield and Powers' backup, Morgan Murphy, took over behind the plate. Fred "Bones" Ely, a 38-year-old National League veteran, then claimed the position but was not an improvement. Mack was determined to fill the shortstop hole before the beginning of the 1902 season and move everyone back to their natural positions.

Lajoie, who had made his name in Fall River as a catcher, was talented enough to play anywhere, but Mack was not interested in seeing his superstar play anywhere but second. "Lajoie is without doubt the greatest second baseman in the business," said the manager to the local reporters. "His reach is so long and he is as fast as lightning, and to throw to second is ideal. Any catcher who has played with him will tell you that he is the easiest man to throw to playing ball. He is sure of everything; high, low, or wide of the bag, it's all the same to him. And his arm is as good as any of them. Combine all this with his batting power and there isn't a ballplayer in the business that compares with him."[14]

9

"A Bright, Particular Star"

Not since the days of old "King" Kelly has such fame come to a baseball player as has fallen on Napoleon Lajoie, the Philadelphia American League team's second baseman. No player is more talked of today than he is, and all the hub-bub is due principally to his accomplishments.... His eye is as good as ever too, this season, for in the [exhibition] game with Jersey City on Sunday [April 6] he made five safe hits, two of which were two-baggers. And it was his first game of the season. "If ever a player was worth $7,000 a year," remarked a critic after that game, "it is that Frenchman." Those who heard the remark agreed. —New York Evening World, April 8, 1902

The Athletics played their last game of the 1901 campaign on September 28, but Larry Lajoie's baseball season was not yet over. He accepted an offer from promoter Joe Cantillon, an umpire and future major league manager, to head up a team of American League stars on a post-season tour of New England and the Midwest, followed by an ambitious trip to California for a series of contests from late November to mid–January. Dubbed the All-Americans, Lajoie's team also featured his Philadelphia teammates Harry Davis and Bill Bernhard, Washington pitcher Win Mercer, Cleveland third baseman Bill Bradley, Baltimore outfielder Mike Donlin, and several other well-known players. On September 30, in a nod to Lajoie, the All-Americans played their first game in Woonsocket, Rhode Island, defeating a local semipro club, the Gyms, by a 14–0 score. When Lajoie strode to the plate in the first inning, local officials interrupted the game and presented their favorite son with a watch. After a bit of speechmaking, Larry walloped the first pitch he saw into the Blackstone River, which ran behind right field. Though the nervous Gyms committed 13 errors that day, the Woonsocket fans were thrilled to see their hero in action.

The All-Americans played their way across the Midwest, then set off for California in early November. They were joined by another team assembled by Cantillon, a group of National League stars (the All-Nationals) with Cincinnati Reds first baseman Jake Beckley serving as captain. The All-Americans proceeded to the Bay Area and took on the Oakland, San Francisco, and Sacramento teams, while the All-Nationals traveled to Los Angeles to play the minor league teams there. After a few weeks, the two clubs switched places so the people of California could see both groups of all-stars in action. The climax of the tour was a 13-game series between Lajoie's All-Americans and Beckley's All-Nationals in San Francisco, in which the American Leaguers impressed the fans and sportswriters with their skill.

76

The All-Americans were far superior to the All-Nationals contingent, said one writer, because "the Nationals do not play with the vigor and snap of Lajoie's men."[1]

The tour concluded on January 20, and though Cantillon received an offer to take both teams to Mexico for another series of contests, the players were anxious to get home. They arrived in Chicago at the end of the month, "their pockets bulging with gold," as *Sporting Life* put it. "Their season on the coast has been a success," wrote A. B. Cole, *Sporting Life*'s Oakland correspondent. "After paying all expenses each player has pocketed $500. One and all played fine ball, behaved well and made many friends here."[2]

The 1902 season looked promising for the Athletics, and not only because of Lajoie's brilliance. The club had closed the 1901 campaign with 40 wins in its last 60 games, and help was due to arrive thanks to another round of defections from the Phillies. During the winter months, Mack strengthened his team by signing Elmer Flick, Lajoie's old sparring partner, who had batted .336 in 1901, and right-handed pitcher Bill Duggleby, a 19-game winner, away from his crosstown rivals. Mack also solved his shortstop problem with Monte Cross, another veteran Phillie who had played for Mack at Pittsburgh several years before. This series of raids, coupled with Ed Delahanty's desertion to Washington of the American League, virtually destroyed the Phillies, who would not challenge again for a pennant for more than a decade. The Athletics were now the top dog of Philadelphia baseball, and many observers picked Mack's team to beat out Charles Comiskey's White Sox in the race for the American League pennant.

The American League survived its initial major league campaign in relatively good shape, despite some controversies and difficulties. "There were plenty of troubles, though," recalled Lajoie in an interview many years later. "Three players were banned for slugging umpires and others jumped from one club to another like grass-hoppers." There were also a few scheduling problems. "One afternoon," said Lajoie, "Boston came to Philadelphia to play us and found the Washington club taking batting practice. It was discovered that Boston should have been in Baltimore."[3] Still, the circuit's first season was mostly successful. Some, but not all, of the eight franchises in the circuit had performed well at the gate and on the field, and Ban Johnson moved to shore up the weaker teams. Because the Milwaukee Brewers had failed to gain a foothold in the Wisconsin city, Johnson moved the club to St. Louis, where it took the name Browns and raided the crosstown Cardinals (the former Perfectos) for talent. Seven Cardinals, including future Hall of Fame members Bobby Wallace and Jesse Burkett, signed with the Browns and dealt another blow to the reeling National League.

The senior circuit fought back, filing suit against the Browns in an attempt to retrieve its lost ballplayers. The National League also assembled a $100,000 fund for raiding Ban Johnson's league, hoping to entice American League stars back to the National. Their main object of persuasion was the Triple Crown winner, Napoleon Lajoie, who reportedly received a three-year offer of $10,000 per year from Horace Fogel, manager of the New York Giants, to quit the Athletics. Such a move must have been tempting for Lajoie, whose salary would have nearly quadrupled from the $2,600 he had received from the Phillies just two years before. Lajoie, whose defection would have dealt a possibly fatal blow to the new league, turned Fogel down. "I have received nothing but the best treatment from President Shibe and Manager Mack," he told the *New York Evening World* on April 4. "I am under contract to the American League club for two years longer. My contract does not expire until the fall of 1903. I have no intention of repudiating that contract, and all of the offers of the National League will not induce me to desert the American League."[4]

Colonel John Rogers, however, would never have allowed the Giants to gain possession of Lajoie. He still saw Larry, Bill Bernhard, and Chick Fraser as the property of the Phillies, and had, as promised, appealed the case of *Philadelphia Ball Club v. Lajoie* to the Pennsylvania Supreme Court. The case wound its way through the legal maze for nearly a year, and a resolution was due in the spring of 1902. Opinions were mixed on what the outcome of the case would be, but higher courts tended, then as now, to be more conservative, and to offer stronger protections for employer rights, than lower courts. While Connie Mack conducted workouts for his team at Columbia Park, he and the affected players could only wait for their futures to be decided at the state capital in Harrisburg.

Lajoie professed to be unconcerned. "Well, Colonel John I. Rogers is having his second round with me," he told *The Sporting News*, "but I am not worrying over the outcome of the suit in the least. No, we didn't leave the colonel a great deal from last year, but at the same time we left him with more than I would have done if I had had my whole way about it."[5]

The court released its long-awaited decision on April 22, 1902, and gave Colonel Rogers and the Phillies a stunning victory. In a major blow to the Athletics and the American League, the six justices ruled unanimously that Lajoie's contract with the Phillies, reserve clause and all, was valid. Lajoie, ruled the court, was still the property of the Phillies and was not only bound to the National League club for the 1902 season, but for the 1903 campaign as well. The justices disagreed with the Superior Court in Philadelphia, which had invalidated the standard National League contract for lacking mutuality; this court decided that a baseball player's salary was just compensation for such features as the reserve clause and the ten days' notice. "Upon a careful consideration of the whole case," ruled the justices, "we are of opinion that the provisions of the contract are reasonable and that the consideration is fully adequate. The evidence shows no indications of any attempt at overreaching or unfairness."[6]

They also upheld the ten days' notice. "Owing to the peculiar nature and circumstances of the [baseball] business," the court declared, "the reservation upon the part of the plaintiff to terminate upon short notice does not make the whole contract inequitable."[7]

The justices further ruled that Lajoie was, in fact, irreplaceable, and that his absence would cause great harm to the National League club. The decision, which made banner headlines across the nation, read as follows, in part:

> The defendant in this case contracted to serve the plaintiff as a baseball player for a stipulated time.
>
> During that period he was not to play for any other club. He violated his agreement, however, during the term of his engagement, and in disregard of his contract arranged to play for another and a rival organization. The plaintiff by means of this bill sought to restrain him during the period covered by the contract. The Court below refused an injunction, holding that to warrant the interference prayed for the defendant's services must be unique, extraordinary, and of such character as to render it impossible to replace him, so that, his breach of contract would result in irreparable loss to the plaintiff. In view of the Court the defendant's qualifications did not measure up to this high standard. The trial Court was also of opinion that the contract was lacking in mutuality, for the reason that it gave plaintiff an option to discharge the defendant on ten days' notice without a reciprocal right on the part of defendant.
>
> The Court below finds from the testimony that the defendant is an expert base ball player in any position; that he has a great reputation as a second baseman; that his place would be hard to fill with as good a player: that his withdrawal from the team would weaken it, as

would the withdrawal of any good player, and would probably make a difference in the size of the audience attending the game.

We think that in thus stating he puts it very mildly, and that the evidence would warrant a stronger finding as to the ability of the defendant as an expert ball player. He has been for several years in the service of the plaintiff club, and has been re-engaged from season to season at a constantly increasing salary. He has become thoroughly familiar with the action and methods of the other players in the club, and his own work is peculiarly meritorious as an integral part of the team work which is so essential. In addition to these features, which render his services of peculiar and specific value to the plaintiff, and not easily replaced, Lajoie is well known, and has great reputation among the patrons of the sport for ability in the position which be filled, and was thus a most attractive drawing card for the public. He may not be the sun in the base ball firmament, but he is certainly a bright, particular star.

We feel therefore that the evidence in this case justifies the conclusion that the services of the defendant are of such a unique character and display such a specific knowledge skill and ability as renders them of peculiar value to the plaintiff and so difficult of substitution that their loss will produce irreparable injury in the legal significance of the term to the plaintiff.[8]

Indeed, Lajoie's brilliant 1901 season, in which he established himself as the premier player in the game, worked to his detriment. The original decision had allowed him to remain with the Athletics because the court, while acknowledging his excellence as a player, had rejected the notion that he was so immensely talented that he could not be replaced. A year later, after winning the batting title by 86 points and leading the league in almost every major offensive category, no one could argue that the "king of ballplayers" was replaceable.

Lajoie was disappointed, but remained defiant. "The decision is very unexpected, as we had received no intimation of its being handed down at so early a date," he said. "The Supreme Court may enjoin me from playing on the Athletic team, but it cannot compel me to play on any club I do not want to play on. I am under contract to manager Mack, and will do just exactly what he wants me to. We shall have a conference with Attorney Richard C. Dale tomorrow, and will probably abide by his advice. I will not, however, bind myself to do so. If manager Mack wants me to play for his club, either in this city or outside of it, I will do so. I am under contract to him, and will faithfully live up to the terms of it, irrespective of what the Court may decide."[9]

Rogers, who bellowed, "I am vindicated! I am vindicated at last!"[10] when he heard the news, immediately announced plans to take similar legal action against the other former Phillies who had abandoned the National League for the American. "We shall proceed at once," he said, "against the following players: Delahanty, Wolverton, Orth and Townsend, of Washington; Monte Cross, Flick and Duggleby, of the Athletics; Donahue, of St. Louis, and McFarland, of Chicago. I shall apply at once, in view of the Court's decision, for an injunction against these players, which will be issued in the ordinary course of events, as the Supreme Court's decision is imperative and will go into effect at once." He closed his comments with a threat. "It is impossible for me to say at this early date what action the players may take, or whether they will return to our club this year. One thing is certain, however, that if they do not play on the Philadelphia National League Club they will not be permitted to play on any other."[11]

Stunned by the ruling, the Athletics traveled to Baltimore to open their 1902 season on April 23. More than 12,000 people packed the stands to see the Orioles take on the Athletics, while Connie Mack nervously awaited word from Philadelphia about another hearing

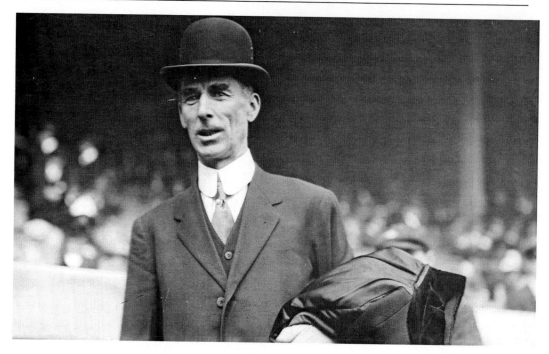

Connie Mack, Lajoie's manager in 1901 and again in 1915 and 1916 (Bain Collection, Library of Congress).

that was held that afternoon. Colonel Rogers had, as promised, filed a request for an injunction that would prohibit Lajoie for playing for any team but the Phillies, and while the game proceeded in Baltimore, the lawyers made their motions and argued their points in a Philadelphia courtroom.

Mack, who decided to keep all the former Phillies in his lineup until forced to remove them by court order, put Lajoie at second base, Elmer Flick in right field, and Bill Bernhard on the mound against the Orioles. Lajoie, who batted fifth in the lineup, contributed a single in four times at bat, while Bernhard dominated the Orioles in an 8–1 win.

During the bottom of the eighth inning, a messenger handed Mack a telegram from the Athletics' attorney, William J. Turner. The telegram informed the manager that the court had granted a five-day temporary injunction requested by Colonel Rogers, and that Napoleon Lajoie was, for the time being, officially enjoined from playing for any team besides the Phillies in the state of Pennsylvania. The temporary injunction would no doubt be made permanent in short order, and because the unanimous Supreme Court decision appeared unlikely to be overturned, Lajoie's career with the Philadelphia Athletics was over. To make a bad situation worse, Rogers had filed two more injunction requests against pitchers Bill Bernhard and Chick Fraser. Those cases were scheduled to be heard on the following Monday, April 26, and because Rogers' case against Lajoie had proved successful, it was a near certainty that not only Bernhard and Fraser, but all the other ex–Phillies on Mack's roster, would soon be lost to the Athletics as well.

With Lajoie due to bat in the top of the ninth inning against the Orioles, Mack had a decision to make. He could have left his star second baseman in the game, because the injunction covered the state of Pennsylvania and the game was being played in Maryland. On the other hand, the manager did not want to anger the judges by appearing to defy their order. After weighing the situation, Mack pulled Lajoie out of the game. He sent Socks Seybold in to pinch-hit for Lajoie in the top of the ninth, while Lou Castro took the field at second base in the bottom of the inning. Bill Bernhard, who was not yet enjoined from playing, remained on the mound and finished the contest.

After the game, Mack called the team's lawyers, who advised the manager to leave Lajoie on the bench for the next two games in Baltimore and the following three in Washington. The other former Phillies remained in the lineup, but Lajoie, the biggest star in the game, was now a mere spectator. He watched the next several games from the bench, in full uniform, and pondered his next move.

On Monday, April 26, the destruction of the Athletics continued apace. While the rest of the team took on the Senators in Washington, Lajoie, Bernhard, Fraser, and Mack attended a hearing in Philadelphia before the same panel of judges that had ruled in their favor a year before. Now, however, Colonel Rogers was on a winning streak, and the judges dealt the American League another blow. They continued the injunction against Lajoie and issued new ones against the other two players. All three injunctions were to be made permanent as soon as the necessary legal paperwork was complete, and a satisfied Colonel Rogers announced plans for a new round of filings against pitcher Bill Duggleby and outfielder Elmer Flick.

Bill Shettsline, manager of the Phillies, had already sent a telegram to Lajoie and his affected teammates. It read, "Supreme Court overrides court below in Lajoie case; decides our contracts absolutely binding on you. You are hereby ordered to report forthwith to me at Philadelphia Ball Park for performance of duties under your contract. Refusal to obey this will be at your peril."[12] This threat had its intended effect upon Bill Duggleby, who signed with the Phillies on May 5, and Chick Fraser, who returned to his former employer two weeks later. Napoleon Lajoie, though, was not intimidated. He could no longer play for the Athletics, but he would take his time in deciding his next move. He might return to the Phillies, but would do so on his terms.

The Phillies celebrated their legal victory, but other judges in other cities handed down different rulings. In St. Louis, the Cardinals failed to compel the Browns to return their seven former players, and though the National League team planned to file an appeal, the Browns were sure to remain intact for the time being. In a District of Columbia courtroom, Colonel Rogers demanded that the Washington Senators return Ed Delahanty, pitcher Al Orth, and infielder Harry Wolverton to the Phillies, but the judge turned down the request.

These decisions offered a glimmer of hope to the American League, though one newspaper report stated that the league was panicked by the thought of losing it biggest drawing card, and "there has been some talk of making Lajoie an umpire."[13] However, the permanent injunctions against Lajoie and the others applied only to the state of Pennsylvania, and because the judges in other states could be persuaded to see the matter differently, there was a chance that Lajoie's presence in Ban Johnson's circuit could somehow be salvaged. Obviously, he could not stay with the Athletics, because he could only play road games if he did so. On the other hand, he could sign with another American League club and continue playing, so long as he stayed out of Pennsylvania. Perhaps Colonel Rogers and the Phillies had done Lajoie a favor. They had annulled his contract with the Athletics and made him, in every state in the Union but one, a free agent.

Most histories of the American League's formative years have, until recently, stated that because Napoleon Lajoie was legally prevented from playing for the Athletics, Connie Mack transferred, sold, or traded his superstar to another team. Thanks mainly to the

Lajoie in a studio pose in 1901 (National Baseball Hall of Fame Library, Cooperstown, New York).

research of baseball historian Norman Macht, Mack's biographer, we now know that Mack had no further claim on Lajoie's services, and because Lajoie's contract with the Athletics had been invalidated by the court, he was a free agent. He was free to return to the Phillies (though he showed little enthusiasm for that option), or he could sign with any of the other seven American League clubs, though he would not be allowed to play road games at Columbia Park in Philadelphia, at least for the time being. The decision, as Macht made clear in the first volume of his biography of the longtime Athletics manager, was solely Lajoie's. In mid–May of 1902, while he entertained offers from several other clubs, *Sporting Life* reported that Mack and co-owner Ben Shibe "both declare that they have no intention of bartering off the services of the great second baseman, and they also add that they would have no right to do so, even if they were so disposed."[14]

Though Chick Fraser and Bill Duggleby returned to the Phillies, Elmer Flick charted a different course. A native of Bedford, Ohio, just outside of Cleveland, he had always dreamed of playing for the local team. The Cleveland fans had always cheered for him enthusiastically whenever the Phillies played there, and Flick saw his chance to better himself. He played in 11 games for the Athletics in April and early May of 1902, but when his name was added to the list of enjoined players, Flick slipped out of Philadelphia before court officers could serve him with papers. He took a train to Cleveland on May 7, and soon signed to play for the Cleveland ballclub, then called the Bronchos and now known as the Indians.

Larry Lajoie and Bill Bernhard were in no hurry. The second baseman and the pitcher were good friends, and Bernhard decided to wait and see what Lajoie would do. Offers rolled in from teams in both leagues, and the papers reported that the New York Giants of the National League and the Detroit Tigers of the American would go as high as necessary to secure the services of the "king of ballplayers." The San Francisco club of the independent California League also weighed in with a proposal. Lajoie, who no doubt realized that the offers would only get better as time passed, was content to watch and wait. He spent a few days in Detroit, where he consulted with James McNamara, part owner of the local American League club, and set off a flurry of speculation that the Tigers would have Lajoie in uniform in a matter of days. Lajoie, however, was not yet ready to commit himself.

Lajoie's situation, as it existed in May of 1902, is unique in baseball history. No other star of Lajoie's magnitude has ever found himself cast adrift during a season, while the owners of other teams competed for his services in a flurry of high-stakes bidding and record-setting salary offers. Perhaps the closest parallel to Lajoie in this regard was Ken (Hawk) Harrelson, a hard-hitting outfielder who was released by the Kansas City Athletics after a dispute with team ownership in August of 1967. Harrelson, who earned $12,000 per year with the Athletics, signed a multi-year deal with the Boston Red Sox a few days later for a total of about $150,000. He played a key role in Boston's drive to the 1967 pennant, and led the American League in runs batted in the following year. However, Harrelson was no Napoleon Lajoie. If Willie Mays or Henry Aaron had been set free in such a fashion, then they would truly compare to Lajoie.

The second baseman also had the option of signing with the Phillies, and perhaps out of courtesy, he met with Billy Shettsline and John Rogers during the second week of May. Returning to the employ of Colonel Rogers, distasteful though it may have been to Lajoie, presented certain advantages. For one, it would bring an end to his legal problems. He was tired of courtrooms, lawyers, and legal maneuvering, and was ready to get back into uniform. Furthermore, Lajoie liked Billy Shettsline, and because Ed Delahanty was now plying his trade for the Washington Senators, Lajoie might be in line to become captain of the ballclub. He had performed well in that capacity for the Athletics in 1901, and except for one minor behavioral incident in September of that year (when he refused to take his turn at bat and forced Connie Mack to pinch-hit for him) he had displayed a newfound maturity. His return to the Phillies would have crippled the American League, perhaps fatally, but might have worked to his personal advantage.

Shettsline, Rogers, and Lajoie negotiated for several days, and for a while it looked like the Phillies had convinced their former second baseman to return to the fold. On May 15, Lajoie cleaned out his locker at Columbia Park, setting off another round of newspaper speculation, and on May 17 the papers reported that he worked out at the Phillies' ballpark while the club was on the road. To most observers, it appeared to be only a matter of time before Colonel Rogers recaptured baseball's biggest star and scored another decisive victory over the American League.

However, the arrogant Colonel overplayed his hand. His salary offer was lower than those Larry had received elsewhere, and he also, in a startling burst of bad judgment, demanded that Lajoie pay a penalty for the time he missed with the Phillies. This was an insult that the proud superstar, who still believed that the Phillies had cheated him out of $400 in his 1900 contract, would not accept, but Rogers stood firm. Time passed without an agreement, and the Colonel turned up the pressure. "Lajoie knows that he is legally bound to play with us," he told the local reporters, "and really wants to come back. We have made him our offer, which will be adhered to, and it would be unfair to some of our other players to accede to Mr. Lajoie's terms, especially under the existing circumstances. We are now awaiting the player's decision."[15]

The colonel's intransigence opened the door for another suitor to swoop in and carry off the prize. The Cleveland Bronchos, who had already signed Elmer Flick, set their sights on the game's premier second baseman, with the encouragement of American League president Ban Johnson. Negotiations with the Phillies had stalled, so Lajoie and Bill Bernhard traveled to Cleveland on May 26 and huddled with team owners Charles Somers and John Kilfoyl. Lajoie liked what he heard. Though the Bronchos had struggled to a seventh-place finish in 1901, Somers and Kilfoyl appeared willing to spend the money necessary to make the club a contender. Signing Lajoie would not only boost the weak Cleveland franchise, but also keep the star in the American League and deal another blow to the National. The Cleveland owners, after conferring with their lawyers and determining that the Pennsylvania court injunction could not be made to apply in other states, drew up a contract that pledged to pay Lajoie a guaranteed salary of $7,000 per year for four years, the largest sum ever promised to a player in the game's history up to that time.

Lajoie was impressed by the offer, and on May 27 he told a Philadelphia reporter that his negotiations with the Phillies were all but dead. "If I play anywhere in the American League," said Lajoie, "it will be with Cleveland. Will I go back to Colonel Rogers? I hardly think I will. He had his chance to get me, and failed to take advantage of the opportunity."[16] Two days later, Cleveland team president John Kilfoyl held a press conference. He announced that Napoleon Lajoie, the best player in the game, was now a Cleveland Broncho and would play his first game at home on June 3 against the Boston Americans. "Lajoie will not join a team," said the *Washington Post*. "It will join him."[17]

10

Cleveland

The town is base ball mad. The addition of Lajoie and Bernhard has set the town afire, and now nothing is talked about except base ball. The big French-man is the hero of the town, and everywhere he goes he is surrounded by an admiring crowd. From a business standpoint the acquisition of Lajoie was a wonder stroke on the part of the Cleveland management, and only goes to prove that if you have the attractions you can get the patronage. —Sporting Life, 1902[1]

Cleveland's American League team came into being in 1900, after the National League, which had dropped its four least profitable franchises after the 1899 season, left the city without a presence in major league baseball. The contraction also left League Park, a wooden structure on Cleveland's east side that was built in 1891 and held about 9,000 people, without a tenant for the 1900 season. Seizing an opportunity, two young Cleveland businessmen, Charles Somers and John F. Kilfoyl, bought the failing Grand Rapids, Michigan, franchise of the Western (soon to become the American) League and moved it to Cleveland. Frank Robison, the owner of the St. Louis Cardinals and former owner of Cleveland's National League team, the Spiders, still held title to League Park, but after some initial resistance, Robison agreed to sell the facility to the two entrepreneurs.

Charles Somers, only 31 years old in 1900, was already a millionaire. His father had founded a coal shipping business and built it into one of Cleveland's most profitable enterprises, but Charles, after learning the business, had set out on his own, buying and leasing mining properties and selling them for a profit. As one of the wealthiest young men in the city, he was able to bankroll not only the Cleveland entry in the new American League, but several other teams as well. His money, coupled with Ban Johnson's vision, made it possible for new franchises in Boston, Philadelphia, and Chicago to stay afloat during the difficult early days of the new circuit. Somers emerged as owner of the Boston club when no local investors came forward to buy the franchise, so he put the nominal ownership of the Cleveland team in John Kilfoyl's hands until he finally sold his Boston holdings before the start of the 1903 campaign. His deep pockets were vital to the success of the American League, and it is not an exaggeration to say that the league could not have survived its first season without him.

John F. Kilfoyl, the other main investor in the Cleveland ballclub, was a local haberdasher and baseball fan who hated to see the National League leave town and convinced his friend Somers to throw in his lot with Ban Johnson's circuit. Not nearly as wealthy as Somers, Kilfoyl was respected for his management skill, so Johnson installed Kilfoyl as president of the Cleveland franchise, with Somers as vice president of both the team and the league itself.

The new Cleveland franchise, with longtime Spiders star Jimmy McAleer as its manager, fought for survival during its first two seasons. In 1900, the club, usually called the Blues (or Bluebirds) but sometimes referred to as the Lake Shores, finished in sixth place and drew only 84,000 fans to League Park. In 1901, the Blues fell to seventh position but raised their attendance to 131,000, though that figure ranked last in the league. Somers and Kilfoyl insisted that Cleveland was a potentially great baseball town, but the local fans were slow to embrace the American League brand of baseball. The team needed some star power, and Somers, who had lured Jimmy Collins and Cy Young away from the National League and put them in Boston uniforms, now gave Cleveland a dash of excitement with the signing of Napoleon Lajoie, the biggest star in the game.

The Cleveland ballclub, which took the name Bronchos and hired Bill Armour as manager after Jimmy McAleer took the reins of the new American League team in St. Louis, possessed some talent. The hard-hitting Elmer Flick signed on with his hometown team after leaving the Athletics and provided a solid bat in right field, while Harry Bay, proclaimed by many as the fastest man in baseball, ruled in center. Third baseman Bill Bradley, after a fine 1901 season, was considered a future star at age 24, and pitcher Earl Moore, a 16-game winner as a rookie in 1901, looked like a dependable anchor for the pitching staff.

Perhaps the most important newcomer, with the exception of Lajoie, was a hard-throwing pitcher named Adrian (Addie) Joss. Joss, a gangly 22-year-old right-hander who had spent the previous two seasons with Toledo of the Interstate League, joined Cleveland in April despite a protracted contract dispute with Toledo management, which believed that the youngster had broken a legal agreement to play with the Mud Hens for one more season. The Toledo club filed suit against Joss and the dispute wound up in front of a grand jury, which dismissed the case and freed Joss to pitch for the Bronchos. To ease any hard feelings, Cleveland owner Charles Somers sent the Mud Hens a prospect in partial payment for the right-hander. Joss, despite the bitterness of his departure from the Mud Hens, later made his home in Toledo and lived there for the rest of his life.

Joss paid dividends immediately. In his first major league start on April 26, Joss held the St. Louis Browns without a hit through the first five innings. With none out in the sixth, Jesse Burkett of the Browns lifted a short fly ball to left field, where Cleveland's Zaza Harvey raced in, slid on his knees, and caught the ball mere inches above the ground. Umpire Bob Caruthers, who probably did not have a good view of the play, ruled that Harvey trapped the ball and awarded Burkett a single. That hit was the only one of the game for the Browns, as Addie Joss completed a one-hit shutout in his initial major league contest.

The shortstop position, however, remained a major weakness for the Cleveland Bronchos. Several players had tried, and failed, to fill the slot adequately in 1901, and in 1902 the team signed John Gochnaur, who had played for manager Bill Armour at Dayton in 1900 and 1901. Gochnaur had earned a reputation in the minors as a good fielder with a strong arm, but his erratic play in the majors resulted in 48 errors in 1902. He followed that up with an eye-popping 98 errors, the highest single-season total at any position in American League history, in 1903. Gochnaur also could not hit major league pitching, compiling an identical .185 average in each of his two seasons with Cleveland. Baseball historian

Mike Attiyeh, writing at the BaseballGuru.com web site, has unkindly suggested that Gochnaur was, in fact, the worst major league player of all time. "Few have been worse than Gochnaur with the bat," wrote Attiyeh in 2003, "and fewer still might have been worse than Gochnaur in the field, but none combined the two-way futility quite the way Gochnaur did."[2] The Cleveland club thus treated its fans to the sight of Napoleon Lajoie, the top second baseman in the game, and John Gochnaur, the worst shortstop, playing next to each other on the infield.

Bill Armour, the Cleveland manager, was a small, dapper 32-year-old who had played the outfield in the minors but never came close to a major league promotion. He had spent the previous five years in Dayton, Ohio, where he led the local Interstate League team to two pennants and developed several future major leaguers, including Lajoie's new teammates Elmer Flick, John Gochnaur, and Earl Moore. He, like Larry's old Phillies manager George Stallings, directed the team from the bench in street clothes, calling the pitches and positioning the fielders. Like Stallings, Armour was well respected for his baseball knowledge, though he did not display the dictatorial tendencies that had so distressed Lajoie in Philadelphia. Armour got along so well with his new superstar that he and Lajoie opened a cigar store together on the corner of Superior and Bond (East Sixth) streets in downtown Cleveland before the year was out.

Despite the presence of talents such as Flick, Bradley, Joss, and now Lajoie, the team was seriously undermanned, especially in the pitching department. The Bronchos had enticed Luther Taylor, a deaf-mute pitcher who had posted an 18–27 record for a bad New York Giants team in 1901, to jump to Cleveland, but Taylor pitched in only four games and hopped right back to the Giants. Taylor's defection and mounting injuries forced Armour to use Addie Joss, who was not a good hitter, at first base and catcher Bob Wood at second. In August, Armour was so desperate for pitching help that he asked Henry Edwards, the longtime columnist of the *Cleveland Plain Dealer*, to publicize a tryout camp at League Park for local semipros and amateurs. A 24-year-old left-hander named Otto Hess, who had never played professional ball, impressed Armour, who gave the young man a uniform and put him on the mound in relief against the Washington Senators that same weekend. Two days later, Hess beat the Senators with a ten-inning, complete-game victory. Another pitching find, an amateur named Charlie Smith, was plucked out of the stands one day when the Bronchos found themselves short-handed on the mound. Smith, who had paid his way into League Park that day, became the hero of the game when he defeated the first-place Philadelphia Athletics by a 5–4 score.

The Bronchos held last place with an 11–24 record when Lajoie and Bernhard joined the team the first week of June. They had completed a disastrous four-game series in Baltimore against the Orioles, winning only one game and losing the other three by scores of 12–4, 10–7, and 14–1. Still, the team had played only ten home games and looked forward to spending more time at League Park than on the road during the rest of the season. In addition, they were only ten and a half games out of first place; it was unlikely, but not impossible, that the presence of Lajoie and Bernhard might give the team a boost into the first division by the end of the season. Using the previous nickname for the club, one paper commented after Lajoie's arrival, "The Blues have a strong team, having stolen most of it."[3]

The signing of Lajoie was front-page news in the Cleveland papers, and the team reported that more than 3,000 extra tickets were sold for his scheduled debut on June 3. That Tuesday contest was rained out, but the skies parted on Wednesday, June 4 (though the League Park field was still muddy) and nearly 10,000 people turned out to see the rebirth of Cleveland baseball. Batting fourth in the lineup, Lajoie, who was appointed captain of the team upon his signing, belted a double off the left field wall, made two acrobatic fielding plays, and led his new team to a 4–3 win over Boston. The Lajoie era in Cleveland had begun, and the *Cleveland Leader* paid tribute to the city's newest star in print:

> Lajoie gave the entire team that confidence that works wonders in baseball. Every time he came up to bat the outfielders went back as far as the ropes, which had been stretched along the back field to confine the crowd. His only safe hit was one up against the fence, and it missed going over by just two feet. It was a great hit.... It was his fielding that attracted the greatest attention, however, and was right here that the game was won. He participated in two lightning double plays, his throws each time to first base being accurate.[4]

The only ominous note was struck by Frank Robison, owner of the National League's St. Louis Cardinals and former owner of the Cleveland Spiders. Robison, flanked by two National League lawyers, attended the contest for the purpose of witnessing an "overt act" that could be used against Lajoie in court. The overt act in question was his participation in the game and his appearance on the field in a Cleveland uniform in direct defiance of the Pennsylvania court, which had ordered him to return to the Phillies. "I doubt if Cleveland will be able to play this great player,"[5] said Robison on his way out of League Park.

"Lajoie Day" was a grand success, and the new captain started his Cleveland tenure on a hot streak. On June 5, Boston pitcher Cy Young won his own game when he hit a grounder that rolled under the scoreboard in center field for a home run, and though Lajoie belted a double and a single, Young defeated Addie Joss before nearly 4,000 fans. Three days later, at a Sunday game in Dayton (the Bronchos were not allowed to play on Sunday in Cleveland) nearly 5,000 people witnessed a loss to the Orioles. Lajoie hit his first home run as a Broncho on June 9, one of his four hits that day, and two days later he walloped a three-run homer in a losing effort against the Athletics. On June 12, in his ninth game for Cleveland, the Athletics held Lajoie hitless for the first time, but he turned two sharp double plays in a 5–4 win.

On that same day, a process server strode to the Cleveland bench before the game and handed Lajoie a sheaf of papers. Colonel Rogers had succeeded in getting the Common Pleas court in Pennsylvania to issue a charge of contempt against Lajoie and pitcher Bill Bernhard. He then filed suit in an Ohio court to force both men out of uniform. At issue was the question of whether or not an Ohio court would enforce a decree from another state. The American League lawyers expressed confidence that the Ohio courts would not, but the colonel's filing promised another round of courtroom arguments, legal motions, and off-field headlines.

After a crowd of 6,000 saw the Bronchos lose to the Americans on a hot Sunday afternoon in Canton on June 15, Lajoie returned to Cleveland while his teammates proceeded to Boston. The Cleveland team always traveled to the eastern states through Pennsylvania, and the ballplayer, on the advice of his lawyers, decided not to set foot in the state. That advice turned out to be correct, because on Tuesday, June 17, the Common Pleas court in Philadelphia issued contempt citations against Bernhard and Lajoie (though Judge Robert Ralston turned down Rogers' request to cite Cleveland co-owner Charles Somers as well). Lajoie now lived under threat of arrest in Pennsylvania, and his legal status played a key role in the 1902 pennant race. The Bronchos began to climb the standings when Lajoie joined the team, but he and Bernhard would be required to miss future games against the league-leading Athletics in Philadelphia for the rest of the season, if not longer. On June 25,

Rogers traveled to Cleveland and filed suit against Lajoie, Bernhard, and Elmer Flick in U.S. District Court, with a hearing set for July 1.

While the legal wheels turned, Lajoie earned his salary on the field, batting .442 during his first 13 games and perking up the formerly moribund ballclub. Attendance at League Park shot upward, and the Bronchos became the league's most popular road attraction. The publicity generated by the drawn-out legal battles, dueling injunctions, and courtroom theatrics had brought attention to Lajoie and his new team and kept his name in the national headlines. Colonel Rogers' single-minded pursuit of Lajoie had made the Cleveland second baseman a national celebrity, and the fans could not wait to see the next installment of the long-running drama.

Lajoie drew another large crowd on Saturday, June 21, as 10,000 fans filled League Park and saw the Senators defeat the Bronchos by a 14–9 score. Three days later, Lajoie belted the first grand slam homer in Cleveland's American League history in a 12–4 decision over the Browns, and on June 30 he, Charlie Hickman, and Bill Bradley walloped consecutive homers in a 17–2 win over St. Louis. The Bronchos finally climbed out of last place on July 11 while sweeping a three-game set against Detroit. Two days earlier, District Court Judge Francis J. Wing had dismissed Rogers' suit against Lajoie, Flick, and Bernhard, ruling that his court had no jurisdiction in the case. Colonel Rogers was angered by the decision. "We did not receive fair play in Cleveland," he complained. "The cases were not really tried. Judge Wing objected to sitting in court during such hot weather, and so he simply threw us out to bring the session to an end."[6] He vowed to fight on, though to most other observers, it appeared that the battle was over.

The three players were still subject to arrest in Pennsylvania, and when the Bronchos traveled to Boston on July 20, the ex–Phillies took a longer route through Detroit, Ontario, and Buffalo before rejoining the club. This did not stop the Pennsylvania authorities from stopping the Cleveland club's train and executing a thorough search, hoping to catch Lajoie or his mates hiding in a baggage compartment. Manager Bill Armour found the search intrusive, but decided to have some fun with the officers. The star second baseman "took French leave," said Armour with mock seriousness. "That's Frenchie's worst habit. He jumped your Philadelphia club too, didn't he?" When Lajoie met up with his teammates in Boston, his teammates regaled him with tales of the unsuccessful search. Said Lajoie years later, "I've always regretted that I wasn't witness to one of those receptions. The boys entertained me with many a funny story of the futile searches, but I would have liked to have been a spectator."[7]

A four-game sweep of the Americans pushed Cleveland up to sixth place, but four losses in a row against the Athletics (without Flick, Lajoie, and Bernhard) dropped the Bronchos back to seventh for the time being. The three players enjoyed themselves in the resort town of Atlantic City, New Jersey, while the Bronchos played in Philadelphia, and during their short vacation, Phillies manager Bill Shettsline paid a visit to Lajoie and reportedly offered him $10,000 a year to return to the National League. These reports may have been exaggerated, as Colonel Rogers could have signed Lajoie a few months earlier for much less, but Larry listened politely to his former manager. "You know, Billy, how much I think of you," the ballplayer replied, "and the $10,000 sounds very tempting, but I am under contract to Cleveland."[8] Though the Phillies and Giants kept trying to entice Larry back to the National League, the newest Cleveland star was not interested. He liked his situation in Cleveland, and turned a deaf ear to the entreaties of the senior circuit.

Perhaps Lajoie felt at home in Cleveland because League Park, home of the Bronchos, greatly resembled Philadelphia's Huntingdon Street Grounds. The left field area was deep, with a distance of 385 feet down the left field line and 460 to center, while the right field fence, which paralleled Lexington Avenue, stood only 290 feet from home plate. Lajoie, a right-handed batter, hit few home runs in Cleveland, but piled up doubles and triples to left and center field. With his great range at second base, and a small outfield area behind him, Lajoie ran the risk of slamming into right fielder Elmer Flick, which had caused problems for both men in Philadelphia. However, Flick and Lajoie had patched up their differences, and no reports of friction between the two future Hall of Famers were ever made public.

However, rumors popped up every now and then that Lajoie had changed his mind and abandoned the Bronchos. On Monday, July 29, he was ejected from a game in Baltimore in the first inning after a heated argument with umpire Jim Johnstone. Because the Cleveland club was due back in Cleveland on Wednesday for a series against the White Sox, he decided to skip the Tuesday game in Baltimore and take his usual circuitous route back to Ohio. However, the train schedules were fouled up due to a series of accidents, and he did not arrive at League Park on Wednesday in time to take part in the game. His absence from the field for two days in a row, and his quick ejection on Monday, caused the Cleveland fans to fear that he had deserted the American League. They had no reason to worry, as Lajoie played on Thursday as usual.

John Rogers refused to give up, filing suit against Lajoie and others in Common Pleas court in Cleveland after failing in U.S. District Court a month before. The New York Giants also stepped up their pursuit of Lajoie after Baltimore Orioles manager and part-owner John McGraw executed a scheme in which the Giants of the National League bought the Orioles outright and transferred all the best Baltimore players to New York, with McGraw as manager. This volley in the baseball war decimated the Orioles franchise and strengthened the Giants, who then went after Lajoie with a new determination. He held fast, however, and on August 16 Judge Theodore L. Strimple rebuffed Colonel Rogers' latest suit in Common Pleas court, refusing to issue an injunction that would have driven Lajoie back to Philadelphia. The courtroom war was over, at least for the moment, leaving Lajoie and the Bronchos free to attend to on-field matters.

The seemingly endless legal battle drove a wedge between Colonel Rogers and his longtime partner, Al Reach, who took the unusual step of blasting the Phillies co-owner in the papers. The relationship between the two men had been strained for several years, but Rogers' handling of the Lajoie affair moved Reach to speak out.

> We could and should have had Lajoie, and no one is to blame for the fact that we didn't get him but the Philadelphia Club. I think the Philadelphia club made the greatest mistake of its career in letting Lajoie get away. Why, I understand that he was actually out on our grounds one day for practice. Everything was fixed except some little hitch as to salary, and I don't think the club should have allowed any amount of money to stand in the way of bringing back Lajoie. It would have been the greatest thing that could have happened for the National League, and would have turned the crowds back to our grounds. Besides, if Lajoie had joined the Phillies, I also think that many of our other players would have returned. I am thoroughly disgusted with the state of affairs.[9]

Rogers reacted angrily, claiming that Lajoie's demands were unreasonable, but now the rift between Rogers and Reach was a matter of public record. Within a year, both men would sell their shares in the Phillies and leave the sport that had brought them nothing but trouble during the never-ending baseball war.

The Bronchos, despite a knee injury to star pitcher Addie Joss, went on a 10–2 streak in early August and rose a notch into fifth place, with a .500 record and a first-division finish in their sights. Lajoie, Bill Bradley, and Charlie Hickman stroked four hits apiece on August 11 in a 17–11 win over the ragtag Orioles, who borrowed players from the other American League teams in order to finish the season. When the Cleveland team made another visit to Philadelphia in late August, Lajoie, Bill Bernhard, and Elmer Flick traveled to Whittinsville, Massachusetts, to pick up some extra money playing for the local semipro team. More than 8,000 people paid to see the major league stars in action, and Lajoie and his mates split $500 for their efforts. A week later, the Bronchos topped the .500 mark with a 23–7 win over the Orioles in which Harry Bay belted five hits and Lajoie four.

At season's end, the Bronchos, who were 13 games under the break-even mark when Lajoie joined the club, finished two games above it at 69–67, claiming fifth place after being last in the league as late as mid–July. Attendance at League Park topped the 275,000 mark, more than double the 1901 total, mostly due to the presence of Napoleon Lajoie. The Cleveland second baseman battled his old friend Ed Delahanty for the league batting title, and the two men wound up in a near dead heat after Delahanty finished his year with 21 hits in his final 36 times at bat. Not until the official statistics were released by Ban Johnson's office that fall did the public learn that Delahanty, at .376, had topped Lajoie by seven points. More than 90 years later, researchers pored over the box scores and discovered four extra hits for Lajoie in the 1902 statistical record, raising his average to .378. Though the American League still recognizes Ed Delahanty as its 1902 batting champion, many sources now give the honor to Lajoie despite the fact that he missed about 50 games that season due to his legal problems.[10]

Surprisingly, the Philadelphia Athletics overcame the absence of Lajoie, Flick, Duggleby, and Bernhard and won their first American League pennant. After losing Lajoie, Connie Mack experimented with several candidates at second base before signing Danny Murphy from the Connecticut League. Murphy was no Lajoie, but proved a solid performer who would spend more than a decade with Mack's club. Mack also picked up a valuable catcher in Ossee Schreckengost, let go by Cleveland to make room for Flick, and improved the team's shortstop play with ex–Phillie Monte Cross. Perhaps the most important addition was pitcher Bert Husting, released by Boston after pitching only one game and losing by a 14–5 score in April. Mack, who had managed Husting in Milwaukee, coaxed 14 wins out of the right-hander. Perhaps Boston should have held on to Husting, who helped the Athletics win the flag by five games over the Americans.

The Athletics, despite their constantly changing cast of characters, owned one large advantage over the rest of the league. Not only were Lajoie and Flick (as well as Bernhard) legally prevented from playing against Mack's ballclub at Philadelphia, but former Phillie Ed Delahanty of the Washington Senators was enjoined from

Lajoie in the *St. Louis Republic* in September 1902 (author's collection).

appearing in Philadelphia that season as well. This meant that the Athletics did not have to face three of baseball's greatest hitters when playing at home, and contributed to their 56–17 record at their home field. The Athletics were nine games under the .500 mark on the road, but their outstanding record at the Columbia Park grounds brought Connie Mack the first of his nine American League titles.

For the second year in a row, Joe Cantillon and Win Mercer persuaded Lajoie to head up another All-American team, which planned to spend the month of October barnstorming through the Midwest before heading to California to play winter ball. The tour had made money the year before, and Lajoie's presence was so crucial to the enterprise that *Sporting Life* referred to the venture as the "Napoleon Lajoie Base Ball Touring Company." Cantillon and Mercer hatched even bigger plans for their 1902 winter tour, even talking up a scheme to travel to Hawaii and play ball on the islands for two weeks in January. Philadelphia's Harry Davis and Lajoie's teammates Addie Joss, Bill Bernhard, and Bill Bradley played on the All-Americans for the second year in a row, and were joined this time by Boston pitching star Cy Young and Chicago catcher Billy Sullivan, among others.

The tour began with a four-game series against the National League champion Pittsburgh Pirates, with the first two contests scheduled to take place in Pittsburgh on October 7 and 8. Lajoie and Bernhard, who still faced arrest in Pennsylvania, sat those contests out as Pittsburgh's Sam Leever defeated Young in the first game and Deacon Phillippe topped Addie Joss in the second. Lajoie joined the All-Americans for the third game in Cleveland on October 10, and went hitless as Joss and Leever battled to a scoreless tie that was stopped by darkness after 11 innings. The series closed at League Park the next day as Young won a 1–0 duel against Phillippe, with Larry again failing to make a hit.

The series was notable, not only because it was "the nearest approach to a world's championship series possible this Fall,"[11] as Francis C. Richter described it in *Sporting Life*, but also as a confrontation between the two top players in the game. Honus Wagner, the Pittsburgh utility man (he did not move to shortstop, the position for which he is most famous, on a permanent basis until the following year), had won the first of his eight batting titles for the Pirates in 1900 and led the league in both runs batted in and stolen bases in 1901 and 1902. He had established himself as the most valuable player in the National League, and won the head-to-head contest with Lajoie, stroking five hits in 15 trips to the plate against the All-Americans while Lajoie went hitless in seven times at bat. These two would meet again and renew their rivalry, while fans and sportswriters debated which man was the better player.

Lajoie initially intended to remain with the All-Americans, but changed his mind in mid–October and pulled out of the tour after the Pittsburgh series. He told the press that he wanted to stay in Cleveland and tend to his cigar store, which had become a popular hangout for sporting types in the city and showed promise of being a profitable enterprise. The tour went ahead anyway (with Joss, Bernhard, and Bradley representing the Cleveland club), but the trip to Hawaii never materialized.

His absence from the barnstorming tour saved Lajoie from dealing with a tragedy that occurred in California on January 12. Win Mercer, the tour treasurer and co-organizer, had been named manager of the Detroit Tigers for the 1903 season. He had also recently married, and it appeared that his life was peaceful and prosperous. It came as a shock to everyone in the baseball world to hear that Mercer, beset by personal problems and facing mounting debts, may have gambled away some of the tour receipts (though Addie Joss said later that the tour participants received all the money due them). Rather than face the consequences of his actions, Mercer committed suicide in a San Francisco hotel room, writing a tragic coda to what had been a moderately successful tour.

Perhaps Lajoie decided to pass up the barnstorming trip not because of the success of his cigar store, but because the talk of sailing to Hawaii made him nervous. Lajoie was never comfortable traveling by water; it was said that when the Naps sailed across Lake Erie between Cleveland and Detroit, he made his own arrangements, traveling by train and meeting up with his teammates later. In 1913, Chicago White Sox manager Jimmy Callahan organized a round-the-world tour and tried to sell Lajoie, still one of the biggest stars in the game, on joining it. As Callahan later related the story to writer G. W. Axelson, he explained to Lajoie that the trip would pass through California, then embark for Hawaii and Japan before making its way to Europe. "Clear around the world, did you say?" inquired Lajoie. Callahan answered in the affirmative. "I suppose it will all be by land?" asked the Cleveland star with suspicion. The White Sox manager allowed that some sea travel would be required, at which point Lajoie lost interest. "Too damp for me," he said with finality.[12]

During the fall of 1902, the papers were full of speculation that Lajoie, despite all his previous denials, would nonetheless wind up in New York with the Giants. People who claimed to be close to the National League team insisted that John McGraw, who still played the infield for the Giants on occasion, hoped to sign Lajoie and manage from the bench from then on. In the meantime, Lajoie acted like a man who intended to make Cleveland his permanent home. He rented an apartment near the downtown area, within walking distance of his cigar store, and settled in for the winter in his new home city.

11

The Cleveland Naps

Later, after Ed [Delahanty] died in that tragic way at Niagara Falls, the big hero of all the kids in Cleveland became Napoleon Lajoie, the Cleveland second baseman. What a ballplayer that man was! Every play he made he executed so gracefully that it looked like it was the easiest thing in the world. He was a pleasure to play against, too, always laughing and joking. Even when the son of a gun was blocking you off the base, he was smiling and kidding with you. You just had to like the guy. — Tommy Leach, Pittsburgh Pirates outfielder[1]

At the end of the 1902 season, the war between the leagues showed no signs of abating, despite the fact that several teams in each circuit were dangerously close to financial collapse. The Philadelphia Phillies, who lost Napoleon Lajoie, Ed Delahanty, and all their other key players (except for Roy Thomas) to the new league, finished 46 games out of first place in 1902 and surrendered their dominant position in Philadelphia baseball to the rival Athletics. The once-proud Boston Beaneaters, decimated by the city's American League entry, fell to last place and stayed there for years, while the Washington Senators (who signed Delahanty away from the Phillies) and the Baltimore Orioles teetered on the brink of extinction. Rumor had it that the struggling Detroit Tigers of the American League were ready to move to Cincinnati or Pittsburgh, while Pittsburgh Pirates owner Barney Dreyfuss, dissatisfied with his treatment by the National League, seriously considered shifting his ballclub to the American. The fans were tired of the constant upheaval, and most of the club owners, though not all, were ready to call a truce.

Nonetheless, the winter months brought a new raft of player defections and contract disputes. Ed Delahanty, who found himself in deep financial trouble after sustaining large gambling losses, broke his contract with the Senators and hopped back to the National League, signing a lucrative deal with the New York Giants. The aging slugger now had three teams claiming his services, as Colonel John Rogers of the Phillies still demanded his return. Delahanty's salary grab, his third distasteful contract controversy in three years, turned many of his fans against him, and after the two leagues finally made peace, the man whom the papers called the "human grasshopper" was nearly banned from baseball for his contract jumping. The Giants, who led the effort to drive Ban Johnson's league out of business, also snatched pitcher Al Orth from the Senators and shortstop George Davis from the White Sox, but received a shock when their own young star, Christy Mathewson, defected to the

St. Louis Browns. Johnson then decided to turn up the heat on the National League. He moved the moribund Baltimore team to New York to do battle with the Giants, and stepped up his campaign to convince the Pittsburgh Pirates to quit the National League and join his circuit.

For the second year in a row, rumors abounded that the Giants were making an all-out effort to sign Larry Lajoie away from the American League. The papers reported that Horace Fogel, a part owner of the New York club, had offered Lajoie an unprecedented $10,000 per year to quit Cleveland. Lajoie, however, rebuffed all advances from the senior circuit. He had found a home in Cleveland, where he was the undisputed star of the team and the idol of the local fans. His cigar store on East Sixth Street was a thriving enterprise, he got along well with the local sportswriters, and he earned the highest salary in the game. Fogel and John McGraw, who had abandoned the American League and emerged as manager of the National League Giants in July of 1902, tried mightily to induce the "king of ballplayers" to jump back to the National League, but Larry, despite his friendship with McGraw, was not interested.

Though McGraw and Giants majority owner John T. Brush wanted to keep fighting, the other National League magnates were willing to negotiate with the American League. Representatives of the two leagues met in January of 1903 and hammered out a truce that created two equal eight-team circuits, governed by a three-man National Commission. All existing teams (except for Baltimore's American League entry, which was allowed to move to New York) remained where they were, and the negotiators dealt with about a dozen disputed contracts on a case-by-case basis. Delahanty, though he had already spent the advance money he received from the Giants, was ordered back to Washington, while Davis was sent back to the White Sox, Orth to the Senators and Mathewson to the Giants. The long, ruinous baseball war was over, and the fans could now enjoy the action on the field and ignore the legal maneuverings off it.

A few issues remained, however. John McGraw railed against the peace agreement and refused to give up George Davis, who played four games for the Giants in April before being ordered off the field by the new National Commission. Davis, who did not want to return to Chicago, sat out the rest of the 1903 campaign in protest. Another complication involved Cleveland's Napoleon Lajoie and pitcher Bill Bernhard, who were still in legal jeopardy in the state of Pennsylvania; specifically, the two players had been cited for contempt of court when they decamped for Ohio the year before, and still faced arrest if they set foot in the state. This legal mess had forced Lajoie and Bernhard to miss seven games (all of which the Naps lost) in Philadelphia in 1902, and because the two men were leery of even passing through the tip of the state by train from Cleveland to Buffalo, they were obliged to travel separately from the rest of the team on road trips to Boston, Baltimore, and Washington. The travel difficulties kept Lajoie out of a few games in those cities as well, and promised to cause more trouble for the club in 1903.

A more serious problem put Napoleon Lajoie's 1903 season in jeopardy months before it began, and for once his legal issues played no part in the difficulty. During the last week of December in 1902, he came down with a lung infection that graduated to a full-blown case of pleurisy, a painful disorder in which fluid collects in the lungs and makes breathing painful and difficult. "His condition is becoming alarming," said a Youngstown newspaper on January 4. "It is feared now that pneumonia has already started."[2] It was serious enough that his doctors found it necessary to make an incision in his side to drain the congestion from his lungs, a process they repeated several times. The Cleveland star was confined to bed for nearly two months, and not until late February was he able to leave his apartment and make an appearance at his cigar store. Not wanting to miss his first spring training in a Cleveland uniform, he made the trip to the team's camp at New Orleans in March as planned, though he was not yet strong enough to participate in strenuous activities. He was noticeably weak, and some feared that he would not be able to play until late in the season, if at all.

While Lajoie worked to regain his strength, the *Cleveland Press* conducted a contest to find a new nickname for the club. The Cleveland team had been known as the Lake Shores in 1900, and in 1901, when the American League declared itself a major circuit, the team was called the Blues (or Bluebirds) after the color of its uniform letters and stockings. Cleveland management, no doubt looking for a more interesting moniker, introduced the name Bronchos for 1902,[3] but no one much liked that designation, and many newspapers around the nation still referred to the club as the Blues. Because Lajoie's arrival had stirred unprecedented fan enthusiasm in Cleveland, the *Press* figured that a more exciting nickname was in order.

The *Press* hyped the contest to the hilt, printing daily updates and stating, "The genius of the fans has produced almost everything to be found in dictionaries and encyclopedias and a good many suggestions not to be found there or elsewhere."[4] Finally, on April 6, the paper announced the final tally of more than 5,000 votes cast by its readers. The winning name was Napoleons, with 365 votes, with Buckeyes (281) in second place and Emperors (276) in third. "'Metropolitans,' 'Giants,' and 'Cyclops' were nicknames that found considerable favor," said the *Press*, "but the fans sought to honor the greatest living ball player, and succeeded in so doing by casting a plurality of the votes for 'Napoleons.'"[5]

Quickly shortened to "Naps," the name would identify the Cleveland ballclub for more than a decade, as long as Lajoie remained with the team. It also provided the player with a new handle. He had always been referred to as Napoleon or Larry, but when his team became the Naps, he became Nap Lajoie to many fans and sportswriters. "They didn't call me Nap until I went to Cleveland,"[6] said Lajoie to *The Sporting News* years later. On another occasion, he remarked to Eugene J. Whitney of the *Cleveland Plain Dealer*, "In later years, many baseball fans thought 'Napoleon,' my real given name, was a nickname."[7]

Though Bill Armour was the manager of the club, the name "Armour-clads" received only 114 votes, and the balloting provided proof that the Cleveland nine was now Lajoie's team in the eyes of the public. Armour, like Philadelphia's Connie Mack, managed from the bench in street clothes, but while Mack had firmly established himself as the face of the Athletics franchise, Armour, by all appearances, had been relegated to the background by Lajoie's star power. As captain of the team that was now named for him, Lajoie was the dominant presence on the Cleveland baseball scene; indeed, many fans were already calling for him to be named playing manager. Armour, a mild-mannered man in a straw hat whose previous experience in baseball consisted of five seasons as manager of a minor league team in Dayton, Ohio, could not hope to outshine the biggest star in the game. Nonetheless, he was a force in his own right and had the support of the Cleveland team owners. Armour, not Lajoie, directed the team on the field, calling pitches and positioning his fielders.

Despite Lajoie's illness, many sportswriters proclaimed the newly-named Naps as the favorites to win the 1903 pennant. With a solid pitching corps headed by Addie Joss, Earl Moore, and Bill Bernhard, a rising star in third baseman Bill Bradley, and the hard hitting of Elmer Flick and Larry Lajoie, the Naps, on paper, appeared to own more talent than most other American League teams. The catching looked solid with Harry Bemis in charge,

Lajoie during his early years in Cleveland. The Naps wore these dark road uniforms in 1903 and 1904 (National Baseball Hall of Fame Library, Cooperstown, New York).

and the outfield of Flick, Jack McCarthy, and speedster Harry Bay was one of the fastest in the league. The shortstop position was still weak, but the Naps believed that the error-prone John Gochnaur could not possibly play as poorly as he had in 1902, and even a small improvement on Gochnaur's part might be enough to boost the team into contention. Besides, Bill Armour, who had managed Gochnaur in Dayton a few years earlier, still believed in his shortstop and kept him in the lineup despite his .185 batting average the year before.

The Naps lost their first three games of the season at Detroit, but their slow start did nothing to dampen the excitement of the Cleveland faithful. Expecting a large Opening Day crowd, Charles Somers and John Kilfoyl ordered the construction of a large temporary grandstand in right field, adding a few thousand seats to League Park. Their foresight was rewarded as the home opener on Tuesday, April 22, drew 19,870, by far the largest attendance ever recorded in Cleveland up to that time. Larry Lajoie, though he felt pain whenever he swung the bat, nonetheless chipped in with a single and a stolen base. The game was marred by a near-tragedy when the hastily built wooden stands collapsed with a roar in the sixth inning, trapping dozens of fans in a pile of lumber and bodies. Though two people were knocked unconscious and taken by horse-drawn ambulances to a nearby hospital, there were no serious injuries. The game resumed after a brief cleanup, and the Naps defeated the St. Louis Browns by a 6–3 score behind Addie Joss.

The Naps won their second home contest as well, but lost the next four in a row to the Browns and White Sox. Lajoie was not hitting, and his condition, exacerbated by cold, rainy weather, appeared to be getting worse by the day. The Naps, the preseason favorites of many observers, found themselves in last place after the first two weeks of the campaign with a 2–7 record. The Cleveland star tried to ignore his physical problems, but he could not go to his left, said Detroit catcher Deacon McGuire, and was "a ghost of his former self."[8] He barely topped the .200 mark after the first week of the season, mainly because of sharp pains in his shoulders and side, an indication that his lungs had not yet fully healed. He missed games on May 1 and 2 due to a severe cold and its accompanying chest congestion, and after playing poorly in a few more contests, he removed himself from the lineup on doctor's orders. He left the team and traveled to the spas at Mount Clemens, Michigan, for a rest.

Lajoie returned to the lineup on May 11, playing first base and contributing a triple to a 6–5 win over the Boston Americans. He looked more like the Lajoie of old, and acted like it on May 12 in a 10–5 loss to the Americans. In the seventh inning, Boston baserunner Hobe Ferris was called safe at second by umpire Tommy Connolly, though Lajoie had not only tagged Ferris, but blocked him off the base with his leg. Enraged by what he regarded as a blown call, Lajoie used such strong language in arguing his case that the arbiter not only ejected the Cleveland captain from the game, but filed a complaint with the league that brought him an indefinite suspension.

Charles Somers was not happy to see his highly-paid superstar on the sidelines. "That comes pretty hard, I tell you," complained the magnate, "when one has to pay a man a big salary, and he is barred from playing. Probably it is true that Lajoie lost his head in talking to Connolly, but he should also have considered his employers as well. Still, I don't believe that Lajoie deserved the penalty that has been given him. We will have to make the best of it, but this base ball business is really getting very tiresome to me."[9] Three days later American League president Ban Johnson, having made his point, lifted the suspension and reinstated the Cleveland second baseman.

The Naps, despite Lajoie's early slump, began to recover from their 2–7 start and by May 11 had climbed to the .500 mark at 11–11. With Lajoie's average on the rise, the Naps prepared to make a challenge for the pennant. However, the team faced a nagging problem that needed to be resolved. With ten road games against the Athletics on tap for 1903, Lajoie and Bill Bernhard were still required to stay away from the ballpark whenever the Naps played in Philadelphia. All parties wanted the situation resolved, so club management began to work behind the scenes to settle the matter. With the baseball war over and Colonel

John I. Rogers, having sold his stake in the club, no longer in control of the Phillies, all indications were that the problem would be solved peacefully on the Naps' first trip to Philadelphia in June. These assurances eased Lajoie's fear of arrest, and in early June, he joined his teammates on a train trip from Cleveland through Erie, Pennsylvania, on the way to Boston. It was his first visit to the state in more than a year, and because there were no detectives searching for him this time, the trip passed uneventfully.

In June, when the Naps made their first road trip to Philadelphia, Lajoie and Bernhard were ready to solve their legal problems once and for all. Fortunately for the two ballplayers, the new owners of the Phillies were ready to put the Rogers era behind them. They had no interest in reigniting the baseball war, which was a settled issue as far as almost everyone else in both leagues was concerned, and were prepared to bring this lingering legal drama to its conclusion. To that end, the two ballplayers agreed to surrender themselves to the Pennsylvania authorities and appear in court to resolve the matter.

On the morning of June 11, a few hours before the Naps were due to face the Athletics at Columbia Park in Philadelphia, Lajoie and Bernhard, accompanied by a phalanx of lawyers representing both the Athletics and the Phillies, appeared before judges Robert Ralston and G. H. Davis in Common Pleas Court Number 5. Attorney William J. Turner explained to the court that he, as the legal counsel of the Athletics, had advised both players a year before that they were obligated to heed the dictates of the court and return to the Phillies, but they instead chose to follow the advice of the Cleveland club and simply remain outside the state. Now, he said, all parties requested that the court invalidate the injunction against the two men and, because they had appeared before the bar voluntarily, dismiss the contempt charges against them.

Judge Ralston asked Turner if Colonel Rogers had been notified of the proceedings, and when Turner answered in the negative, Ralston ordered court personnel to contact Rogers by telephone and ask him to put in an appearance. A few minutes later, the former Phillies club owner strode into the court. Gone was the defiance and bluster that had characterized the Colonel's dealings with his players. Now, because Rogers no longer owned the club and had mostly disengaged himself from the sport, he harbored no wish to see the players punished. Rogers explained to the court that he had consulted with the Phillies' attorneys and had agreed with their opinion that the injunction issued at his behest in 1902 was no longer necessary. The Colonel, in an uncharacteristic show of magnanimity, asked the court to deal with Lajoie and Bernhard with the utmost leniency.

After a short recess, the two judges returned to the courtroom. Judge Ralston said,

> The question before the court is whether the two defendants are to be punished for contempt or not. Punishment for contempt in such a case would be a serious matter. We don't believe in allowing persons to violate the law and evade the execution of the Court's mandate, and then inflict only nominal punishment. Such persons ought to be severely fined or imprisoned. Nominal punishment would be merely trifling."

However, the voluntary nature of their surrender carried the day. Continued the judge,

> There is no doubt that the mandate of this Court has been violated by these two defendants. But all the parties have settled their differences, and the two defendants have acknowledged their error by appearing and surrendering. If these men had been brought in by force, then I would say they were very deserving of severe punishment. As the matter now stands, a severe punishment would not establish the dignity of the Court. In view of all the circumstances, the defendants are purged of contempt, and the prayer of the petition is granted.[10]

Their legal problems resolved, Lajoie and Bernhard then proceeded to Columbia Park for their first on-field appearance in Philadelphia in more than a year. Lajoie, who received a rousing ovation from more than 7,300 fans when he came to bat in the first inning, belted a sharp line drive that shortstop Monte Cross stabbed just off the ground for the out. In the eighth, however, with the score tied at 2, Lajoie doubled and scored on two long flies to the outfield. That run proved to be the winning tally in a 3–2 Naps win.

While Lajoie reclaimed his place at the top of the league's hitting statistics, his old teammate Ed Delahanty found nothing but turmoil. Delahanty had abandoned the Phillies after the 1901 season and signed with Washington of the American League. Still a dangerous hitter at the age of 35, he won the batting title, his second, for the Senators in 1902. Despite his fine performance, he was unhappy playing for the cash-poor Washington ballclub, and with the baseball war still in full swing, John McGraw of the National League Giants signed Delahanty to a contract for 1903. McGraw also gave Delahanty a large advance, which the ballplayer quickly spent.

Unfortunately for the aging slugger, the peace agreement between the leagues mandated that Delahanty return to Washington at his previous salary. "The Only Del" was not only stuck with the Senators, but also owed the Giants a large amount of money that he could not repay. The ballplayer grew ever more despondent as the 1903 season progressed. Weighted down by family problems, financial issues exacerbated by his penchant for gambling, and harsh criticism by the local press, Delahanty drank heavily and his behavior grew increasingly erratic, leading to conflict not only with manager Tom Loftus, but also with his teammates. His hitting fell off, and his fielding and baserunning deteriorated so badly that he could not remain in the lineup. In late June, the Washington club suspended Delahanty indefinitely.

Delahanty then decided to quit the Senators, who were in Detroit for a series against the Tigers, and travel to New York, where he hoped to convince McGraw and Giants owner John T. Brush to break his Washington contract and allow him to play in the National League. There was little, if any, chance that McGraw and Brush would have done so, as such an act on the Giants' part would have torpedoed the peace agreement and set the two leagues at war again. Besides, George Davis had tried, and failed, to accomplish the same thing a few months before. Nonetheless, Delahanty, not thinking clearly after an extended bender, left his Washington uniform in his Detroit hotel room and boarded an eastbound train on July 2. As the locomotive crossed southern Ontario, the drunken ballplayer threatened his fellow passengers and was so disruptive that the conductor put him off the train at Niagara Falls. What happened then is a matter of conjecture, but apparently Delahanty ran across a railroad bridge after the departing train, lost his footing, and fell into the Niagara River. Missing for a week, his body was discovered below the falls, 26 miles downstream, on July 9.

News of the tragedy stunned the baseball world, and the ballplayer's death was greatly mourned in his hometown of Cleveland. Delahanty had always drawn enthusiastic cheers at League Park whenever the Phillies or the Senators played there, and had often been the subject of trade rumors that would have transferred him to the local ballclub. Napoleon Lajoie, his friend and former road roommate with the Phillies, was unable to attend the funeral, as the Naps were on an extended eastern road trip at the time and would not return to Cleveland for another two weeks. John McGraw, however, served as one of Delahanty's pallbearers.

Delahanty's death was a cautionary tale for major league players, as was the suicide earlier that same year of Detroit pitcher Win Mercer, who had gambled away money from a barnstorming tour and had no way of recovering the losses. Delahanty and Mercer, like too many ballplayers, had destroyed their lives after falling into the grip of alcohol abuse, gambling problems, and financial pressures. Napoleon Lajoie might have joined them had he continued on the destructive path he started upon early in his career, but fortunately he proved to be more mature than the highly talented but emotional Delahanty. Lajoie had turned his behavior around, and though he still let loose with tirades against umpires, his off-the-field exploits were no longer a source of concern for his employers. In 1906, after he had become manager of the Naps, a friend of his was moved to tell a reporter, "Not a drop of malt or spiritous liquor has passed the lips of Lajoie since he assumed the management of the Clevelands. Furthermore, I understand that Larry does not smoke much, goes to bed early, attends to business strictly and otherwise sets a good example for the players of the Blues."[11]

Lajoie's friend was probably overstating the case, but the ballplayer had apparently curbed what *The Sporting News* called his "wolfish thirst for liquor" during his trouble-marred 1897 season. Delahanty's drinking was so out of control that shortly before his death, his family had forced him to take a sobriety pledge in front of a Catholic priest. Lajoie, like Delahanty a Catholic, never needed such an intervention. "I never took any pledge," he said many years later. "Why should I? I always liked a glass of beer and never made any secret about it."[12] He had become a respected team leader and may have already been thinking about a future career as manager of the team that was named for him. Few would have looked upon Lajoie as managerial material during the dark days of 1897, but his transformation was remarkable. He was the most popular player in the American League, as well as its best all-around player, and he wore that distinction well.

The only criticism of Lajoie in the national press centered upon his contentious relationships with the umpires. Though league president Ban Johnson strongly discouraged players from abusing his arbiters, Lajoie, as captain of the Naps, fought hard whenever he believed that a bad decision might cost his team a game. The Cleveland star, usually a friendly sort off the field, could display an explosive temper on it, as shown on the Fourth of July. On a muggy, hot day in Washington, he blew up at umpire "Parisian Bob" Caruthers, the one-time pitching star of the St. Louis Browns, who called the Senators' Kip Selbach safe at second on a steal attempt. He raged so violently at Caruthers that the umpire called the local police to hustle the Cleveland captain off the field. Though Ban Johnson soon dismissed Caruthers from his umpiring staff, he also handed Lajoie another indefinite suspension, his second of the 1903 season, which ended after five days.

Another eruption of the Lajoie temper occurred on August 8 in Cleveland. The contest that day against the Tigers went into extra innings, and the visitors scored in the top of the 11th to take a 6–5 lead. In the bottom of the 11th, Detroit catcher Fritz Buelow threw an old, grass-stained ball into play. The ball was so dark that Lajoie and the other Naps complained that they could not see it in the late afternoon light, but umpire Tommy Connolly refused to remove the sphere from play. Lajoie, who was fighting a batting slump at the time (he had made only four hits in his previous 23 times at bat), refused to accept Connolly's decision. He grabbed the ball and heaved it over the grandstand, after which Connolly declared the game a forfeit to the Tigers by a score of 9 to 0. This decision prompted the Cleveland fans to surge onto the field and threaten the umpire, but cooler heads prevailed, and Connolly exited the diamond safely. For once, Ban Johnson decided not to issue another suspension, and Lajoie missed no games as a result.

Perhaps Lajoie's outburst stirred the Naps out of their funk, for the club won 13 of its next 14 games, all at home, and jumped back into the race for second place. The Boston Americans ran away with the pennant that year, and the Naps, Athletics, and Highlanders, the other first-division clubs, harbored no illusions about catching them. Still, second place was a desirable prize, and on August 21 the Naps defeated the Washington Senators to pass the Athletics and take over the runner-up slot.

The most dramatic incident of the 1903 season occurred off the field. In the early morning hours of August 29, the St. Louis and Cleveland teams were asleep on a westbound train, traveling on the Wabash Railroad to Missouri for a weekend series. The engineer reportedly misread a signal, causing the special train's three cars to derail at a crossing. The cars lurched off the tracks and landed on their sides in a ditch, hurling the ballplayers and team officials out of their berths. Miraculously, no one on the train was seriously injured in the wreck, though Addie Joss was knocked briefly unconscious when infielder Charlie Hickman landed on top of him. The baggage car was wrecked so completely that all the luggage aboard was destroyed, but the only player hurt, aside from those with cuts and bruises, was Lajoie, who suffered a sprained right knee and a cut on his face.

The railroad put the players on another train for St. Louis, and the two teams played that afternoon, though the scheduled doubleheader was changed to a single game due to their late arrival in the Missouri city. Lajoie, despite his knee injury, singled in four times at bat against Jack Powell, who shut out the Naps that day. On Sunday, he belted five hits, including a home run, in seven trips to the plate as the Naps swept a doubleheader behind Addie Joss and Red Donahue.

Addie Joss won his 19th game of the season that day against the Browns, but his 7–4 victory proved to be his final appearance of the 1903 campaign. The Naps boarded a train to Detroit for a series against the Tigers, and on the trip Joss fell ill with a deep cough and a fever that surpassed 100 degrees. The club sent him to a hospital in Cleveland, where doctors ruled out typhoid (mostly because no other players were sick) but could not find a reason for the pitcher's illness. Joss remained in bed for two weeks, and was so weak that he had to walk with a cane for some time afterward. He was finished for the season, as was Earl Moore, who had been hit in the arm with a batting practice liner off the bat of Charlie Hickman on July 24. Moore, still fighting the effects of the injury, lost to the Browns on August 31 and pitched no more that year. Bill Bernhard had been lost to the team a month earlier with a broken finger, and the absence of three leading starters left the Naps at a distinct disadvantage in the pennant chase.

In the end, the Naps held onto second place until the last weekend of the season, when two losses in their last three contests allowed the Philadelphia Athletics to pass them in the standings by half a game. The Naps, at 77–63, won two more games than Mack's club (75–60), but ties and rainouts that were not made up gave Cleveland five more decisions than the Athletics and left them slightly behind in winning percentage. On the whole, it was a good year for the Naps, who drew more than 311,000 fans to set a new attendance record. For Larry Lajoie, his slow start and the introduction of the foul strike rule (in which foul balls were counted as strikes in the American League for the first time) resulted in a batting average of .344, which was his lowest in several years but still good enough to cop his second batting title by a margin of nine points over Detroit's Sam Crawford.

He also enjoyed a celebration in his honor in Fall River, where he had made a name for himself in his first professional season eight years before. On September 15, the Naps traveled to the Massachusetts city for an exhibition game against the local minor league club, an event billed as "Lajoie Day." More than 3,000 fans filled the stands to see their most famous former player, and when he came to bat in the first inning, a delegation led by the city's mayor stopped the game for a presentation. Mayor Grime reeled off an appropriately flowery greeting, telling the guest of honor, "Your success has demonstrated to our youth that earnest endeavor and diligence will receive its proper reward.... We consider it a special honor that the Fall River club has furnished to the baseball firmament the greatest and brightest star that thus far has ever appeared in its galaxy."[13] After a few more well-chosen platitudes, the mayor presented Lajoie with a scarf pin valued at $200, and the game resumed. The fans went home happy, not only because they were able to cheer for Lajoie again, but also because the locals defeated the Naps by a score of 6 to 2.

In October, while the Boston Americans and the Pittsburgh Pirates faced off in the first modern World Series, the Naps and the Cincinnati Reds met in the "All-Ohio Championship," a nine-game series that featured games not only in Cleveland and Cincinnati, but in Newark and Columbus as well. Unfortunately, bad weather kept many fans away, and the players, who expected to clear about $500 apiece, earned only $216.32 for their efforts. Nonetheless, it was a hard-fought series, with the Naps winning six of the nine contests and notching a victory for the American League over the National.

The series ended with a riot in Cincinnati. Though the Naps had already clinched the All-Ohio Championship with a doubleheader win in Cleveland on October 10, the two teams met in Cincinnati the next day for the final two contests. The Reds won the first game, and led the second contest by a 1–0 score in the seventh as darkness approached. The unruly Cincinnati fans demanded that umpire Tim Hurst call the game at that point, but Hurst ordered the teams to play on and called in the local police to prevent the surging crowd from storming the field. After Cleveland scored two runs in the eighth and one in the ninth to win the game, the angry Reds supporters formed a mob and attacked the Cleveland players as they raced for the team bus. Rocks and bottles flew through the air as Lajoie and his teammates took cover.

After the visitors reached safety, Lajoie made light of the situation, telling local reporters,

> Cincinnati is the best town I ever played in. Why, they think so much of the visiting teams down there that the fans make them presents after the games. They were simply stuck on us Sunday, and when we got in our bus to leave the park we were handed a few bricks and stones. Most of us dropped to the bottom of the bus and escaped as the driver whipped up his horses. But all did not come through without some marks. I was hit twice on the head with rocks, while Elmer Flick was struck in the face with a brick. His nose and upper lip were cut, and he had two teeth loosened. That our list of injuries was not greater was due to the fact that the Cincinnati toughs ran out of ammunition. Yes, Cincinnati's a nice town and what I like best about the base ball fans is that they are such cheerful losers.[14]

Lajoie, who had nine hits in the nine games, drew praise for an act of kindness he performed for a blind man in Columbus. As the players milled about outside their hotel in that city after the third game of the series, the Cleveland captain spotted a beggar in dark glasses nearby. He struck up a conversation with the blind man, who assured the ballplayer that he could identify any coin by touch alone. Lajoie gave the man a penny, and when the man correctly recognized it as such, the ballplayer handed over larger coins. He also convinced his teammates to do the same, and a parade of Cleveland ballplayers showered the beggar with coins. As *Sporting Life* described the scene, "Down at Columbus, Larry gave a blind man a handful of silver. The double affliction of being blind and having to live in Columbus would appeal to even harder hearts than Larry's."[15]

Lajoie had come a long way since his days in Philadelphia, where he had often been described as moody, and because he was popular with the fans and got along well with the press, the nation's sportswriters were willing to give him positive publicity whenever possible. In mid–1903, shortly after his blowup with umpire Bob Caruthers had resulted in a five-day suspension, the *Washington Post* revealed his relationship with a Cleveland orphan named Peetie Power. Lajoie had met the boy in early 1903 and made him an unofficial member of the Naps, decking him out in both home and away uniforms and bringing him along on road trips during the summer months, when school was not in session. The boy carried a suitcase with "Peetie Power, Mascot" printed in white letters on the side, a gift from his benefactor, who also paid for the boy's schooling and clothes. The *Post* concluded that despite his rough treatment of Caruthers and other umpires, "Lajoie is not such a bad fellow."[16]

This opinion was seconded by a reporter for the *Cincinnati Times-Star*.

It is a pleasure to meet a base ball player who, despite the fact that he has earned fame and has had fame thrust upon him, keeps his equilibrium and does not have to put his hat on with the aid of a solution of slippery elm or Vaseline. Usually when a player reaches the pre-eminent class in base ball he looks down upon the other members of the profession much as an elephant would look at an ant. Such is not the case with Lajoie of the Clevelands. Although reckoned as one of the two greatest players in the business — Hans Wagner, of the Pittsburgs, being the other — Lajoie never allows one to feel that his prowess as a ball player entitles him to homage or gives him licenses that the other members of the team do not enjoy. He is just a big-hearted, good-natured, hail-fellow-well-met man off the field, and one can feel as much at ease with him as with the most insignificant man in base ball to-day.[17]

12

Batting and Fielding

*If he ever had a weakness, no one was able to find it. About the best thing for
a pitcher to do when Larry came to bat with the score tied and men on second
and third was to offer up a prayer, throw in the general direction of the plate,
and trust to luck.* — Ed Walsh, 1916[1]

Napoleon Lajoie was the sixth player, and the first second baseman, elected to the
Baseball Hall of Fame in Cooperstown, New York. Since 1939, when the first group of 25
inductees was honored at the opening of the baseball museum nearly 300 other players,
umpires, and executives have earned plaques on the wall in the museum's gallery. Those
bronze tablets display a likeness of the individual and a brief summation of the person's
career.

The words "great" and "greatest" occur on many of the plaques, while others contain
adjectives such as "durable" and "colorful" and "fiery." However, during the first 50 years
of the Hall of Fame's existence, only one man was described on his plaque as "graceful."
That man was Napoleon Lajoie.[2]

Lajoie, by all accounts, was a "natural" ballplayer, not one who spent years developing
his skills. He was blessed with superior eyesight, strength, and reflexes, and because he was
both remarkably well coordinated and bigger and stronger than most other players of his
era, Lajoie discovered early in his career that he could succeed, and excel, on sheer physical
talent alone.

Lajoie was no keen student of the art of batting. Ty Cobb, the most notable example
of what the sportswriters called the "scientific" ballplayer, studied opposing pitchers and
defenses, adjusted his swing to place the ball on the ground or in the air to different parts
of the field, and did his best to out-think and out-strategize his opponents. A later multiple
batting champion, Ted Williams, wrote a book called *The Science of Hitting* in which he
discussed the proper angle of the swing (he recommended a slight uppercut, not the chop-
ping motion of Cobb and others), hip rotation, footwork, and other elements of the successful batting style. By contrast, the method employed by Lajoie, Shoeless Joe Jackson,
and other so-called "natural" hitters could be succinctly described as "see ball, hit ball."
Lajoie had a few theories, but for the most part, he simply stepped up to the plate and
belted the first good pitch he saw.

Before setting himself in the batter's box, Lajoie drew a line in the dirt beside the plate
with his bat. Only then would he look up to face the pitcher. Like Ty Cobb, he held his

hands apart on the bat, a style rarely seen today but much more common a century ago. He could adjust his hand position as the ball made its flight to the plate, allowing him to swing mightily with his hands together or slap at the pitch with hands apart. During his early days with Cleveland, Lajoie created a strange-looking bat with two knobs on it; the higher knob, called the shoulder, was designed to keep the hands apart at a consistent distance. It also allowed the player to choke up on the bat with both hands above the shoulder and still have a knob under his fists to support his swing. Wright and Ditson, a Boston sporting goods company, sold the "Lajoie bat" to the public in 1903, in four different sizes, for a dollar and a quarter apiece, but the idea did not catch on, and it soon disappeared from the market.

Like a later slugging second baseman, Rogers Hornsby, Lajoie stood deep in the box. He strode toward the plate and swung his long bat through the ball in one graceful motion. He once explained:

> I am ready to step in any direction with my right foot for pivot. I bat mostly with a wrist movement, as you can get a quicker move on and allow the ball to come closer before timing it.... A ball wide of the plate can be chopped off to right field, while one a bit close can be turned to account by a proper swing. This can be accomplished by taking the bat up short, as it requires less swing and can be worked with a snap, which will have just as good effect when it meets the ball and the batter is less likely to send up weak flies.[3]

Lajoie, like Hornsby, was protective of his eyesight. Hornsby refused to read anything after sundown and declined all invitations to go to movies, fearing that artificial light would weaken his vision, and apparently Lajoie shared that view, at least in part. "The secret of batting is in the eye," he said. "I never read at night, for I believe it is bad for the eyes. When your eyes go back, even a little, you are done."[4]

In another respect, Lajoie and Hornsby were as unalike as could be. Hornsby's batting motto, which he repeated to teammates and, later, to pupils such as a young Ted Williams, was "Get a good pitch to hit." Hornsby reasoned that if the batter refused to swing at balls outside the strike zone, he could force the pitcher to put the ball over the plate for the batter to hit, or send him to first base with a walk. Lajoie, on the other hand, hated to walk and did not believe in waiting for the pitcher to deliver an acceptable ball to swing at. "I go to the plate with the idea of hitting the first good ball sent up," he once said, "as I believe in working on the aggressive. In this way I am seldom caught for a strike unless where I miss the ball."[5] Because he would swing at almost any kind of pitch, over the plate or not, high or low, the concept of "plate discipline" held little meaning for Napoleon Lajoie.

According to one oft-quoted story, Phillies manager Billy Nash was scouting the New England League in 1896 and asked Lajoie, who was batting over .400 for Fall River, what pitches gave him trouble. There weren't any, replied the rookie, "only the ones I can't reach."[6] This tale first appeared in *Sporting Life* in August of 1896, before Lajoie had played in a major league game, and concisely illustrates Lajoie's approach to the art of hitting. Arthur Irwin, a former Phillies manager, told a reporter in 1899 that Lajoie actually preferred to swing at bad balls. "[Lajoie] claims that he can get a stronger and cleaner swing on a wild pitch," said Irwin, "and that a wild one that connects with the end of his bat is bound to travel."[7]

Lajoie's distaste for the walk was noted during the first month of his major league career. In September of 1896, after the newest Phillie had been in the lineup for less than four weeks, Francis Richter of *Sporting Life* told his readers, "Lajoie does not wait for bases on balls. He can hit anything and 'goes right at 'em.' ... He can't bunt, though."[8] In 21

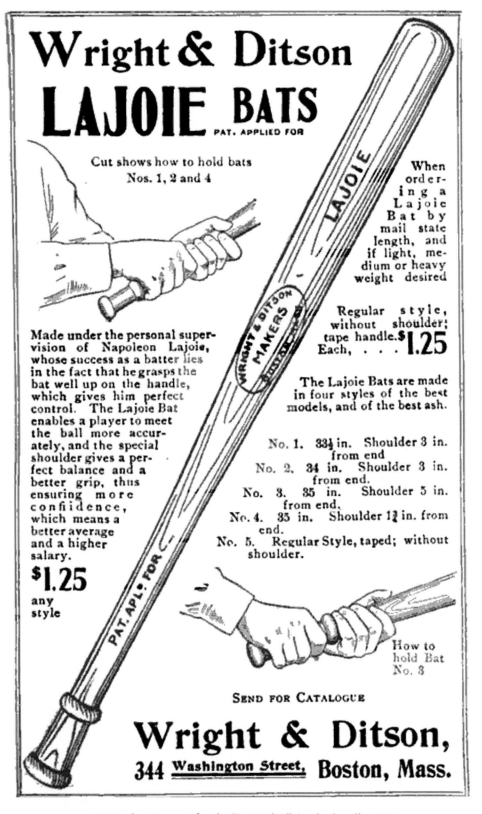

A 1903 advertisement for the "Lajoie bat" (author's collection).

major league seasons, encompassing more than 10,400 plate appearances, Napoleon Lajoie walked only 516 times, according to statistics compiled by the Baseball Reference web site. His walk total is the lowest of any of the 28 major leaguers with 3,000 or more career hits (as of the end of the 2012 season).[9] Hurlers found it incredibly difficult to pitch around Lajoie, and perhaps some of them became frustrated enough to simply issue what was then called a "Red Cross walk"—that is, to send Lajoie to first by hitting him with a pitch. He received such painful free passes 134 times, a large total for a batter who was not known for crowding the plate.

On the other hand, a Larry Lajoie strikeout was an even rarer occurrence than a walk. He never went down on strikes more than 27 times in any season, and in only five campaigns did his total exceed 20. In 1901, when he batted .426, hit 14 homers, and drove in 145 runs, Lajoie struck out only nine times. Perhaps he swung at outside pitches to avoid taking a called third strike due to a plate umpire's bad decision, but no one knows if he consciously adopted this strategy to take the outcome of his time at bat out of the umpire's hands. In any case, he almost always made contact at the plate. His career total of 346 strikeouts is remarkable, especially when one considers that the single-season record for whiffs is now over 200. His greatest contemporary rivals for batting honors, Honus Wagner (737 career strikeouts) and Ty Cobb (680) were retired on strikes far more often than he was.

Lajoie did not try to out-think the pitcher, and did not limit himself to certain pitches. "I never care to anticipate the kind of a ball the pitcher is about to deliver," he explained, "as I find a low ball no more difficult than a high one."[10] On one occasion, he expressed himself even more directly. "The pitcher's thoughts are his own," he once remarked to F. C. Lane of *Baseball Magazine*. "I am no mind reader. I don't know what he is thinking about and I don't care. It doesn't matter to me whether he throws a curve or a fast one so long as he gets the ball over the plate where I can reach it."[11] The ball did not even have to be over the plate, because Lajoie perfected a one-handed swing to swat at balls far outside. Like Joe Jackson, Honus Wagner, and some other outstanding hitters of the era, he had very long arms, and he could hold the bat with his right hand only and belt deliveries well out of the strike zone.

An oft-quoted tale describes an incident that may or may not have actually happened. In a game between the Cleveland club and the New York Highlanders in 1910, Lajoie faced Russ Ford, a rookie right-hander who won 26 games that season with a new pitch, the emery ball, which he created by scuffing the surface of the baseball with a piece of sandpaper hidden in his glove. As the story goes, Ford decided to walk the Cleveland star on purpose every time he came to bat that day, but in the first inning Lajoie, sensing the pitcher's intentions, reached across the plate and slapped an outside pitch to right for a hit. In Lajoie's next plate appearance, Ford threw the ball even farther off the plate, but Lajoie belted that one to the outfield as well. The same thing happened a third time, after which Ford decided to adopt a new strategy. On Lajoie's fourth at-bat of the day, Ford threw four pitches behind the Cleveland slugger's back and sent him to first.

Lajoie, at six feet one inch in height and 195 pounds, was a big player for the era, and the muscles he developed driving horse teams in Woonsocket gave him a strong set of arms and shoulders. When he connected with a ball, he produced ferocious line shots that sometimes frightened his opponents. Pitching legend Cy Young once stated, "Lajoie was one of the most rugged hitters I ever faced. He'd take your leg off with a line drive, turn the third baseman around like a swinging door and powder the hand of the left fielder."[12] On the final day of the 1910 season, when the St. Louis Browns apparently allowed Lajoie to bunt his way to the batting title over Detroit's Ty Cobb, rookie third baseman Red Corriden backed up almost onto the outfield grass against the Cleveland slugger. Corriden, called upon to explain his defensive positioning, replied, "I want to remain in baseball for some years. I was not going to get killed playing in on Lajoie. I might have gotten some of the bunts, and at the same time broken a nose or lost a couple of teeth. Lajoie is known as a hard hitter, and I played far back."[13]

On two occasions during the 1899 season, Lajoie hit a ball so hard that the cover tore open and, according to witnesses, the rubber core in the middle of the sphere broke in two. In a game played the following year, Chicago catcher Tim Donohue, with Lajoie due to bat with men on base, reportedly shouted to his infielders, "Get back, you chumps, get back." Pointing to Lajoie, Donohue cried, "Do you want this man arrested for manslaughter?"[14] Facing right-hander Buck O'Brien of the Boston Red Sox in 1912, Lajoie walloped a liner that caromed off the hip of shortstop Heinie Wagner, O'Brien's roommate. Wagner limped to the mound and snarled at his pitcher, "Buck, if you throw that big Frenchman any more pitches like that, you won't get into the room tonight."[15] Lajoie was also credited with the Paul Bunyanesque feat of killing not one, but two, birds with a single line drive.

Lajoie was not as attached to his bats as some players. Joe Jackson, for example, gave names to all his bats and regaled the Cleveland writers with stories about "Black Betsy," "Blond Betsy" and "Big Jim." Lajoie did not relate to his lumber in such a colorful way, and he was usually happy to share his bats with his teammates. Still, he had his favorites, and was distressed when Cleveland pitchers borrowed his bats during pre-game practice. Said Larry,

> They don't know how to bat anyhow, and the first thing you know they hit the ball with the end of the bat. It breaks, they throw it to the ground and think no more of it. But I do, for invariably the broken bat is one that I've broken in and am just beginning to get the bingles with. Of course, I can get a new one for 75 cents, but that isn't the idea. It's being accustomed to a bat, and getting used to its heft and tricks so that I can grab the hits. Why, I've had fellows break 75-cent bats on me when I wouldn't have sold one of 'em for $100.[16]

However, he could hit with any bat, and sometimes, after a particularly good day at the plate, gave the bat he used that afternoon to a friend as a souvenir.

He was as natural in the field as he was at the plate. Talented enough to play any position on the diamond, he began his professional career in 1896 as a center fielder and part-time catcher and infielder. He played first base during his first season and a half with the Philadelphia Phillies before moving to second base, where he gained his greatest fame. During his career, he saw action at shortstop and third base, acquitting himself well, and never pitched only because he was not interested in becoming a hurler.

With his superior reflexes and instincts, Lajoie was routinely described as "graceful" no matter where he played on the field, and performed with such apparent ease that some observers regarded him as "nonchalant" or "diffident," and concluded that he was not trying very hard. Lajoie rejected that notion. "It pays to keep on your feet," he once said, "although at times the spectators have an idea that the man rolling about in the dust is doing the most effective work."[17] When asked by his friend Grantland Rice if he planned his movements in advance, Lajoie answered,

> No, I merely make the play as it comes. When a ball is batted to a man there is but one right place to make the play, and he should be able to know that place without wasting time thinking about it. By the time the bill has reached me, the flash of an eye shows what the base runners are doing, and the rest is easy. Any man who has to think out a play has his mind

Fielding practice, about 1910 (National Baseball Hall of Fame Library, Cooperstown, New York).

taken off the ball, and this leads to a good many fumbles and misplays. When a man is eating he doesn't have to stop and think, does he, just how high he shall lift his fork at every bite or how wide open he must hold his mouth?[18]

Of necessity, Lajoie had to employ more strategy in the field than at the bat. In 1905, invited to write a piece on "How to Play Second Base" for a baseball guide put out by player-turned-sportswriter Tim Murnane, he described his style of infield play:

I play a deep field and change my distance from the base according to the style of pitching I am backing up. If a weak fielding pitcher, who will allow medium hit balls to go through the box, I play closer to second. Then again you must size up the man at the bat and know the style of ball the pitcher is to feed him. It is always best to go in and meet the ball and smother it if you find it coming with a shoot. I never make up my mind how to take the ball until it is very close, for it may take a jump if you set yourself for the regulation bound.

I always have a perfect understanding with the shortstop and catcher, as to who will cover the base, and play a bit closer when out for a double play. It is not a bad idea to take your cue from the third baseman after he sends you a ball for a force-out. If there is no chance for a double you should hold the ball. A tip to let the ball go will help, as you feel there is a good chance to get the man. In turning to throw, step in front of the base and throw regardless of the man coming down, as he will generally look out for himself, and is not anxious to get hit with the ball.[19]

Some of Lajoie's ideas on second base play may not find favor in the present day. For example, he saw little difference in fielding a ball with one hand or two, because he was so sure-handed. "[Lajoie] is the only ball player I ever saw that can handle a ball as well with one hand as with two," said John McGraw in 1903. "If he can get to a ball with either hand it is usually all up with the batter."[20] Like many players of the time, he cut a hole in the palm of his glove so he could feel the ball against his bare hand, a practice that disappeared decades ago. He also had a novel theory on fielding short popups. When a fly ball is hit just behind the infield, most experts believe that the outfielder coming in has a better chance to catch the ball than the infielder, who is running away from the infield, usually with his back to the plate. Lajoie disagreed. "A second baseman should go for short flies," he wrote, "and depend on the outfielders for the coaching, as they are in a better position to judge the ball."[21]

This attitude may have contributed to his collisions with right fielder Elmer Flick early in his career, but his statement illustrates one important facet of Lajoie's fielding style. He was so supremely confident in his ability that he wanted to handle every ball that he could reach. He topped his league in putouts five times and in double plays six times (while never leading the league in errors), partly because of his skill and partly because he dominated his team's infield play, especially in Cleveland. He wanted to handle everything, and his infield mates, for the most part, deferred to him.

Bill James, in his *New Historical Baseball Abstract*, examined the fielding statistics compiled by Lajoie and his fellow infielders during Larry's career in Cleveland. While playing for the Naps, Lajoie led the American League in putouts in 1903, 1906, and 1908 (he had also topped his circuit with the Phillies in 1898 and with the Athletics in 1901). He missed out in 1902 because he sat out for more than a month while waiting for his contract situation to be cleared up. He failed to lead in 1904 because he spent 44 games at shortstop that season, and he was out of the lineup with injuries for long stretches of 1905, 1907, and 1909. Still, Cleveland second basemen as a group, Lajoie and others, also led the league in putouts in 1902, 1904, and 1910. In fact, as James points out, the team's second sackers made more than the league average in putouts in every season of Lajoie's career in Cleveland except 1905 and 1907, when he was injured. James also notes that Cleveland shortstops compiled a below average number of putouts in every one of Lajoie's 13 years with the Naps.

To James, the explanation for these figures is simple. "*Lajoie took everything at second base*," he wrote, italics his. " Nap Lajoie was not only the team's superstar, after 1905 he was also the manager. He was more than that — hell, the team was actually called the 'Naps' in his honor, as if he *was* the team. If Lajoie was in the habit of covering second base [on] every play, the shortstop certainly wasn't going to tell him not to."[22]

Perhaps Lajoie learned to dominate the middle of the infield due to the caliber of his keystone partners. In 1898, his first season as a second baseman, the Phillies shortstop was Monte Cross, who led the league in errors with 93. He was out of the lineup for much of 1899 and 1900, and in 1901, he joined the Athletics and played next to the mediocre Joe Dolan and the 38-year-old Fred (Bones) Ely. When he arrived in Cleveland in 1902, he paired up with the error-prone John Gochnaur, sometimes called the worst regular shortstop of all time. Terry Turner, a much better fielder than Gochnaur, took over in 1904, but by then a pattern had been set. Lajoie took every throw, caught every pop-up, and tagged out every runner that he could reasonably reach. His eagerness to make every play, and his remarkable skill in doing so, made Lajoie's fielding statistics look so good that John Thorn and Pete Palmer's statistical encyclopedia, *Total Baseball*, ranked him, in its various editions, as either the number one or number two defensive player of all time, at any position.

Lajoie could have played anywhere, but the second sack was his preferred position.

"Second base gives a player an opportunity to show up better than any other position," said Lajoie in 1905, "as it is truly styled 'the key to the infield,' and I believe a player will last longer in the game in this position than any other, if he is a natural and not a made ball player."[23] Lajoie showed up well indeed, as he compiled a .338 career batting average, made more than 3,200 hits, and led his league in fielding categories on a regular basis. In 2001, Bill James ranked Lajoie as the sixth-best second baseman in baseball annals, a rating that appears too low to many observers. Lajoie was routinely described as the greatest second baseman in the game's history at the time he retired and for many years afterward, and it was not difficult to find those who considered him the best player of all time before Ty Cobb, 12 years his junior, came along. He deserves to stand with Joe Morgan, Eddie Collins, and Rogers Hornsby at the top of the second base rankings.

13

Fourth Place

There is no greater road attraction today than the Cleveland team. This is due partly to Lajoie's personality, but more largely to its great batting ability, which always holds out to patrons the promise of action. As a matter of fact there was never yet a noted batting team that was not a card on the road. Regardless of what foul-strike rule proponents may say, the public likes batting above any other feature of baseball.—Sporting Life, June 1904[1]

The Naps finally gave up on shortstop John Gochnaur, who batted .185 and set a league record with 98 errors in 1903. In his place, the team signed Terry Turner, a 22-year-old who had spent the previous two seasons with Columbus of the American Association. Turner, who had received a two-game tryout with the Pittsburgh Pirates in 1901, was a feisty redhead who carried the nickname "Cotton Top" and slid headfirst into bases, a rarity at the time. He was, according to Cleveland sportswriter Gordon Cobbledick, "a little rabbit of a man with the guts of a commando."[2] He weighed only 150 pounds but was ready to give his new team a dose of competitive fire that Bill Armour believed was lacking. Turner proved to be a talented, but fragile, performer, but despite his many injuries and illnesses, he played for the Cleveland club until 1918 and set the team record for career games played, which he holds to this day.

With Turner shoring up the infield defense, the Naps appeared to have solved their most glaring weakness. The club featured strong pitching, with Addie Joss, Bill Bernhard, Earl Moore, and Red Donahue in the starting slots. Cleveland still lacked a left-hander, but Armour held high hopes for Otto Hess, who had pitched briefly for the Naps two years before and spent 1903 with Kansas City of the Western League. The outfield of Elmer Flick, Harry Bay, and veteran switch-hitter Billy Lush was the fastest in the league, and although catchers Harry Bemis and Fred Abbott were weak at bat, they were solid defensively. The Naps, with Lajoie in the cleanup spot, were the best hitting team in baseball, and the most imposing, with several men (Joss, Bernhard, Lajoie, Moore, and others) over six feet tall, a fact which led Ban Johnson to tell the newspapers that the Cleveland team should be called the Giants. The team leaders, manager Armour and captain Lajoie, set out to turn this physically impressive club into a pennant contender.

Major league teams had traditionally conducted their spring training in Georgia, Florida, Alabama, and at Hot Springs in Arkansas, but in 1904 four clubs set up camp in Texas for the first time. The St. Louis teams, the Cardinals and Browns, went to Dallas and

Corsicana respectively, the Chicago White Sox trained in Marlin Springs, and the Naps traveled to San Antonio, the westernmost city in the state. Bill Armour expected to find hot and dry weather in west Texas, but unseasonably cold and rainy conditions kept the

Naps indoors for much of the spring and prevented the team from working out as much as Armour desired. Several local exhibition contests, which the Naps relied upon to pay for their training costs, were cancelled, as were games in Louisville and Indianapolis just before the start of the American League season. As a result, several pitchers, including Moore and Joss, complained of sore arms due to a lack of work, and other Naps suffered from boils. The club found the sanitation in San Antonio not up to standard, and the Naps never trained in San Antonio thereafter.

The Naps opened their 1904 season on April 14 in Chicago, where the temperature hovered near the freezing mark and the ground was still stiff from the winter cold. Lajoie went hitless, but the Clevelanders defeated the White Sox by a 6 to 1 count. Lajoie's bat came alive as the Naps split two more contests in Chicago, then traveled to St. Louis, where the club that the papers called "Lajoie's Fence Breakers" supported Bill Bernhard with 16 hits, five of them by Lajoie, in a 10–4 win. Though the game attracted only 1,000 people on a rainy day, the local papers made much of the batting exhibition put on by the vis-

Bill Armour, Cleveland manager from 1902 to 1904 (author's collection).

itors from Cleveland. "Lajoie, as befits his dignity as captain of the Blues, led his team with the willow," wrote a reporter for the *St. Louis Republic*. "Five hits were all he made, but he can be excused for not doing better, as he faced the pitcher only five times, and when one considers that two of his hits were for doubles, his performance is altogether satisfactory to all concerned except the pitchers."[3]

Opening day at League Park in Cleveland on April 22 drew nearly 15,000 people, who overflowed the 9,000-seat ballpark and required team management to put rope barriers in the outfield for the fans to stand behind. The umpires ruled that any ball hit into the standing-room area behind the ropes would be called a triple, and as a result, the game featured four three-baggers by the Naps and three by the White Sox. Lajoie once again went hitless, but Billy Lush belted three hits, rookie Terry Turner drove in four runs, and the Naps took a 10–2 win. The next day, more than 10,000 fans saw Bill Bradley and Larry Lajoie wallop back-to-back homers in the first inning off Chicago pitcher Doc White, though the White Sox took advantage of six Cleveland errors and won the game with three runs in the eighth.

During the first few weeks of the season, the Naps displayed their usual inconsistency, alternating brief winning streaks with equally short losing skids, and floating near the .500 mark before six wins in a row pushed them into second place at 19–12, three games behind the defending champions from Boston, by May 28. Lajoie, as expected, stood atop the league batting race, but other Naps battled maladies and injuries which Armour blamed on the lack of proper conditioning during spring camp. The most serious health problem belonged to Terry Turner, who fell ill in Boston and was diagnosed with a life-threatening case of typhoid. Turner was laid up in bed for weeks, as was right-hander Addie Joss, who contracted a fever and was unable to shake it. Joss sat out for more than a month and pitched only sporadically for a while after he returned to the team in mid–June.

American League president Ban Johnson did not have to wait long for the first Lajoie eruption of 1904. On Sunday, May 29, the Naps faced the White Sox in Chicago and led 2–0 in the eighth inning with left-hander Otto Hess on the mound. Hess, after dominating for the first seven innings, issued three walks, a double, and a single to put the White Sox in the lead by a 3–2 score. A fourth run came in when a Chicago batter missed a bunt attempt and the ball bounced off the glove of catcher Fred Abbott. Because both Abbott and Lajoie, playing shortstop that day, insisted that the pitch was a foul ball, an argument ensued with umpire Frank Dwyer, a former pitcher whom Lajoie and other players called "Blinky." As Lajoie remembered it years later, he ran to the plate and demanded, "What's the idea, Blinky?"

"He didn't foul the ball, Larry," replied the umpire.

Dwyer stood his ground as the Cleveland captain raged about the call. "I figured I had lost the argument," recalled an older Lajoie, "and I was so mad I wanted to hit him, but I wouldn't do that. Instead, I did something that I guess was worse."[4] Dwyer thumbed him out of the contest, and he took the wad of tobacco out of his mouth and threw it in the arbiter's face. Lajoie soon left the field, but accosted Dwyer outside the park after the game (which the Naps lost) to resume the argument. Only the intervention of some Chicago players kept the angry Cleveland star from punching the umpire. Unfortunately for Lajoie, the American League office was based in Chicago, and President Johnson attended the game that day and witnessed the scene. Johnson suspended Lajoie indefinitely.

Johnson told the press that he intended to "make an example" of the Cleveland star, but Lajoie, to the astonishment of the rest of the league, did not miss any games. The next three scheduled contests in Chicago between the Naps and White Sox, including a Decoration Day doubleheader, were rained out, after which the Naps headed home to Cleveland to take on the Boston Americans on Wednesday, June 1. The local chapter of the Fraternal Order of Eagles had scheduled a presentation to its favorite player and fellow Eagle, Napoleon Lajoie, for that day, and had reserved more than 600 seats in the grandstand at League Park for the occasion. The national leaders of the Eagles prevailed upon Johnson to rescind the suspension, so Johnson, not wishing to back down on his "example" statement but also not wanting to anger a major ticket-buying organization, steered a middle course. He lifted the suspension, but fined Lajoie $50 for his transgression.

Given Johnson's oft-stated opposition to, and punishment of, rowdy behavior on and off the field, Lajoie's escape from serious sanctions shocked and angered many in the sporting press. Johnson had virtually driven John McGraw out of the American League two years earlier for constantly battling the umpires, but now the league's biggest star and gate attraction was hardly punished at all for something far worse than anything McGraw ever did. *The Sporting News*, in an editorial, blasted the Cleveland star for his actions:

> Lajoie's course at Chicago was indefensible and he should have been suspended for 10 days or more for his outrageous treatment of an American League umpire and under normal conditions his punishment would have been commensurate with the offense.

All that Lajoie has to commend him is his ability to play ball. He is not a man of education or refinement and, so far as his conduct shows, is peevish and puerile on the ball field. His habits are better than when he entered the base ball profession, but he has not mastered his temper and when in anger goes beyond bounds.

Manager Armour does not pretend to exercise authority over him.... Lajoie, when away from Cleveland has been a free lance.

Star players, who indulge in rowdy tactics, need not expect to escape penalties imposed for like offenses on ordinary players.[5]

Many years later, the same newspaper interviewed Lajoie and asked the aged ex-ballplayer about the incident. Of his punishment, minor though it was, Lajoie refused to criticize Johnson. "I don't blame him" for the suspension, Lajoie recalled. He also denied that he held any animosity toward the umpires. "When I got mad at an umpire like that," he said, "it was a temporary thing and lasted only while I was on the field. I have never had any enemies off the field."[6] Still, the incident brought attention to the fact that Lajoie, who had been suspended several times during the previous two years for his actions toward the arbiters, seemed to have a problem with authority. He possessed many positive personal traits, but owned an explosive temper that he needed to bring under control for the sake of his team.

With Joss absent for five weeks and Turner on the sidelines for nearly two months, the Naps struggled to maintain their place in the first division. In Turner's absence, Bill Armour moved Lajoie to short for 44 games and put Charlie Hickman on second base, though out-fielder Elmer Flick and catcher Harry Bemis also saw some action at the second sack. Lajoie fielded well at short, but Hickman, who was a mediocre first sacker, was worse than average at second. The Naps fought hard to remain in the pennant race, but mounting injuries took their toll as the club drifted further behind the league-leading Americans and Highlanders.

Seeking talent to shore up his depleted infield, Armour left the team in late June and went on a scouting trip to the Midwestern states. In Burlington, Iowa, he found a first base-man who would play a major role in Cleveland baseball, and in the life of Napoleon Lajoie, during the next several seasons. George Stovall was a smooth-fielding 26-year-old from Kansas City whose older brother Jesse had pitched for the Naps in 1903. George was a good hitter and a born leader with the scrappiness that Bill Armour liked to see in his players. "There is a homely grace in his six feet-one of solid tendon and muscle," said F. C. Lane in *Baseball Magazine*. "There is an impressive power in his firm, protruding jaw, a seasoned endurance in his entire physical makeup. He has a keen brain, ready wit, a blunt philosophy. But he is no man to be trifled with."[7] He had managed the Burlington club for a few weeks before Armour bought his contract for $700 and brought him back to Cleveland. Stovall, a popular fellow whom his teammates called "Brother George," solidified the first base position and batted .298, though with little power, in 52 games.

As the 1904 season progressed, Bill Armour grew frustrated at the maddeningly inconsistent play of his team. Though many believed that the Naps, led by the game's best player, owned the premier collection of talent in the league, the club alternated winning streaks with losing skids and looked sloppy and disorganized. On July 13, Larry whacked three triples, tying the league record, and added a single in a 16–3 mauling of the Highlanders in New York, but on the next afternoon the Naps committed nine errors in a 21–4 loss to the same team. The injury-riddled Naps appeared listless and disinterested much of the time, and although they drew large crowds on the road, mainly due to Lajoie's star power, attendance at League Park leveled off as the club's pennant chances slipped away.

Armour believed that the Naps lacked a fighting spirit. He had tried to rectify that situation by signing Terry Turner and George Stovall (and acquiring catcher Fritz Buelow from Detroit in mid-season), though nothing short of a major roster overhaul would have turned the Naps into a band of fighters. Worst of all, confided Armour to the local reporters, was the fact that his captain, Larry Lajoie, was too easy-going to be an effective team leader. Lajoie's diffident attitude, said Armour, infected the rest of the Naps, who took their cues from him.

By August the Naps had settled into fifth place, and the players began sniping at Armour. Charlie Hickman, a solid hitter but a poor fielder, resented losing his starting spot to the newly-arrived George Stovall and clashed repeatedly with the manager. The two exchanged heated words in the clubhouse one day, and on August 6, after Hickman dropped two popups and made a wild throw to the plate in a loss to the Highlanders, Armour traded him to Detroit for Charlie Carr, a weaker hitter but a much better glove man. More importantly, the papers reported that Armour and Lajoie, despite their co-ownership of the cigar store in downtown Cleveland, were not on speaking terms. All involved denied the reports, but Hickman and Lajoie were good friends, and it appeared that the club had divided itself into pro–Armour and anti–Armour factions.

The injury wave continued into late August, as Earl Moore tried to pitch with a strained muscle in his side, catchers Harry Bemis and Fritz Buelow were banged up, and outfielders Harry Bay and Billy Lush fought leg problems that robbed them of their speed. Nonetheless, the Naps won five of six late in the month to pull within four and a half games of the lead on August 29, led by Lajoie, whose average hovered near the .400 mark. Their optimism was short-lived, as a 3–6 skid put the Naps eight and a half out by September 6 and, with four teams still ahead of them, out of the race for good. In the end, Boston and New York battled down to the wire for the 1904 pennant, in a race that ended with a doubleheader between the two clubs on the season's final day. The Americans clinched the flag by winning the first game, scoring the go-ahead run in the ninth inning when New York pitcher Jack Chesbro, who won 41 games that year, uncorked a wild pitch that allowed a Boston runner to score from third.

Many observers, in Cleveland and elsewhere, wondered aloud why the Naps, with what many regarded as the most talented roster in the game, had failed to stay in the race. The team led the American League in most of the important hitting categories, including runs, hits, batting average, and slugging percentage, and also featured a strong starting staff and a solid defense. Mostly, many questioned why any ballclub with Napoleon Lajoie, widely hailed as the "king of ballplayers," would need a late-season surge to finish in fourth place, as did the 1904 Naps. The Cleveland ballclub was unlucky in the frequency of its injuries and illnesses, but the pennant-winning Boston Americans dealt with their share of physical problems as well. The Naps did not perform up to their potential in 1904, and some placed the blame for their ultimately failed season at the feet of their captain and biggest star.

One blast of criticism came from a surprising source. In June of 1904, Connie Mack, Larry's former manager, made his feelings about Larry's leadership capabilities known in an unexpectedly blunt way. In an article that appeared in the *Washington Times*, Mack said:

> If I had kept Lajoie and the rest of that bunch the American League took from the Philadelphia National League club, I never would have won the pennant in the American League in 1902. Lajoie has some of the worst ideas on how to play baseball of any practical ballplayer I have ever known.
>
> It was a lucky thing for the club that we lost Lajoie and that bunch, in some ways. They

were thoroughly imbued with the ideas that had prevailed for so long a time on the old National League club that slugging the ball was good ball playing. Of course, there must be plenty of good stick work, but there must be team work, "inside baseball," as well. "Inside" baseball was absolutely unknown to Larry and is nearly so today, though Armour has brought him to the point where he will attempt to bunt the ball in a close game with a man on first and no one out. But Lajoie is not a success as a batter in this department and chafes under the restraint that compels him to do it. He wants to "hit it out," as the bleacherites say.

In saying this of Lajoie I am not belittling his ability as a ball player. He is undoubtedly without an equal in the game today and probably never has had for general all-around play. As a sticker he is the greatest and as a fielder there are none to approach him. But on what is known as "scientific" ball playing, the "inside" of the game, he is deficient and I am thoroughly convinced that the Athletics could never have won the pennant in the American League in 1902 had that aggregation been retained.

At the time, we made a desperate fight to hold them, but the State courts were against us. Since that I have changed my mind about the usefulness they would have been to me.[8]

On September 8, to the surprise of team owners Charles Somers and John Kilfoyl, Bill Armour submitted his resignation, effective at the end of the season. He released a statement explaining his decision. "I came to Cleveland when the team was in last place and built a strong team," said Armour. "We have had bits of bad luck, however, in the way of injured players, and the showing of the club has been a disappointment to me; consequently as I think I have a chance to better myself, I thought I would see if the club would not make a better showing under some other manager."[9] Few blamed Armour for his withdrawal; as Henry Edwards of the *Cleveland Plain Dealer* explained, "No better judge of a ball player's ability than Bill Armour lives, and not a small point necessary to win games escapes him. But the ability of the players to carry out his plans has, oftimes, been lacking."[10] Armour remained on the bench for the rest of the season, though he turned over the direction of the club to captain Lajoie.

With Lajoie in charge and the pennant out of reach, the Naps were able to relax and cause problems for Boston and New York, who fought down to the wire for the flag. The Naps bested the Highlanders in late September, winning two games and tying one of a three-game set, then took three in a row from the Americans. In the first game of the Boston series on September 27, Cleveland right-hander Bob Rhoads carried a no-hitter into the ninth inning, losing it on Chick Stahl's single with two out. One inning before, with Elmer Flick on first base, Boston manager Jimmy Collins called for a pitchout, but Lajoie stepped across the plate and belted the wide delivery into the right field stands for a home run that provided the winning margin.

Later in the month, Lajoie took to the bench to nurse a sore leg. He put Flick at second base and was pleasantly surprised when Flick, who had spent some time at the position in the minors, played errorless ball. Flick, who had boasted about his prowess as a pitcher, begged Lajoie to let him take the mound for the last game of the season on the road against the Tigers, with Lajoie as his catcher, but the captain, after much consideration, turned down the request. Instead, the Naps and Tigers split a doubleheader on a muddy field with only 400 people in the stands. Under Lajoie's leadership, the Naps closed with 21 wins in their final 34 games and edged into fourth place, seven and a half games behind the pennant-winning Boston club.

Though the New York Giants, champions of the National League, refused to play the Boston Americans in what would have been the second modern World Series, the Cleveland Naps represented the American League in a post-season clash. They agreed to meet the

Pittsburgh Pirates, fourth-place finishers in the senior circuit, in a five-game set in early October, just after both teams had concluded their regular campaigns. Barney Dreyfuss, owner of the Pirates, had proposed that each National League club battle its American League counterpart, but only the two St. Louis clubs joined the Naps and Pirates in staging interleague matchups. These games were allowed, but not sanctioned, by the sport's governing body, the National Commission, so Dreyfuss and Cleveland owners Charles Somers and John Kilfoyl set the schedule, agreed on playing rules, and hired a minor leaguer named Bill Klem to umpire the contests.

The Naps-Pirates matchup promised a showdown between the game's two brightest stars. Napoleon Lajoie and Pittsburgh's Honus Wagner had played against each other in the National League from 1897, when Wagner joined the Louisville Colonels, to 1900, Lajoie's final year with the Phillies. Since then, each man had staked his claim as the premier performer of his league, with each winning multiple batting titles and leading his circuit in major offensive categories. Lajoie, baseball's top second baseman, and Wagner, the sport's outstanding shortstop, dominated their respective leagues on offense and defense, and the nation's sportswriters suggested that the post-season clash between the two superstars might settle, once and for all, which man more richly deserved the title "King of Ballplayers."

Most American League fans gave the unofficial designation of "the game's best player" to Lajoie, though the 30-year-old Wagner, who was about six months older than his Cleveland counterpart, drew support for the honor in many quarters. Lajoie, the reigning American League batting champion, edged the Pirates star in career batting average (.363 to .343), slugging percentage (.544 to .493), runs, hits, and runs batted in. Wagner was faster, holding a significant edge in stolen bases, but Lajoie's hitting stats, at this point in their careers, were easily the more impressive of the two. In the field, Lajoie's range, surehandedness, and strong throwing arm made him the best in baseball at this position, as did his graceful movements. "Lajoie glides toward the ball," said the *New York Press*, "[and] gathers it in nonchalantly, as if picking fruit."[11]

However, Wagner's adherents could point to several markers in the Pirate's favor. For one thing, he was more durable than Lajoie, who had missed significant parts of the 1899, 1900, and 1902 seasons with injuries and legal problems. Though Wagner's major league career started the year after Lajoie's, he had played in more games and batted more times by the end of the 1904 season. Wagner, an awkward-looking, bowlegged man, had none of Lajoie's grace in the field, but had no peer at the most demanding position on the infield. Wagner was such a skilled defender that he had played every position on the field except catcher, and played them so well that the Pirates did not move him to shortstop until 1903, his seventh season in the National League. Most importantly, the "Flying Dutchman" had led the Pirates to three National League pennants. Larry Lajoie, despite his individual brilliance, had not yet ended any season in a position higher than third.

Both teams hoped for large crowds, but the weather refused to cooperate, and the Naps-Pirates series became an afterthought to the fans of Cleveland and Pittsburgh. The first game, played at League Park on October 10, drew fewer than 4,000 fans on a cold, wet day and ended in a 2–2 tie after five innings due to rain. Lajoie did not make a safe hit, while Wagner smashed a liner to center field that rolled under the scoreboard and allowed the Pirates star to charge around the bases for a homer. In the second game, both men stroked two hits as the Pirates won a 7–4 decision. The third contest was a 14-inning pitching duel between Addie Joss and Charley Case that ended in a 2–2 tie. Wagner, suffering from rheumatism, decided to play at the last minute and borrowed a uniform and a pair of spikes

Napoleon Lajoie and Pittsburgh's Honus Wagner shake hands before the series between the Naps and the Pirates in 1904 (author's collection).

from pitcher Sam Leever, who was taller and thinner than he was. In this uncomfortable garb, he whacked two singles, as did Lajoie. The series concluded with two Cleveland victories on wet grounds in Pittsburgh, as Bob Rhoads and Otto Hess held Wagner to one single in eight trips to the plate. In the end, neither man played well, with Lajoie belting five hits and Wagner six. Perhaps the star of the series was umpire Bill Klem, whose even-handed work led the National League to hire him for the 1905 season, marking the beginning of a 35-year major league career that culminated in his election to the Hall of Fame.

Despite his disappointing performance against the Pirates, Larry Lajoie compiled one of his greatest seasons in 1904. He won his third batting title with a .376 mark, topping the second-place finisher, New York's Willie Keeler, by 33 points. Lajoie also led the American League in hits (208), doubles (49), runs batted in (102), slugging, and total bases. In a league with only five .300 hitters, Lajoie's offensive dominance rivaled his outstanding performance with the Athletics three years earlier. Lajoie was in a class by himself in the field as well. He failed to lead the league's second basemen in putouts and assists only because he played 44 games at shortstop for the Naps in mid-season.

Despite Lajoie's offensive dominance, the Naps had failed to win the pennant, and some lay the blame on the shoulders of its biggest star. Lajoie was routinely described as "graceful" and "effortless," and even "diffident" in his manner at bat and in the field. This demeanor appeared, to some, as lethargic and uncaring, and because players tend to follow the stars in their midst, Lajoie's attitude, some said, kept the Naps from winning. The Naps were a good team that, given their talent level, should have been a great one, and in mid–September, Elmer Bates of the *Cleveland Press* wrote a piece that described Bill Armour's difficulties in getting the Naps out of their mediocre rut.

> The cause which lies directly back of the resignation of Manager Armour is the refusal of the Cleveland team to play the kind of ball he wants it to play. Captain Lajoie is not what is known in baseball as a "fighter." While he has on occasions lost his temper on the field and gotten himself into trouble by violent outbursts, he is not ordinarily an aggressive player. With the game running smoothly and Cleveland a little in the lead, or a little behind, Larry is content with what might be termed a quiet and dignified style of play, with just enough coaching to keep the base runners posted.
>
> And what is said of Lajoie in this respect applies equally well to the rest of the team, with the exceptions of Buelow [who had come over from Detroit in mid-season], Stovall, and possibly Flick. These three have a habit of keeping up some sort of action all the time — coaching, shouting encouragement to the pitcher, a little kidding of the opposing players — anything to inject a little ginger into the game and keep things moving. It is this kind of a game that Armour wanted all the Naps to play. He has asked them to do it, if not for the sake of themselves, then for the sake of the spectators, who pay to see live baseball, and of the club owners, who are dependent on the spectators. But most of the players have stood firm with the assertion that quiet baseball was just as good to win games as any other kind.
>
> There have been many differences of opinion between Armour and Lajoie. While they have been friendly enough on the ball field, and while each has appreciated the ability of the other, they have failed to agree upon the way the team should be run. There has been no open revolt by Lajoie to any instructions of Armour's; there has simply been a continual friction that has seemingly resulted in that absence of life and teamwork upon which everybody who has seen the Cleveland club play ball has commented.
>
> The inevitable result has come. Armour has found that he cannot get good work out of the Cleveland club, has decided that he would better cast his lot elsewhere, and let Somers and Kilfoyl find someone else to better take up his burden.[12]

Bill Armour was quickly hired to manage the Detroit Tigers, while the Cleveland owners considered several candidates for their managerial post. One possible new leader was Joe Cantillon, the former umpire and organizer of winter barnstorming tours. Cantillon, however, reportedly did not want to leave Milwaukee, where he managed the Brewers of the American Association in 1904, so his withdrawal left the field open for the man who everyone figured would get the job in the end. Larry Lajoie was the premier player in the American League, a three-time batting champion, and the most popular man in Cleveland. He had captained the Athletics in 1901 and the Naps during the previous three seasons, so leadership was nothing new to him. Also, said Jay Knox of the *Cleveland Press*, "Larry has been a hard man for any manager to handle, because he does not like to be 'bossed,' and the only way to get the greatest benefit out of his work seems to be to let him do the bossing."[13]

Perhaps Charles Somers and John Kilfoyl saw the situation in the way the *Press* described it. Lajoie, with his star power and local popularity, had dominated the Cleveland baseball scene and relegated Bill Armour, the manager of the club, to a supporting role. Lajoie, a superstar at the peak of his fame in 1904, would have overpowered anyone Somers and Kilfoyl could have brought in from outside the organization. The rational, and popular, course would be to make Lajoie the manager of the club that was, after all, named in his honor. On October 28, 1904, the Cleveland owners confirmed that Napoleon Lajoie would manage the Naps in 1905.

Somers and Kilfoyl made it clear to Lajoie that he had full control of the team, including the responsibility for signing players and making trades. Nonetheless, Lajoie paid little attention to baseball matters during the next few months, preferring to wait until the new year to concentrate on the upcoming campaign. He tended to his cigar store, spent two weeks visiting friends in Philadelphia (where, as rumor had it, he was ready to become engaged to a local woman), and generally took it easy. "Anything doing in baseball? No, not a thing,"[14] he told the press in late December. The work, and the pressure, would begin soon enough. "Manager Napoleon Lajoie certainly will have a great chance to show his managerial ability next year," declared *Sporting Life*. "He has ample material to work with, that's certain."[15]

14

Boss of the Naps

I am the president, secretary and sole employee of the Lajoie Clipping Bureau. Everything I can find that has been said in print about my appointment as manager I have put in a big scrap book. Looking it over today I find that the number of critics who think I will fall down outnumber the others. But I'll try to fool them. — Napoleon Lajoie, November 1904[1]

During his nine major league seasons, Napoleon Lajoie had played for two managers who believed in tightly controlling all the moves their players made on the field, those being George Stallings and, to a lesser extent, Bill Armour. Lajoie had clashed repeatedly with Stallings and, according to the Cleveland papers, had grown distant from Armour as time went on. He had also played for Billy Nash, Bill Shettsline, and Connie Mack, who believed in letting the players figure things out for themselves on the field and allowed them a great deal more latitude in their decision-making. Only Nash among them was a playing manager, and because he was often undermined by Colonel Rogers, he was unable to exercise true authority over his men. Shettsline had never played professional ball, and was more of a front office figure than a field leader. Mack, however, was Lajoie's favorite manager, and when the Cleveland star became the boss of the Naps, Mack was the man he consciously tried to emulate.

Henry P. Edwards of the *Cleveland Plain Dealer* wrote a detailed description of what he called "Lajoie's methods" and compared the new Cleveland manager to his immediate predecessor:

It is true that the Lajoie method of playing the game will differ very materially from the Armour method. Bill Armour is a bench manager and he is one of those bench managers who dictate practically every move made by his players on the field. Every man who goes to bat is told by Armour whether he is to bunt or hit it out and he is expected to follow those instructions to the letter. Armour has signs to inform the base runners what he has instructed the batter to do and they are expected to work together. Experience has shown, however, that the base runners often failed to get the signs from the bench and, as a result, there was a lack of what is generally called "team work" with the result that run after run was thrown away.

The Armour method is often a great handicap to the team using it. The team that wins in a major league today must do the unexpected and it is practically impossible to do this under the Armour method. If a batter goes to the plate with certain instructions he is compelled to turn and look at the bench to get those instructions changed and his action is a straight tip to the opposing club to look for something new. If one can judge from what has been seen of Manager Lajoie's methods in the training quarters up to date, the Cleveland Club this year will not play ball by any such iron clad rules as were laid down by ex–Manager Armour.

This does not necessarily mean that there will not be just as much "team work" as has been shown in the Cleveland ranks during the past three years. It does mean, however, if the Cleveland players are as great exponents of the game as they have been credited with being, there is a chance for more effective "team work" than has ever been shown at League Park in the American League history of the Forest City Club. There is an erroneous impression as to what constitutes "team work." The average fan has been educated to believe "team work" consists in obeying the instructions of the manager to the letter. That definition would be more nearly correct than it is if it were possible for each player to carry out those instructions in action according to the theory which prompts them. But such is not the case. Not once in three times will the batter be able to successfully do the thing which his manager would like to have him do when he goes to bat. A better definition of "team work" than that given above would be that the base runners know what the batter is going to try to do and act in such a manner as to get the best possible results in case the batter succeeds.

It is believed that this will be the keynote of the Cleveland style of play this year. In the games played at Atlanta the batters have been sent to the plate to use their own judgment. Every major league ball player of any experience whatever knows what is the proper thing to do theoretically. Manager Lajoie seems to be impressing his men with the fact that it is up to them to use their brains and judgment and to know when theory must give way to practice. For instance, if there are runners on first and second and no one out, the batter knows that, according to the theory of the game, he ought to bunt. The opposing players know this also, and it is Lajoie's salary against a bag of peanuts that the infielders are going to start toward the plate on a run as soon as the ball is pitched. When Armour was on the bench a Cleveland batter had to bunt just the same, but Manager Lajoie is teaching the men to use their heads, and they have permission, if they think that they can cross the opposing infielders, to try and hit one through the infield. The batters will be expected to sign to the base runners what they are going to try to do and this will constitute real "team work."

Under Lajoie the players will find that they are supposed to have brains of their own and they will be on their mettle to prove that this assumption is correct. The result will be a far greater interest in the game by the individual members of the club and there should be more ginger in evidence than in past years. Every man on the team will have a chance to prove that he knows the game and this opportunity for individual action may prove just the thing, which the Cleveland team has needed to make it a contender for the championship. We shall see. The average spectator does not know it, but Connie Mack seldom says anything else to players on the bench except "You fellows will have to get together," meaning that they will have to work intelligently among themselves, just as Manager Lajoie is trying to have the Cleveland players work this spring. If Lajoie succeeds as well along this line as Mr. Cornelius McGillicuddy, the Cleveland patrons will be well satisfied.[2]

Connie Mack's dictum —"You fellows will have to get together"— became Napoleon Lajoie's motto as a manager. Lajoie had always wanted his bosses to trust him to do the right thing on a ball field, and because he was now a playing manager, perhaps he had neither the energy nor the inclination to dictate every move on the diamond in the manner of a John McGraw or a George Stallings. He knew how to play the game, and because the other Naps were major leaguers like him, he believed they should know how to play the game as well.

There was one huge difference between the situations faced by Connie Mack and Larry Lajoie. Mack had founded the Philadelphia Athletics franchise and literally built it from the ground up, having constructed the ballpark the team played in mere weeks before the club's first American League game in 1901. Mack, a co-owner of the club, had filled an empty roster with his own hand-picked players, ones with both the talent and the brainpower to play winning baseball without being strictly regimented. He took chances on talented eccentrics such as pitcher Rube Waddell, but most of Mack's men were serious, businesslike individuals like himself. On the other hand, Lajoie held no ownership stake in the Cleveland club, and had inherited an existing cadre of players, four of whom (Bill Bradley, Elmer Flick, Earl Moore, and Addie Joss) had arrived in Cleveland before him. Lajoie, unlike Mack, was called upon to direct a team full of players who had, until recently, been his equals.

After spending the previous spring in San Antonio, Texas, the Naps gathered in Atlanta, where Lajoie directed his first training camp. The weather was cold and wet, and by early April several of the Cleveland players, including the manager, were fighting off injuries and illnesses. Lajoie was hobbled by a severe cold, as was Elmer Flick, while catcher Harry Bemis and infielder George Stovall suffered from hand injuries and pitcher Red Donahue fought a pulled muscle in his side. Pitcher Earl Moore practiced a spitball, which New York's Jack Chesbro had used to win a league record 41 games in 1904, while Addie Joss, promised a $500 bonus by team management if he won 20 games, looked to be in excellent shape. So was Lajoie, who reported to camp at 195 pounds, ten less than his usual spring weight.

Though the Naps did not get as much work in as they would have liked, Lajoie expressed optimism in his team's chances. He had sent pitchers Joss, Bernhard, Donahue, and Moore, along with catcher Bemis, to Hot Springs, Arkansas, three weeks before the official start of spring camp, and the pitchers appeared to profit from the extra work. Because the Naps had been caught short at the catching position due to injuries in 1904, Lajoie decided to carry three backstops, not the usual two, in 1905. One of the three was Jay "Nig" Clarke, whom the Naps had bought from Atlanta of the Southern League the previous August. Clarke did not play often, but kept the regulars, Fritz Buelow and Harry Bemis, from being overused.

Now that Lajoie was the manager, he was required to deal with the often fickle Cleveland press corps on a regular basis. It did not take long for the local writers to stir up controversy in the Cleveland camp involving one popular Naps star who had been with the ballclub since 1901. A rumor floated around camp that third baseman Bill Bradley nursed managerial ambitions and was miffed about being passed over for the job in favor of Lajoie. The new boss decided to meet that particular problem head-on during the first few days of camp. The new manager said to the press,

> In all my years in baseball, there has never been anything more difficult for me to understand than the story so persistently circulated that Bradley and I are not the best of friends. There has never been the faintest, remotest reason for such a story. From the time we first met on the ball field when he was with Chicago and I with Philadelphia we have been the greatest of friends, even sharing each other's confidences in a good many things. There has never been a misunderstanding or a quarrel of any kind not even a word. How such a story could be set afloat and kept going I am unable to understand.

"Same here," agreed Bradley. "No one living ever heard me say a word about Larry except in praise. He is my friend and I am his, and always have been."[3]

In late March, the American League's biggest star crossed paths with the undisputed king of the boxing world. Jim Jeffries, who had won the world heavyweight title six years before, stopped in Atlanta, where he was touring with a stage show, "Davy Crockett." Jeffries, who loved baseball, stopped by the park to see the Naps, and especially Lajoie, play ball. Afterward, Lajoie and Jeffries went to lunch together and formed a friendship. The Cleveland manager even attended Jeffries' stage show with a group of Naps one evening. These two men, both at the top of their respective fields, found much to admire in each other. "He's the only fighter in the world," said Lajoie after the show. "All other ball players look alike to me," said Jeffries. "The Frenchman towers above them so far you can't see his head for the clouds."[4]

Jeffries was not the only boxer who held Lajoie in high regard. In a syndicated article that appeared in the nation's newspapers that spring, John L. Sullivan, the former bare-knuckle heavyweight champ, sang the praises of his fellow New Englander, Napoleon Lajoie. Specifically, Sullivan expressed admiration for the way that Lajoie embraced sobriety, unlike not only himself, but other prominent athletes that included the late baseball star of the 1880s, Mike (King) Kelly. Wrote Sullivan (or his ghostwriter):

> When King Kelly passed out, the future Emperor Napoleon Lajoie was driving an ice cart in Woonsocket. Prosperity almost carried the Frenchman off his feet, but the lesson of Mike Kelly and some more of us foolish ones was drilled into him. He cut out the "red eye," got a bank book, and today he is king of them all and getting rich. He didn't intend to get off the water wagon again and go back to the ice cart. The difference between King Kelly and Emperor Lajoie is the difference between the old style and the new in all kinds of sport, and the stayer is the man behind the pledge.
>
>   Kelly died early. Lajoie grows better every year, and if he were to take up boxing he could sprint faster than Corbett, punch as hard as myself, get away as quick as Fitz and handle his fists like Tommy Ryan. Moreover, his hat fits. I call the attention of all the temperance lecturers to Larry Lajoie as one of the best examples they can use in their business.[5]

The Naps planned to start their season with a four-game set at home against Detroit, but the scheduled opener at League Park on April 14 was rained out. The weather on the following afternoon was not much better, but the Naps and Tigers played anyway (though the opening ceremonies were cancelled). Lajoie, in his first official game as manager, belted three hits as Earl Moore pitched a 6–2 win in front of 7,544 fans. The next two games were rained out, and the Naps then hit the road for three games at St. Louis and four at Detroit. On May 7, though Lajoie had yet to find his hitting stride, the Naps grabbed first place with a 2–0 win at Chicago behind a two-hitter by Bob Rhoads. Not since 1900, when the American League was still a minor circuit, had the Cleveland club held the top spot at any time in any season.

The league was tightly bunched in May — the last-place Boston club was only three and a half games behind on May 15 — and the Naps stayed close to the top for several weeks before opening a two-game lead with an eight-game winning streak at home late in the month. The streak began after Lajoie benched first baseman Charlie Carr, a good fielder who struggled at the plate, and put the better-hitting George Stovall in his place. Stovall was not Carr's equal as a glove man, but proved to be adequate, and his bat gave the team a boost. So did Lajoie, who found his groove at the plate and began to climb the batting list.

Lajoie went hitless against Washington on May 12, but played a key role in an unusual ninth inning in Cleveland. The score was tied at four in the bottom of the final frame, and after Elmer Flick singled with two out, pitcher Albin (Beany) Jacobsen decided that he did not want to face either of the next two batters, Lajoie and Bradley. He intentionally walked both men, loading the bases and bringing the less dangerous Terry Turner to the plate. Jacobsen's strategy backfired when he walked Turner, forcing Flick across the plate with the winning run. "Still another surprise," said the *Washington Times*, "was Lajoie who never got a sign of a hit and struck out once. With Jacobsen making doubles [the pitcher had two hits of his own that day] and the mighty Napoleon fanning it's a hard job doping baseball."[6]

The first-place Naps left Cleveland for a three-week eastern trip on June 1, and a reporter for *The Sporting News* asked the ebullient Cleveland manager about his expectations. "Eleven out of 15 will about suit me," said Lajoie. "Unless the Eastern teams have improved wonderfully since they were here, we should take three out of four from New York, Boston, and Washington.... The Athletics are the team we have got to beat out if we win the pennant and there is a possibility of some of the other clubs bothering us."[7] While the White Sox and Naps fought for the lead, Connie Mack's Athletics stayed close enough to pose a threat. The top teams had begun to separate from the pack, leaving a three-team race among Chicago, Cleveland, and Philadelphia. The long road trip promised to make or break the Naps, unfamiliar as they were with the pressure of a pennant race.

Lajoie decided to deploy his pitchers in a four-man rotation of Joss, Moore, Hess, and Rhoads, with veterans Bill Bernhard and Red Donahue in reserve, and the scheme appeared to work. On June 4, Addie Joss and Chicago's Nick Altrock hooked up in a three-hour duel that was not resolved until the 16th inning, when singles by Flick, Lajoie, and Bradley loaded the bases. Terry Turner cleared them with a triple, and though Joss allowed one run in the bottom of the 16th, the Naps escaped with a 4–2 win and a two and a half game lead. Nine days earlier, left-hander Otto Hess had shut out the Highlanders for ten innings, then won his own game with a run-scoring single in the bottom of the inning.

Always an aggressive hitter, Lajoie outdid himself on June 19 in Washington. In a 12–5 victory over the Senators,[8] he went to bat six times and saw only seven pitches. He swung at every pitch thrown to him that day, drilling five singles and lifting a fly ball to center. The other delivery was a foul ball. A reporter for the *Washington Times* was amazed. "Maybe that isn't batting some," he wrote, "and doesn't justify the posters announcing the only Larry as an added attraction when his team comes to town. He was able to reach out and get everything that was sent him and if they came too close to his chest all he had to do was stand back to give himself a little more leeway and bang the ball on the nose."[9]

The new Cleveland manager, whose confrontations with umpires had made headlines in past seasons, played the role of peacemaker on June 9 in New York. Umpire Frank (Silk) O'Loughlin endured abuse from both teams that day, and in the fifth inning the usually mild-mannered Addie Joss let his frustration boil over and threw his glove at the arbiter's head. This brought both teams rushing onto the field, and when catcher Fritz Buelow and New York manager Clark Griffith nearly came to blows, a full-scale riot appeared imminent. Eventually, O'Loughlin restored order and ejected Joss, Buelow, and Griffith from the contest. The New York papers strongly criticized the Naps the next day, with one columnist insisting that Joss had "outraged public decency" and that Lajoie should have been removed from the field by the police for interfering with the umpire. O'Loughlin disagreed. "Lajoie did remain out of the way," he explained. "In fact, he tried to prevent his men from acting disorderly and to stop the row which was starting between Buelow and Griffith. Had the others acted as quietly as Larry, there would have been no trouble."[10] Joss and Buelow were suspended by the league for five games each, while Lajoie, who had thrown tobacco in Frank Dwyer's face 12 months before, was not sanctioned.

The pennant-starved fans of Cleveland responded to the success of their club. On Friday, June 23, the Naps completed their road trip with their third loss in a row to the

Philadelphia Athletics. Still in first place by two games, the Naps returned to Cleveland on Saturday morning and were surprised by 10,000 cheering fans at the Euclid Avenue train depot. The Cleveland rooters blew whistles and honked horns while a band played and the tugboats in the harbor sounded their greetings. The fans escorted their heroes to their rooms at the Kennard House, and a few hours later, more than 11,000 people filled the stands at League Park for a game against the St. Louis Browns. The contest ended badly, with the Browns defeating Addie Joss and the Naps by a 6–2 score while the fans, protesting a call by umpire Jack Sheridan, threw hundreds of seat cushions onto the field. Despite the loss, Lajoie's men maintained a one-game lead at day's end.

The Naps were riding high, and despite an alarming wave of injuries (to Elmer Flick, Bill Bradley, and George Stovall, among others) the club maintained a grip on the league lead before disaster struck on July 1. The Naps played Detroit at home on that Saturday afternoon and put on a hitting display in a 14–3 win. Lajoie managed only one hit, but Elmer Flick belted five safeties and Jim Jackson four before the contest was stopped in the eighth inning to allow the Naps to catch a train to St. Louis. Late in the game, Detroit shortstop Charley O'Leary slid into Lajoie at second base and gashed the Cleveland manager in the left foot with his spikes. Lajoie, who had suffered spike wounds often while playing the infield, ignored the pain and finished the game. The Naps quickly headed for the railroad station and boarded a Missouri-bound train for a doubleheader against the Browns, one of the few teams in baseball that played games on Sundays.

When Lajoie woke up in St. Louis the next morning, his foot was so swollen that he could not put a shoe on it. He could barely walk, so he remained at the team hotel while the Naps earned a rain-soaked 3–2 victory over the Browns. The second game of the twin bill was halted by rain in the fifth inning, after which Lajoie and the Naps returned to Cleveland. When the players arrived in their home city on Monday morning, an off-day for the Naps, Lajoie rushed to the office of Dr. Morrison H. Castle, the Cleveland team physician, for treatment.

Lajoie had played through pain and injury before, but his foot was so discolored and distended that Dr. Castle was alarmed by its appearance. A serious infection had set in, and early word from the doctor's office indicated that the spike wound, which the manager had regarded as a minor cut, had graduated to a full-fledged case of blood poisoning. Dr. Castle ordered the Cleveland star to bed, but the foot became even worse during the next two days. On Wednesday morning, Lajoie returned to Dr. Castle's office with burly pitchers Bob Rhoads and Red Donahue in tow. The doctor administered chloroform and, with Rhoads and Donahue holding the patient down, lanced the swollen foot near the site of the wound.

For a while, some feared that the injury put Lajoie's career in jeopardy, and reports surfaced that the infected leg was so badly damaged that it might have to be amputated. Fortunately, the foot began to heal, however slowly, and the Naps manager was soon out of danger. He stayed in bed for about three weeks, then ambled about in a wheelchair for a while after that. By the end of July he was able to put a shoe on the injured foot, and in early August he was walking again and making plans to return to the team.

Though Lajoie's infection most likely could have been avoided by thoroughly washing and cleaning the wound soon after it occurred, news reports at the time blamed the case of blood poisoning on the blue dye in the player's socks. On July 4, three days after the injury, the *Boston Globe* explained the circumstances by stating, "some of the dye in his stocking got into the wound and affected it." A few months later, a reporter for the *Washington Post*

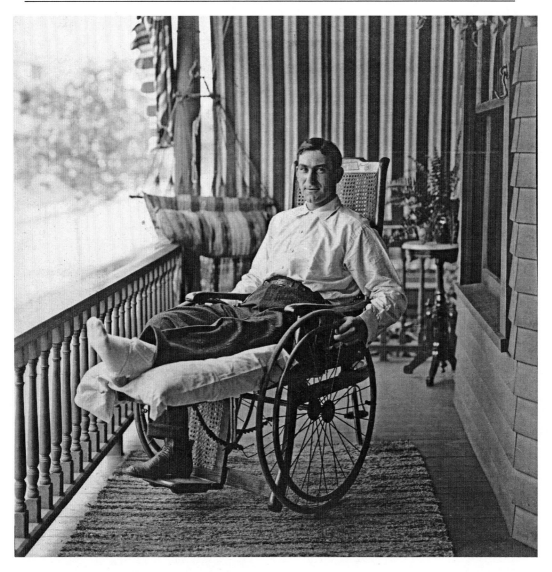

Lajoie in a wheelchair during his recovery from a serious case of blood poisoning in 1905 (Library of Congress).

wrote that the Cleveland players "will hereafter wear pure white stockings to avoid the possibility of blood poisoning."[11] In any case, many players, fearing a repeat of Lajoie's career-threatening illness, began to wear all-white socks under their uniform hose. Wearing two pairs of thick woolen socks at once proved uncomfortable, so some unknown individual decided to cut the toe and heel out of his colored socks to make them fit easier inside his shoe. With that, the colored uniform stirrup was born.

In Lajoie's absence, the "Napless Naps," as the local papers called them, continued their fight for the pennant under the direction of veteran third baseman Bill Bradley. They stayed in the race for a while, largely due to the pitching of Addie Joss and the hitting of Bradley and Elmer Flick, and on July 19 and 20, Cleveland swept two doubleheaders against Boston at League Park. The injured manager could not yet walk, but put in an appearance to support his men. Said the *Boston Globe*, "Napoleon Lajoie sat in his easy chair in the shade of the grand stand and wore a continuous smile."[12] However, the Naps depended so much on Lajoie, on both offense and defense, that the team could not succeed for long without him. "With Lajoie out of the game," said Boston manager Jimmy Collins, "the Cleveland boys are not a team, and are likely to find a very rough trip ahead."[13]

The Naps (some of the papers were moved to call the club the "Brads" for the time being) suffered another major injury when a New York Highlander drilled a liner off Earl Moore's right foot on August 1. Moore, who had compiled a record of 13–7 to that point, played through the pain but posted a 2–8 log the rest of the season. Injuries piled up, and nine losses in a row at Boston and New York dropped the club from first place to third as the Naps, with catcher Harry Bemis at second base and infielder George Stovall in center field, struggled to put a complete team on the field. Pitchers Bob Rhoads and Otto Hess saw action in the outfield, Addie Joss played a few games at first and third, and rookies Nick Kahl and Bill "Jap" Barbeau tried to fill Lajoie's spot at second. Lajoie wanted to travel to Boston on August 3 to support his fading team, but Dr. Castle forbade him to do so, and he could only sit by helplessly while his foot healed slowly. Still, he maintained an optimistic attitude. "There are about 60 regular scheduled games to come, nearly half of them at home," he said, "and luck is bound to turn. It is doubtful if any American League club ever ran up against it so hard as we have, but as showing there is mettle in the boys they have not faltered, although they have had every reason to become disheartened."[14]

Perhaps the Cleveland players believed their manager's words, at least for a while, but in late August the last embers of Cleveland's pennant chances died out. Lajoie rejoined the lineup as a first baseman on August 28 in a home game against the Highlanders, going hitless but providing an emotional lift in a 5–4 win. Third sacker Bill Bradley, however, had been fighting a deep cough for more than a week, and was so weak from lung congestion that the team feared that he had contracted tuberculosis. Bradley's doctors decided otherwise, calling his illness "consumption," which was still serious enough to drive Bradley to the sidelines. He played a few more games but left the team in early September and checked into a sanitarium in Geneva-on-the-Lake, outside of Cleveland.

Lajoie, still nursing a sore foot and ankle, stubbornly remained in the lineup during a four-game home series against the Athletics, though he managed only four singles in 15 trips to the plate. The Naps lost all four contests to Connie Mack's team, and on August 31, the last game of the series, Lajoie fouled a Rube Waddell pitch off his aching ankle. He collapsed from the pain and lay sprawled on the infield grass for more than five minutes. The joint swelled up immediately, driving him from the game and, as it turned out, from the lineup as well. Dr. Castle, once again called upon to treat the Cleveland star, decreed that the injured ankle was too damaged to play on, so Lajoie reluctantly retired to the bench. He continued to manage the Naps, but as a player, his 1905 season was over.

The Naps, who began the season with such optimism, totally collapsed after Lajoie's season-ending injury. In third place, 12 games above the .500 mark, before the disastrous series against the Athletics, Lajoie's men won only 15 of their final 44 games, dropping to fourth place with one week left in the season. In early October, after losing the third of three straight in Boston, the Naps, who had led the league for 77 days, fell to fifth place, where they remained. "When the game was over," said the *Boston Globe* the next day, "manager Larry Lajoie, with his handbag, led the Cleveland boys out of the grounds the most disappointed bunch that trod a ball field."[15] To make matters worse, the Cleveland fans gave up on the club. On September 5, a cold and windy day, only 225 fans filed into League

The 1905 Cleveland Naps. Front row, from left: George Stovall, Bob Rhoads, Addie Joss, Lajoie, Bill Bernhard, and Bill Bradley. Second row: Otto Hess, Fritz Buelow, Terry Turner, Harry Bemis, Jim Jackson, and Harry Bay. Third row: Elmer Flick, Claude Rossman, and Nig Clarke (far right). Fourth row: Bunk Congalton, Harry Fells, Howard Wakefield, Ralph Cadwalader, Hi West. Back row: Happy Townsend, Bill Shipke, Jap Barbeau, Scotty Ingerton, unknown (Baseball-Fever.com).

Park to see the Browns shut out the Naps in a sloppily played game that a St. Louis paper called "a farce comedy instead of a ball game" as the tiny crowd "hooted itself hoarse."[16] The next day, with better weather, another contest against the same team attracted only 645 people. Despite the enthusiasm of the early season, the Naps finished sixth in the league in attendance, with only Detroit and Washington drawing fewer fans per game through the turnstiles.

The Naps ended their up-and-down season at 76–78. Napoleon Lajoie's .329 average was the highest in the American League, though he missed out on the batting title because he played in only 65 games. Addie Joss earned his $500 bonus by winning 20 games for the first time, while Elmer Flick, at .308, won the batting crown with the second-lowest winning mark in league history. Only Boston's Carl Yastrzemski, who hit .301 in 1968, posted a lower average by a champion. Still, many sources ignored the fact that Lajoie played in fewer than half of his team's scheduled contests and listed the Cleveland second baseman as the 1905 batting champ for several years thereafter.

Larry was still the American League's "king of ballplayers," but the jury was still out on his performance as a manager. The sports columnists of the four main Cleveland newspapers were a demanding bunch, and as the season slipped away, they filled their pages with so much criticism that in November of 1905, John Kilfoyl found it necessary to declare that he would indeed return as field leader in 1906.

> You can say definitely for the club that Lajoie will be the man. I am surprised to think that there should be a doubt of it in anyone's mind. We have never had a better manager than Larry.... Larry as a manager was a success right from the start. The fact that the team slumped when Larry was hurt, instead of being a basis of attack against Larry, is, as a matter of fact, one of the strongest proofs of his managerial ability. The club is wholly satisfied with Larry at the helm, and we never even dreamed of any change. There is absolutely no question of Larry's being manager of the Cleveland team."[17]

15

Pennant Race

If Napoleon Lajoie broke a leg or an eardrum in today's game of ball, or in anywise dismantled himself so that his second-basing days were over he would not need to worry about whether the neighbors would bring in something to eat. The big Frenchman has about 25,000 cold, metallic simoleons stowed away in various safe places.... Lajoie has earned his little fortune, if ever a man did. He has drawn hundreds of thousands of lovers of the national game through the turnstiles to see "the greatest player in the world," and nine days out of ten has made good. — Cleveland News, *August 1906*[1]

Since the birth of the American League in 1901, Napoleon Lajoie had earned the top salary in the new circuit and, unlike many other ballplayers, had managed to save much of it. As a bachelor, he spent less than his teammates who had wives and children. He was never much of a gambler or horseplayer, and by the time he assumed the manager's role in Cleveland, he had given up the wild nightlife escapades that had sometimes marred his early career with the Phillies. As manager of the Naps, his idea of a good time at night consisted of dinner and a low-stakes game of cards with a select circle of friends. This low-key, frugal lifestyle allowed Lajoie to salt away a large amount of his salary each season.

He was not a cheapskate, however. Grantland Rice, who joined the sports staff of the *Cleveland News* in 1906, became a friend and admirer of Lajoie when Rice wrote for the *Atlanta Journal* and covered the Naps at their 1903 spring camp in Georgia. When Rice and his wife Anna were married, Lajoie surprised the newlyweds with a large barrel of china. Though Rice and his wife had not yet picked out an apartment, said the writer, "my bride had enough chinaware to stock a hotel."[2] Lajoie was also generous in support of his widowed mother Celina, who still lived in Woonsocket, as did all of his siblings and their growing families. He visited his home town whenever the Naps played in Boston, and always gave his mother a gift of a few hundred dollars, though the ballplayer admitted that she was unwilling to spend the money on herself. Instead, the ever-frugal Celina, like her son, preferred to put the money in the bank.

By 1906, Larry had built up enough of a nest egg that he did not need his paycheck to pay his daily and monthly bills. Instead, he invested his money with his boss, team owner Charles Somers. As the *Cleveland News* described the arrangement, "Larry did not draw a cent of his salary last year. His checks were made out to his employer, Charles W. Somers, who borrows the money of Lajoie, using it in his coal business, and pays the Naps' manager six per cent instead of the four he would get from a bank. There is thrift for you."[3] Such a scheme was unusual, to say the least, and though both parties benefited from the arrangement, it served as an indication that Somers' finances may not have been totally solid. It is never a good sign for a business when the owner borrows money from his highest-salaried employee.

Despite Somers' reported wealth, reports of financial hardship had hit the headlines in the past. The franchise had experienced a potentially embarrassing money crunch in 1904, when the Naps held their spring training camp in San Antonio, Texas. Somers planned to use the receipts from the final two training games, on a Saturday and a Sunday, to pay his expenses for the trip. When rain washed out those two potentially profitable games, Somers found himself $1,600 in the hole, with no funds available to pay the hotel bills and meal expenses for his Naps. According to longtime *Cleveland Press* sportswriter Franklin Lewis, the problem was made known to the players, and pitcher Bob Rhoads told Somers not to worry. Rhoads scraped together some cash and headed for a nearby gambling hall, emerging a few hours later with more than enough money to cover the shortfall. Rhoads handed the cash to Somers, who paid all the bills and split the rest among the players.[4]

The continuing local ban on Sunday ball was one factor that threatened the viability of the Cleveland franchise. In 1902 and 1903, the team moved scheduled Sunday games to four different cities (Canton, Dayton, Columbus, and Fort Wayne, Indiana), but the results were disappointing, and the team did without Sunday crowds thereafter. The politically powerful ministerial association of Cleveland was determined to keep League Park silent on Sundays, and their intransigence handed a distinct financial advantage to the St. Louis Browns and Chicago White Sox, who drew hugely profitable crowds on the Christian Sabbath.

Lajoie, however, was as popular as ever on a national basis, and his presence on the Naps made the Cleveland team the league's leading draw on the road, even if the crowds were disappointing at League Park. In early 1906, the Cleveland star lent his name and face to *Napoleon Lajoie's Official Base Ball Guide*, a compilation of statistics, photos, and features similar to those put out on an annual basis by Albert G. Spalding and Al Reach. In the preface, Lajoie proclaimed that his book was "the first Base Ball guide ever published by a Ball Player actively engaged in playing Base Ball,"[5] which it was; manager John McGraw of the New York Giants, who put out a similar guide the year before, still played every now and then, but not on a regular basis. Lajoie's guide, which featured several contributions from his friend Grantland Rice of the *Cleveland News*, was well received and added to Lajoie's stature as the premier personality in the sport.

The guide also highlighted Lajoie's growing popularity as a commercial endorser. The book showed the Cleveland second baseman in advertisements for Coca-Cola, Heptol Splits laxative, the "Napoleon Lajoie Official League Ball" from a Cincinnati manufacturer, Louisville Slugger bats, and the like. The most striking ad was the simplest one. On one page of the guide, plain black letters on a white background informed the reader that "Lajoie chews Red Devil Tobacco. Ask him if he don't."

On the first day of training camp in Atlanta, the Cleveland manager lined his players up on the field and delivered a piece of advice. "I want you all to get out and hustle," he said. "Hustle first, last and all the time. Hustle as much in the ninth inning as you do in the first. Hustle as much in September as you do in April, and think while you hustle. That's all."[6] After a few weeks of workouts, Lajoie announced that he would set his lineup with Harry Bay, the speedy outfielder, in the leadoff spot, followed by Bill Bradley, Elmer

Flick, himself, shortstop Terry Turner, outfielder Jim Jackson, and first sacker George Stovall, followed by the catcher and the pitcher. Bradley had usually batted fifth or sixth in the order in the past, but Lajoie believed that Bradley was his best bet to move Bay around for the sluggers to drive in.

As for the pitching staff, Otto Hess, 10–15 in 1905, looked much improved and promised to finally give the Naps a reliable left-handed starter. Addie Joss was healthy, though Earl Moore, whose foot was still sore from his injury of the previous September, was a question mark. Moore claimed that he was well, but James "Bonesetter" Reese, the well-known Cleveland osteopath who worked with injured players, told the press that the muscles of Moore's injured foot had torn loose and made the pitcher flat-footed. Moore angrily denied the claim, though he did not pitch much down South. Bill Bernhard worked hard to make a comeback at the age of 34, while Bob Rhoads, a 16-game winner in 1905, rounded out what appeared to be a strong starting corps.

Lajoie, after an injury-marred 1905 season, proclaimed that his foot and ankle were totally healed. He encountered no problems during spring workouts and hit the ball as well as ever. Entering his 11th major league season at the age of 31, Lajoie's career batting average of .361 was now the highest in the history of the game (he had passed Willie Keeler during the 1905 campaign), while he had held the career record for slugging percentage since passing Dan Brouthers in 1902. He was widely considered, as the cover of his baseball guide put it, "the champion batter of the world," and needed only a World Series berth to cement his legacy as both a player and a manager.

The Naps played their first 11 games on the road in 1906, winning six and tying one, then opened their home schedule against the Browns on April 29. After only two wins and one tie in their first seven contests at League Park, Lajoie shook up his lineup, shifting Elmer Flick to the leadoff spot and moving Harry Bay into second place and Bradley in third, with himself batting cleanup. He also pulled the slumping Jim Jackson out of center field and replaced him with Bunk Congalton. The team responded with a 15–1 win over the White Sox, belting Chicago spitballer Ed Walsh out of the box and continuing the assault against reliever Frank Smith. Walsh had mesmerized the Naps with a one-hit shutout only four days before in Chicago. Lajoie's men then won 13 of their next 15 games on an eastern swing to pull into second place. On June 15, after winning three of four from the Highlanders at home, the Naps held first place by percentage points over the New Yorkers.

Though Earl Moore's foot did not respond to treatment (he pitched in only five games for the Naps), the starting corps of Hess, Joss, Rhoads, and the rejuvenated Bill Bernhard kept the Naps in the middle of a four-way fight for the pennant with the Athletics, White Sox, and Highlanders. Harry Bay split a finger at bat on June 13 and was lost for two weeks, but the Naps, with Flick and Lajoie belting the ball day after day, held either first or second place during the next month. The Cleveland club's pennant chances looked better than ever, and the flag-starved local fans dared to hope for a berth in the World Series. On July 4, the traditional midway point of the season, the Naps defeated the Tigers in both ends of a doubleheader and retained their hold on first place by a game and a half.

With Earl Moore unable to pitch, Lajoie made Addie Joss the workhorse of the pitching staff. Joss sometimes rested for only two days between starts, and in one seven-day stretch, he made three starts and one relief appearance. The 26-year-old pitcher appeared to be well on his way to another $500 bonus for winning 20 games, but his health had been fragile in the past, and it remained to be seen if the Cleveland ace would hold up to his increased workload. For a while, Lajoie's strategy worked, as Joss threw nine shutouts and led the league in wins at mid-season. On July 18, after team co-owner John Kilfoyl appeared in the Cleveland dressing room and promised the Naps a $5,000 pot to split if they won the pennant, Joss responded with a 5–0, complete-game win over the Highlanders.

The Athletics, defending American League champions, collapsed in July and fell out of the race, but the White Sox and Highlanders held firm. Cleveland, despite Lajoie's league-leading batting average, was the next to falter as a wave of injuries struck the Naps in mid-July. Harry Bay was lost for the season on July 18, the day of Kilfoyl's $5,000 offer, after he wrenched his knee while avoiding a collision with shortstop Terry Turner. Elmer Flick moved to center field, but Jim Jackson and rookie Ben Caffyn could not make up for Bay's speed and fielding prowess, and right field, once a strength, was now a weakness for the Naps. A more serious injury occurred on July 19, when New York pitcher Bill Hogg threw an inside fastball that broke Bill Bradley's wrist (after which Hogg reportedly boasted, "The big Frenchman is next on my list"[7]). Bradley, like Bay, was sidelined for the rest of the season, robbing Cleveland of one of its strongest hitters and defenders.

The loss of Bay and Bradley exposed the Cleveland club's lack of depth. Jackson (who hit .214 in 1906) and Caffyn (.194) were insufficient substitutes for Bay, while Bill (Jap) Barbeau, a 24-year-old rookie, batted only .194 while filling in for Bradley at third. Lajoie kept shuffling his lineup, even putting himself at third base for 15 games and at shortstop for seven while searching for a winning combination. In September, Lajoie shifted George Stovall, who had shared first base with Claude Rossman, to third, but the move came too late. The Naps suffered through an 11–14 record in August while the White Sox ran off a league record 19 wins in a row to take control of the race. The Naps were still in the hunt, but barely, when Addie Joss went down with arm soreness and went home to Toledo to recuperate. Lajoie, desperate for help in the outfield, had put Addie in center field for two games, and the fans wondered if the manager had ridden his star pitcher too hard. Joss returned after two weeks, though his arm was still tender, and relied on control and changing speeds for the rest of the season.

The Naps, so close to a pennant, did their best to ignore even the most serious injuries and stay on the field. On September 2, Lajoie suffered a spike wound just above his left ankle that produced so much blood that "some of the players were sickened just by looking at the wound,"[8] reported *Sporting Life*. The memory of Lajoie's blood poisoning drama of the year before was still fresh in everyone's minds, but the Cleveland manager refused to leave the lineup with an important Labor Day doubleheader against the first-place White Sox on tap the next afternoon. Lajoie, against his doctor's advice, took two stitches in the wound, washed it as thoroughly as possible, and played the next day. He went six-for-eight in the doubleheader (though he was ejected from the first contest for throwing a handful of dirt at umpire Jack Sheridan) as the Naps swept the twin bill to keep their fading pennant hopes alive.

George Stovall also declined a seat on the bench in September, though he had been complaining about a sharp pain in his hip for weeks. Finally, after the pain became so bad that the tough infielder could not take it any more, he went to the Cleveland team physician, Dr. Morrison H. Castle, who put the hip under his X-ray machine. Dr. Castle found that Stovall's hip was broken, as a piece of it had chipped off and had been rubbing against the rest of the bone. The doctor designed a splint to keep the offending bone chip from moving, and allowed Stovall to remain in the lineup.

The doubleheader win against the White Sox on Labor Day shaved two games off Chicago's lead and lifted the Naps into third place, five and a half games out of first, but the White Sox won 11 of their next 13 to keep the Naps at bay. The Clevelanders fought valiantly, but Chicago's 19-game win streak in August proved too much for the Naps to overcome in September. In the end, the "Hitless Wonders" from Chicago took the flag by four games over New York and five and a half over the Naps.

On a personal note, Napoleon Lajoie stayed healthy all year, missing only five games, and nearly copped another batting title, batting .355 but losing out to George Stone of the Browns by three points. Lajoie led the league in hits (214) and doubles (48), and finished second in runs batted in with 91, though he did not hit a home run all season. Elmer Flick, too, avoided injury and illness, playing in every game and leading the circuit in triples, stolen bases, and runs scored. The hard-hitting duo of Flick and Lajoie was the most feared twosome in the American League, and drew comparisons to the Lajoie-Delahanty tandem on the Phillies so many years before. Nonetheless, personal statistics could not make up for losing a pennant, and Lajoie, after 11 years in the major leagues, had still never played for a championship team.

Lajoie's men ended their 1906 season with a 7–5 win in St. Louis on Sunday, October 7, after which the Naps returned to Cleveland to collect their final paychecks and take their leave until the following spring. The Cleveland manager told friends that he would be out of town for a few days, because he was headed to Buffalo, New York, to take care of some unexplained "legal business." The "legal business" involved a female admirer whom the ballplayer had been dating for a while, and when Lajoie returned to Cleveland, he brought the admirer back to the city with him as his wife.

Myrtle Ivy Smith,[9] née Wallace, was a stylish, handsome, 30-year-old brunette who had run a boardinghouse near League Park and rented rooms to Lajoie and several other Cleveland ballplayers. Born in St. Joseph, Missouri, she had lived for a time in Philadelphia and been married to a man named Bill Smith, who was described in the papers as a bookmaker, "well known in base ball circles."[10] The union had dissolved, Mrs. Smith having been granted a divorce on a charge of desertion. After moving to Cleveland, Myrtle became a regular at the ballpark, where she sat in a box seat and cheered for Napoleon Lajoie. The two began dating and continued their relationship even after she sold her boardinghouse and moved to Buffalo, where she "managed a corset-fitting establishment,"[11] according to a report in *Sporting Life*. The same paper also said that Lajoie had previously been engaged to a woman in Philadelphia, though that relationship had ended "by mutual consent" sometime in 1905.

Lajoie, who liked to keep his personal life as private as possible despite his celebrity status in Cleveland, slipped out of town and took a train to Buffalo, where he collected Myrtle and

Myrtle Ivy Smith, née Wallace, who married Napoleon Lajoie on October 11, 1906 (author's collection).

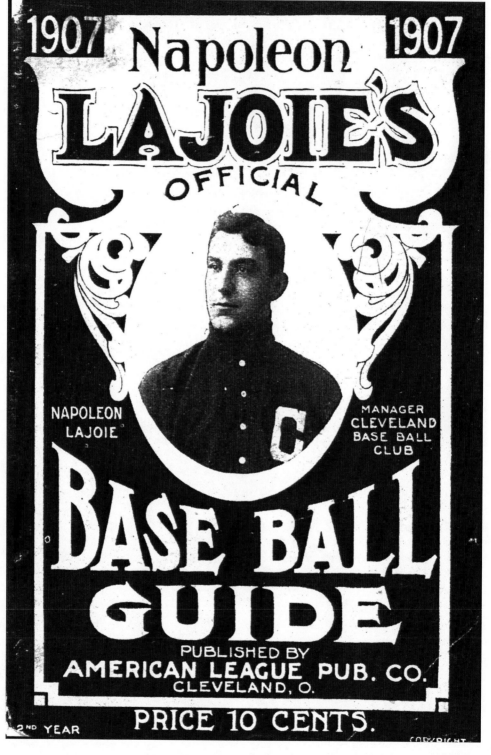

The cover of Napoleon Lajoie's Base Ball Guide for 1907 (Transcendental Graphics/theruckerarchive. com).

crossed the Niagara River into Canada. In Niagara Falls, then as now a marriage mecca, the couple headed to the office of a local magistrate on the morning of October 11, 1906. There, he and Myrtle were married in a short, no-frills ceremony. They spent their honeymoon in the Niagara Falls area, then returned to Cleveland to set up housekeeping and introduce the new Mrs. Lajoie to his circle of friends and admirers.

By almost every measure, the Cleveland Naps were the best team in the American League in 1906. They led the circuit in runs scored, batting average, slugging percentage, and doubles, all by wide margins. Their pitchers compiled the lowest earned run average in the league and allowed the second lowest total of runs, with only the pennant-winning White Sox giving up fewer tallies to their opponents. Cleveland fielders turned more double plays and committed fewer errors than any other American League team. The Naps boasted the league's top hitter, Napoleon Lajoie, and three 20-game winners (Joss, Rhoads, and Hess) in the starting rotation. Still, the Naps finished five games behind Chicago, a club with such an anemic offensive attack that the name "Hitless Wonders" became a permanent part of its legacy.

Though the White Sox batted only .230 as a team (in contrast to the Naps, who posted a .279 average) and featured several regulars in their lineup who batted under .200 in 1906, they compiled a healthily positive margin in run production, scoring 570 runs and allowing 460. The Naps, however, plated 663 runs against 481 for the opposition, a much more impressive mark. Baseball historian Bill James, in his *1980 Baseball Abstract*, introduced a metric called the "Pythagorean winning percentage," a formula with predicts a team's won-lost record by its differential in runs scored and allowed. By this measure, the Naps should have won the pennant easily with a record of 98–55, instead of the 89–64 mark they actually earned, while the White Sox should have finished at 90–61 instead of their actual 93–58 log.

The American League pennant was ripe for the picking in 1906, as all of Cleveland's main competitors faced serious problems. The Boston Americans, flag winners in 1903 and 1904, dropped to fourth in 1905, endured a 20-game losing streak early in 1906, and joined the Browns and Senators at the bottom of the league. Connie Mack's Philadelphia club, the 1905 title holder, held first place in late July of 1906, then collapsed utterly and fell out of the race. The Chicago White Sox could not hit to save their lives, and the Detroit Tigers suffered so many injuries that in early August, out of sheer desperation, they called Lajoie's old Phillies teammate, 46-year-old Sam Thompson, out of retirement to fill in for a few games. The only team that could compete with the Naps, at least on paper, was New York, which had pitching woes and turned fewer double plays than any team in the league.

Why did the Naps fall short of the pennant in 1906 (and also in 1904, when their won-lost record was nine games worse than their expected performance, using Bill James' Pythagorean metric described previously)? James attributed large swings between actual and predicted performance to offensive inefficiency (scoring lots of runs in blowouts, while producing fewer when it counted), or to mere luck. The Naps, indeed, were the unluckiest team in the league in regard to injuries, being hobbled year after year by ill-timed accidents to Lajoie, Bradley, and the pitchers. However, Cleveland compiled a poor record in close contests, going 21–25 in one-run games in 1906 while the White Sox recorded a 29–19 log. The Naps also fattened their record against second-division teams, while posting losing marks against Chicago (10–12) and second-place New York (10–11). The Naps, under the direction of Napoleon Lajoie, were solid in every phase of the game, but a constant stream of injuries and an inability to win the close games kept them from taking the long-awaited and much-desired pennant.[12]

The Cleveland star appeared in advertisements for Coca-Cola (as seen here) and many other products at the height of his fame (Transcendental Graphics/theruckerarchive.com).

Many people believed that Lajoie's managerial style was to blame. The Cleveland manager was no clever strategist like New York's Clark Griffith, who had once dared to walk Lajoie intentionally with the bases loaded in a tight game. Lajoie was not a meticulous team builder like Connie Mack, nor was he a shrewd manipulator like John McGraw. Instead, the Naps, like the Phillies of Lajoie, Delahanty, and Thompson a decade before, relied on clubbing their opponents into submission. "The backbone of the Cleveland team is old fashioned slugging," complained a columnist in the *New York American*.

> Theorists who have mapped out on paper will get a sickening setback if Lajoie leads his hitters into the top place. There isn't any "inside" work in the Cleveland efforts. Bunting and other shows of science are not highly regarded by the burly leader. Lajoie's order from the bench is invariably, "Clout it." Mr. Lajoie is highly fortunate in having a sturdy lot of assistants. A weak batting team would collapse under the Cleveland plan. The Cleveland pitching staff isn't any better than the Yankees. Joss is the lone star. He has some mates who often break into the sunshine of victory, but mostly through the terrific attack of the Naps on opposing pitchers.[13]

In November of 1906, a month after the end of another disappointing season for the Naps, Grantland Rice of the *Cleveland News* attempted to diagnose the problem.

> To begin with[,] Lajoie has the hardest ball club in the league to handle. This doesn't mean that dissension reigns or that disobedience to orders crops out upon the field of battle. It doesn't mean that the individual members of the Cleveland team are not doing their best to win. Nor does it mean that they can't play high-class base ball. But it DOES mean that without an exception there is not a member on the squad upon whom Larry can depend for help or advice in a game, nor a single man who ever attempts to pull off anything in a crisis or do anything else except play straight mechanical base ball wherein the noodle doesn't figure at all. If there is an exception George Stovall is the man, but even George is of the quiet, subdued type that hasn't much to say unless called upon.
>
> The Cleveland Club ... by nature is built up of reserved talent. Bill Bradley is a great ball player in every way, but Bill hasn't anything to say, no matter what is going on. A grander infielder than Terry Turner never lived, but Terry never cut away from his own job to flash any new line of thought. You can't blame the men for this, as changing one's nature is almost as hard as chasing the proverbial blotches off the leopard but to say the least, it's an unfortunate incident that the full roster should include only this type. When they think for themselves they are not generous with their thoughts, and so no one else is any the wiser for what may be whirling around their brain pans. Winning a pennant by sheer brute strength is not as easy as picking cherries from the bottom limb of a stubby tree.[14]

Grantland Rice was one of the Cleveland slugger's greatest admirers — he once re-wrote *Casey at the Bat* with Lajoie in the starring role — but he voiced the frustration of many Clevelanders with the continuing inability of the Naps to win a pennant. The fans were impatient after enduring 25 years of major league ball (with the Spiders in the National League and the Naps in the American) without a championship. That frustration was reflected in the League Park attendance numbers, as fan support in Cleveland was only the sixth-best in the eight-team league, despite the presence of the "king of ballplayers" as star and manager. The Cleveland franchise would have to win a pennant, and win one soon, to retain the allegiance of its fans and avoid the fate of the failed National League Spiders of the previous decade.

16

"Just One of Those Things"

Did you ever watch Lajoie's eyes as he talked to you? They are sharp, piercing, dark eyes, always restless. His gaze may be centered upon you and yet you seem to feel that he can see at each side of you—maybe in back. As he talks, those eyes shoot over and around you, then through you.—Detroit News, 1907[1]

Napoleon Lajoie had made a remarkable transformation by the beginning of the 1907 season, his 12th in major league baseball and sixth with the Cleveland Naps. When he joined the Philadelphia Phillies as a rookie in August of 1896, he had seen nothing of the world outside of New England. He fell in with the hard-drinking contingent of Phillies and, despite his outstanding play on the field, found enough trouble off it that team management was obliged to put a temperance clause in his contract every year. He had even crippled the Phillies' pennant chances in 1900 by engaging in a clubhouse fight with teammate Elmer Flick. Now, seven years after that embarrassing episode, Lajoie was not only "the greatest natural hitter in the world,"[2] as Athletics pitcher Jack Coombs described him, but was also the manager of the team that took its nickname from him. Few would have regarded the moody and unpredictable younger Lajoie as managerial material, but now he ranked with such respected baseball leaders as Connie Mack and John McGraw. There were only 16 managerial positions in major league baseball, and Cleveland ownership had entrusted Napoleon Lajoie with one of those coveted slots.

Now that Lajoie was married (a "benedict," as the newspapers of the time put it), life in a rooming house near the ballpark came to an end. He and Myrtle found a small farm in South Euclid, about ten miles east of League Park, and moved there during the early months of 1907. There, the couple kept a flock of chickens and raised dogs. The ballplayer had always loved dogs, the larger the better, and a farm was the perfect place to keep them.

The early days of spring training were usually quiet, even sleepy affairs, but a controversy erupted in the Detroit camp at Augusta, Georgia. A young outfielder named Ty Cobb had joined the Tigers in August of 1905, and showed enough promise to stick with the team in 1906, when he was still only 19 years old. Cobb, a Georgia native, had blossomed as a hitter, batting .320 during his first full major league season, but his contentious relationships with his teammates had made him a virtual pariah in the Detroit clubhouse. High-strung, mercurial, and quick to take offense, Cobb had fought several of his teammates during the 1906 season, and distrusted them so intensely that he took to sleeping with a loaded pistol. In

August of 1906, Cobb left the lineup with what the team called "stomach problems," though other sources insist that the troubled young outfielder had suffered a nervous breakdown.

On the first day of spring practice in 1907, Cobb took offense to a greeting from an African-American groundskeeper at the Augusta ballpark, then slapped and choked both the man and the man's wife, who tried to intervene. Soon after, Cobb engaged in an ugly brawl with catcher Charley Schmidt, who upbraided him for hitting a woman. This scene was enough for Hugh Jennings, the former Baltimore Orioles shortstop who had recently been hired as manager of the Tigers. That evening, Jennings sent a telegram to Cleveland manager Napoleon Lajoie, whose Naps had begun spring practice at Macon, Georgia, 100 miles west of Augusta. In the telegram, Jennings proposed to trade the 20-year-old Cobb for the 31-year-old Elmer Flick.

Flick, the best hitter on the Cleveland team after Lajoie, was not present in camp at Macon. He was staging another of his annual holdouts, which irritated team owners John Kilfoyl and Charles Somers no end but had always been resolved peacefully in the past. Lajoie considered the offer, but the Naps played 22 games against the Tigers each year, and he had heard all the stories of rancor and infighting that had come out of Detroit with dismaying regularity during the 1906 season. The offer was tempting, but Lajoie and Somers were in no hurry. They let a day or two go by without an answer as they contemplated the situation.

Jennings may have been eager to get rid of Cobb, but team ownership was not. On March 18, 1907, Tigers owner Frank Navin wrote a letter to Jennings in which he cautioned against trading Cobb for Flick. "It seems hard to think that such a mere boy as Cobb can make so much disturbance," wrote Navin. "On last year's form, he has a chance to be one of the grandest ballplayers in the country. He has everything in his favor. It would not surprise me at all to see him lead the league this year in hitting and he has a chance to play for 15 years yet." Besides, Elmer Flick was too independent for Navin's taste. "Flick is a dangerous man to bother with," the Detroit owner wrote, "for the reason that he has about all the money he cares for, does not care about playing ball, except as a means of livelihood, and is liable to quit on you at any time, besides being a great deal older than Cobb."[3]

After discussing the matter for a day or two, Somers and Lajoie turned down the deal. "We'll keep Flick," Somers told Jennings, as reported by Cleveland sportswriter Franklin Lewis. "Maybe he isn't quite as good a batter as Cobb, but he's much nicer to have on the team."[4] Lajoie suggested a trade of outfielder Bunk Congalton, a .320 hitter in 1906, for Cobb, but Jennings rejected the offer, and although at least three other teams made bids for the young outfielder, Cobb remained with the Tigers for the next 20 seasons. The Georgian played his last major league game in 1928, a dozen years after Lajoie retired and 18 years after Flick's final game.

Elmer Flick could also be a difficult character, and a few weeks before the proposed trade for Cobb hit the papers, Flick had made noises about quitting the game and retiring to his farm near Bedford, Ohio. He was tired of the travel and of being away from his family during the summer. He, like Lajoie, had managed his money carefully, and although he was still one of the American League's best hitters and was only 31 years old, he knew that his career would not last forever. Flick said to Cleveland writer Ed Bang,

> I do not believe in hanging on to baseball until I am played out and a back number before taking up some other business. They all tell me that I am good for several years yet in baseball. That may be true, but why wait until I am too slow and too ancient? Why not quit when I am still rated a capable player? ... I feel that I would not be leaving the Cleveland club in

the lurch if I quit the team now, for they have four good men in Birmingham, Bay, Congalton and Hinchman, and I might not be missed.[5]

Lajoie wanted to be sure that his pitchers were ready to start the season, so he borrowed a page from Connie Mack's managerial textbook and sent four of his starters — Hess, Bernhard, Moore, and Rhoads — to spring training in Hot Springs, Arkansas, a week before the other Naps were due to report to Macon. This strategy worked, as the pitchers performed well during the early weeks of the 1907 campaign, though the hitters, Lajoie included, fell into a funk. The Cleveland offense sputtered, and the Naps failed to reach the .500 mark until a 7–5 win at Chicago on May 8 left them with a 10–10 record. "I know our work on the bases and in the field has been punk," said the Cleveland manager to the local reporters, "but if we were hitting we wouldn't look half so bad at that. Any club which is clouting the ball and making the runs can pull off a lot of poor work in other departments of the game and get away with it, but when you aren't making any hits or scoring any runs every little slip stands out like a sore thumb."[6]

Manager Lajoie was also called upon to flex his disciplinary muscles. Pete O'Brien, a reserve infielder acquired in a trade with the Browns before spring training, stayed out all night after a game in May and did not show up at the team hotel until the next morning. Lajoie fined the misbehaving player $50 and suspended him indefinitely, sending a message to the other Naps that such shenanigans would not be tolerated. Lajoie was an easygoing manager, as compared to a John McGraw or a George Stallings, but he could be pushed to the limit, and proved that he was not afraid to act. Team ownership supported the manager, and O'Brien, by all accounts, shaped up, though Lajoie traded him to the Senators two months later.

With 15 wins in their next 17 games, all at home, the Naps pushed their way into the thick of the pennant chase, ending the winning streak with a 1–0 win over Detroit in the first game of a Decoration Day doubleheader. The Tigers won the second contest, starting the Naps on a four-game losing skein, but seven wins in their next eight boosted Lajoie's men into second place, one game behind the White Sox. By June the race had narrowed to four teams, with the White Sox leading, Cleveland hanging close, and the Tigers and Athletics a few games behind. On June 24, a 7–5 win at Chicago gave Cleveland the league lead by percentage points over the White Sox, with Detroit six games out and Philadelphia seven back. The Naps were playing their best ball of the season, and though the White Sox regained the top spot a few days later, Cleveland took the lead again by defeating Chicago at League Park on July 3. However, Lajoie's team lost both ends of its Fourth of July doubleheader to the Sox, falling two games back at the traditional midpoint of the season.

Though the Naps mounted a strong challenge for the pennant, the Cleveland fans stood aloof from the team. They had been disappointed so often in the past that they found it difficult to trust the local club, and the Naps, still the leading road attraction in the league, stood sixth in the circuit in home attendance, with only the Senators and Browns drawing fewer fans. The Cleveland players could only marvel at the White Sox, who in late September of 1907 attracted 23,607 fans, the largest crowd in American League history up to that time, to a Sunday game against Lajoie's club.

The Naps were not the only game in town. The city of Cleveland boasted a strong amateur baseball scene, and on the same day that the Naps lost two games against the White Sox on July 4, two local nines, the Brooklyn Athletic Club and the East Side All-Stars, staged a historic contest at Brookdale Park. The game lasted nearly six hours and required

30 innings to complete before a Brooklyn pitcher named O'Leary, who struck out 21 men that day, belted a three-run homer just before dusk to seal a 4–1 win. The game made national headlines as the longest contest, professional or amateur, in baseball annals, and Cleveland fans buzzed about it for weeks, relegating the Naps to the background.

Many observers regarded the Cleveland team as the unluckiest in the game, and on July 10, the Naps received another crippling blow when Napoleon Lajoie was spiked by Boston's Bob Unglaub. In the first game of a doubleheader at League Park that afternoon, first baseman George Stovall covered home on a play at the plate and then wheeled around and threw to Lajoie at first in an attempt to catch Unglaub off the bag. As Unglaub lunged back to the base, his spikes tore through Lajoie's left shoe and sliced into his instep, leaving a serious wound and causing a significant loss of blood. Somehow, Lajoie stopped the bleeding and played the second game of the twin bill, but packed the wound in ice after the game and reported to the team physician, Dr. Morrison Castle, for treatment.

Dr. Castle ordered Lajoie to keep the foot iced for two days, but swelling set in and forced the manager to the sidelines. Fortunately, Lajoie did not develop a career-threatening infection, as was the case two years earlier, but the wound was slow to heal. After nearly three weeks of enforced idleness, Lajoie consulted a specialist in Boston when the Naps played a series there during the last week of July. The specialist determined that Unglaub's spikes had damaged several bones in the foot, and that rest was the only treatment. In all, the Cleveland star remained on the sidelines for nearly four weeks, returning to the lineup for a doubleheader in Philadelphia on August 5. The club could not afford to lose Lajoie, as Bill Bradley had come down with a persistent high fever, raising fears that he had contracted typhoid. The third baseman, who had been complaining of fatigue all year, eventually recovered, but left the team in late July and did not return that season.

Another key player who lost significant time was Elmer Flick. Few paid attention when Flick, who was leading the American League in hitting at the time, gave an interview to the *Cleveland Press* in June of 1907 in which he claimed that "playing the game day in and day out [was] ruining his health," that he was "on the verge of physical collapse," and that "the time of his retirement [was] not far distant."[7] This time, however, he meant it. He demanded a vacation in mid-season to rebuild his strength, and Lajoie granted the right fielder's wish. Flick left the team in late July and traveled to Mount Clemens, Michigan, the usual recuperation spot for ballplayers in that era. After a week or so at Mount Clemens, Flick returned to his farm in Bedford, while local sportswriters criticized him for enjoying himself at the racetracks in Detroit and Cleveland while his teammates were exerting themselves on the diamond.

Perhaps the other Naps resented Flick's mid-season vacation, because some of the players started to grumble among themselves about their manager and his leadership style. Lajoie, who had faced down one disciplinary problem earlier in the season, was now forced to deal with an unhappy clubhouse, weak fan support, and inconsistent performance on the field. Forceful, demanding leadership did not come naturally to the Cleveland manager. Said Lajoie in an interview a few years later:

> I am, I suppose, what would be called fairly easy to my men. Ball players are generally intelligent people, and it is pretty safe to trust their welfare in their own hands. The player who fails to take care of himself is always the heaviest sufferer, and if he hasn't got interest enough in his own affairs to do this, it is doubtful if the manager can compel him to. When a man is in uniform, of course, he is expected to live up to certain rules, which he does. But after the game is over I believe in allowing a considerable amount of freedom.[8]

An older Lajoie expressed the same sentiments to *The Sporting News* in 1953. "If I had a fault it was probably being too lenient with the players," Lajoie said. "But I always figured that once a player reached the big league, he ought to know enough to go his own way. I treated them as men, not boys."[9]

One familiar incident is often used to illustrate Lajoie's easygoing style of management. In August of 1907, Lajoie moved first baseman George Stovall, mired in a season-long slump, from the third spot in the lineup to the eighth. The move angered the sensitive Stovall, and after brooding about the perceived slight for a while, Stovall confronted his manager in the dining room of the Hotel Aldine in Philadelphia. An argument ensued, and Stovall picked up an oaken chair and hurled it at Lajoie. Pitcher Bob Rhoads deflected the chair in mid-flight, but the heavy piece of furniture struck the manager in the head as it sailed by. Asked by a reporter from *The Sporting News* nearly 50 years later if he punished his attacker, Lajoie answered in the negative. "He's a good player and we need him," reasoned Larry. "That chair episode was just one of those things."[10]

Contemporary newspaper accounts, however, painted a different picture of the event. Ed Bang, the Cleveland correspondent for *Sporting Life*, reported that Lajoie not only suspended his first baseman, but fined him $100 and sent him home to Cleveland to await further developments. On that same day, he suspended reserve outfielder Frank Delahanty, younger brother of the manager's departed Phillies teammate Ed, because his "physical condition was not up to the standard of the athlete,"[11] as Bang delicately described it. Stovall was still angry a day later, and declared, "I will never submit to a fine. Rather than pay the money I will quit baseball. So far as the incident in Philadelphia in which I had a row with Manager Lajoie goes, I am done. All overtures must now come from the other side." Such defiance boded ill for the first baseman's continued employment with the Naps, and the *Pittsburgh Press* spoke for many when it stated, "It is improbable that Stovall will ever again appear in a Cleveland uniform."[12]

Both Stovall and Delahanty cooled their heels in Cleveland, where Stovall settled down and perhaps perceived the situation with a clearer head. The controversy blew over, and after nearly two weeks on the sidelines, both players were allowed to rejoin the club. Lajoie's memory, nearly half a century later, proved faulty, as no major league field leader, in that era or any other, would have kept his position for very long had he not meted out severe punishment for such a transgression. Stovall paid his fine and did not rejoin the team until August 15, when he batted eighth in the lineup in a 3–2 loss to the Philadelphia Athletics. However, the story of Lajoie's leniency persists, and his supposed weakness as a disciplinarian became an accepted part of his legacy.

In truth, the fact that Lajoie kept Stovall on the team at all after the incident set him apart from most of his contemporaries. One can only imagine how John McGraw or Frank Chance would have responded to a similar assault by a player. Baseball in that era was a rough sport, populated by tough characters, and fisticuffs between teammates, or between a manager and his charges, occurred on a regular basis. "Many players hated their managers and didn't attempt to conceal their enmity," said Lajoie in an interview years later. "They didn't rush to the boss to complain, though. They were told to settle their differences with the manager or get off the team." Ballplayers, who were strong, strapping young men, often settled disputes with their fists. As Lajoie recalled, "It wasn't uncommon to have a player threaten to crown a waiter with a chair if the steak was too tough or if he had to wait too long before being served."[13]

Stovall, who became the manager of the Naps a few years later, thought little of Lajoie's

This advertisement appeared in Lajoie's 1906 baseball guide (author's collection).

leadership style. In an interview long after the altercation, Stovall said of Lajoie, "He wasn't what I would call a good manager. 'Bout all he'd ever say was 'let's go out and get them so-and-so's today.' He knew he could do his share but it didn't help the younger fellows much." He held no grudges, however, over the chair-throwing incident. "It never amounted to as much as they said," claimed Stovall, who also led the St. Louis Browns for a while after leaving the Naps. "Guess we'd be good friends now if we met."[14]

As a manager, Lajoie was no brilliant strategist or game tactician in the mold of John McGraw or Connie Mack. He had a habit of passing defensive signals to his fielders by wiggling his fingers behind his back, and his sign system, such as it was, was easily deciphered by opposing players and managers. He was also not much interested in the teaching aspect of the job. "You can't win in the major leagues unless you have players who know the game," he said to Cleveland writer Franklin Lewis. "We don't have time to teach and train youngsters up here. We're here to win pennants, not run schools."[15] It appears that his idea of managing involved nothing more complicated than setting an example and expecting the other Naps to follow it.

Lajoie's hands-off policy extended to the pitching staff. He had disliked micromanagers such as George Stallings in Philadelphia and Bill Armour in Cleveland, who called most of the pitches from the bench, so he left his hurlers to figure things out for themselves. In later years, he told how Heinie Berger, a right-hander who joined the team in 1907, once loaded the bases against Detroit with the dangerous Sam Crawford advancing to the plate. Berger turned around and looked pleadingly at Lajoie, who ignored him. Finally, Berger called to his manager, "What do I do now?"

Larry replied in an irritated voice, "You filled 'em up without any help from me and you can unload 'em the same way. Get in there and get to work on him and quit looking around at me. I'm not a pitcher."[16]

Like many great players who tried their hand at managing, Napoleon Lajoie found it difficult to lead players who possessed only a fraction of his talent. As New York writer Tom Meany put it, "The great player-artist rather disdained the subtleties of the game and responsibility sat heavily upon him. He failed to lift up lesser players to the batting and fielding heights that he had attained so easily. He knew how to do a thing, but to impart to another how it should be done eluded him."[17]

Indeed, the impatient Cleveland fans, though they still regarded Lajoie as their favorite player, began to flood the mails with suggestions that the namesake of the team should be replaced as manager. "Poor Lajoie!" remarked Ed Bang, one of Larry's staunchest supporters. "While cripples, bad luck, quitters and weight-throwers are doing all they can to make his every-day life a busy joy, the Cleveland critics have sprung demands in chorus that he resign. Dodging insults on the field, roasts in the papers and chairs in the clubhouse, he has about as vivid an existence as anybody we can think of offhand."[18]

The Naps had problems with misbehavior and drunkenness in the ranks, as did virtually every team in that era. However, the Cleveland club's struggles in 1907 were caused by offensive ineptitude, ill-timed injuries, and uncertain pitching. Though Addie Joss enjoyed his finest season, Otto Hess, the Swiss-born left-hander who won 20 games in 1906, fell to a 6–6 mark and left a void in the rotation that neither Walter Clarkson nor Jake Thielmann could fill. The sore-armed Hess made four appearances for the Naps in 1908, all in relief, before returning to the minors. He never pitched again for Cleveland, though he resurfaced with Boston in the National League a few years later, and his absence deprived the Naps of their only reliable left-handed starter.

Wednesday, September 5, was "Lajoie Day" at League Park, and a large crowd gathered to watch the Naps take on the Tigers and to celebrate Lajoie's 32nd birthday (although everyone assumed it was his 31st, because all contemporary sources cited 1875, not 1874, as his birth year). Before the game, the fans presented him with a portable wooden wine chest called a cellarette, along with "a large library, a floral horseshoe, a big Napoleon hat in flowers, a purse, and a small brown sheep."[19] The animal was intended to be a mascot for Lajoie and perhaps for the team, and because he and his wife lived on a farm outside Cleveland, people figured that the sheep would make a home with its new owner. However, he had other plans for the creature, and two weeks later *Sporting Life* reported that it "is now being served in roasts and chops a la mint sauce. Lajoie regarded it as a 'hoodoo.'"[20]

After the ceremony, Addie Joss put on one of the greatest performances of his career, shutting out the Tigers 3–0 on one hit. The only safety made by the Tigers that day was a single by pitcher Ed Killian, and except for one walk, no other Detroit batter reached first base. This victory propelled Cleveland into a virtual tie for third place with the White Sox and left them only two games behind the first-place Athletics and the runner-up Tigers. The Naps would get no closer to the lead, as three losses in their next three games, to the Tigers and Browns, dropped Cleveland back to fourth, where they stayed for the remainder of the season.

Lajoie was not yet ready to give up, although the Naps would have to climb over the Athletics, Tigers, and White Sox to win the flag. "Hope is a long way from being dead in my mind," he told a reporter for the *Washington Times* in early September. "My players feel the same way about it. We can and must win the pennant this year, an honor we have been cheated out of several times by most unfortunate accidents. If bad luck does not come to us at this stage of the contest, as it is coming to all the others, we will win. Not only are we playing the best ball of the four first teams but the other three are weakening beyond hope at this critical stage. We are intact and capable of putting in our very best on the field in every game."[21]

Cleveland's most important series of the season, and their wildest, was a five-game set played at Detroit during the second week of September. On September 11, Addie Joss held the Tigers to five hits in a 3–0 shutout on a rainy, muddy afternoon. This game set the stage for a doubleheader the next day which drew more than 10,000 fans, the largest weekday crowd ever gathered in Detroit. A mixture of excitement and danger filled the air, especially after a spectator collapsed and was carried onto the field, where he died on the outfield grass, delaying the game for a time. A few innings later, a section of the center field stands collapsed and dashed about 50 fans to the ground, though no serious injuries resulted. Despite all the distractions, Tigers right-hander "Wild Bill" Donovan gave up only two Cleveland hits, winning by a 2–0 score in ten innings. In the second contest, Lajoie drove out two singles and a double, but the Naps scored only twice, and the game was called due to darkness after eight innings with the score tied at two.

On the following afternoon, with two more games on tap, about 4,700 people saw the Naps win the opener by a 4–1 score. Because the first contest lasted so long, the two teams agreed to a time limit for the second game, and with Addie Joss on the mound, the Naps looked forward to sweeping the doubleheader. However, Detroit scored three times in the first inning and added four more runs in the third for a 7–0 lead. With the time limit approaching, Lajoie ordered his players to stall. The Naps allowed the Tigers to steal bases at will, let fly balls drop in the outfield, and repeatedly stopped the action to adjust their equipment and tie their shoes. The game became a farce, and the angry Detroit crowd

Right-handed pitcher Addie Joss (author's collection).

seemed poised to storm the field as the sun sank on the horizon. Somehow, the Tigers managed to make enough outs to complete an official game, and won the contest by a 10–0 score in six innings.

League president Ban Johnson took a dim view of Lajoie's unusual strategy. After receiving reports on the contest from the umpires, Tim Hurst and Tommy Connolly, he levied a $300 fine on the Naps. Charles Somers, upset that Johnson failed to get the Cleveland side of the story (and ignored the fact that Detroit had employed similar stalling tactics against Cleveland several weeks before), appealed the fine to the National Commission. Johnson lost his temper and, on Saturday, September 30, sent a telegram to the Naps in which he threatened to suspend Lajoie indefinitely unless the Naps paid the fine within 24 hours.

Some claimed that Frank Navin, owner of the Tigers, had convinced Johnson to take a hard line, but if that was true, Navin put his team's pennant chances in jeopardy. Cleveland was out of the race, leaving Detroit, Philadelphia, and Chicago to slug it out during the last week of the season. The Naps had five games left — two against the Athletics and three against the White Sox — and if Johnson suspended Lajoie, Detroit's two main challengers would have a much easier time of it, especially since Terry Turner was out of the lineup with an injury. To avoid an unnecessary controversy, Somers paid the $300 and kept his second baseman and manager in good standing with the league. A few weeks later, the National Commission dealt Johnson an embarrassing defeat when it overturned the fine and returned the money to Somers.

In the end, Detroit, with young Ty Cobb winning the batting title, won its first American League pennant, with the Athletics one and a half games back, the White Sox five and a half out, and the Naps eight games off the pace. Philadelphia fans, and manager Connie Mack, protested the outcome bitterly, mostly because a controversial umpiring decision on September 30 prevented the Athletics from winning a 17-inning marathon against Detroit that ended in a tie. The two teams were supposed to play a doubleheader that day, but the tie game lasted so long that the second contest could not be started, and the Tigers left Philadelphia with a lead that they would not relinquish. Teams were not then required to make up tied games and rainouts, and at season's end Detroit (92–58) had played five more contests than Mack's club (88–57). Had those five games been played, or even if only the tied contest and the canceled second game of September 30 were completed, the Athletics might have caught the Tigers from behind. As it was, the Detroit club went on to face the Chicago Cubs in the World Series, while the Athletics could only dream of next year.

Cleveland fans were disappointed with a fourth-place finish, though some of the players performed well. Addie Joss, at 27–11, compiled his best season and won 20 games for the third year in a row. Right fielder Elmer Flick batted .302, a fine average in a pitching-dominant year, and led the league in triples for the third season in a row, though he finished the campaign in a 7-for-63 slump. However, the other two outfielders, Bill Hinchman and Joe Birmingham, hit .228 and .235 respectively. First sacker George Stovall (.236) and third baseman Bill Bradley (.223) also underperformed at the bat, while several of the bench-sitters (Harry Bay among them) failed to reach the .200 mark. Lajoie, perhaps weighted down by his managerial responsibilities, batted .299 with a slugging percentage of .393, setting new career lows in both categories.

The Naps finished 16 games above the .500 mark, a respectable showing, though they boosted their record by beating the second-division doormats on a regular basis. Still, the club had reason for optimism entering the 1908 season. The Cleveland club had split its 22 games with the pennant-winning Tigers in 1907, and despite Lajoie's long absence and the lack of a left-handed starter, Lajoie's charges had finished only eight games out of the lead. No one expected the Naps to hit as poorly again, and if even a few of the Naps improved at the bat in 1908, the club expected to climb in the standings and challenge for its first American League pennant.

17

Half a Game Out

Of course I want to win the pennant, more on account of the boys than myself.
I have met with disappointments galore in my time and suppose I could stand
another, but the boys are playing their heads off to win and it would be a sore
disappointment for them to miss landing the flag. It means a handsome sum
of money to each of us if we get in the world's series, and, of course, that is a
big consideration. — Napoleon Lajoie, September 28, 1908[1]

When Napoleon Lajoie joined the Phillies in 1896, batting averages were at their highest level in baseball history. Entire teams, pitchers included, hit over .300 for the season, and an average of well over .400 was usually required to win a batting title. Twelve years later, as the 1908 campaign dawned, pitchers dominated the game, as averages plummeted and runs scored per contest fell to record low levels. Lajoie's .378 average in 1899 was only the fifth highest in the National League, but his .299 mark in 1907 was good enough for sixth place in the American. Though the fans loved hitting, the more of it the better, baseball became a defensively oriented game during the first decade of the twentieth century.

The foul strike rule, adopted by the National League in 1901 and by the American two years later, played a part in the game's offensive decline, but the introduction of the spitball accelerated the trend. The wet pitch, which may have been developed by a journeyman National Leaguer named Elmer Stricklett, became a pitching fad during the middle of the century's first decade. In 1904 Jack Chesbro, a New York Highlanders right-hander who learned the sharp-breaking spitball from Stricklett, used the delivery to win 41 games and boost a mediocre team to within one game of the pennant almost single-handedly. Other pitchers copied the secret to Chesbro's stunning success, and by 1908 the spitball had made life miserable for batters, especially in the American League. Ed Walsh of the White Sox won 40 games in 1908 with a spitter that Detroit slugger Sam Crawford described as nearly unhittable. "I think that ball disintegrated on the way to the plate," said Crawford to interviewer Lawrence Ritter, "and the catcher put it back together again. I swear, when it went past the plate, it was just the spit went by."[2]

In early 1908, Larry Lajoie was asked about the general decline in hitting and his own dearth of home runs (he had hit only two in 1907 and none at all in 1906).

Why don't I make so many home runs as formerly? I guess the foul strike rule and spit ball are to blame. Nowadays you have to pay more attention to hitting the ball and placing it in fair territory than to putting all your weight into the swing. If you swing your head off on a spit ball, you would look mighty cheap. Then, again, you have got to try to keep from hitting the ball foul. Foul strikes hurt, you know. Those may not be the reasons, but that is how I figure it out. It may be, however, that the pitchers are getting better and the outfielders play deeper.[3]

Pitchers had also developed new ways to doctor the baseball. They darkened it with grass stains and tobacco juice, carved ridges in its cover, and loosened or broke its seams to make it lopsided. The league magnates, no doubt as a cost-saving measure, had instructed the umpires to keep used baseballs in the game as long as possible, so a sphere's condition deteriorated as a game wore on. Team employees retrieved foul balls from the stands whenever possible and tossed them back into play. Baseballs grew darker and softer as the innings marched by, making the task of the hitter that much more difficult.

Pitchers were not the only ones who altered baseballs. The infielders of Lajoie's day kept supplies of needles and thread in their clubhouses, using them to sew sheets of emery paper into their gloves. It was not unusual to see a small group of ballplayers form their own sewing circle in the clubhouse, working busily at the task of attaching emery paper to their gloves. The infielders used the abrasive sheet to damage the surface of a baseball before allowing their opponents to bat against it. "When a new ball was put into play," recalled an older Lajoie, "the first baseman whistled at the pitcher, who turned around and permitted the catcher's throw to roll out to the shortstop or second baseman. Emery paper and tobacco juice had done a good job on the ball before it was tossed back to the pitcher, who then worked on the seams. It wasn't unusual to have a pitcher scrape the cover of the ball with his spikes to give it grooves and cause it to wobble through the air."[4]

From the 1920s to the mid–1950s, major league ballplayers often left their gloves lying in the field between innings, but Lajoie and his contemporaries were more careful with their equipment. "If you forgot to take your glove in," said Larry, "it meant another sewing job the next day. Opponents ripped out the emery paper if they found a glove lying on the field."[5]

Such gamesmanship by pitchers and fielders was legal under the rules of the time, and though many observers expressed their opposition to these activities, the magnates and league presidents took no steps to curtail them. As a result, hitting became more difficult with each passing year. In 1905, Elmer Flick won the American League batting championship with a mark of .308, while Detroit's Ty Cobb took the crown three years later with a .324 average. Napoleon Lajoie's percentage dipped below the .300 mark for the first time in his career in 1907, and though his raw numbers made it appear that he slumped at the bat, he finished sixth in the batting race.

When the Naps gathered at Macon, Georgia, for spring training in March of 1908, Lajoie presented them with a unique plan. He divided the team into two separate units, one captained by himself and the other led by ace pitcher Addie Joss. Lajoie told his charges that the two teams would not cooperate or compare notes; instead, they would devise their own plays to use while playing two five-inning games against each other, one in the morning and one in the afternoon, on most days. Only at the end of camp would the two teams come together and share what they had learned, keeping strategies that worked no matter which team had devised it. In this way, manager Lajoie hoped to keep his men interested and involved during the training period.

Lajoie, as always, auditioned new players during spring training, one of whom was a 23-year-old first baseman named Jake Daubert. Daubert was too raw to displace George Stovall at first, so the Naps sent him to Nashville of the Southern League. Several years later, Daubert became a star in the National League and won two batting titles with the Brooklyn Dodgers. Another young hopeful, a 22-year-old left-handed pitcher from Canada named Jack Graney, made a poor first impression upon his manager. The newcomer was assigned to pitch an early-season batting practice session, and as Graney recalled many years later,

> The fourth batter was the manager, Lajoie, who also played second base. I knew all about him ... every kid in America did.
>
> I was pretty cocky and had a crazy idea I could strike Lajoie out. I wound up, reared back and cut loose with a fastball that was supposed to get past him before he ever saw it. But it didn't. Though Lajoie tried to duck, the ball hit him above the left ear and he went down like a load of bricks. Instead of striking him out, I knocked him out.
>
> That evening I was told Lajoie wanted to see me. I went to his room and found him with an ice bag on his head. I started to tell him I was sorry, but he stopped me. He said, "They tell me the place for wild men is out west. So you're going west, kid, so far west that if you went any farther your hat would float. Here's your railroad ticket."[6]

Graney spent the next two seasons with Portland of the Pacific Coast League, returning to the Naps in 1910 as an outfielder.

The optimism surrounding the team, however, was tempered by the serious illness of Elmer Flick. The Cleveland right fielder had arrived at camp on time, but came down with a gastrointestinal malady that caused him to lose an alarming amount of weight. This was not the usual "train sickness," which doctors often blamed for stomach problems during the first few days of training camp, but something much more troublesome. Flick lost 20 pounds in two weeks and the team physician was alarmed enough by his weakened condition to send him home to Cleveland for further study.

Flick, who was seen as something of a chronic complainer, had often grumbled about hot weather and the rigors of travel. He reportedly staged holdouts almost every spring not because he was dissatisfied with his contract, but because he disliked training in the South, exercising in its humid climate and eating unfamiliar Southern cooking. Few paid attention when Flick, one of the few .300 hitters in the American League at the time, gave an interview to the *Cleveland Press* in June of 1907 in which he claimed that he was "on the verge of physical collapse."[7] The Cleveland right fielder was only 32 years old, and appeared to have several productive seasons ahead of him. Still, he may have given indications of deteriorating health in September of that year. He entered the month near the top of the league in batting with a .329 mark, but finished it with only seven hits in his last 14 games as his season-ending average fell to .302. Now, as his doctors tried to figure out what was wrong with him, it appeared that he would be lost to the team for a few months at least.

When the Naps moved to New Orleans for a series of games in late March, Lajoie's teammates saw another side of their manager. He had always enjoyed New Orleans, and one day he took several Naps on a visit to the French Quarter. There, his charges stood in awe as the manager engaged the French-speaking residents and shopkeepers in animated conversations, not a word of which the players could understand. Lajoie had never lost his ability to speak French; indeed, his aged mother, who still lived on Sayles Street in Woonsocket, had never learned English, so the family home in Rhode Island was still a French-speaking one. Lajoie thoroughly enjoyed himself that day, while his players could only watch him in amazement.

The Naps started the season strongly despite their usual wave of injuries. Lajoie was bothered for weeks by a case of neuralgia that he picked up during spring practice, though he played through it, while Terry Turner displaced a muscle in his right shoulder on April 25 against Detroit and was driven to the bench. Bill Bradley strained his side so severely that the Naps left him behind in Cleveland when the team traveled east for a road trip in May, while Elmer Flick remained at home with his mystery illness. Nonetheless, Addie Joss won eight of his first ten decisions, Bob Rhoads and Glenn Liebhardt offered solid pitching support, and the Naps stayed close to the lead through May. As one of five teams bunched tightly at the top of the standings, the Naps never fell more than two and a half games off the lead during the season's second month. On May 31, a 3–2 loss to the Browns dropped the Naps to fifth place, though they were only a game and a half behind the first-place Tigers. Two days later, after sweeping a single game and a doubleheader in Detroit, the Naps vaulted all the way to first.

They did so despite one major handicap. The Naps had tried for years to develop a left-handed starter, and for a while Otto Hess, who won 20 games in 1906, appeared to be the answer. Hess began to fade in 1907, and in 1908 he pitched in only four games, all in relief, before the Naps gave up on him. Another lefty, rookie Bill Lattimore, made four starts in April but failed to impress, and the wild Canadian, Jack Graney, pitched in two games before going to the minors for more seasoning. No other left-hander pitched an inning for the Naps that year, and other American League teams loaded their lineups with left-handed batters whenever possible when they played the Cleveland club.

As usual, injuries caught up with the Naps. Elmer Flick returned to the team but played in only nine games before dropping out. Terry Turner's bad shoulder kept him mostly out of the lineup until August, and the club suffered a cruel blow in July when Detroit pitcher Ed Willett ran into George Stovall at first base, breaking Stovall's wrist. By midsummer Lajoie was forced to juggle a patchwork lineup, with pitchers playing the outfield on some afternoons. The Naps held fourth place, nine games out, on July 29, and looked to be too far behind to remain a factor in the chase. No other team was able to pull away, however, and when Cleveland won 14 of its next 16 games, they found themselves in third place, only five games behind, by August 17. Reversing the trend of past seasons, the Naps refused to fold, and were still within striking distance of the lead despite their injury troubles. Said the manager to the *Washington Post* in late August, "We have been playing good ball and with a little luck I think we have a chance to get to the top before the season is over."[8]

All the while, Lajoie led by example. Plagued by injuries in previous seasons, Lajoie was healthy enough in 1908 to appear in every scheduled game, the only Nap who did so. His batting average hovered near the .280 mark all season, but 1908 was a pitchers' year, with averages plunging to new depths in both major leagues. In the field, he was never better, setting a new American League record for assists in a season and leading the circuit in putouts, double plays, and fielding percentage. Lajoie, who had never played for a pennant winner during his 13 seasons at the big league level, was determined that this would be the year to break his string of failure.

After beating the league-leading Tigers in Detroit on September 1, the Naps were still in fourth place, but only two and a half games out of first. Five losses in a row at Detroit and Chicago knocked Cleveland for a loop, but Lajoie's men recovered with a doubleheader win over the White Sox on Labor Day, followed by four wins in five games against the Browns. By the time they split a Sunday twin bill at home against Chicago on September 13, the Naps were back in the race to stay, bolstered by the excellent pitching of Addie Joss, Bob Rhoads, and Heinie Berger. The four-team pennant race excited the city of Cleveland, while fans across the country rooted for Lajoie and his Naps to win. "If they do [win the pennant]," said *Sporting Life* in a front-page story, "they deserve extra credit because they have played clean ball. They have not 'baited' the umpire, they have not resorted to the ancient and long since repudiated tricks of the sandlots to gain a point, they have not disgraced themselves by outbursts of profanity on the diamond. They have played a sportsmanlike game. That is why Larry's nine is the most popular ball team, with the possible exception of the Giants, in the land today."[9]

The Naps, who spent the last two weeks of September at home, took advantage of their familiar surroundings, reeling off nine wins in a row as the Cleveland fans responded with an enthusiasm never before seen in the city. On September 17, Addie Joss matched shutout innings with Boston's Cy Young in a game that remained scoreless until the bottom of the ninth when singles by Bill Hinchman, Larry Lajoie, and George Stovall gave the Naps a 1–0 win. The next day, Bob Rhoads pitched a no-hitter, the first in Cleveland's American League history,[10] in a 2–1 win over the Boston Red Sox (formerly called the Americans), and on September 19, a crowd of 15,600 filled League Park and watched the Naps and Red Sox take a 5–5 tie into the bottom of the ninth. When Bill Bradley drove in the winning run with a single, the crowd surged onto the field and carried the third baseman around on their shoulders. Others pounded drums and blew horns, parading around the field for more than half an hour before dispersing. This was the pennant race that the fans had waited for since the days of the National League Spiders.

Three more wins against the New York Highlanders pushed the Naps past the Tigers and White Sox into first place by a game and a half on September 23. The lowly Senators broke Cleveland's winning streak on September 24, when a 20-year-old fastball pitcher named Walter Johnson held the Naps to three hits. Washington, the seventh-place team, handed the Naps another loss the next day, but on Saturday, September 26, a crowd of 16,836 cheered the Naps to a 5–4 come-from-behind win over the Senators that left Cleveland in first by half a game.

Lajoie's team was off the next two days, but Detroit defeated Philadelphia and Washington to grab the top spot by half a game, with Chicago lurking close behind. Because the Browns had fallen back, it was now a three-team fight to the finish. The Naps closed September with three wins against the Athletics, but because Detroit kept winning, October began with the Tigers on top, Cleveland half a game out, and the White Sox one game back. The Naps did not play on October 1, and when the White Sox arrived at League Park for Cleveland's final two home games of the season, the stage was set for the wildest finish of any American League pennant race in history.

On Friday, October 2, 10,598 fans paid their way into League Park to see Addie Joss face off against Ed Walsh, the Chicago spitball expert who had kept the White Sox in the race almost by himself. Though Joss had won 23 games to that point, Walsh was looking for his 40th of the 1908 season. Manager Fielder Jones

Chicago pitcher Ed Walsh, who struck out 15 Naps on October 2, 1908, but lost to Addie Joss' perfect game (author's collection).

had no qualms about putting the "ironman" Walsh on the mound whenever the team needed a win, and the spitballer had won both games of a doubleheader against the Red Sox only three days before, pitching all 18 innings. He was the most, and perhaps the only, dependable pitcher the White Sox owned, and though Walsh had already pitched more than 400 innings that year, the Chicago club would win or lose with him.

Joss and Walsh were both on the top of their form that afternoon. Walsh's famous spitter broke so sharply that catcher Ossee Schreckengost had a hard time catching it, and Schreckengost's troubles led to the game's only run. In the third inning Cleveland's Joe Birmingham singled with no one out, then lit out for second when Walsh attempted to pick him off. First baseman Frank Isbell threw the wet ball wildly, and the sphere hit Birmingham in the back of the head and bounded into the outfield. Birmingham made it to third, aching head and all, and stayed there as Walsh struck out shortstop George Perring and pitcher Joss, who tried and failed to bunt the runner home. Birmingham scored when a spitball to the next batter, Wilbur Good, got past Schreckengost and rolled to the backstop.

Birmingham's single was one of only four hits for the Naps that day (Birmingham had two, Lajoie one, and Perring one). Walsh struck out 15 batters, one short of Rube Waddell's American League record for a nine-inning game, and the movement on his spitball was so unpredictable that one of his deliveries broke Schreckengost's finger in the eighth inning and drove the catcher from the game. Lajoie, who rarely struck out, went down on strikes twice, while Wilbur Good fanned four times. Though Walsh gave many outstanding performances during his Hall of Fame career, he was never more dominant than he was on this day.

Joss, however, was even better, as only two Chicago batters came close to reaching base during the first eight frames. In the top of the third, Freddy Parent hit a sharp grounder to Perring, who made a wild throw to first that Stovall corralled with a diving catch. In the eighth, Lajoie, who made several good stops on balls that might have skipped past a second baseman with less range, knocked down a bad-hop grounder by Patsy Dougherty and recovered to make the play. In all, Joss struck out only three men, but gained 16 outs on ground balls, most of them weakly hit. Lajoie threw out eight batters at first, and Joss retired five.

As the contest wore on, the Cleveland crowd began to cheer both pitchers with roughly equal enthusiasm. The fans realized that the greatest pitching duel in baseball history was unfolding before them, and in the eighth, when Walsh struck out his 15th Cleveland batter, the fans let out a roar that shook the wooden stands of League Park. They immediately hushed themselves, as if prompted by an invisible hand, as Joss took the mound to face the White Sox in the top of the ninth. The Cleveland pitcher had retired the first 24 Chicago batters and needed only three more outs to complete a perfect game.

As Joss threw his warmup pitches, the previously boisterous crowd was so quiet, "a mouse working his way along the grandstand floor would have sounded like a shovel scraping over concrete,"[11] as one reporter described the scene. The tension mounted as Chicago manager Fielder Jones sent Doc White, a good-hitting pitcher, to the plate to bat for Schreckengost's replacement, Al Shaw. White rolled a grounder to Lajoie, who threw to Stovall at first for the out. Jiggs Donahue pinch-hit for Lee Tannehill, and struck out on three pitches. Jones then sent his third pinch-hitter of the inning, John Anderson, in to hit for Walsh.

Anderson, a solidly built, Norwegian-born outfielder in his 14th and final major league season, slashed one of Joss' deliveries down the third base line, but the ball curved foul by a foot or so. He drilled the next pitch on a bounce to third baseman Bill Bradley, who fumbled the ball briefly, but gained control of it and fired to Stovall at first. The throw was low, but Stovall reached far to his left, dug it out of the dirt, and toppled to the ground, landing on top of Anderson, who slid into the bag. Umpire Silk O'Loughlin called Anderson out, and the fourth perfect game in major league history was complete.

Joss was fully aware that he was pitching a perfect game. He told a reporter for the *Cleveland Plain Dealer*,

> About the seventh inning I began to realize that not one of the Sox had reached first base. No one on the bench dared breathe a word to that effect. Had he done so, he would have been chased to the clubhouse. Even I rapped on wood when I thought of it. I did not try for such a record. All I was doing was trying to beat Chicago, for the game meant much to us, and Walsh was pitching the game of his life. I never saw him have so much. In the third inning with Birmingham on third I tried to bunt and actually could not get my bat out in time. In giving credit for my feat that now appears wonderful, don't forget that the boys played grandly behind me, while Larry killed three drives that would have been hits for ordinary second basemen.[12]

Walsh was magnanimous in defeat. He said,

> I am sorry we lost, of course, but seeing that we did have to lose, I am glad that Addie took down a record that goes to so few. It is something to be proud of—keeping a team like Chicago from reaching first base — and I guess way down in my heart I was sort of glad when "Silk" called Anderson out in the ninth. It would have made no difference anyway. Yes, I pitched a fairly good game myself, but [Joss] pitched better. Maybe I did strike out fifteen men, but they got four hits off me and we got none off Joss. I passed a man and Joss passed none. That shows how much better ball he pitched.[13]

Detroit defeated the Browns at home that afternoon, so Joss' gem left the Naps one-half game behind the Tigers, with the White Sox, two and a half games out, facing elimination.

Detroit	88–61	.591
Cleveland	88–62	.587
Chicago	85–63	.574

The Tigers had one more game to play against the Browns on Saturday, October 3, before closing the season with a three-game set against the White Sox in Chicago. Meanwhile, the Naps were scheduled to face Chicago on Saturday before ending their campaign on the road with three contests against St. Louis. Because Detroit and Chicago were due to play each other, Lajoie's men could not count on both clubs to falter. Instead, the Naps realized that their best chance at the pennant lay in winning all four of their remaining games; even then, Detroit would clinch the flag by winning all four of theirs. The Naps could only play their best and pray for Detroit to stumble at least once.

On Saturday, an even bigger, more enthusiastic crowd of 20,709, the largest in Cleveland baseball history, filled League Park to watch the Naps play the White Sox one more time. Lajoie sent Glenn Liebhardt to the mound, while Fielder Jones, who no doubt wished that he could start Ed Walsh in every game, gave the nod to right-hander Frank Smith.

In the most important game of his career so far, Napoleon Lajoie played inconsistent baseball. He belted two doubles off Smith in the early innings, but mishandled a throw from catcher Harry Bemis on a steal attempt in the second, leading to a Sox rally that netted two runs. The Naps scored in the bottom of the second, but the Sox knocked Liebhardt out of the box in the sixth with another tally. Lajoie waved Bob Rhoads in from the bullpen to put out the fire, and although the White Sox did not score again, they entered the seventh with a 3–1 lead. The Naps rallied in the seventh, with George Perring whacking a double to lead off the inning. Pinch-hitter Nig Clarke struck out, but Josh Clarke's infield single sent Perring to third. Clarke raised the pressure on Smith by stealing second, and after Bill Bradley walked to fill the bases, Jones made a pitching change. Smith took a seat on the bench as Ed Walsh, who had already pitched 449 innings that season, took the mound.

Walsh got Bill Hinchman to ground a sharp-breaking spitball to third baseman Lee Tannehill, who threw home to force Perring. There were now two out, the bases were loaded, and the crowd buzzed excitedly as Lajoie dug in at the plate.

Walsh, one of the most analytical pitchers in the game, had an unusual theory on how to pitch to Lajoie. "Now, if the Frenchman had a weakness," said Walsh years later, "it was a fast ball, high and right through the middle. If you pitched inside to him, he'd tear a hand off the third baseman and if you pitched outside he'd knock down the second baseman."[14] He threw two spitters to Lajoie, one inside and one outside, and the Cleveland manager fouled both of them away. Now, with a two-strike count, catcher Billy Sullivan called for another spitter, but Walsh did not respond. Sullivan repeated the signal, but still Walsh refused to acknowledge his request.

"Sully signaled for another spitter, but I just stared at him," said the pitcher. "Then Billy walked out to the box. 'What's the matter?' Bill asked me. 'I'll give him a fast one,' I said, but Billy was dubious. Finally, he agreed." Sullivan returned to his position as Lajoie waited for play to resume. Walsh set himself and delivered a rising fastball, high and over the center of the plate. Lajoie was so surprised by the pitch that he did not attempt to swing at it. "He watched it come over without even an offer," said Walsh. Umpire Silk O'Loughlin called Lajoie out on strikes, and, said Walsh, "Lajoie sort of grinned at me and tossed his bat toward the bench without ever a word." Walsh, who threw a no-hitter three years later and had once struck out 12 men in a World Series game, nonetheless called his strikeout of Lajoie with the bases loaded "the high spot of my baseball days."[15]

Walsh finished the game, preserving the 3–1 victory as the White Sox dealt a blow to Cleveland's pennant hopes. Lajoie's men were not mathematically eliminated yet, but because Detroit defeated the Browns again that afternoon, the Naps found themselves at the end of their rope, one and a half games off the pace with three games left. The Naps could only win the flag by sweeping the final three contests from the Browns and hoping that the White Sox could beat Detroit at least once. The White Sox, despite their win against the Naps, were still two and a half out and needed to win all of their final three games against Detroit to take the title.

Detroit	89–61	.593
Cleveland	88–63	.583
Chicago	86–63	.577

The Naps, with their season hanging in the balance, received a scare on Sunday morning when they arrived in St. Louis for the final three games of the campaign. As the players hurried off the train and hailed cabs to take them to their hotel, Addie Joss, who had pitched so brilliantly two days before, fainted and dropped to the ground. He regained consciousness in about a minute, and though he refused to go to a hospital, speculation abounded that the staff ace was so exhausted that he would not be able to pitch against the Browns.

Bob Rhoads, who had no-hit the Red Sox two weeks before, started for the Naps that Sunday afternoon but was ineffective, giving up two runs in the second inning and one in the third. In the fifth, Lajoie called Heinie Berger out of the bullpen, but Berger was wild. He walked George Stone, and after Tom Jones sacrificed Stone to second, the Cleveland reliever walked Roy Hartzell. After he threw two balls to Danny Hoffman, Lajoie had seen enough. He waved Addie Joss into the game. Joss completed the walk to Hoffman, loading the bases with one out and Dode Criss at the plate.

Joss, showing no ill effects from his fainting spell, induced Criss to pop up to third baseman Bill Bradley and struck out Jimmy Williams on three pitches to end the inning. The Cleveland ace held the Browns at bay the rest of the way, and the Naps chipped away at the lead, scoring one run each in the fifth, sixth, and seventh to tie the contest.

The Naps nearly won the game in the top of the ninth when Joss walked and, with two out, Bradley doubled to the gap, putting runners on second and third. Bill Hinchman then drove a liner past the pitcher's head, but shortstop Bobby Wallace made a one-handed stop and threw to Tom Jones at first as Hinchman streaked for the bag. Joss crossed the plate and Bradley rounded third as the ball and the batter converged at first.

The infield umpire that day was Jack Egan, who had endured several heated arguments with Lajoie and his men that season and was probably the least-liked arbiter in the league, at least by the Cleveland players. Egan had been assigned to the game at the last minute by league president Ban Johnson, who believed that the three-game set in St. Louis was important enough to require the use of two umpires instead of the usual one. Egan set out for the ballpark that morning, but because his train ran late, he did not step onto the field until the third inning. Late-arriving extra umpires did not usually enter a game that was already in progress, but Silk O'Loughlin, who worked the first two frames by himself, was happy for the assistance and welcomed Egan onto the field. Now, in the ninth inning, Egan was called upon to make the most important decision of the game, and perhaps of the season as far as the Naps were concerned.

Taking no chances, first baseman Jones caught Wallace's throw and ran toward home in a bid to keep Bradley from scoring behind Joss. As Bradley slammed on the brakes and scrambled back to third, Egan suddenly thrust his right arm into the air. He called Hinchman out at first, ending the inning and removing Joss' run from the scoreboard. The Cleveland half of the ninth inning was over and, with darkness approaching, the game was still tied at three runs each.

Lajoie and the Naps charged at Egan and raged at his decision, but Egan stood firm in his belief that the throw had beaten Hinchman to the bag by a split second. Egan reportedly told Lajoie that Hinchman had "loafed" on the way to first, an accusation that dogged the outfielder as "Bill Hinchman's Boner" for the rest of his career, though it may or may not have been true. Perhaps Hinchman merely trotted down to first because he did not think Wallace could reach the ball. At any rate, the Cleveland papers were predictably apoplectic in their game reports the next day, with the *Plain Dealer* describing the call in a headline, "Weird Decision on a Play Not Even Close." Though Lajoie stormed and ranted, the argument ended with the contest still tied. Joss retired the Browns in the bottom of the ninth, and the game went into extra innings.

The Naps nearly pulled the game out in the tenth. Lajoie doubled to lead off the inning, and George Stovall followed with a single that sent the manager to third with no one out. Lajoie failed to advance on an infield out by Nig Clarke, and Joe Birmingham popped up for the second out. George Perring then belted a liner to short, but Bobby Wallace caught it to end the threat. Neither team scored again, and as dusk fell, the umpires called the game at the end of the 11th.

The 3–3 tie on Sunday was disappointing for Lajoie and his charges, but at least the White Sox kept Detroit from winning, defeating the Tigers 3–1 behind Doc White. Rather than extend the season one more day, the Naps and Browns agreed to play a make-up contest as part of a Monday doubleheader, with the season ending in a single game on Tuesday as planned.

Addie Joss, after throwing nine innings on Friday and five more on Sunday, was unavailable to pitch, so Lajoie chose Glenn Liebhardt to face veteran right-hander Bill Dinneen of the Browns. Liebhardt, like Bob Rhoads the day before, ran into trouble early, but held the Browns to a single run during the first five frames. Stovall scored for Cleveland in the fourth, and the teams entered the sixth tied at one.

In the bottom of the inning, the Naps fell apart. Danny Hoffman grounded to Lajoie, who made an uncharacteristically wild throw to first that eluded Stovall and rolled to the grandstand. Hoffman reached second on the play, and Dode Criss then sent a blooper down the left field line out of the reach of Bill Hinchman. Some of the local reporters charged afterward that Hinchman, who had been accused of loafing in the critical play at first the day before, failed to hustle after the ball, which bounced near the left field line as Hoffman scored the go-ahead run. Criss rounded second and headed for third as Hinchman finally caught up to the ball and relayed it to Bill Bradley, but Criss avoided Bradley's tag and slid in safely. Criss scored when Jimmy Williams singled, and the Browns led by two runs. Dinneen, who held the Naps to only four hits, completed a 3–1 St. Louis win that eliminated the Naps from the race.

Years later, Napoleon Lajoie still lamented the pennant that got away. "You know what beat us that year?" he told an interviewer in 1953. "A pinch single by a part-timer player for the Browns named Dode Criss. You'd call it a blooper now, a ball that hit off the handle of his bat and went about ten feet over the head of my third baseman and landed fair by one inch on the left field line. If that ball had gone foul, we'd have won the pennant. But that's the way things go in baseball."[16]

Lajoie at home in a photo taken around 1909. He and his wife Myrtle raised chickens on their farm in South Euclid, Ohio (Library of Congress).

The next morning, as the Naps boarded their omnibus to go to the ballpark, the Republican presidential candidate, William Howard Taft, and his campaign team arrived at the hotel. Taft, a baseball fan as well as an Ohioan, greeted the Naps and shook hands with Lajoie and the other players. Lajoie, still smarting from the loss the day before, nonetheless wished Taft well, saying, "I hope you have better luck than we did." Taft smiled and answered, "I hope to win, and I'm sorry that a team from my home state didn't land the pennant. But you did well."[17] Cleveland won its last two games of the season to finish with 90 wins and 64 losses, while the Detroit Tigers, who beat the White Sox on the season's final day to win their second straight flag, played one fewer game than Cleveland and won on percentage points at 90–63. The Tigers had not made up a rainout earlier in the season against the Senators, and because American League teams were not then required to do so, Detroit was able to win by a mere half-game in the closest pennant race in history.

William Howard Taft won his race in November, but Napoleon Lajoie had fallen short once again, this time in agonizing fashion. Injuries to Bill Bradley and Terry Turner, the absence of Elmer Flick, and a bad umpiring decision had all factored into the loss of the pennant. Now Lajoie, at age 34, and the core players of his veteran-laden team were getting older. Joss, Bradley, Flick, and Lajoie had all joined the Cleveland club in 1901 and 1902, and all except Joss were now in their thirties. They were running out of time, and the pressure was on. If Lajoie and his men failed to rebound from the disappointment of 1908 and win the long-desired pennant in 1909, perhaps they never would.

18

Stepping Down

I wouldn't care to say who was the best hitter I ever faced. I never saw Hans Wagner, but I have faced [Rogers] Hornsby, but only in an exhibition game when he wasn't in his best form. No, I am not in a position to judge just how good he is. Undoubtedly he has developed greatly in recent years. I am inclined to believe that the hitter who impressed me most of all those that I have faced was Lajoie. It is hard for me to believe that anybody could be a greater hitter than the Frenchman. — Walter Johnson, 1925[1]

Because Lajoie's batting average had fallen below the .300 mark in two consecutive seasons, some wondered if he, at the age of 34, was on the decline as a hitter. Lajoie himself had remarked upon how the stress and responsibility of managing had a negative effect on the performance of a playing manager, and many observers pointed to his statistics for 1907 and 1908 to find proof of his assertion. On the other hand, the absence of Elmer Flick's big bat in the lineup removed some of his protection in the order, and may have allowed opponents to pitch him tougher. Additionally, the 1908 campaign represented the height of pitcher domination of what later historians called the "Deadball Era," and Lajoie's .289 average in 1908 was not a bad mark when Ty Cobb's .324 was good enough to lead the league. Still, there were a few opposing pitchers who claimed to have diagnosed his weakness at the bat, and were not afraid to trumpet their claims.

One such hurler was Detroit Tigers right-hander George (Spec) Winter, who insisted to a reporter early in 1909 that he had found a fatal flaw in Lajoie's approach to hitting.

The first time I ever pitched against the Cleveland club was at Boston. Now I'd always noticed in my college ball games that when a big fellow came up to the plate and stood straight up with his feet together he had difficulty in hitting a curve ball that broke around his knees. I didn't know what the other fellows had been throwing to Larry, but he seemed to demand the prescription, though the catcher didn't signal it. Larry missed the first two and rolled the third one over to [third baseman Jimmy] Collins.

"My goodness, Spec," Collins said when I came in after the inning was over, "don't ever hand that big fellow a low ball again. He murders it. Just shut your eyes, say a little prayer and shoot one up, fast and high."

"But I got him, didn't I?"

"Yes, but you were mighty lucky."

Well, to cut a long story short, I pitched two games of one series against Cleveland and won both of them. Lajoie didn't get a single safe hit, and, inside of two weeks, all the pitchers on the other teams were pitching him the same thing. He hits it once in a while and, now and then, somebody tries to fool him with something else, but usually wishes he hadn't.[2]

Winter, who had been released in mid-season by Boston after going 4–14 for the Red Sox and finished the 1908 campaign with a 1–5 log for Detroit, might not have been the most convincing witness, but word around the league was that, for the first time, American League hurlers might have found a way to muzzle the mighty Lajoie.

The loss of the 1908 pennant by a mere half-game gnawed at Napoleon Lajoie for the rest of his life. He had always dreamed of leading his team into the World Series, and by 1909, with batting titles and other personal honors galore to his credit, the World Series was the sole remaining goal of his career. The lack of a pennant was a gaping hole on his baseball resume, especially because Pittsburgh shortstop Honus Wagner, Lajoie's main rival for "best player in the game" honors, had led his Pirates to three National League pennants (and would win his fourth in 1909) while Lajoie tried, and failed, to win his first. Detroit's budding superstar Ty Cobb, a dozen years Lajoie's junior, had already appeared in two Series and would play in yet another that season. Though Lajoie was still the most popular player in the American League, Cleveland's repeated pennant failures threatened Lajoie's status as "King of Ballplayers" with Wagner and now Cobb making strong cases for that unofficial title.

Though the mysterious illness of Elmer Flick may have been the biggest factor in Cleveland's failed bid for the flag, Lajoie, many years later, told sportswriter Tom Meany that a recently married player may have caused the loss of the pennant that year. Said Larry,

> It may have been my fault Cleveland lost the flag in 1908. I fear I may have been too strict with Nig Clarke.... Well, late in August of 1908 [Clarke] got the idea that he ought to take a run home and see his new bride. I refused permission. Clarke sulked, then picked up his glove when I told him to work with [Addie] Joss.
>
> Darned if he didn't deliberately stick his right forefinger into one of Addie's fast ones. He came back to the bench bleeding, and the bone could be seen peeking through the flesh of his shattered finger. He stuck his hand out toward me and said, "Well, I guess I can go home now, can't I?"[3]

At Cleveland's spring training camp in Mobile, Alabama, 11 pitchers battled for eight spots on the roster. A lack of pitching depth had hindered the Naps in their fight for the pennant the year before, so Lajoie, determined to develop some of these raw talents into reliable major leaguers, hired Jim "Deacon" McGuire, the former manager of the Boston Red Sox, as a coach. McGuire had caught in the majors for more than 20 years and owned a reputation as a pitching expert, and Lajoie was happy to allow McGuire to act as an assistant manager during camp.

The most important addition to the Cleveland pitching staff for the 1909 season was Cy Young, who had already won more games than any pitcher in the history of baseball. Young was the oldest pitcher in the game in 1908, but had pitched 299 innings for the Red Sox, winning 21 games and posting a 1.26 earned run average for a sub–.500 team. At season's end the Red Sox, perhaps in a cost-cutting move, decided that the aging legend was past his prime and sent him to the Naps for $12,500 and two younger hurlers, Charlie Chech and Jack Ryan. Neither Chech nor Ryan lasted long with the Red Sox, and the deal appeared to be a steal for the Naps. Lajoie, who had faced Young dozens, if not hundreds, of times in both the National and American leagues, was impressed that the pitcher could still perform so well at his age. On March 29, the occasion of Young's 42nd birthday, Lajoie said that he would like to play as long as Young. "If I can stick till I'm forty-two I will be satisfied," he said. "I have been in baseball for some time and can see no reason why I should not remain."[4]

The Naps had tried to work out a deal with the Red Sox for Lou Criger, a 37-year-old veteran who had served as Cy Young's personal catcher for the previous 13 seasons on three different teams, but the Boston club sent Criger to the St. Louis Browns instead. The Naps then picked up catcher Ted Easterly, a rookie from the Pacific Coast League. Aside from the additions of Easterly and Young, the Naps entered the 1909 season with virtually the same ballclub that had lost the flag by a paper-thin margin the year before. For this reason, many national columnists hailed the Naps as the pre-season favorites to win the 1909 pennant.

Lajoie arrived in camp about ten pounds heavier than his usual playing weight, but he was not concerned. He declared that he was running and hitting as well as ever, and that the extra poundage would keep him from wearing down as

Cy Young, baseball's winningest pitcher, joined the Naps in 1909 (author's collection).

the season progressed. Elmer Flick, who played in only nine games in 1908, insisted that he was finally healthy, though he needed to rebuild his strength. Onlookers stated that Flick could run from home to first as speedily as ever, but became winded if he had to run out a double or triple. Within a week or so, Flick's weight dropped from 170 pounds to 155, and he returned to Cleveland for more consultations with his doctors. On a positive note, Terry Turner appeared to be recovered from a serious beaning the previous August, and he, too, was expected to resume his normal workload after appearing in only 60 games the year before.

Once again, the Naps broke camp and headed north without any left-handed pitchers on their roster, a weakness that other teams had learned to exploit since the decline and release of Otto Hess. The Naps opened their 1909 season on April 14 in St. Louis, defeating the Browns behind Addie Joss, and followed with another win the next day as Cy Young pitched a 4–3 victory. Three losses in a row, to the Browns and Tigers, followed, but a 12–2 win in Detroit on April 20 evened their record at 3–3. The Cleveland home opener on April 22 drew more than 9,000 fans, who went home disappointed as the Browns roughed up the Naps by a 6–4 score.

Pitching, which was expected to be a strength for the Cleveland ballclub, failed to live up to expectations. Lajoie had declared that he would work his two star hurlers, Joss and Young, every five days instead of the usual four, but the remaining starters failed to pick up the slack. Heinie Berger fought to reach the .500 mark, while Bob Rhoads and newcomer Fred "Cy" Falkenberg alternated strong performances with poor ones. The fast start that the Naps hoped for did not materialize, and at the end of April the Naps held seventh place with a 4–8 record. The Naps were playing so poorly at the time that they rejoiced when an entire three-game series in Chicago against the streaking White Sox was washed out by rain.

The annual rash of injuries started earlier than usual for the Naps in 1909. On April 17, in the fourth game of the season, the Naps caught Detroit's Ty Cobb off third base on a botched squeeze play. Catcher Nig Clarke threw to third baseman Bill Bradley in time to retire Cobb, but the Detroit star kicked at Bradley's glove with his spikes and knocked the ball free. He also slashed Bradley's thumb open, putting the talented but fragile third sacker out of the lineup for several weeks. Clarke had to be restrained from attacking Cobb on the field, and the incident would be remembered by Cleveland players and fans for years afterward. On May 2, in a Sunday afternoon game at St. Louis, Jimmy Stephens of the Browns slid into second base on a force play and spiked shortstop Terry Turner, cutting the Cleveland infielder's ankle to the bone and forcing him to the sidelines for nearly a month. The loss of Turner and Bradley exposed the lack of depth on the Cleveland roster.

The three-day rest due to rain late April was good for the Naps, and the team rebounded with four wins in six games against the White Sox in early May, bringing their record to within one game of the break-even point. The Naps then lost six in a row at home to the Red Sox and Highlanders, a disastrous skid that soured the fans on the ballclub after the high expectations of the preseason. One of the games against Boston drew only 1,089 fans to League Park, and none of the weekday contests in mid–May drew as many as 3,000 people. Lajoie frantically shuffled his lineup as the losses mounted, and the team began to recover after he placed outfielder Bris Lord in the cleanup spot and dropped himself to fifth. This lineup clicked with four wins in six games against the Senators and Athletics, though the Naps were still mired in seventh place at the end of their May homestand. Still, they were only seven games behind the league-leading Tigers, and with Bradley and Turner restored to the lineup, the Naps appeared poised to climb the standings. Elmer Flick also reported to the club in late May, looking healthy and eager to play.

Despite the fact that the season was barely a month old, the Cleveland papers were full of criticism for the Naps and their manager. Ed Bang of the *Cleveland Press* was particularly harsh, and on May 17, during the Naps' six-game skid, Bang penned a column for *Sporting Life* under the title, "Cheerless Cleveland." Wrote Bang, "Never since the days of the old Cleveland Misfits [the horrid 1899 Spiders] has a team proved such a disappointment to the fans as the Naps of 1909. The great finish of the Larrupers in 1908 put the fans on the edge of expectancy for still greater things this year. It's no wonder that they dreamed of their idols comfortably situated in first or second place when one takes into consideration the amount of money expended to strengthen the team."[5] Other papers expressed similar sentiments, and though Lajoie's batting was much improved over the previous two seasons (his average stayed steady around the .330 mark), the Naps could not help but feel the waves of negativity from the fans and the press.

A 13–2 streak in June boosted the Naps into third place and relieved the pressure for a while, but on June 23, another ill-timed injury to Napoleon Lajoie put a damper on Cleveland's pennant chances. Lajoie, playing first base in place of the injured George Stovall, reached across the bag for a throw from the infield when baserunner Patsy Dougherty of the White Sox collided with him. Dougherty ran into Lajoie's outstretched arm and gave the Cleveland manager a sprained wrist and an injured hand. The wrist injury swelled up so painfully that, two days later, Lajoie's doctor was obliged to perform a surgical procedure to drain fluid from the joint. Lajoie, whose batting average placed him near the top of the league, was knocked out of the lineup for nearly a month. He directed his injury-riddled team from the bench, his hand and wrist encased in bandages.

While the Naps fought to stay in the pennant race, Charles Somers had instructed two Cleveland scouts, Tom O'Brien and Deacon McGuire, to search the nation for pitching, particularly of the left-handed variety. They started their tour of the country in the South, where they signed left-hander Harry Otis from Goldsboro of the Eastern Carolina League and right-hander Red Booles from Shreveport of the Southern League. In Texas, they were impressed by left-hander Willie Mitchell of San Antonio, who had recently struck out 20 Galveston batters in a nine-inning game. McGuire and O'Brien bought Mitchell's contract, then traveled to the West Coast and uncovered several more likely candidates, including Vean Gregg, a 21-year-old pitcher with Spokane of the Pacific Coast League. Gregg, who found later success with the Naps, was due to arrive in Cleveland in 1910, but Mitchell, Otis, and Booles reported to the Naps in mid-season of 1909. Mitchell, who was only 19 years old, was worth keeping, but neither Booles nor Otis made much of an impression, and both were gone by the start of the following season.

Despite Lajoie's absence, the Naps made a charge in early July, winning 12 of 13 during a homestand to claim fourth place and move close enough to threaten the league-leading Tigers. After the Naps took three of four from the second-place Athletics in Cleveland, Connie Mack told the local papers, "We don't fear Detroit. We have had it on the Tigers all season and can't understand their high position in the race. The Naps have been the thorn in our sides. We fear Lajoie's team more than any other. If we don't win the flag, I believe the Naps will."[6] On July 15, the Naps were virtually tied with the Red Sox for third position, with both teams five games out. The Athletics were only a game and a half ahead of the Naps, and if the Cleveland club could stay close to the leaders, the return of Lajoie might provide the boost it needed to pass the teams ahead of it.

That was the high point of the 1909 season for the Cleveland ballclub, as mounting injuries drove the Naps out of contention. Addie Joss, with an 11–3 record in mid–July, complained of back pain and won only three of his remaining 13 decisions, while Elmer Flick's recurring illness restricted the once fearsome hitter to 66 games and a .255 average. Cy Young pitched well for a 42-year-old man, winning 19 games to lead the pitching staff, but he could not carry the rest of the team on his aging shoulders. The fans stayed away from League Park as the Naps, so close to a pennant in 1908, faded in the heat of late July and early August.

The most memorable play of the campaign occurred on July 19 at League Park. In the first game of a doubleheader against the Red Sox, Boston's Heinie Wagner led off the second inning with a single. Jake Stahl then beat out a bunt, moving Wagner to second and bringing Amby McConnell to the plate. McConnell drilled a liner past pitcher Cy Young's head. George Perring, substituting for Lajoie at second base, was too far away to catch the ball, but shortstop Neal Ball leaped for it.

In an interview, Ball explained what happened next. "It was on the rise," said Ball, "and I didn't think I had any chance of getting it. But I gave it a try, and there was the ball, traveling over second. I jumped, and sure enough, it stuck in my glove. After that, there was no trouble. Wagner had already rounded third, and all I had to do to get him was step on second. Stahl was racing to second when I caught the ball. He couldn't stop and ran right into my hands. I actually waited for him."

Ball had completed the first unassisted triple play in major league history. The inning was over, but no one besides Ball appeared to realize what had happened. As Ball tossed his glove aside and headed for the dugout, the other Naps remained in their places, and the next Boston hitter approached the plate to take his turn at bat. Not even Cy Young, the 20-year veteran, caught on. Young fixed Ball with a look and asked, "Where are you going, Neal?"

Ball replied, "That's three outs."[7]

There were 11,000 fans in the stands in League Park on that Monday afternoon, and when they finally realized what Ball had accomplished, they let loose with a roar that rivaled the ovation awarded to Addie Joss after the last out of his perfect game nine months before. The contest was delayed by more than 20 minutes as groundskeepers removed hundreds of hats that had been flung onto the field in celebration. When play resumed, Ball gave the crowd another thrill when he lined a drive over Tris Speaker's head in center field and charged around the bases for an inside-the-park home run. Ball, whose nine putouts at the shortstop position that day set a major league record, keyed the Naps to a 6–1 win over the Red Sox.

Neal Ball, a journeyman infielder with a career batting average of .250, enjoyed the game of his life that day. His unassisted triple play made him famous, and most likely prolonged his career, which lasted until 1913. Only 14 other men, all infielders, have performed an unassisted triple play in major league action since Ball turned the trick more than 100 years ago, and his name pops up whenever such a play occurs. The glove Neal Ball used that day is on display at the Baseball Hall of Fame in Cooperstown, New York. Eight days after the famous play, league president Ban Johnson presented Ball with a gold medal, studded with pearls and diamonds, to commemorate the accomplishment during a pregame ceremony at League Park.

Lajoie returned to the lineup on July 21, though his wrist and hand were still sore. He would have stayed out of action longer, but Terry Turner broke a finger on his throwing hand while catching a pop-up against the Athletics, and Bill Bradley, ill with tonsillitis, was confined to his bed at home in Cleveland. George Stovall was back, so Lajoie returned Stovall to first, kept Neal Ball at short, and moved George Perring to third. This patchwork lineup, coupled with pitching woes, boded ill for the Naps, who started losing games and drifted away from the league leaders. Fan enthusiasm, temporarily buoyed by Neal Ball's heroics on July 19, faded quickly, and the Cleveland writers attacked the team and its management with renewed vigor. Fans and writers joked that the team should be called the Napkins, "the way they fold up."[8]

In mid–August, the Naps lost four in a row at Boston, closing out a road swing that saw the club move from eight games over .500 to one game below it. The club played listless and uninspired baseball, and with the Cleveland writers filling their columns with waves of criticism on a daily basis, Larry Lajoie decided that he was tired of the stress and strain of managing. He was becoming increasingly bitter and sarcastic toward his players, attributes that had turned him against George Stallings in Philadelphia so many years before. The Naps were not responding to his leadership, and his dream of managing a pennant winner in Cleveland appeared to be further than ever from fruition. On August 17, 1909, he decided to step down. On that morning, he wrote a letter of resignation and delivered it to team management.

Cleveland, O., August 17, 1909.
The Cleveland Ball Club Co., city.

Gentlemen:

  I herewith tender my resignation as manager, to take effect as soon as you can select someone to take up the duties of the position.

  I feel that my obligations to you, to the public and to the players compel me to take this action at the present time. You have given me liberal support as manager for the last five years, and I feel that if anyone can accomplish more with the club than I have been able to do, you deserve to have an opportunity to take advantage of same.

Lajoie shows his batting form (Transcendental Graphics/theruckerarchive.com).

The Cleveland public has been very loyal to me under many trying circumstances. I feel that any criticism directed toward me in the past or at the present is not due to any personal feeling against me, but has been and is solely because of a conscientious desire to see Cleveland have a winner, and it is natural for them to put the blame on the manager who does not give them one. It has been my desire to manage Cleveland's first pennant winner, but, if someone else can do this more quickly than I can, I feel that it would be a mistake for me to allow my personal ambition to stand in the way, because I want just what the public wants — a winner — and I know that it is much more important that we all get our desire than I should be manager.

Besides my obligation to yourselves and the public as above stated, I feel that it is my duty to the other players on the club to give them relief from the abuse and criticism which is being heaped upon them. Just at present the boys are being subjected to a lot of abuse because of our failure to win, and they are unjustly accused of not trying and being unwilling to play for me. In my heart I feel that the players are being wronged. Not a man on the club has ever refused to do anything I have asked of him. My retirement should certainly put a stop to this criticism of the players, because it will remove the opportunity of charging them with disloyalty.

In conclusion I wish to pledge myself to the patrons of the club, who have always treated me so royally under all circumstances, that I shall work just as hard as a player to give them the winner which they so richly deserve.

I wish to thank you and the public for the loyal support which has been given me during the last five years, and each and every player on the club for the hard and conscientious work he has done under my management.

Very truly yours,
N. LAJOIE.[9]

Charles Somers asked his manager to reconsider, but Larry's mind was made up. "I am glad to be relieved of the worry," he told a reporter for the *Cleveland Press*. "It is a great load off my mind. I want to continue to play on the team, and to do my level best."[10] More than 40 years later, he still regarded his resignation as the right move. "That was all right with me," said Larry in a 1953 interview. "I figured I might continue to make a better record as a player without the worries of managing, which was a thankless job."[11] Indeed, the papers reported that Larry had, on at least two previous occasions that summer, offered to give up his leadership role, only to be talked out of it by the team owners.

Unable to convince Lajoie to delay his resignation until the end of the season, Somers asked him to remain in charge of the team until a replacement was ready to take over. He agreed, and after a week-long flurry of newspaper speculation, Somers appointed Deacon McGuire, the Cleveland coach and scout who had managed the previous two seasons at Boston, to take Lajoie's place. McGuire was then on a scouting mission in California, but hurried eastward when he received news of his appointment. Lajoie voiced no objections to McGuire's elevation, and was the first Nap to publicly pledge his loyalty to the new manager. He did not even mind McGuire's decision to appoint first baseman George Stovall as captain. "It's one more load off my shoulders,"[12] he said.

News of the managerial change seemed to energize the Naps, who swept two home doubleheaders against the Browns in two days after Lajoie's resignation letter became public. However, the Naps fell back to earth, dropping three straight against the Athletics to leave the team at 57–57 for the season. McGuire arrived in Cleveland on Sunday, August 22, and directed the team the next day in a 12–6 loss to Philadelphia, the fourth Cleveland defeat in a row. "With our pitching staff in its present condition we cannot expect to do miracles," cautioned the new manager. "But we'll do the best we can."[13]

Deacon McGuire was a baseball "lifer," an old-time catcher who had started his major league career with Toledo's American Association entry in 1884. Never a star, he was nonetheless a good hitter and a durable performer who played for 11 teams in three major leagues during his long career, one that lasted well into his forties. All of his managerial experience, with Washington in 1898 and Boston in 1907 and 1908, had come with bad teams. The 1909 Naps, despite their mediocre record, possessed more talent than his previous clubs, and McGuire waxed optimistic about the Cleveland team's future prospects.

Lajoie was more than happy to surrender his leadership role, one that had proved more difficult to handle as the years wore on. In later years, Lajoie referred to his decision to take the manager's position in 1905 as the greatest mistake of his baseball career. In a 1941 interview with Eugene J. Whitney of the *Cleveland Plain Dealer*, Lajoie expressed regret that the rigors of managing detracted from his production as a player. "It didn't take long for me to realize my mistake," he said. "I had the job and didn't want it, but I wasn't going to give it up without a fight. With the added responsibility of directing the club, I soon learned that my work at bat and in the field was beginning to suffer. I tried too hard to make up for the team's shortcomings and, as a result, often failed to hit in the pinches and made errors at the wrong time."[14] Indeed, Lajoie batted at nearly a .400 clip in the first 20 games after he surrendered the reins of leadership, boosting his average to .345 in early September.

Still, Lajoie's record as a manager was not a bad one, statistically speaking. Other all-time greats, including Ty Cobb, Walter Johnson, George Sisler, Frank Robinson, and Ted Williams, also served as managers and, like Lajoie, failed to win a pennant. His winning percentage of .550 is the best of all the aforementioned stars (except for Johnson, who also compiled a .550 mark), and only a quirk of the schedule kept him from leading the Naps into the 1908 World Series, which would have added luster to his record. A Series win would have put Lajoie in the company of Rogers Hornsby, Lou Boudreau, and Tris Speaker among field leaders who won championships as playing managers.[15]

The *Cleveland Press*, which had conducted the contest which selected the team nickname six years before, used Lajoie's resignation as another opportunity to stir up reader interest. The paper announced a new contest to determine whether the name Naps should be retained or replaced, and offered a 1910 season pass to the winner of a 100-word essay contest explaining why, or why not, the team appellation should be changed. For a week, readers wrote in with their ideas. One early responder nominated the name Farmers, and another suggested that the team should be called the Bullets, "for that's what it takes to kill the Tigers." Others defended the status quo; as one writer opined, "Nap Lajoie never did anything to bring dishonor to the Naps," and in the end, Lajoie's personal popularity carried the day. The contest winner, a fan named Ben Bomstein, wrote, "No matter whether Larry is manager or player, as long as he is the mighty Lajoie and a member of the Cleveland team, the name Naps should be kept and made a synonym for champions."[16]

Because the Naps had fallen well out of the pennant race by the time Lajoie stepped down as manager, Deacon McGuire spent the last five weeks of the season giving extended playing time to rookies and prospects. As a result, the Naps, after posting a 57–57 mark under Lajoie's leadership, won only 14 of the remaining 39 games for McGuire. The Cleveland ballclub finished the 1909 season in sixth place, 27½ games behind the Tigers, who won their third pennant in a row (and would lose their third consecutive World Series, this time to the Pirates, in October). The city of Cleveland, after 26 seasons of representation in major league baseball, would have to wait at least one more year for its first league champion.

Lajoie slumped during the last two weeks of the 1909 season, but his season-ending average of .324 was the third highest in the league, trailing only Ty Cobb of Detroit and Philadelphia's Eddie Collins in the batting race. Though his tenure as Cleveland's manager was over, he had compiled his best hitting performance in three years and given notice to American League pitchers that he was not yet finished. Now free of the worries of managing and the stream of constant criticism from the newspapers, he was prepared to battle Cobb and Collins, and any other challengers that might arise, for hitting supremacy in 1910.

19

The Great Race

No managers ever worked harder than Lajoie. No manager ever fought more fiercely than he for the supreme laurel crown of the baseball world, the pennant. And yet this elusive banner floated ever just beyond his reach, and try as he would, he could never reach it. He worried over this failure more probably than anyone will ever know. His work suffered in consequence.... Lajoie allowed his own record to become sadly marred solely through a desire to reward his employers and the good people of Cleveland who had supported him so long with what they so much desired, the pennant of the American League. — F. C. Lane, *Baseball Magazine*, 1912[1]

Though the Naps suffered from low attendance in 1909, Charles Somers decided that, with most of the other 15 major league teams either building new ballparks or planning them, the Cleveland ballclub needed to get with the program and replace the aging League Park with a modern, twentieth century stadium. Immediately after the close of the 1909 campaign, workmen demolished the 18-year-old wooden structure and began to raise a new League Park. Like Shibe Park in Philadelphia and Forbes Field in Pittsburgh, both of which had opened a few months before, the new stadium was a marvel of concrete and steel, with a stately brick façade and two decks containing more than 21,000 seats. The previous structure had space for only 9,000 people, so the new League Park stood as a symbol of optimism for American League baseball in Cleveland.

It also represented, at long last, a sense of stability for the Cleveland franchise. The future of professional baseball in the city was by no means a settled issue before Napoleon Lajoie joined the club in June of 1902; had he signed with another American League team, or returned to the Phillies of the rival circuit, the Cleveland ballclub might have moved (as did the Baltimore team after that season) or folded. Lajoie not only performed at a high level during his first eight seasons with the club, but also gave the team its identity. Lajoie and the Naps were synonymous, and despite the club's disappointing failure to win a pennant, baseball in Cleveland might not have survived without him. The bright, gleaming new League Park was a symbol of success, and much of the credit for that success belonged to Napoleon Lajoie.

Deacon McGuire, starting his first full season as manager of the Naps, decided to reconfigure his infield. He acquired Simon Nicholls from the Athletics in a trade for outfielder Wilbur Good, and inserted the newcomer at shortstop, with Terry Turner moving

On the field before the game (National Baseball Hall of Fame Library, Cooperstown, New York).

to second base and Lajoie to first. "I've decided I can get the most strength in the infield by switching Larry to first and bringing Turner and Nicholls into the infield," said McGuire. "Turner is one of the country's greatest players and I've got to have him in the game. There's a better chance of his playing the season at second than at short, where the throw might strain his arm. Lajoie will play first. Nicholls is an inside ball player, fast on the bases and a good left-handed hitter, and he ought to be good at short."[2] George Stovall was the odd man out, but McGuire planned to make "Brother George" available as a pinch-hitter and a substitute in case of injury to Lajoie or Turner. Given Turner's injury history and Lajoie's advancing age, the plan appeared reasonable, so Lajoie worked out at first during spring training in Alexandria, Louisiana.

The Naps began the 1910 season on the road, winning two of three against the defending league champion Tigers before traveling to Chicago and taking two in a row from the White Sox. On April 20, the final game of the road trip, Addie Joss pitched the second no-hitter of his career, defeating Chicago by a 1–0 score and becoming the only pitcher in major league history to no-hit the same team twice. The Naps, for once, had made a strong start to their season, and returned to Cleveland for their home opener in first place by a game.

On April 21, 1910, the Naps played their first contest in their new park. The weather was cold and overcast, but more than 18,000 people braved the elements and saw American League President Ban Johnson preside over a ceremony that included several other team owners, local politicians, and Cincinnati Reds owner Garry Herrmann, head of baseball's National Commission. Cy Young, who had pitched the first game in the previous version of League Park in 1891, drew the opening day assignment for the Naps against the Tigers. Young, at age 43, showed his age on this historic day, losing to the Tigers, 5–0.

Cleveland's fast start gave the fans a sense of hope, but the positive feelings dissipated quickly. The Naps lost five of their first six contests in their new stadium and fell to fifth place before April was over. Simon Nicholls, the key to McGuire's reconstituted infield, utterly failed to hit and played in only three games, all as a defensive replacement, before drawing his release in early May. The oft-injured Bill Bradley stopped hitting almost entirely, batting below the .200 mark and giving every indication that his career was drawing to a close. After two weeks, McGuire ended his infield experiment, shifting Lajoie back to second base and restoring George Stovall to his former slot at first.

Terry Turner showed a welcome durability, missing only four games all season, but the left side of the infield was a disaster area. Eight different third baseman and eight different shortstops saw action for the Naps that season, with only Turner performing well. Jack Graney, a one-time pitcher who learned to play the outfield in the minor leagues, claimed the right field job (and brought to the team a pet bulldog, which he named "Larry"), but newcomer Art Kruger hit only .179 in left. Elmer Flick, fighting the effects of his mysterious illness for the third consecutive year, was finally finished at the age of 34 and drew his release in mid–August, while Joe Birmingham, the center fielder, gave his usual fine defensive performance but hit weakly. The Naps had stayed with their veterans (Flick, Bradley, and others) for too long, and the aging ballclub was in dire need of a makeover.

One of the few Naps who performed well, and remarkably so, was Lajoie. While most of his teammates struggled to connect at the plate, Lajoie played like a much younger version of himself, showing a strong resemblance to the man who won three batting titles in four seasons earlier in the decade. Said Ed Bang of the *Cleveland Press*, "The one man of whom great things were expected, Napoleon Lajoie, has delivered. He has made one-third of the team's total of hits on the home lot, but Larry can't win the games all by his lonesome.... If [light-hitting shortstop Neal] Ball is kept in the game for his fielding ability, it will be necessary for Larry to hit about .700 to hold Neal up in the batting end."[3] The move back to his familiar spot at second base seemed to rejuvenate Lajoie, who carried a .450 average as April turned into May.

Though the Naps kept losing, Lajoie continued to wallop the ball. Free from the worries of managing, no longer concerned with directing the activities of the eight other men on the field with him, Lajoie, at age 35, showed the league that he still deserved to rank with Ty Cobb and Honus Wagner at the pinnacle of the sport. Ed Bang of the *Cleveland Press*, always one of Lajoie's biggest boosters, fairly gushed over the Cleveland star in print. Wrote Bang,

> The veterans are legion in stating that had Larry never accepted the management of the Naps, he would have set a batting record for himself that would have stood for all time. Now that everything is said and done and Larry is no longer the leader of the Naps, but one of the rank and file, we are pleased to note that he is batting where he left off when he became manager and are delighted to join the vast army of fans and worship at the shrine of the Greatest Player of All Time.[4]

Lajoie avoided the injury bug that had interfered with his play so often during the previous few years, and by mid-season it was clear that, with an average of .411 on June 16 (according to *Sporting Life's* tallies), he had another batting title in his sights. Ty Cobb, Detroit's three-time title holder, was in second place at .388, with the third-place hitter, Boston's Tris Speaker, about 50 points behind Cobb. The batting race was a two-man affair from May on, and the competition between the aging superstar Lajoie and the much younger Cobb grabbed the nation's attention.

To make things more interesting, Hugh Chalmers, a Detroit automobile magnate, declared his intention to award his company's flagship product, a Chalmers 30 roadster, to the man with the highest batting average in the major leagues at the close of the season. Chalmers was a 38-year-old businessman and baseball fan who believed that a spirited batting race would bring attention to his line of cars. There were many challengers to Henry Ford's preeminent position among Detroit automakers at the time, and Chalmers relied on a keen sense of marketing and publicity to separate his products from those of his competitors.

The Chalmers automobile was not the first instance of a post-season prize in the baseball world. In 1868, the *New York Clipper*, a much-read weekly newspaper of the day, awarded gold medals to the nine best ballplayers, one at each position, in the nation. Professional baseball magnates, however, frowned on such rewards, fearing that the pursuit of individual honors would tempt players to perform selfishly, protecting their statistics at the expense of winning team play. Newspapers and fan groups had presented trophies and medals to star players in the past, but the Chalmers 30, a top-of-the-line automobile with a list price of $1,500 (as compared to a price tag of $450 to $600 for a Ford Model T), became the first, albeit unofficial, approximation of a Most Valuable Player award in baseball history.

Cobb thought the proposal a good idea. "I am glad that something besides medals and trophies is offered for the championship in batting," he said. "I think the offer of a Chalmers 30 is simply great and I hope to be lucky enough to own a new Chalmers next fall."[5] Apparently it made no difference to the ultra-competitive Detroit star that he already owned one of the company's products, a Chalmers-Detroit Bluebird racing model that he bought in

Lajoie and Cobb in a Chalmers 30 roadster (Transcendental Graphics/theruckerarchive.com).

1909 and drove in a tour from New York to Atlanta that October. Cobb loved cars, and as the biggest sports celebrity in the town that was quickly earning the name "Motor City," he was keenly interested in the burgeoning auto industry. He knew Hugh Chalmers and many of the other business leaders of the city, and was determined to see that the car, manufactured in his team's home city, remained in Detroit.

While Lajoie enjoyed his best season at the bat in years, Cleveland fell out of the pennant chase early. A 1–11 skid on the road put the Naps in fifth place by May 28, and the team would not again crack the first division in 1910. Addie Joss, after his fine start, was sidelined with arm problems and won only five games, while Cy Young, at 43, showed his age with a 7–10 record. Many believed that it was time for Young to end his 21-year career, but the oldest starting pitcher in the game resisted. "Quit the game, well, I guess not," he told one Cleveland reporter. "I'd be awfully lonesome, and you know this is a healthy game. I'll not quit until I have to."[6] Cy Falkenberg led the Naps in wins with 14 that season against 13 losses, while 20-year-old left-hander Willie Mitchell showed promise with 12 wins. Falkenberg and Mitchell, not Joss and Young, represented the future of the Naps, and it was obvious that the team needed to import younger players and substantially remake its roster if it hoped to challenge for a pennant (and fill the 21,000 seats in its new stadium) in the near future.

There were changes off the field as well. John Kilfoyl, who had served as president and co-owner of the franchise since its inception in 1901, wanted to sell out for health reasons, so Charles Somers bought his shares and took full control of the ballclub in July. Somers pledged to rebuild the club, phase out the old guard, and bring in new talent, and he started the overhaul in August when he released veterans Bill Bradley and Elmer Flick. He also swapped an outfielder named Bris Lord to the Philadelphia Athletics for infielder Morrie Rath and the rights to a promising young Southerner named "Shoeless Joe" Jackson, a three-time minor league batting champion who had failed in two previous trials with Connie Mack's team. Somers paid a reported $6,000 to the New Orleans club for Jackson, a 22-year-old who hit from the left side. Jackson finished his minor league season at New Orleans, then joined the Naps in early September.

The Cleveland owner insisted to all that Napoleon Lajoie, who turned 36 on September 5 of that year, was safe from the turnover. Nonetheless, the Boston papers reported that a deal between the Naps and the Red Sox, in which Cleveland would acquire third baseman Harry Lord for Lajoie, was in the works and due to be completed in a matter of days. This proposed trade was a pipe dream by the Boston press, because Lord had recently been suspended by the Red Sox, and Lajoie was so popular in Cleveland, and performing so well, that such a deal might prove fatal to the franchise. At the same time, the *Washington Times* hyped a possible trade of Lajoie to the Senators, mainly because he had always hit so well in the nation's capital. Somers was not in the least bit interested in trading his most popular star, and he remained with Cleveland while ownership turned over the rest of the roster. By September, only Lajoie, Joss, and 35-year-old catcher Harry Bemis remained from the Naps who had nearly won the pennant only two years before.

Because the pennant races in both leagues were over by August (the Philadelphia Athletics and Chicago Cubs ran away with the flags of their respective circuits), baseball fans across the nation focused their attention on the batting race. The offer of a car to the game's leading batter made the race more interesting, and the public reaction to the prize surpassed even Hugh Chalmers' highest expectations. Across the nation, newspapers kept a running tally of the battle between Ty Cobb and Napoleon Lajoie for the "gasoline steed," and though Lajoie held the lead until late July, Cobb roared back with an August surge to claim first place. Cobb's Tigers, like Lajoie's Naps, had no chance to win the pennant, so the fans in both Detroit and Cleveland rooted for their local heroes to win the car.

On a national level, Lajoie emerged as the popular favorite. Cobb, the winner of the previous three batting crowns, had angered fans and opponents with his win-at-all-costs tactics, and even the level-headed Connie Mack declared, "Organized baseball ought not to permit such a malefactor [as Cobb] to disgrace it"[7] after an incident in which the Detroit star spiked third baseman Frank Baker in August of 1909. Cleveland's Bill Bradley had seen his thumb ripped open by Cobb's spikes earlier that same year, while even some of Cobb's teammates had traded punches with their fellow Tiger off the field. Cobb's burning intensity turned opponents into mortal enemies, while the friendlier Lajoie enjoyed great popularity with other teams. "Even when [Lajoie] was blocking you off the base, he was smiling and kidding with you. You just had to like the guy,"[8] said Pittsburgh's Tommy Leach. Lajoie, too, was driven to win, but managed to do so in a less threatening way. For that reason, the majority of interested parties, on the field and in the stands, pulled for Lajoie to win the title.

On September 5, with about one month left in the 1910 season, *Sporting Life* reported that Lajoie held a seven-point lead:

	Hits	AB	Avg
Lajoie	184	494	.372
Cobb	167	458	.365

However, no one knew the exact totals. Newspapers kept their own tallies of statistics, and because papers printed their own box scores from their own score sheets, one paper might record a fumbled ball as a hit while another in the same city might mark the same play as an error. Big cities at the time had many competing papers (Cleveland had four major dailies), all of which printed their own stats. The American League released its official statistics only at the end of the season, so in the meantime, the public had to be content with what the papers provided on an unofficial basis.

On September 6, when the Naps and Tigers opposed each other in Detroit, Lajoie and Cobb both stroked two hits. The two clubs then traveled to Cleveland for four more contests, but Cobb stayed behind in Detroit. He was having problems with his vision, and his eye doctor diagnosed the outfielder with an inflammation of the optic nerve. Cobb remained on the sidelines for all four games in Cleveland, and when the Naps returned to Detroit a week later for a three-game series, Cobb batted only once, striking out in a pinch-hitting role. Though the Cleveland papers criticized Cobb for failing to oppose Lajoie head to head, his eye problems were real, and he sat in the stands, wearing smoked glasses, while Lajoie soldiered on with the Naps. Cobb did not return to the Detroit lineup until September 20, when he hit two singles in eight times at bat during a doubleheader against the Athletics.

Lajoie, who had not yet missed a game in 1910, hit a brief slump while Cobb was out of action, and on September 15, the *Washington Times* had Cobb in the lead by one point:

	Hits	AB	Avg
Cobb	167	459	.364
Lajoie	190	523	.363

Both men closed the month of September with a rush, though Lajoie suffered a bruised shoulder during a doubleheader against the Red Sox on September 27 and sat out two games, the only ones he missed all season. The race for the Chalmers was a seesaw affair, with first one man, then the other, taking the lead and holding it for a brief time. Most of the papers had Lajoie in front by a few points before Cobb belted four hits in five tries at St. Louis on October 2, while Lajoie went hitless that same day against right-hander Doc White in Chicago. Neither the Tigers nor the Naps played on October 3 and 4, and when the teams met in Detroit for a doubleheader on October 5, Cobb and Lajoie played to a draw, with both men swatting three hits in six times up. The Detroiter was now slightly ahead by most tallies, but Lajoie inched closer on October 6 with three hits in St. Louis while Cobb was belting two safeties against the White Sox.

Lajoie and the Naps were idle on Friday, October 7, while Cobb went 2-for-3 at Chicago in what would prove to be his final contest of 1910. The Detroiter's average was now in the low .380s, with Lajoie between six and eight points behind, so Cobb, believing his lead to be safe, passed up his team's last two games of the season. Instead of playing the scheduled contests on Saturday and Sunday in Chicago, Cobb journeyed to Philadelphia, where a team of American League all-stars was slated to play the league champion Athletics in a series of tune-up matches before the start of the World Series. While the Tigers finished their season without Cobb, Lajoie and the Naps closed their campaign with three games against the Browns in St. Louis, one on Saturday and a season-ending twin bill on Sunday. Lajoie made only one safe hit in four tries on Saturday, and it was clear to everyone that only an offensive eruption of historic proportions on the final day would allow the Cleveland second sacker to pass Cobb and win the car.

On Sunday morning, the Cleveland papers expressed cautious optimism. "Nap Lajoie's chances of owning the automobile presented to the leading batsman of the country are mightily slim," reported the Sunday edition of the *Plain Dealer*. "In fact, they are practically obliterated unless the 'official' figures prove that 'unofficial' figures are radically incorrect. Cobb, according to the *Plain Dealer*'s estimate, is batting close to .383, while Lajoie's present mark is slightly in excess of .378." The paper went on to tweak Cobb for leaving his team in the lurch. "Cobb left the Detroit team Friday night, departing for Philadelphia where he will be a member of the All-Star team that will practice with the Athletics. The Georgian declared that he was not feeling very well. The fact that he was ahead in the auto race and feared that he might take a slump in the two games yet to be played may have had something to do with the sudden decision."[9]

To win the car, Lajoie needed to hit safely at least eight or nine times during the Sunday doubleheader in St. Louis. He didn't know it yet, but the Browns were willing to help him do just that.

"Rowdy Jack" O'Connor, manager of the last-place Browns, was a rough, tough ex-catcher who had played for the Cleveland Spiders during the 1890s. He also served as manager Patsy Tebeau's right-hand man and chief enforcer for the brawling Spiders, whose hell-raising and misbehavior both on and off the field were the stuff of legend. No one knows if O'Connor hated Cobb, liked Lajoie, or some combination of the two, but the St. Louis manager decided that his cellar-dwelling team, with nothing at stake on that Sunday afternoon, would play a key role in the most controversial batting race in American League history. If Lajoie needed eight or nine hits, decided O'Connor, the Browns would help him get them.

Rowdy Jack was 44 years old and had not played a major league game in three years, but he put on the catching equipment and wrote his own name on the lineup card. He also ordered third baseman John "Red" Corriden, a 23-year-old rookie who had played only 11 games at the position for the Browns, to play as far back as he could. When Lajoie came to bat in the top of the first inning, he found the oldest, slowest catcher in the game behind him and a third sacker standing only a few steps in front of the outfield grass. The message was clear; if he cared to bunt his way on, the Browns would not stand in his way.

The Cleveland veteran did not catch on right away. Instead of accepting the obvious gift, he belted a fly ball to center, where outfielder Hub Northen showed little interest in catching it. The fly fell for a triple, giving Lajoie his first hit of the day. The Browns won the first game by a 5–4 count, but the real story was Lajoie, who batted three more times and in each instance found the Browns totally unprepared to field even a mediocre bunt. He laid three bunts down the third base line and beat each one out easily, completing a 4-for-4 game and closing the gap on Cobb.

The second game proceeded in the same manner as the first. In this contest, Lajoie tapped five bunts down the left side, four to Corriden and one to shortstop Bobby Wallace. Official scorer E. V. Parrish, who was not involved in the scheme, ruled one of the bunts a sacrifice instead of a base hit, and a few innings later a messenger boy handed Parrish a note. The note read, "Mr. Parish — If you can see where Mr. Lajoie gets a B. H. instead of a sacrifice I will give you an order for a $40 suit of clothes — sure."[10] No one knows who sent the note, though O'Connor and his coach, former spitball pitcher Harry Howell, emerged as the chief suspects.

At day's end, Lajoie had compiled one of the greatest batting lines in baseball history, with eight hits in eight official trips to the plate (the sacrifice did not count as a time at bat). In the view of most observers, he had passed Cobb and won the Chalmers.

However, the controversy was just beginning. While the *Plain Dealer* celebrated Lajoie's apparent victory with a headline that read, "Lajoie Wins Auto In Final Stretch," the paper acknowledged the something was not right. In a subhead titled, "St. Louis Papers Say Browns Made It Easy for Nap Slugger," the *Plain Dealer* admitted, "Larry's triumph is tinged with a charge of illegitimacy. St. Louis sporting writers assert that Lajoie was favored by opposing fielders. They say that the St. Louis pitchers pitched the ball where Larry could hit it to best advantage. They maintain that Corridon [sic], the Brown third baseman, did not field to the best of his ability when the Cleveland champion drove the ball into Corridon's territory. They insist that other fielders abetted him and aided Lajoie in his race for highest honors."[11] The *St. Louis Globe Democrat* agreed, criticizing the local club's infield play. "Every time Lajoie stepped up to the plate," said the St. Louis paper, "Corridon walked out to the very edge of the grass almost. The Browns' third sacker was virtually playing a short left field for Larry. This always resulted in the same old thing happening, that of Lajoie bunting down the third base line, Corridon rushing in to field the ball and then not throwing because a throw to first would have been useless."[12]

O'Connor, queried about his unusual, and unsuccessful, strategy, tried to defend his actions. "Lajoie outguessed us," he said. "We figured he did not have the nerve to bunt every time. He beat us at our own game. I will not send any of our players in to play up close to Lajoie when he tries to bunt."[13] Corriden, the rookie infielder, seconded that notion. "I want to remain in baseball for some years," he said. "I was not going to get killed playing in on Lajoie. I might have gotten some of the bunts, and at the same time broken a nose or lost a couple of teeth. Lajoie is known as a hard hitter, and I played far back."[14]

No one knew for sure who the winner would be until the American League released its final statistics, so Lajoie waited patiently while the Naps prepared to take on the Cincinnati Reds in a post-season series for the "All-Ohio Championship." From Cincinnati, Lajoie explained his version of events.

It's too close for me to claim the victory and the auto. Take it from me, I am waiting until Ban Johnson and [league secretary] Robert McRoy tell me whether I have a better record than Cobb or Cobb has me beat. There is such a difference of opinion that I am not counting my eggs before they are hatched or taking a ride in that auto before Johnson and McRoy have poured in a little Cleveland gasoline.

   The talk about my not earning those eight hits in St. Louis, though, makes me tired. The first time up I smashed one to the outfield that went over Northen's head, yet some say he misjudged it. Then I hit one that Wallace was lucky to knock down. If that wasn't a hit, there never was one. Then we get down to those six bunts that I beat out. Suppose Corriden did play fairly well back. If he had played in for a bunt and I had swung hard on the ball, I suppose the youngster would have been roasted to a turn because he did not play deep.[15]

He also sent a telegram to the St. Louis newspapers that read, "After I made my first hit, a clean drive to centre for three bases, the St. Louis men played deep, expecting me to pound the ball every time. I fooled them right along. The pitchers did their best to deceive me, I am certain."[16]

   Despite Lajoie's insistence that the games in St. Louis were played on the level, the controversy continued to grow. President John Taylor of the Red Sox said, "The action of the St. Louis Browns in playing their infield so far back that Lajoie was able to beat out seven bunts was a disgrace to the game. Judging from the reports, there is no doubt but what the St. Louis club did this, as Lajoie is a free hitter, who has probably not beaten out seven other bunts during the entire season."[17] Ban Johnson, who had seen the greatest batting race in league history dissolve in bickering and accusations of "laying down" by the Browns, summoned Jack O'Connor and Red Corriden to his office in Chicago for an explanation. When neither man showed up at the appointed hour, Johnson was furious. He gave them one more day to appear and threatened to drive them both out of baseball if they refused to show. O'Connor and Corriden arrived promptly in Chicago the next day, where they were grilled by the league president, then dismissed.

   Because the controversy over the car threatened to overshadow the World Series between the Athletics and the Cubs, Johnson moved quickly to put the matter to rest. Hugh Chalmers was slated to present the car to the winner at the second game of the Series in Philadelphia on October 18, nine days after the fateful twin bill in St. Louis, so Johnson put his statistician, Robert McRoy, to work. On October 15, after completing his investigation, Johnson released his final statistics and declared Ty Cobb the winner of both the batting title and the automobile. "The records of the American League for 1910," said Johnson to a group of reporters, "show that their respective batting averages are as follows: Cobb, 509 times at bat, 196 base hits; percentage, .384944. Lajoie, 591 times at bat, 227 base hits; percentage, .384084. The margin is meager and each of the contestants has, during his connection with the American League, contributed much to its prestige by his magnificent batting and all-round work."[18]

   Perhaps the figures were compiled in haste, for Johnson's announced percentages were slightly off. Given the reported totals of hits and times at bat, the percentages should have been:

	Hits	AB	Avg
Cobb	196	509	.385069
Lajoie	227	591	.384095

   Nonetheless, Cobb had won the car by the slimmest of margins, and in the end, the official scorer's decision to credit Lajoie with a sacrifice instead of a base hit during the second game of the doubleheader against the Browns cost Lajoie the batting title. Due to the closeness of the race, Johnson correctly surmised that the public would be happy to see both men drive away in a shiny new automobile, so he contacted Hugh Chalmers and offered to buy a matching car for Lajoie with league funds. Chalmers proposed instead to give an identical machine to the Cleveland second baseman, and the league president readily agreed, explaining that the car would be presented to Lajoie "in recognition of his service to the American League ... and for his grand batting record during the season." This, hoped Johnson, would settle the matter to everyone's satisfaction, and when a reporter pressed Johnson about how Cobb and not Lajoie came out on top of the league statistics, he tersely replied, "The Cobb-Lajoie affair is a closed matter."[19]

While Lajoie and the Naps played their "All-Ohio Championship" series against the Reds, Cobb traveled to Philadelphia, where the World Series between the Athletics and the Chicago Cubs opened on October 17, to receive his prize in a pre-game ceremony before Game 2. Lajoie was not present, but Hugh Chalmers and Ban Johnson announced that his new car would be delivered to him in Cleveland the following week. After the ceremony, Cobb watched the Athletics defeat the Cubs, then loaded his wife and infant son into his new vehicle and drove it all the way home to Georgia. Said Cobb, "I am glad I won an automobile and am especially pleased that Lajoie also gets one. I have no one to criticize. I know the games were on the square and am greatly pleased to know that the affair has ended so nicely."[20]

Napoleon Lajoie, too, accepted the outcome, though he could not help letting some of his competitive nature seep through. "I am quite satisfied that I was treated fairly in every way by President Johnson," he said, "but I think that the scorer in St. Louis made an error in not crediting me with nine hits. However, I am glad that the controversy is over. I have the greatest respect for Cobb as a batter and I am glad of his success."[21] Privately, however, Lajoie was steaming, or so say family sources to whom the story of the 1910 batting race has been passed down through the generations. Larry's nephew Lionel Lajoie once claimed in an interview that the Cleveland star "didn't want to accept it," and only did so at the insistence of his wife Myrtle. "He just thought that he, not Cobb, had won that championship and was angry that Cobb had been ruled the winner,"[22] said Lionel. Recalling the epic race years later, Larry said with a smile, "I've always understood that the automobile I got ran a lot better than the one they gave to Ty."[23]

Though Lajoie fell short of the batting title by one hit, he had enjoyed one of his best seasons in a Cleveland uniform. At age 36, he led the league in hits with 227, set a new league record for doubles with 51, and paced the circuit in total bases with 304. He missed only two games all year, set a new personal high in walks with 60, and compiled his highest batting average since his .426 mark with the Athletics nine years before. Even so, one of his new teammates posted a batting mark that was higher than those of both Lajoie and Cobb. Shoeless Joe Jackson, who joined the Naps in early September, batted .387 in 20 games and showed promise of becoming one of the top hitters in the league.

Ban Johnson had declared the Cobb-Lajoie race a "closed matter," but in 1981, long after all the principals in the hotly contested affair had passed on, *The Sporting News* revived the controversy in a front-page article. In it, writer Paul MacFarlane reported that two researchers, Leonard Gettelson and Pete Palmer, had studied the game logs and score sheets for the 1910 season and found that Johnson had incorrectly credited Cobb with two extra hits. Specifically, Gettelson (who had died in 1977) and Palmer, working independently, had discovered that the batting totals of a game played on September 24, 1910, between the Tigers and the Boston Red Sox had been entered twice in the league's final statistics. Johnson and his staff had corrected the mistake for all the Tigers players except Cobb, who went 2-for-3 that day. Therefore, according to Palmer and Gettelson, Cobb received credit for two non-existent hits. They also found two additional unsuccessful times at bat that should have been charged against Cobb and one that was missed in Lajoie's totals. The corrected statistical record for 1910, according to the article, handed the batting crown to Lajoie:

	Hits	AB	Avg
Lajoie	227	592	.383446
Cobb	194	508	.381890

Though many sources now list Napoleon Lajoie as the 1910 batting champ, Major League Baseball still recognizes Cobb as the titleholder. When *The Sporting News* confronted American League president Lee MacPhail with its findings, MacPhail refused to consider changing the official records. He deferred to his long-ago predecessor, stating, "Just to zero in on one isolated record after all these years seems unfair. Ban Johnson certified Cobb as the champion and I'm sure he had good reasons for it." Commissioner Bowie Kuhn also took a hands-off approach, offering his view that "the passage of 70 years, in our opinion, also constitutes a certain statute of limitation as to recognizing any change in the records."[24] Though both players received new cars, the real winner of the Cobb-Lajoie affair was Hugh Chalmers, who received such a windfall of publicity from the batting race and its aftermath that sales of the Chalmers 30 more than doubled from 1909 to 1910.

Did Ban Johnson intentionally leave two extra hits in Cobb's totals to make sure the Detroit star won the car? We will never know, because Johnson, who died in 1931, never mentioned the controversy again. Still, the league president's decision to award the title to Cobb was the neatest available solution to a vexing problem. Lajoie may have actually compiled a slightly higher batting average than his Detroit rival, but Cobb's case is a strong one, largely because the Cleveland second baseman's claim on the prize was tainted by the machinations of his opponents on that final Sunday of the regular season. The 1910 batting race remains a topic of controversy to this day, more than 100 years after it happened, and though Ban Johnson has been roundly criticized for the way he handled it, perhaps his resolution of the matter was the fairest one possible after all.

20

A Season of Change

You know, they tell a story, I can't vouch for it, but I wouldn't be surprised if it were true. Lajoie endorsed a certain kind of chewin' tobacco, as all ball players did in those days, just like they endorse cigarettes and clothes these days. And do you know what happened? The day after the advertisement was in the papers half the kids in the country were sick from chewing. Yeah, they used to follow him around, just like they hung after Ruth. He had what you call "color." He was great, old Nap. — Cy Young, 1950[1]

In a sport that was dominated by players of Irish and German extraction, Napoleon Lajoie's French-Canadian ancestry was a source of both interest and amusement.

Other stars of the era enjoyed colorful, descriptive nicknames. Honus Wagner was the "Flying Dutchman," Christy Mathewson was "Big Six," and Ty Cobb was the "Georgia Peach," to name but a few. Napoleon Lajoie, by contrast, was the "big Frenchman," or simply the Frenchman. There were so few players of French ancestry in the game at the time that the very fact of his Gallic ancestry was sufficient to describe him in only one word. A few prominent players — Patsy Tebeau and Gene DeMontreville among them — had French surnames, but when anyone in the baseball world at the time used the word "Frenchman," everyone knew immediately that the object of the reference was Lajoie.

In those less culturally sensitive times, the terms "frog" and "frog-eater" came easily to the pens of the sportswriters whenever Lajoie, or any other French-surnamed player, was discussed. This particular slur, which had been deployed by the British against their traditional French rivals for generations, was often used at the time in casual conversation. In 1898, *Sporting Life* asked New York Giants captain Bill Joyce to comment on Lajoie's shift from first base to second. "That big Frenchman, Lajoie, fooled all of us," said Joyce. "I thought that [manager George] Stallings was spoiling a first-class first baseman when he turned the frog-eater into a second-bagman."[2] Another example occurred in early 1905, when the *Chicago Journal* announced the arrival of the Cleveland star at the local ballpark in a fashion that no reputable paper would employ today:

SOUTH SIDE PARK! 3:30 PM!
THE ONLY — THE INCOMPARABLE NAPOLEON LAJOIE,
Eating Frogs and Base Hits with Impartiality!
ZE PRIDE OF LA BELLE FRANCE. Three-baggers Manufactured While You Wait!
WOW, WOW, WOW!

ALSO OUCH!
COME AND SEE HIM!
DO NOT MISS HIM — HE WON'T MISS THE BALL![3]

The Sporting News, the St. Louis–based weekly paper that came to be revered as the "Bible of Baseball," was not afraid to refer to Lajoie with a term that most people now regard as an ethnic slur. In 1940 and again in 1941, the paper ran profiles of the long-retired Lajoie under titles such as "The Big Frog Tells of His Historic Hop to A. L. in 1901" and "The Big Frog As He Looks Today." By November of 1953, when the paper printed a two-part celebration of Lajoie's career in consecutive issues, the word "frog" had disappeared. Times had changed, and perhaps it was not a coincidence that the usage of such questionable terms had declined as racial integration, which *The Sporting News* had opposed in its early stages, gained traction.

Lajoie never commented on the matter. As with most other issues in his life, he preferred to take things in stride, and if he ever objected to the term, he left no record of it. During his first few days with the Phillies he had accepted the name "Larry" without complaint, and though in later life he sometimes corrected people who mangled the pronunciation of his last name, he was not one to make a fuss about it.

Similarly, Lajoie was not much interested in celebrating his own accomplishments, though he was undeniably proud of them. After his spectacular 1901 season, league statistics credited him with 229 hits in 543 times at bat, resulting in an average of .422. However, a typographical error in the 1902 Reach Guide, which carried the official American League records, left his number of hits at 220, not 229. More than a decade later, some sharp-eyed statistics buff pointed out that 220 divided by 543 is .405, so his average was changed to .405 in most reference books. This change also took the single-season league record for batting average away from Lajoie and gave it to Ty Cobb, who hit .420 in 1911. Not until 1954 did statistician John Tattersall, writing in *The Sporting News*, correct the mistake and restore Lajoie's .422 mark, making the Frenchman, once again, the holder of the record for the highest average in American League history. Lajoie, when informed of the correction, said only, "Anyway, it was a great year."[4]

Lajoie had enjoyed another great year in 1910, and looked to continue his hot hitting and renew his rivalry with Ty Cobb in 1911. Cleveland was a team in transition, with Elmer Flick and Bill Bradley gone, Cy Young and Addie Joss aging, and young players fighting for spots on the roster. Lajoie, at the beginning of his tenth season in a Cleveland uniform, was still the star of the team and a fixture at second base, while Joss, the senior Nap in time of service, fought to recover from his injury-plagued 1910 campaign. Joss, who had joined the Cleveland club a few months before Lajoie in 1902, was only 30 years old, but his career was at a crossroads. Charles Somers hired a trainer to work on Joss' arm at his home in Toledo during the winter months, and sent the pitcher to the spas at Hot Springs, Arkansas, in February for further rest and rehabilitation. When training camp opened at New Orleans in March, Joss told the sportswriters that he expected to be ready to pitch when the season began.

Lajoie arrived at New Orleans in his usual excellent physical condition, prompting Cleveland scout Bobby Gilks to tell a reporter from *Sporting Life* that Larry was "one of the marvels of the base ball world" and that he would probably be a member of the 1921 Naps.[5] The weekly sports paper also reported that Lajoie wore the same white cap around camp that he sported the previous spring. The veteran second baseman had performed so well in 1910 that he decided that the cap must be lucky. Deacon McGuire, impressed by Lajoie's

Lajoie at the bat in 1908 (author's collection).

spring play, scotched any rumors of a shift to first base, declaring that George Stovall at first, Lajoie at second, and Joe Jackson in center field were settled in their positions. The manager also proposed to bat Jackson third in the lineup, with the 36-year-old Lajoie in the cleanup spot.

The pitching staff was unsettled, partly due to the continuing struggles of Addie Joss. Despite his hard work during the winter months, Joss, whose complete-game victory over the Reds in the Ohio Championship Series the previous October had raised expectations for a return to form in 1911, complained of arm pain during spring practice. The pitcher thought his elbow had healed, and he was at a loss to explain the latest discomfort. "One day my arm feels great and the next day it hurts," he said. "I've tried every way I know to find out except the x-ray. I'm going to try that next week."[6] On April 3, while visiting with teammates on the field in Chattanooga, Tennessee, before a game with the local minor league team, Joss suddenly fainted and collapsed to the ground. His breathing was labored, but the doctors blamed his fainting spell on the heat, and he boarded the train for Cincinnati with the rest of the Naps at the end of the game.

Joss experienced chest pains on the train, so the team sent him home to Toledo for treatment. There his condition worsened, and by April 9, when he asked Charles Somers for permission to remain at home to recuperate, he had lost a considerable amount of weight and his speech was slurred. His family doctor diagnosed his illness as pleurisy, a lung inflammation, but the pitcher's condition deteriorated so quickly that Somers dispatched Dr. Morrison Castle, the team physician, to Toledo for a second opinion. Dr. Castle examined his patient and delivered grave news. Addie had tubercular meningitis, and the disease was too advanced to hope for recovery. On Friday morning, April 14, two days after his 31st birthday, Addie Joss died, leaving a wife and two young children.

The Naps received the tragic news at their hotel in St. Louis, where they had lost their first two games of the 1911 season to the Browns and were preparing to play again that afternoon. Deacon McGuire delivered word of the pitcher's death to his charges, many of whom wept openly before offering their thoughts to the reporters in the hotel lobby. "In Joss's death, baseball loses one of the best pitchers and men that has ever been identified with the game," said a shaken Napoleon Lajoie to a writer for the *Cleveland Plain Dealer*. "In saying that he had no superior as pitcher or player I am only expressing the sentiment of every one who has known him intimately. I am feeling very glum that my friend and teammate is no more."[7]

The pitcher's funeral was scheduled for the afternoon of Monday, May 17, in Toledo, a date when the Naps were slated to play the second game of a weekend series against the Tigers in Detroit (the first was on Sunday, which the Naps lost by a 5–2 score). Charles Somers asked the Tigers to postpone the contest by one day so the Naps could attend the funeral, but American League president Ban Johnson insisted that the game go on, instead suggesting that the teams hold a memorial ceremony before the contest and wear black arm bands in Joss' honor. The grief-stricken Naps would have none of that. Team captain George Stovall announced that the Naps would go on strike rather than play the game on Monday, and when Deacon McGuire tried to quell the threatened rebellion, Stovall stood firm. "I may be captain, but I'm still a ballplayer,"[8] Stovall declared, and when the rest of the Naps supported his stance, it looked for a day or two as if the American League would see its first player strike.

Cooler heads prevailed, and probably at the insistence of Somers and Detroit owner Frank Navin, Johnson reluctantly agreed to postpone the Monday game. The Naps, except for a few rookies who did not know Joss well, arrived in Toledo by train on Monday morning, accompanied by Ty Cobb and a contingent of Detroit players. Lajoie and his teammates heard Billy Sunday, the old Chicago outfielder who had left baseball for the ministry and become the most popular evangelist in the nation, deliver an emotional eulogy that brought most of the mourners to tears. At day's end, after the Cleveland ballplayers had visited the Joss home and paid their respects to Addie's widow Lillian, they returned to Detroit, where they lost to the Tigers the next day before heading for Cleveland to open their home schedule.

The Naps were deeply shaken by the death of their pitching ace, and their grief was reflected in their play. The club seemed unable to concentrate on the task at hand, and although both the veteran Napoleon Lajoie and Shoeless Joe Jackson, the up-and-coming star, started the season in top hitting form, the Naps played poorly. A rash of illness that spread through the team in April (a "wholesale visitation of the grip," as *The Sporting News* put it) was partly to blame, but several members of the club were also angry with McGuire and his initial resistance to canceling the game in Detroit on the day of Joss' funeral. Perhaps the players, upset by their grief and their poor play, made McGuire the target for their anger. McGuire, though no dictator, was nonetheless never personally close to his charges, and the upheaval of April made him even less popular with his men.

The 1911 campaign would have been a season of transition in any case. Such veteran standbys as Elmer Flick, Bill Bradley (who signed with Toronto of the Eastern League), and Addie Joss were gone, while the fragile Terry Turner was hurt again and out of the lineup. Cy Young fell ill with bronchitis during spring training and did not start the season with the team, instead repairing to his farm in eastern Ohio to recuperate. First base (Stovall), second base (Lajoie) and center field (Jackson) were solid positions for the Naps, but the team had plenty of holes to fill in almost all other areas. The Naps, only three years after losing the American League flag by half a game, appeared to be at least several years away from challenging for a pennant, and the small April crowds at League Park reflected that.

The death of Addie Joss, the continuing decline of Cy Young, and a rash of injuries left the Naps with only six wins in their first 17 games, and by early May Deacon McGuire had reached the end of his rope. The Cleveland ballclub had fallen back into its usual listless rut, and McGuire saw no way out of it, perhaps because of the hard feelings caused by his actions in the controversy over Joss' funeral two weeks before. The Naps had already fallen hopelessly far behind the red-hot Tigers, who won 21 of their first 23 games, so on May 2, McGuire paid a visit to Charles Somers and asked to be relieved of his duties. Somers tried to convince him to stay, but McGuire's mind was made up, and his tenure as Cleveland manager came to an end.

Lajoie was not interested in taking the managerial reins, so Somers promoted first baseman George Stovall, who had been McGuire's captain, to the post on a temporary basis. Stovall's appointment proved popular with the players, especially after he cancelled morning practices and relaxed the rules on curfews. "Brother George" was more of a friend than a manager, often buying drinks for his men because, as he explained to a reporter, he figured that they would be less inclined to imbibe on the sly if he provided the refreshments. His slogan, "Two kegs of beer if we win, boys, and one keg anyway,"[9] marked a sharp contrast to the attitude of his predecessor, and the Naps responded to his leadership. Though the local papers described Stovall as an interim pilot and speculated on other candidates for the position (with Lajoie's old Phillies manager George Stallings prominently mentioned), the players were happy with Stovall and supported his bid for the permanent appointment.

However, Somers had named Stovall as manager because his preferred candidate for the job was not yet available. Philadelphia Athletics first baseman Harry Davis had acted as Connie Mack's lieutenant for more than a decade, serving as field captain and managing the club whenever Mack was absent or indisposed. Somers and Mack were good friends, and because Davis, at age 39, was coming to the end of the line as a player, Mack wanted his longtime assistant to realize his dream of managing a major league club. That club turned out to be Cleveland. Mack was not yet ready to set Davis free, preferring to wait until the 21-year-old Jack "Stuffy" McInnis was ready to take over first base on a full-time basis, but McInnis was progressing quickly, and Mack assured Somers that Davis would be available by the spring of 1912. Accordingly, Mack and Somers agreed to a plan that would land Davis in the Cleveland manager's chair at the start of the following season no matter how well George Stovall performed.

Stovall and Lajoie had long since patched up their differences, and the chair-throwing incident of four years before was virtually forgotten by both men by the time Stovall became manager. In 1908, Lajoie had praised Stovall's play in glowing terms, declaring that he would not trade Stovall for the Yankees' Hal Chase, then considered the best in the game at the position. Stovall, in turn, described Larry to reporter Ed Bang as "my best friend in baseball, and if I am in doubt about anything I often consult with him and he is glad to lend me his advice."[10] Perhaps Stovall was selling his relationship with the namesake of the team a little too extravagantly, but it appears that manager Stovall and ex-pilot Lajoie got along well.

The Naps, still reeling from Joss' death, started slowly under Stovall, but two bright spots emerged that spelled hope for the club. One was Napoleon Lajoie, who continued his hot hitting of 1910 and walloped the ball, with his .394 average placing him among the league leaders after two weeks. The other cause for optimism was Joe Jackson, who shot to stardom in his first full major league season, batting well over .400 as April turned into May. On April 21 he belted a long home run over League Park's 40-foot right field wall, a feat that only Detroit's Sam Crawford had yet performed, and on May 7 he won an extra-inning game against the Browns with a bases-loaded, inside-the-park homer. Shoeless Joe could run (he stole 41 bases that year), hit for power and average, and make incredible throws from the outfield, and Cleveland fans wondered how a shrewd operator like Connie Mack could have cast Jackson aside. Jackson's hitting actually improved as the season wore on, and the youngster from South Carolina seemed poised to join Napoleon Lajoie and Ty Cobb in the ranks of the American League's biggest stars.

"Shoeless Joe" Jackson, Lajoie's Cleveland teammate who batted .408 in 1911 (author's collection).

Unfortunately for the Naps, Lajoie suffered a leg injury in that game in St. Louis on May 7, and he was absent from the lineup the next day with what the *Cleveland Press* described as a slight charley horse. It was much worse than that. He limped around for a few days before his doctors determined that he had severely pulled, or partially torn, a ligament in his leg, and once again the Cleveland second baseman faced a long recovery period. Indeed, he missed the rest of May and all of June. He rejoined the team in early July, but did nothing but pinch-hit until the end of the month, when he entered the lineup at second base.

While Lajoie was laid up at home in Cleveland, the Naps came together under the leadership of George Stovall and started to win games. Cy Young, the 44-year-old legend, was finished — he won only three of the seven games he pitched before the team released him on August 15 — but rookie Vean Gregg won 23 games and gave the club the reliable left-handed starter it had lacked for years. Left-hander Willie Mitchell and right-handers Gene Krapp, Fred Blanding, and Cy Falkenberg also made progress, and the Naps were suddenly well fixed for pitching even without Joss and Young. Joe Jackson continued his rampage at the bat, keeping his average well over .400 through the summer months, and the Cleveland fans, so apathetic in April and early May, rallied around the team.

Perhaps the turning point in fan support came not at the ballpark, but in Ohio's state legislature, the General Assembly. A bill to allow Sunday baseball was introduced in that body in early 1911, and despite the fierce opposition of the churches in Cleveland and other large cities, the legislators passed the bill by a narrow margin on May 6 and sent it to Governor Judson Harmon. The governor, who had vetoed a similar measure a year before, nonetheless allowed the law to take effect without his signature. Charles Somers immediately scheduled a contest for Sunday, May 14, against the New York Yankees (the former Highlanders), and held a ceremony before the contest at which he presented State Representative Joseph Greeves, the sponsor of the Sunday baseball bill, with a gold lifetime pass. More than 15,000 fans stormed League Park to watch their Naps, without Lajoie, defeat the visitors by a 14–3 score, and the enthusiasm generated on that day gave the team and the city a lift. The Naps put together a five-game winning streak the following week, culminating in an 8–1 win on Sunday, May 21, in front of 14,000 people.

Lajoie, though unable to play the field when he rejoined the team, proved to be a good pinch-hitter. On July 1, batting for Jack Graney in the eighth inning with two out and the bases loaded, he drove a liner over the center fielder's head that scored all three runners and led the Naps to a 5–2 win over the White Sox. On July 18 he drove in two runs with a single against the Yankees, and two days later he won a game against the Red Sox with another two-run single. In all, he pinch-hit 12 times in July, with four hits and three walks, before he returned to the daily lineup on July 29.

The Naps gave up one of their off days to do a favor for Mrs. Addie Joss and her children. On Monday, July 24, the Cleveland club put on a benefit exhibition game to raise money for the family of the late pitcher. Opposing the Naps that day were the stars of the other seven American League teams, an aggregation assembled and directed by Washington Senators manager Jimmy McAleer. It proved to be an amazing assemblage of talent, one that probably had never been surpassed on any field at any one time in the game's history to that point. The All-Star contingent boasted a starting outfield of Ty Cobb (Tigers), Tris Speaker (Red Sox) and Sam Crawford (Tigers), while the infield featured Frank Baker (Athletics), Bobby Wallace (Browns), Eddie Collins (Athletics), and Hal Chase (Yankees). Gabby Street of the Senators handled the catching duties, while Joe Wood of the Red Sox started the game on the mound for McAleer's team.

Washington second baseman Herman "Germany" Schaefer did not get into the game, but kept the fans entertained with his clowning during infield practice, juggling baseballs and making exaggerated diving stops while Larry Lajoie hit grounders to him. Lajoie, who had not yet played in the field since his leg injury on May 7, was not in Cleveland's starting lineup, but declared himself ready for duty if needed. No doubt for sentimental reasons, manager Stovall sent a close friend of Joss, the 44-year-old Cy Young, to the mound to start the game for the Naps. Young, on his last legs as a major league pitcher, faced the most formidable lineup of his long career that afternoon, one that featured six future Hall of Famers. Ty Cobb, burdened by a heavy cold, did not expect to play, but changed his mind at the last minute and borrowed a Cleveland road uniform for the occasion.

More than 15,000 fans in League Park that day saw the All-Stars score twice in the first inning on a single by Speaker, a triple by Collins, and a single by Cobb. They tallied again in the second on a sacrifice fly by Wood, and were never seriously threatened, especially after Wood gave way to another future Cooperstown inductee, Walter Johnson, in the third inning. Young lasted only three innings, and though the Naps pushed across one run in the second and two more in the eighth, Johnson and his successor, Russell Ford of the Yankees, held them in check the rest of the way. One notable feature of the game was Larry Lajoie's first appearance in the field in two and a half months. He took over at first base for Stovall in the sixth inning and failed to get a hit in two trips to the plate against Ford, though he belted a long drive to center in the eighth that Washington's Clyde Milan, substituting for Speaker, hauled in for the out. The All-Stars won the game by a 5–3 score, and the contest raised nearly $13,000 for the Joss family.

By the time Lajoie returned to full-time duty on July 29, going hitless in four trips in a loss to the Senators, the Athletics and Tigers had pulled away from the pack and turned the pennant chase into a two-team race. Cleveland held sixth place, but the three teams immediately in front of them (New York, Chicago, and Boston) were only a few games ahead and easily catchable with a hot streak or two. Lajoie started hitting like the Lajoie of old in early August, and with Joe Jackson still marauding through the league with a .400 average, the Naps now possessed the most dangerous one-two batting punch in the game, with the possible exception of Detroit's tandem of Ty Cobb and Sam Crawford.

On August 29, a 2–1 loss to the Senators left the Naps in sixth place, 18 games behind the league-leading Athletics but only two and a half games out of third position. The Naps then reeled off a ten-game winning streak and vaulted into third place, a spot they held for the remainder of the season. Much of the credit for the surge went to George Stovall, who, with little prior experience as a manager, had the Naps hustling and scrapping for wins. "The team lacked pepper, but Stovall got them all up on their toes, and today they jabber away like a lot of poll parrots," the *Cleveland Plain Dealer* remarked at the end of the season. "They are full of fight, back up each other like champions, and you can look for them to be very much in next year's pennant race."[11]

Perhaps the Naps performed so well because they liked playing under Stovall's loose rein. Nonetheless, the secret deal between Connie Mack and Charles Somers to install Harry Davis as Cleveland manager for 1912 hit the papers in mid–August. The principals denied the story, mainly because Davis was under contract with the Athletics until the end of October, and Somers did not want to answer charges of tampering. *Sporting Life* reported on August 12 that Davis had already signed a contract with the Naps for the following season, though all involved disavowed all knowledge of any such agreement. The Cleveland players, however, were virtually unanimous in supporting Stovall for the permanent appointment as manager, and no doubt hoped that a strong finish to their season would change Somers' thinking.

Napoleon Lajoie, healthy again, hit the ball with authority while splitting time between second and first base. He did so while dealing with a family crisis involving his oldest brother Jeremie, who had spent his entire adult life as a laborer and hack driver in Woonsocket and was now in the second year of a losing battle with cancer. The ballplayer visited his brother in Woonsocket in early August, when the Naps visited Boston to play the Red Sox, and found that Jeremie's long fight was entering its end stage. On Thursday, September 14, an off day for the Naps, Lajoie received word that Jeremie had passed away. He and Myrtle proceeded immediately to Rhode Island, while the Naps traveled to Boston for a weekend series against the Red Sox. All American League games were rained out on Friday, but the Naps, without Lajoie, played two games in Boston on Saturday and lost both, 6–0 and 3–0. He missed one more game on Monday, a 4–1 Cleveland win, then rejoined the team in New York for a series against the Yankees.

Lajoie's average stood at .393 in mid–September, but his bat cooled off during the last two weeks of the season, and the veteran ended the 1911 campaign, his 16th in the major leagues, with a .365 average in 90 games. Joe Jackson, Cleveland's newest star, never stopped hitting and finished at .408, setting a new Cleveland team record that stands to this day. Jackson also scored 126 runs and belted 233 hits. He had no chance for the batting crown, because Detroit's Ty Cobb, still smarting over the Chalmers controversy from the year before, was determined to win the title free and clear in 1911. Cobb batted .420, the highest average of his career, to win his fifth consecutive championship.

The Naps, behind the hitting of Lajoie and Jackson and the improved starting pitching (highlighted by rookie left-hander Vean Gregg's 23 wins), held onto third place and finished the year with an 80–73 record, a fine performance after their 6–11 start. Though the Cleveland papers praised Stovall's leadership, his term as manager was finished. The deal between Somers and Connie Mack to put Harry Davis in the Cleveland managerial post was the worst-kept secret in baseball during the summer of 1911, but the season was over and Stovall's time was up, despite his team's surprising third-place finish. Charles Somers wanted Harry Davis, not George Stovall, to lead his club, and the Naps owner was a man who got what he wanted. "Brother George" was out and, immediately after the close of the World Series, Davis was in. On October 27, Harry Davis signed a contract to manage the Naps in 1912.

21

The Silver Horseshoe

The season of 1912 will open with the best of prospects in Cleveland. With a magnificent ball park equipped with the finest of modern improvements, with a new and wide-awake manager and some of the greatest stars in baseball as the nucleus of a club, the fans of the Forest City are more than justified in expecting a gilt-edged quality of baseball. — Baseball Magazine, *March 1912*[1]

The appointment of Harry Davis as manager of the Cleveland Naps continued a pattern that had held form since the franchise entered the American League. The club had alternated strict managers with permissive ones since Jimmy McAleer, the first leader of the team, gave way to Bill Armour before the 1902 campaign. Armour, a disciplinarian, was replaced by Lajoie in 1905, and he, in turn, was supplanted by another authoritarian manager, Deacon McGuire, four years later. The merry George Stovall, who showed little interest in policing his men off the field so long as they played well, led the Naps to a third-place finish in 1911 but failed to impress Charles Somers. Now Harry Davis, a Connie Mack acolyte, would have his turn. Lajoie, who played with Davis on the Athletics 11 years before, pledged his support. "I want to see the Naps succeed under Harry Davis," he told reporter Ed Bang. "In fact, nothing would please me more than to see Davis win the pennant his first year as a big league manager. I will give my all to bring about this result."[2]

Davis got off on the wrong foot with his new team almost immediately, when he traded George Stovall to the Browns for pitcher Lefty George on February 17. Stovall was popular with his fellow Naps, not only for his personality but for his loose managerial rein. Davis explained that the club needed more left-handed pitching, which had been a problem for the Naps for several years, and that he could move Napoleon Lajoie to first, with Neal Ball, Ivy Olson, and several others fighting it out for the second base and shortstop positions. It appeared, though, that Davis was uncomfortable with the presence of the popular ex-manager in the playing ranks. Somers had offered the managerial post in Toledo to Stovall, who turned it down and attempted to buy his release so he could pursue an opening with the Chicago Cubs. The Naps owner might have allowed Stovall to continue his career in the senior circuit, but when the first baseman failed to clear waivers, Somers had no choice but to trade him to another American League team.

Davis was determined to show more firmness than the departed Stovall, and instituted several rules of conduct for the Naps. He outlawed dice-playing in the clubhouse, which had been a popular pastime during the Stovall regime. "I don't object to a small game of poker, but I do draw the line on craps," said Davis. "Some players carry around gambling debts and they cannot do justice to themselves in the games."[3] Davis also banned fraternization between the Naps and opposing players before and during the games, and tightened the rules on curfew, which Stovall had often ignored. He even took issue with the players' caps, ordering new ones after telling the papers that "he never saw such a punk selection of headgear in all his experience as a ball player."[4] Davis was determined to set a businesslike tone similar to the one his mentor Connie Mack had established with the Athletics, but it remained to be seen how his new charges would accept the more restrictive atmosphere.

The new manager intended to manage from the bench in street clothes, but during the first week of training camp in Mobile, Alabama, he donned a uniform, because, as *The Sporting News* explained, "He complains that the Naps do not show the snap and ginger they should, and he has found that the only way to drive them is to work in uniform with them."[5] Sundays were an off day in training camp, but not totally. "Every player must take some exercise," Davis told his charges. "You may play golf, tennis, walk, or go fishing, but you must do something besides loafing around the hotel. A cross-country walk of four or five miles would not hurt some of you fellers. So if you don't play golf or tennis, it's a walk for you."[6] This was a departure from the way Lajoie had run things a few years before, as he had allowed his players much more free time. Still, Davis did not work the players as hard as had Deacon McGuire the previous spring, so the Naps took a wait-and-see attitude toward their new leader.

Stovall's departure opened a hole at first base, and Davis reviewed several candidates for the job at Mobile. Art Griggs had hit fairly well in a 22-game trial for the Naps the year before but needed more seasoning, while Eddie Hohnhorst, who played at Toledo in 1911, appeared to be more ready to claim the position. Though Davis had starred at first for more than a decade with the Athletics, he was not interested in playing the position himself, as he was nearly 40 years old and wanted to lead the team from the bench. With a surplus of middle infielders (Neal Ball, Ivy Olson, Griggs, and others) fighting for jobs, Davis raised the possibility of moving Napoleon Lajoie to the first sack. Lajoie worked out at first base, the position he played for the Phillies during his first two seasons, and proclaimed himself ready to play there if asked.

In mid–March, though spring training had barely begun, Davis expressed frustration with the attitudes of some of his men. "They haven't any ginger," he complained to the press. "They seem to need waking up."[7] To rectify what Davis saw as a general lack of hustle, he named shortstop Ivy Olson as captain of the team, reportedly after Lajoie, who wanted to concentrate on his playing, turned down the position. Olson was a chatterbox on the field, and though his constant nattering bothered many of his teammates, Davis believed that the team needed a strong dose of pep. Olson's appointment was not well received, as the shortstop had played for the club for only one year and his swaggering, self-confident personality irritated many of those around him. He was also deeply unpopular around the league. As Casey Stengel, a childhood schoolmate of Olson's, once said, "They tell me he was a rough cookie on the bases in the Pacific Coast League before coming up. I hear he spiked his name and forwarding address on practically every infielder in the league."[8] Many Naps believed that Joe Birmingham, the veteran center fielder, deserved the captaincy, but Davis wanted an infielder to hold the job. The fact that Olson was not much of a hitter and faced competition from Terry Turner, Neal Ball, and others for a starting position apparently did not factor into the new manager's thinking.

The Naps opened their season at home on Thursday, April 11, in front of more than

19,000 fans, the largest League Park crowd since the closing days of the 1908 pennant race, and rewarded their supporters with a 3–2 win over the Tigers. During the win, the Tigers exposed one of Cleveland's weaknesses. Jackson, batting third, belted three singles that day, two of which came with two out. The Tigers purposely walked the next batter, Lajoie, on both of those two-out occasions, and then retired Buddy Ryan, a rookie from Portland who had taken over right field. Pitchers had learned to walk Lajoie intentionally without giving him a chance to swing at a pitchout, and the men behind Jackson and Lajoie (Ryan, first baseman Hohnhorst, and third baseman Terry Turner) were much weaker hitters. Lajoie provided protection for Jackson in the order, but the Naps needed someone to protect their veteran slugger.

Lajoie was passed intentionally four times during the four-game series against Detroit, but the one time the Tigers elected to pitch to him, the 37-year-old made them pay. On Friday, April 12, the Naps and Tigers were tied at two in the bottom of the eighth when Lajoie came to bat against Edgar Willett. Ivy Olson was on third and Joe Jackson on second, and because first base was open, everyone in the park expected Willett to walk Lajoie. Instead, the Tigers pitched to the Cleveland star, and Lajoie whistled Willett's first pitch into right field for a single that scored both runners. This hit proved the winning margin in a 4–2 Cleveland victory. The Tigers prevailed on Saturday, taking advantage of nine Cleveland errors in a 12–4 win, and on Sunday, in front of 17,975 fans (the biggest Sunday crowd ever in Cleveland), the Naps lost again by a 1–0 score, with Detroit right-hander Tex Covington outdueling Cleveland's George Kahler. Ty Cobb, the five-time batting champion, scored the only run of the game when he was hit by a pitch in the first inning, took second on an error, and rode home on a triple by Sam Crawford.

The Naps defeated the St. Louis Browns twice at home before traveling to Detroit for the first game ever played in the Tigers' new edifice, then called Navin Field and later known as Tiger Stadium. The inaugural contest was scheduled for Thursday, April 18, but heavy rains delayed the opener for two days. On Saturday, April 20, the skies cleared and the Naps and Tigers battled into extra innings, with Detroit pulling out a 6–5 win in the bottom of the 11th. The Naps won a 4–0, ten-inning affair the next day, then returned home and lost three straight to the White Sox, leaving their record at 5–6, before setting off on a western road trip.

While the Naps struggled to play .500 ball, the *Cleveland News* reminded its readers that the tenth anniversary of Lajoie's first game in a Cleveland uniform was fast approaching. Team management had already proclaimed another "Lajoie Day" on June 4, the date of the anniversary, while the *News* hit upon a novel way to commemorate the occasion. The paper requested that 1,000 Cleveland fans donate a dollar apiece to purchase "an immense thousand-dollar silver horseshoe, the same to be presented to the man who has brought everlasting fame to Cleveland as a baseball town, when he comes to bat the first time on June 4 next."[9] The article asked that donations be sent to the "Lajoie Fund Editor" for the purchase of 1,000 silver dollars. The Cleveland Athletic Club was also involved in the effort, and by the third week of April, *Sporting Life* reported that about $300 had been raised. The *News* and the Athletic Club expressed optimism that they could raise the remainder of the money by June.

The Naps clattered along near the .500 mark during the first few weeks of the season, and Davis started making changes before the end of April. Eddie Hohnhorst opened the season at first base, but failed to hit, and on April 24 in Chicago, Davis benched Hohnhorst and manned the position himself for two games. He then moved Lajoie to first and put

Neal Ball on second base after sending Art Griggs back to Toledo. The left side of the infield was also unsettled, with Terry Turner, Ivy Olson, and rookie Herman Bronkie sharing the shortstop and third base positions. In mid–May, Davis gave up on Hohnhorst and recalled Griggs, who saw action at first and second. Davis continued to change his lineup in search of a winning combination, and the constant shuffling made many of his charges uneasy.

Once again, the injury bug struck Lajoie at a most inopportune time. On May 3, while fielding ground balls at first base during infield practice in Chicago, he twisted his upper body sharply to catch a ball and doubled over in severe pain. It appeared that he had wrenched his back, though a doctor determined that the ballplayer was suffering from pleurisy, a lung inflammation usually caused by a virus or bacteria but which can also result from a chest injury. Lajoie's pain was so acute that he had trouble breathing, and an alarmed Myrtle Lajoie traveled from Cleveland to Chicago to tend to her husband. A few days later, Larry and Myrtle returned to their home in South Euclid, where the veteran ballplayer was ordered to bed for a rest. Lajoie, whose average of .389 led the league at the time, missed 22 games and did not return to the lineup until June 2.

On June 4, League Park hosted another "Lajoie Day," on the tenth anniversary of his first game in a Cleveland uniform. In a ceremony before the contest, Lajoie was presented with a purse filled with 25 five-dollar gold coins from his fellow Naps, and an enormous floral horseshoe with 1,009 silver dollars wired into it. The fans had come through for the Cleveland star, not only reaching the $1,000 goal, but slightly surpassing it. Lajoie had been treated to several "Lajoie Day" celebrations during his career, but this one was special. He later said that the recognition he received that afternoon "meant a great deal to me," though it also was a distraction during the game that followed. "I was worried all through the game that something might happen to [the horseshoe]," said Lajoie, "and afterward we loaded the dollars into sacks and carried them right to the bank."[10] The Naps defeated Boston by a 5–1 score that day, with Joe Jackson belting a homer and Lajoie, in his third game back from the injured list, chipping in with a double, a single, and a sacrifice fly.

Lajoie got along well with Harry Davis, but the new manager's strict discipline rankled several Naps, who grumbled about his leadership as the season wore on. Center fielder Joe Birmingham, still smarting that Davis had bypassed him for the captaincy of the team in favor of the less experienced Ivy Olson, soon emerged as the leader of an anti–Davis clique on the ballclub. The complaining grew louder as the Naps, who rested in fourth place after winning three out of four from the Yankees in early June, dropped nine in a row and stumbled back into sixth position. Discipline problems abounded as the Naps fell further from contention, and although Jackson and Lajoie kept pounding out hits, most of the other Naps played maddeningly inconsistent ball.

Cleveland's two star hitters did their part. On June 30, in the second game of a doubleheader at St. Louis, Lajoie and Jackson belted four hits apiece in a 15–4 win. Jackson scored four runs, and three of his hits were triples, tying the American League record set in 1902 by Elmer Flick and since matched by Bill Bradley, Larry Lajoie, and several others. The Naps then traveled to Detroit, where George Mullin held them to five hits in an 8–2 Tigers win. Three of those hits belonged to Lajoie, who was still hitting as well as ever, even as most of the other Naps struggled at the plate. Earlier in the season, Joe Benz of the White Sox had shut down the Naps on five hits, and Lajoie made three of them that day as well.

Lajoie left the lineup again for two weeks in July, but for once his absence was not the result of an injury. His mother Celina had been ailing for more than a year, and Larry

Lajoie with his silver dollar horseshoe at League Park on June 4, 1912, the tenth anniversary of his debut in a Cleveland uniform (National Baseball Hall of Fame Library, Cooperstown, New York).

visited her for the final time in Woonsocket when the Naps traveled to Boston in late May. On July 11, during a game between the Naps and the Senators at Washington, Larry received the news that his mother had died that morning at the age of 79. Lajoie finished the game, then boarded a train for Woonsocket. Celina Lajoie's wake was held in the home of Larry's sister, Celina Harpin, among a wealth of floral tributes from the Cleveland players and from team owner Charles Somers. Celina Lajoie, who had survived her husband Jean-Baptiste by 31 years, was buried in the cemetery of Precious Blood Church.

The grieving ballplayer did not immediately return to the team, instead remaining in Woonsocket with his wife Myrtle to help settle his mother's affairs. He did not appear in the Cleveland lineup again until July 27, when he reclaimed his position at second base. The Naps had performed abysmally in his absence, falling from one game above .500 to five games below it before winning two contests just before his return. While Lajoie attended to family matters, Davis moved Ivy Olson to second base and auditioned two young prospects, Brown University star Ken Nash and local high-school standout Roger Peckinpaugh, neither of whom was ready for major league competition. Lefty George, the pitcher the Naps received in exchange for George Stovall, failed to win a game in five tries and soon drew his release, leaving the team with nothing to show for the unpopular trade and increasing the pressure on Davis, the man who made it.

Davis, who had hoped to pattern his managerial demeanor after that of his mentor Connie Mack, nonetheless grew bitter and sarcastic as the losses mounted. He enraged some of his charges when the local papers revealed that Somers, at Davis' suggestion, had asked for waivers on more than half of the team. He also unwisely collared the local reporters and blasted his men as "quitters" and threatened to "get new players ... if the ones on the payroll did not act more alive."[11] He moved Joe Jackson from right field to center and back, shuttled Lajoie between second to first, and shifted Ivy Olson all around the infield in a seemingly random fashion. Though he named Olson as his captain, he gave the responsibility for positioning infielders to Neal Ball, undercutting Olson's authority and bypassing Lajoie once again. Davis' moves were unpredictable and often counterproductive, further increasing the anti–Davis sentiment on the club.

The first indication of a brewing player revolt came during the last week of May, after the Naps lost a game in Boston because Olson failed to cover third base on a key play. Pitcher Willie Mitchell confronted Olson after the game, and the two men fought in the clubhouse, with Mitchell getting by far the worst of it. The Naps held a closed-door meeting and decided that they could play no more with Olson as their captain. Several of the players formed a committee and confronted Davis, demanding the dismissal of Olson and the appointment of Joe Birmingham to the post. Word of the meeting quickly got out, and although Davis denied knowledge of the fight, claiming that he had neither witnessed it nor heard about it, it was no secret to anyone close to the team.

More than a week later, Davis finally addressed the matter, telling the press that Olson was still the captain of the team, and that he would take no action until he learned more about the fight. "We'll have harmony in this club or bust," declared the manager. "We've got to have harmony. I can't and won't take any action until I know the different sides of the matter. What action I take then will depend upon what I hear."[12] Shortly afterward, Olson was stripped of the captaincy and Birmingham was appointed to succeed him. Davis had given in to the pressure in the interest of "harmony," and his standing with his players suffered. The Naps put Olson on waivers with the intention of sending him to Toledo, but because the New York Yankees put in a claim for him, the Naps were forced to keep him on the Cleveland roster.

Lajoie, who was out of the lineup at the time (and was on the mend in Cleveland when the players held their meeting in Boston), stayed out of the fray. Despite the turmoil surrounding the team, he and Joe Jackson combined to form a devastating one-two batting punch, much as had Lajoie and Ed Delahanty so many years before with the Phillies. Though Lajoie was now nearly 38 years old and missed 34 games in 1912 due to injuries and absences, he kept his batting average above the .360 mark and fielded as well as ever. Though he failed to hit a homer that season, he drove in 90 runs and struck out only 11 times in 500 plate appearances. Jackson, who like Lajoie paid little attention to his teammates' complaints about their manager, compiled another remarkable season, nearly clearing the .400 mark for the second season in a row and swatting a league record 26 triples.

Harry Davis put a premium on beating Philadelphia, his old team, and appeared to be so intent on proving himself to Connie Mack that the players could not help but feel a measure of unwelcome pressure. When the Athletics came to Cleveland for a four-game series on Sunday, June 9, Davis pulled out all the stops, moving Lajoie back to second base and putting the newly recalled Art Griggs back at first. The result was a 13–2 drubbing at the hands of the defending champions, a defeat that so disheartened the Naps that they lost the last three games of the series, followed by three losses to the Senators and one to the Tigers before they finally halted their eight-game skid. This losing streak dropped the Naps out of the first division, a level they would not reach again in 1912.

In July, the Naps traveled to Philadelphia to play the Athletics, and this series ended in an even worse fashion. The two teams split a doubleheader on Saturday, July 13, then returned to Cleveland for a single game on Sunday which the Naps won. On Monday, back in Philadelphia, the Athletics handed Cleveland a 7–0 defeat, and on Tuesday, the rattled Davis became so unglued in an argument with umpire Harry Westervelt that he had to be escorted from the field by a gaggle of local policemen. To make matters worse, Davis joined with two of his fellow American League managers (George Stovall of the Browns and Nixey Callahan of the White Sox) and filed a formal complaint with the league office against Westervelt. This protest went nowhere and unnecessarily damaged relations between the Naps and the rest of the league's arbiters. Shortly afterward, a 2–12 slide left the Naps ten games below the .500 mark, more than 23 games behind the first-place Boston Red Sox.

Lajoie received a jolt on June 5, when the Naps played the Yankees in Cleveland on the afternoon after "Lajoie Day." In the fourth inning, with the Naps ahead by four runs, Joe Jackson went to bat with two men on and Lajoie on deck. Yankees pitcher Jack Quinn sized up the situation and decided to walk Jackson, preferring to face Lajoie with the bases loaded. No one could remember if any pitcher had ever disrespected Lajoie in this manner, and though the incensed veteran foiled the strategy, belting a single that scored two runs, it appeared that Jackson had supplanted Lajoie as the hitting star of the club. The Naps won the game by a 7–0 count as the aging Lajoie gave notice that he was not yet finished as an offensive threat.

By August, with the club anchored in the second division, the Cleveland papers were filled with complaints about the listless and careless play of the Naps. Fan support dwindled as the losses mounted and Harry Davis' position grew less tenable by the day. A disastrous eastern swing in mid–August brought 13 losses in 15 games, and by the end of the month Davis realized that his time in Cleveland was up. On the morning of September 2, Labor Day, after a 6–3 loss to the Browns (who had hired George Stovall as their manager) the day before left the Naps 18 games below the .500 mark, Davis resigned. He returned to the Athletics in 1913 and remained with Connie Mack for more than a decade thereafter as a coach and scout, but never managed again.

Charles Somers named Joe Birmingham, the good-fielding but light-hitting center fielder who had joined the Naps late in the 1906 campaign, as interim manager for the rest of the season. Birmingham immediately rescinded some of his predecessor's more restrictive rules, and the Naps, who had fallen out of the pennant chase months before, perked up. Lajoie went on a tear, batting nearly .500 in September and raising his average to the .360s

The 1912 Naps. Lajoie is prominently featured in the middle of the first row (National Baseball Hall of Fame Library, Cooperstown, New York).

after the new manager shifted him and Jackson down one spot each in the lineup, with Jackson now hitting fourth and Lajoie fifth. Ray Chapman, a rookie from Toledo, claimed the shortstop position, while the pitching suddenly coalesced and began winning games. In all, the Naps finished with a 21–7 record under Birmingham and convinced Somers, who had considered several candidates for the managerial post, to give the permanent position to Birmingham for the 1913 season.

Birmingham was not as tough and aggressive as Ivy Olson, but he had plenty of self-confidence and had definite ideas about how a team should be run. He came to the Naps in 1906 after a successful career at Cornell University, and though he was not a strong hitter, his speed and strong throwing arm made him a defensive star in center and right field. After his appointment to the captaincy in June of 1912, he shared his opinions freely with his fellow Naps, and was even so bold as to give hitting advice to Joe Jackson and Napoleon Lajoie. Jackson, who hit .395 in 1912, paid little attention, but the proud Lajoie took offense at Birmingham's presumption. Lajoie also believed that Birmingham and others had purposely played mediocre ball in July and August in a bid to get Davis fired.

He was not the only one. Buddy Ryan started the 1912 season in right field for Cleveland and stayed with the team for two years. After the Naps released him to Portland of the Pacific Coast League, Ryan blasted Birmingham in the papers, calling him "the poorest excuse of a manager in the major league." He continued, "[Harry] Davis is one of the brainiest players in the country and could have done a lot with the club. We know pretty well that Birmingham knocked him out of a job by carrying tales."[13]

Napoleon Lajoie was not pleased with the elevation of Birmingham. The center fielder possessed definite leadership qualities, but had also placed himself at the center of opposition to Harry Davis. Lajoie resented the fact that Birmingham had been rewarded for his disloyalty, and though he was not interested in the job himself, he looked upon the selection of Birmingham as a slap in the face to his friend and former teammate Davis. Lajoie and Birmingham had been teammates for seven years, but never close friends, and the circumstances of the new manager's promotion caused a rift between the two strong-willed men and threatened team harmony as the 1913 season approached. Lajoie said nothing publicly to indicate his state of mind, but his distaste for his new manager could not stay under wraps forever.

22

Player vs. Manager

Nap has been a wonder for so long that most people have forgotten when he began to dazzle the circuits with his phenomenal play. He has always been a marvel and he has never played upon a pennant winner ... This is one of the most peculiar of the many peculiar vagaries of baseball. Why defeat should thus dog the footsteps of one of baseball's brightest stars is inexplicable.—*Baseball Magazine*, August 1913[1]

When Joe Birmingham became manager of the Cleveland Naps on September 3, 1912, he inherited a situation that was unique in baseball. His second baseman, Larry Lajoie, was not only ten years his senior, but was also a former manager of the Naps and the man who led the club to the best finish of its existence (second place) four years before. "Birmy" was a fine defensive outfielder with a mediocre bat, while Lajoie was a multiple batting champion who was still the "king of ballplayers" to Cleveland fans. To make matters more complicated, the team itself was named for Lajoie. Though Lajoie had missed a large number of games due to injuries during the previous two seasons, he was still a powerful force on the field and off, and the latest Cleveland manager would have to use all the diplomacy at his command to deal with his aging superstar.

Indeed, Birmingham appeared to recognize that his relationship with Lajoie was a frosty one, and made an effort to praise his second baseman whenever the opportunity arose. In March, the manager made it clear that Lajoie would remain at his preferred position, second base, though some critics had noted the veteran's shrinking range and had suggested that he be moved to first. "Where could we get another second baseman who could equal Larry at putting the ball on a stealer?" asked Birmingham. "Nowhere."[2] In April, after Lajoie handled eight chances, many of them difficult ones, in a win at Chicago, Birmingham was effusive in his praise. "Talk about Larry's going back," he said. "Why, he'll be with the Naps five years hence. He never was greater in his whole career than he is now."[3]

Despite the new manager's expressions of admiration, Lajoie's dislike of Birmingham was no secret around the American League, and as soon as the 1912 season ended, trade rumors began circulating in the nation's sporting press. One scenario had Lajoie joining the Boston Red Sox, who had won the 1912 World Series in an exciting eight-game set against the New York Giants. The Red Sox were solid at second base with Steve Yerkes, but their first baseman and manager, Jake Stahl, was ready to retire as a player and direct the team from the bench. A trade to the Red Sox would not only put Lajoie on a team that had a chance to win a pennant, but would also allow him to finish his career in his home region of New England. Other reports stated that the last-place New York Yankees, who needed help at almost every position after losing 102 games in 1912, were interested in the Cleveland veteran. Terry Turner, the third baseman and shortstop who had joined the Naps in 1904, was also caught up in the discussion, and some reports had him and Lajoie going to Boston, New York, or elsewhere as a package deal.

The rumor mill was working overtime, and in January of 1913 Charles Somers decided to shut it down. "Inasmuch as both Larry and Terry are in excellent health and banking on playing ball next season, there is only one city where they can play, and that is Cleveland," he told the papers. "Lajoie and Turner are neither for sale nor trade. Manager Birmingham wants them to continue as Naps. So do I, as I believe they are a considerable part of our offensive and defensive strength. Then, too, I firmly believe that the fans of the Sixth City are heart and soul with Lajoie and Turner. Larry is slated to play second base and Turner third base for the 1913 Naps. And that goes."[4] To prove his point, he announced on January 21 that Lajoie had signed his contract for 1913 at a salary of $9,000 per year, the same amount he had received in 1912. This proclamation slowed the spread of rumors, though sources in New York claimed that the Yankees were still interested in the former batting champion.

Though the Naps had finished in fifth position in 1912, their 21–7 streak to end the season brought renewed optimism that the city would break its long pennant drought in 1913. Lajoie's good friend Grantland Rice, for one, hoped to see the Naps in postseason play for Lajoie's sake. "Speaking strictly as a noncombatant," wrote Rice, "we'd like to see our old sidekick, Larry Lajoie, get one whack at that World's Series fluff after 17 seasons of stardom, minus any part of it. To say nothing of observing Larry just once up in a championship series with the bases full and the score fairly compact."[5]

Hugh Fullerton thought otherwise. The Chicago sportswriter evaluated the Naps in his nationally syndicated column and laid much of the blame for Cleveland's repeated failures on the Frenchman's shoulders. Said Fullerton:

> The fact that Lajoie, himself one of the greatest players of all time, has failed to get into the spirit of the club and has been the leader among the indifferent ones, has hurt more than anything else.... Lajoie will play second, and a great deal depends upon whether or not his heart is in the game. If he is inclined to make an effort to hustle he will make the team at least one position higher. I have few hopes. Lajoie has grown accustomed to the careless system of ball playing and is indifferent at heart. It looks to me as if there is little hope Lajoie ever will play good ball for Cleveland, and that the only hope of his ever being great except at bat is that he be traded.[6]

After training in Pensacola, Florida, and Mobile, Alabama, the Naps headed north with a host of injuries, especially to the pitchers. Cy Falkenberg and Fred Blanding were not ready to pitch, so Birmingham started the season with Vean Gregg, Bill Steen, Willie Mitchell, and George Kahler in the starting slots. Terry Turner, whose wife was seriously ill, was not with the team, so Ivy Olson took over third base. The outfield featured Birmingham in center, with Joe Jackson in right and Jack Graney in left. The infield looked solid with Olson, Ray Chapman at short, Lajoie at second, and the reliable Doc Johnston at first, while two solid defensive players, Steve O'Neill and Fred Carisch, shared the catching chores for a club that appeared to have more talent than recent Cleveland teams. The Naps had made a habit of disappointing their fans after raising hopes in the spring, but many nonetheless expected the Naps to challenge the Athletics and Red Sox for the pennant.

The weather played havoc with the schedule in April and May of 1913. Flooding along the Ohio River submerged the Cincinnati ballpark and led to a series of cancellations, while heavy rains caused plenty of postponements in and around the Great Lakes. The Naps hoped to draw more than 20,000 fans to their home opener on April 10, but the contest was rained out, and wet weather the next day held the attendance to 14,000. They saw the Naps defeat Chicago by a 3–1 score. Cleveland lost to the White Sox on Saturday in front of 7,000, and the first Sunday game of the season, which usually drew a large crowd, was called off due to rain. Most major league teams suffered from the weather in early 1913, but the Naps may have taken the hardest hit of all. Though fan enthusiasm ran at a high pitch, the Naps were unable to take advantage, and lost thousands of paid admittances to the elements.

Joe Birmingham, like other Cleveland managers before him, wanted his team to play "inside baseball," so the Naps utilized the bunt and the sacrifice to good effect. Joe Jackson, the cleanup batter, and Lajoie in the fifth slot were still expected to belt the ball, but the other Naps stole bases, executed squeeze plays, and worked hard to put runners on the bases for the two sluggers to drive in. Past editions of the Naps had simply waited around for someone, usually Lajoie, to deliver the big hit, but Birmingham's club played aggressive, alert baseball, especially on the base paths. On April 25, Detroit hurler George Mullin pitched out a dozen times in a single game, expecting the Naps to attempt a squeeze play whenever they had a runner on third. Birmingham refused to call for one, and the distracted Mullin lost the game by a 3–0 score.

Joe Jackson and Napoleon Lajoie supplied the power for the energetic Naps, and both men, especially Lajoie, started the season in good hitting form. "[Larry] is clouting them on the nose just as he did half a dozen years ago," said *The Sporting News*. "When will he quit? When they refuse to let him have a uniform."[7] Lajoie also played second base with his usual style, and though some claimed that his range was not what it once was, he was as sure-handed as ever, playing errorless ball until he dropped a pop-up in his 17th game of the season. He had handled his first 94 chances of 1913 cleanly. While Ty Cobb remained out of action in a protracted salary dispute with Detroit owner Frank Navin, Jackson and Lajoie led the batting lists, with Jackson over the .400 mark and Lajoie close to it. Cobb had won the previous six batting titles, but the two Naps stars threatened to make the batting race an all–Cleveland competition.

Cleveland's aggressive style proved unpopular with some of the other American League teams, and on May 7, a physically bruising contest against the defending champion Boston Red Sox resulted in a wild post-game brawl. In the second inning, while Boston catcher Bill Carrigan and pitcher Dutch Leonard conferred between the plate and the mound, the runner on third, Jack Graney, attempted to steal home. Carrigan sprang into action and slammed into Graney before he could reach the plate, knocking the Cleveland runner unconscious as Leonard tagged him out. This act set off a series of retaliations by the Naps during the next few innings. Joe Jackson slid into second base with his spikes high, Ivy Olson collided with Boston's Rube Foster at first base, and Fred Carisch leveled Boston's Hal Janvrin on a play at second. Cleveland won the game by a 4–1 count, and as both teams made their way to the clubhouse, Olson and Boston's Les Nunamaker traded insults, then started throwing punches. Carrigan stepped in to help Nunamaker but was belted by Cleveland's Buddy Ryan, a former boxer, and the fight was on.

The Naps and Red Sox battled under the League Park grandstand for more than ten minutes. Napoleon Lajoie, usually the friendliest of ballplayers, was one of the main combatants, throwing haymakers and taking shots with the rest of his teammates. In time, the battle ended, and almost all the players involved nursed cuts, bruises, and black eyes for days afterward. Tris Speaker, the Boston center fielder, suffered the most serious injuries, having been spiked three times during the fracas. League president Ban Johnson demanded an explanation from both managers, but Boston's acting field leader, Heinie Wagner, denied any knowledge of the incident. "I have heard nothing of any fight," said Wagner afterward. "I was chased from the field and had dressed and gone upstairs before the game ended." Joe Birmingham claimed that he did not see anything either. "I have nothing to say," reported the Cleveland manager. "Some of the boys were pretty hot about the play at the plate and may have called each other something after the game, but I was the last one off the field and did not see anything out of the way. Everything was peaceable when I arrived."[8] All the players involved swore themselves to secrecy, and even the two umpires, Tommy Connolly and Eugene McGreevy, pleaded ignorance when Johnson queried them. In the end, Johnson fined Olson and Nunamaker $25 apiece and, faced with a wall of silence, dropped the matter.

The Naps won three of four from Boston and held second place before the "annual blasting of hopes," as *The Sporting News* described it, threatened to derail Cleveland's pennant chances. On May 11, Napoleon Lajoie fell victim to another major injury when an inside fastball delivered by Ed Klepfer of the Yankees hit the veteran second baseman in the hands, breaking both his right little finger and his left thumb. This calamity put the Cleveland star, hitting .382 at the time, out of the lineup for three weeks and left a hole in the Cleveland offense. The next day, an even worse fate befell center fielder Joe Birmingham, who slid into second base and broke his right leg in two places. He was out for the rest of the season, leaving a void in center field that Buddy Ryan and rookie Harry (Nemo) Leibold struggled to fill.

Lajoie's latest injury left Joe Jackson without a powerful presence behind him in the lineup, and opposing pitchers dealt with the hard-hitting outfielder, who was batting nearly .450 in late May, by walking him with greater frequency. However, other hitters picked up the slack, the pitching proved solid, and the Naps ran off a nine-game winning streak without their veteran star. The final win of the streak came on June 1 at Cleveland in the first game of a twin bill against the St. Louis Browns. In the nightcap, Lajoie made his first appearance since his injury and went hitless as the Naps made six errors in a 6–2 loss. The team traveled to New York and, with Lajoie on the bench, won four in a row from the Yankees at the Polo Grounds, maintaining their hold on second place, a game and a half behind the Philadelphia Athletics.

The rest of the road trip was a catastrophe, as the Naps won only three of their next 12 games and fell six and a half off the pace. Even during their 13–1 run, they failed to gain ground on Connie Mack's club, which ran off 15 wins in a row and extended its lead. The Naps expected the streaking Athletics to hit a slump at some point, but the 1913 edition of the Philadelphia club proved to be one of the deepest and most talented in league history up to that time. The Athletics looked so formidable that by the time the season was half-finished, Henry Edwards of the *Cleveland Plain Dealer* declared that the race was over and the Naps would have to be content with second place.

Lajoie was anxious to return to the lineup, but he could not grip a bat or handle a baseball until his injuries healed. At age 38, he recovered more slowly than in the past, so he could only watch while the Naps fought to keep the Athletics within striking distance. In late May, when the Naps traveled to Elmira, New York, for an off-day exhibition game,

Lajoie's main rivals for American League hitting supremacy — Ty Cobb (left), Joe Jackson and Sam Crawford (author's collection).

he tried to play but retired to the bench when the pain in his hands proved too severe. When Cleveland took to the road on an eastern swing in early June, he pinch-hit twice against the Yankees and once against the Red Sox, failing to reach base all three times, before earning a start at second base in Boston on June 10.

The bad blood between the Naps and Red Sox still simmered, and when Boston catcher Bill Carrigan spiked Ray Chapman on June 11, it might have ignited another brawl. Certainly the Naps believed that the spiking, which occurred when Chapman, like Graney as few weeks before, attempted to steal home, was not accidental. "The spirit of fair play does not exist in the Boston team," fumed Joe Birmingham, managing in street clothes from the bench. "We shall not submit tamely to such methods as they employed in our games here just closed. I never saw such a raw, coarse, mean exhibition."[9] During that 15-inning contest at Fenway Park, pitcher Joe Wood of the Red Sox attempted to walk Lajoie intentionally by throwing inside, not outside, to him. Wood's first pitch sailed past Lajoie's head, and the second glanced off his wrist. Lajoie, who was not injured by the blow, immediately accused Wood of throwing at him. His hands were not fully healed, and the possibility of another injury, especially an intentional one, angered the usually friendly Cleveland star.

Joe Jackson's walks continued unabated even after Lajoie rejoined the lineup, as the sore-handed veteran had trouble gripping the bat properly and failed to give Jackson his usual support. Jackson grew frustrated by his mounting number of bases on balls, and on

June 22, he exploded in a profane tirade against umpire Jack Egan at League Park after Egan called Jackson out at first on a grounder, though the Cleveland slugger had apparently crossed the bag safely. Egan was the umpire who had called Cleveland's Bill Hinchman out at first at a pivotal moment of the pennant race in 1908. Jackson's verbal assault incited the crowd, which showered the unpopular Egan with a hail of pop bottles, though none of the missiles found their mark. Jackson earned an indefinite suspension from the league, though he protested that Egan had cursed him first. The Naps could ill afford to lose Jackson for any length of time, as Lajoie was hitting poorly and Cleveland's annual wave of injuries had already begun.

League president Ban Johnson, never shy about expressing himself on any topic, blamed Joe Birmingham for Jackson's suspension and roasted the Cleveland manager in a particularly intemperate manner. "The trouble provoked by Jackson might have started a riot," fumed the league president, "and anything approaching that would mean the abolition of Sunday baseball in Cleveland. The failure of Birmingham to realize this and to handle his players so as to prevent a disturbance on big days convinces me that he is not competent to handle one of our teams. I shall write Birmingham a scathing rebuke and tell him he cannot take such chances of doing baseball a permanent injury in Cleveland."[10]

Johnson's blast against Birmingham angered the fans of Cleveland, who circulated petitions in support of their manager and sent them to the league office with thousands of signatures attached. Johnson, taken aback by the level of outrage he had unwisely stirred up, summoned Birmingham to the league office in Chicago when the Naps arrived there on Friday, June 27, to begin a series with the White Sox. Birmingham explained his side of the Jackson-Egan confrontation, and the league president, satisfied with what he heard, lifted Jackson's suspension after five days, though he fined the Cleveland star $25.

Shortly after Birmingham left Johnson's office on that Friday afternoon, the tension between Birmingham and Napoleon Lajoie erupted into the biggest controversy of the season. The Cleveland ballclub had played well during the early part of Lajoie's absence, with Terry Turner at second base and Ivy Olson at third, and Birmingham was understandably reluctant to disrupt a winning combination in the middle of a pennant chase. When the sore-handed Lajoie returned to the lineup in mid–June, his average dropped from the .380s to the .320s in only a few weeks. During his layoff, according to Ed Bang in *Sporting Life*, Lajoie "took on considerable avoirdupois. He is now at an age when he takes on weight easily and when the time came for him to break into the line-up again he was far from being in the same excellent physical condition that he was when the Naps came North."[11] The Naps had slumped with Lajoie, who was noticeably slower in the field and on the basepaths, in the lineup, and on June 26, Lajoie committed three costly errors against the White Sox in a 7–5 loss. He was not playing good ball, so Birmingham decided to shake up the club with a move that many thought impossible. The manager put Olson back at third and Turner at second, relegating Lajoie to the bench as a pinch-hitter and utility man.

Birmingham said later that he intended to notify Lajoie of his demotion before the game on Friday, June 27, but was unable to do so because of his conference at Johnson's office. The manager had no time to inform Lajoie, who learned about his benching when he looked at the lineup card before the game that afternoon and saw that his name was not on it. He confronted Birmingham and demanded an explanation. The two men argued, in full view of their teammates, as Lajoie cursed Birmingham and declared that he would rather quit the team than ride the bench. The argument soon abated, and the game began with Turner at second and Lajoie, still fuming, on the bench. Called upon to pinch-hit in the seventh inning, Lajoie delivered a single and was immediately removed for a pinch-runner, after which he returned to his seat on the bench and stewed about the situation.

Lajoie, after the game, tried to put a good spin on his new role, telling Henry Edwards of the *Plain Dealer* that he would "play anywhere they put me. If they like it I'm satisfied."[12] However, the more he thought about it, the angrier he became. Though the *Cleveland Press* reported that Lajoie was "philosophical" about the situation, Edwards ran into the ex-manager later that evening and found him boiling with rage. Lajoie's subsequent tirade, which Edwards recorded, made the front page of the *Plain Dealer* the next morning.

> I do not expect to be in uniform tomorrow. No bush leaguer can make a fool of me. I have been in baseball sixteen years. I have been with Cleveland eleven years and I have never shirked. Consequently I did not expect such treatment as I received today. The only information I had that I was not going to play was when Turner was told to play second base. Fine.
>
> No, I'm not through with baseball. I am far from being all in. But I am not going to be driven out by Joe Birmingham. Going to make me advisory manager, are they? That makes me grin. They have enough wise guys on the bench now as it is. They don't need any more. The trouble with Cleveland is that there is too much of that rah-rah college stuff [Birmingham had attended Cornell] and not enough real baseball. Looks as if the hot weather has got someone and that someone is trying to make me the goat because the club has been losing a few games.[13]

To a *Washington Times* reporter, Lajoie explained himself further.

> I will take no orders from a college player always playing to the grandstand. When I can't be a regular I refuse to be a bench warmer, a substitute, or an assistant manager to a man who does not know as much baseball as I do. This goes, too. If I can't get any justice from Somers, I'm likely to quit the game for good and all. As soon as we get back to Cleveland I shall confer with Somers. If he backs up Birmingham, then I'm through.[14]

This incident, coming as it did in the heat of a pennant race, seemed wildly out of character for Lajoie. Nonetheless, Lajoie was too honest, and too proud, to pretend that the demotion did not anger him. He had slumped in the past, but had always hit his way out of it, so why would he fail to do so now? After 12 seasons in Cleveland, Lajoie believed that he had earned the right to decide when he would leave the lineup. He would not leave that decision to Birmingham, who had batted .300 only once during his career and had taken the liberty of giving batting tips to both Lajoie and Joe Jackson, both of whom were bona fide .400 hitters.

Perhaps Joe Birmingham reminded Lajoie of his least favorite managers, the ones who called every pitch from the bench and demanded a high number of bunts and sacrifices. He had defied George Stallings, stopped speaking to Bill Armour, and now saw his relationship with Joe Birmingham explode in controversy. During his entire career, Lajoie's hitting strategy, such as it was, was a simple one. He walked to the plate and whaled away at the first good pitch he saw. He had little use for the station-to-station style of baseball that typified what historians call the Deadball Era, with its emphasis on bunting, stealing bases, and scoring one run at a time. Birmingham wanted to play that kind of baseball, while Lajoie clung to the game he learned from Ed Delahanty and the free-swinging Phillies of the 1890s. By 1913, Lajoie was one of only a handful of active players who began their careers before the turn of century. He was as popular as ever in Cleveland and around the league, but his style of play was, by this time, an anachronism.

Birmingham moved to shore up his position, telling Henry Edwards,

Mgr. Birmingham   Jackson   Kahler   Hinton   Falkenberg   D. Gregg   V. Gregg   Steen   Johnston   Blanding   Carisch

2nd Row: Bates, Olson, Bassler, Turner, Lelivelt, Chapman, Cullop
Sitting: Leibold, Land, O'Neill, Graney, Mitchell, Ryan, Lajoie

1913   CLEVELAND   FATIMA TURKISH BLEND CIGARETTES   AMERICANS

A Cleveland team picture taken in 1913. Manager Joe Birmingham is at the left in a suit. Notice that Lajoie is not in his usual place in the center; instead, he is at the right end of the bottom row (Library of Congress).

Mr. Somers expects Cleveland to win games. I am running the team. The team is slumping. In order to ascertain the trouble and to put my strongest team on the field, I must make some changes until I hit the right combination. I have another shift in mind which will mean the return of Lajoie to second base. I am not trying to drive him out of baseball and he ought to know me well enough by this time to know that I would not try anything of the kind. I am merely trying to get the best results out of the material I have.[15]

The Cleveland manager, who had successfully obtained the reinstatement of Jackson only to have the Lajoie situation blow up into an embarrassing public spectacle, stood firm. "If Lajoie is at all dissatisfied with his treatment by the Cleveland team," he said the next day, "he doesn't have to stay with it."[16]

Despite his threat to quit the team, Lajoie showed up at the park for the game against the White Sox on Saturday afternoon. He did not play in the 3–2 Cleveland win, and, as Henry Edwards reported in the *Plain Dealer*, Lajoie and Birmingham spent the day avoiding each other at the team hotel. On Sunday, Lajoie walked as a pinch-hitter and was immediately replaced by a substitute runner in a 2–1 loss to the White Sox. The Naps then traveled to St. Louis, where they defeated the Browns on Monday with Lajoie still riding the bench. Tuesday's contest was rained out, leaving Lajoie with only two brief appearances on the field since his disastrous three-error game the previous Thursday.

While Lajoie pondered his next move, several other American League teams contacted the Naps to see if the disgruntled star was for sale. Detroit Tigers president Frank Navin, no doubt seeing an opportunity to put Lajoie and Ty Cobb in the same lineup, placed a long-distance phone call to Charles Somers asking if Lajoie was available. Navin reportedly offered to trade Sam Crawford or Bobby Veach, along with a substantial amount of cash, for Lajoie. Other teams professed interest, but Somers moved to quell any rumors. "There is no chance of Larry being disposed of," said Somers to the papers. "Birmy and Lajoie are good friends. They will patch things up all right, I'm sure, without calling on me."[17] The Cleveland players knew better, having seen the animosity between the two men up close, but no one said so on the record.

After all the fuss, Lajoie's absence from the lineup was a short one. On Wednesday, July 2, Birmingham benched third baseman Ivy Olson, moved Terry Turner back to third, and restored Lajoie to his familiar second base slot for a doubleheader against the Browns. Lajoie went hitless in the first contest, a 2–1 loss, but pounded a double and a single in the second game, a 4–1 win. He remained at second base for the rest of the season and kept his feelings about the unpleasant benching episode to himself while the Naps fought, against ever lengthening odds, to catch the Athletics.

Cleveland held second place from late May to mid–September, and while they occasionally shaved a few games off the gap between themselves and Connie Mack's club, they could never get close enough to mount a real challenge. In early August, Lajoie belted seven hits in 14 trips to plate, including two doubles and a homer, in a four-game set at Philadelphia, but the Naps lost three of the games and left town eight and a half games behind. A week later, the Naps took three of four against the Athletics at Cleveland, but Mack was not concerned. "I told my players," he said, "we only had to win the one game we were after. Chicago, Cleveland, Detroit, or Boston might carry off a series, but the power of doing it would so weaken them that they would lose the next series."[18] He was correct as far as the Naps were concerned, because Cleveland followed up their three wins against the Athletics with five straight losses to the Senators and Red Sox.

The Naps cut the margin to six games in early September, with a five-game series in Washington looming as a make-or-break opportunity to climb closer to first place if another club could beat the Athletics. Unfortunately, the Naps were doomed to fail before their train arrived in the District of Columbia on the morning of September 9. Eight Naps, along with team secretary Bill Blackwood, were stricken with ptomaine poisoning after eating in the dining car. To make matters worse, starting pitchers Cy Falkenberg and Vean Gregg engaged in a friendly wrestling match on the train and injured each other. Falkenberg did not pitch against the Senators, while Gregg started the first game and failed to complete the second inning. The third-place Senators, with two victories from 36-game winner Walter Johnson, won five in a row from the Naps and ended Cleveland's pennant hopes once and for all. Two weeks later, the Naps fell out of second place as the Senators steamed past them. In the end, Cleveland finished third, nine and a half games behind the Athletics and three behind the Senators.

In early October, while the Athletics took on the New York Giants in the World Series, the Naps faced the Pittsburgh Pirates in a replay of their 1904 post-season matchup. This seven-game set proved to be the last on-field meeting between two aging stars, Napoleon Lajoie and Honus Wagner, both of whom had batted over .300 for the final time in 1913. The *Pittsburgh Press* hyped the series, running an interview in which Lajoie graciously named Wagner the "greatest player the game has ever seen"[19] and distributing pictures of the two men under the title, "Here They Are — The Greatest Ever." Despite all the publicity, the fans showed little interest, and the Lajoie-Wagner face-off proved anticlimactic. Neither man performed well, as Lajoie managed only six hits and Wagner four. The series belonged to the pitchers, especially Cleveland's Vean Gregg, who threw a 13-inning, 1–0 shutout in the sixth contest and struck out 19 Pirates. Though the games were close, well-played affairs, crowds in Pittsburgh and Cleveland were disappointingly small, and the Naps, who won the series in seven games, took home only $216.32 apiece for their efforts.

For Napoleon Lajoie, 1913 was an eventful, and ultimately disappointing, season. He batted a healthy .335, though his slugging average dropped as his extra-base power waned. Lajoie was still a solid hitter, but Joe Jackson had long surpassed him as Cleveland's greatest offensive threat. Jackson hit .373 in 1913 with a league record 26 triples, and on June 4, Shoeless Joe walloped what the fans and sportswriters called the longest homer in major league history, a 500-foot shot at the Polo Grounds in New York. The title of baseball's "greatest natural hitter," borne for so long by Lajoie, now belonged to the 26-year-old slugging star. In addition, the Naps once again fell short of a pennant, though they fought valiantly until faltering during the final two weeks of the campaign. Larry Lajoie, who turned 39 in early September, was running out of time. The Naps would have to find a way to defeat the seemingly invincible Athletics, and find it quickly, to give Lajoie a shot at World Series stardom.

23

The Fall of the Naps

I should worry when I still have one friend with me in the crowd. What friend? Who else but Mrs. Lajoie? I suppose she has busted a new pair of gloves, but she can use up a new pair every day if she wants to. She still thinks I am a great ball player if nobody else does. — Napoleon Lajoie, during his late-career troubles in Cleveland[1]

George Stovall, Lajoie's former teammate and manager, had followed a bumpy path after his tenure in Cleveland. Traded to St. Louis by Harry Davis early in 1912, Stovall was named manager of the last-place Browns in mid-season and invigorated the team as he had in Cleveland. However, "Brother George" lost his temper on May 5, 1913, and spat a mouthful of tobacco juice in the face of umpire Charlie Ferguson. (As teammate Jimmy Austin told Lawrence Ritter in an interview for the book *The Glory of Their Times*, "It was terrible. George always did chew an uncommonly large wad, you know."[2]) Though Napoleon Lajoie had assaulted Frank Dwyer in much the same way in 1904 and escaped with little punishment, Ban Johnson suspended Stovall for three weeks, and the incident eventually cost him his position with the Browns. Unable to find another job in the American League, Stovall signed on with a new circuit, one that aimed to challenge the existing structure of major league baseball.

The Federal League came to life in 1913 as an independent minor league, but later that same year its president, Chicago businessman James A. Gilmore, decided to follow the blueprint created by Ban Johnson and the American League 13 years before. After lining up an impressive array of financial backers that included oil baron Harry Sinclair and St. Louis ice magnate Phil Ball, Gilmore declared the Federal League a major circuit and raided the established leagues for talent. Gilmore and his two main recruiters, former Chicago Cubs shortstop Joe Tinker and ex–Cleveland Nap George Stovall, traveled the country during the winter months, offering large salaries to players willing to break their 1914 contracts and join the new organization. They insisted, as had Johnson and the American League in 1901, that the reserve clause and the ten-day notice made major league contracts too one-sided to be enforceable if challenged in the courts. In effect, their plan was to re-argue the case of *Philadelphia Base Ball Club v. Lajoie* and hope for a different outcome.

The rise of the Federal League set off another baseball war, with the American and National leagues threatening legal action against any players who violated their agreements and signed up with the upstarts. The papers ran wild with speculation during the winter months, with the biggest names in the sport rumored to be jumping to or from the new league. Wishing to make a splash, the Feds offered large salaries to stars such as Ty Cobb, Walter Johnson, and Eddie Collins, though Tinker and Stovall were the most recognizable names to take the plunge for the 1914 campaign. In January that year, Gilmore offered to pay Cobb $15,000 a year for five years, which caused many to wonder how the new league, with teams in second-tier cities such as Buffalo, Indianapolis, and Kansas City, expected to survive for long with its big-spending strategy. Nonetheless, though Cobb and other major stars turned the Feds down, the league found enough talent to fill the rosters of its eight teams.

Inevitably, Napoleon Lajoie, the man who gave the new American League its most important dose of credibility in 1901, was mentioned as a possible target for Stovall, Tinker, and Gilmore. Some suggested that a new team in Pittsburgh, with Honus Wagner at shortstop and Lajoie at second, would virtually assure the eventual success of the would-be third major league. Others opined that a Federal League team in Cleveland, with Lajoie as its manager, might so damage the Naps, and the American League in general, that the existing majors would sue for peace. None of these things came to pass, but Ban Johnson was worried enough about the threat of a Federal franchise in Cleveland that he prevailed upon Charles Somers to take some sort of action to prevent it. Somers replied by moving his top minor league team, the Toledo Mud Hens, to Cleveland for the 1914 campaign. Rechristened the Scouts, this club planned to play at League Park while the Naps were on the road, leaving few open dates for a Federal League team to draw fans.

At any rate, Lajoie was not interested in giving a boost to another new circuit. His contract with the Naps paid him $9,000 per year, still one of the highest salaries in the game, and had three more years to run. It was also, at Lajoie's insistence, an "ironclad" contract, lacking both the reserve clause and the ten days' notice that most players found so objectionable. His large salary was guaranteed, and even if he had wanted to break his contract, he could have found no basis to challenge it with those two features missing. Besides, as he told Ed Bang in December of 1913, "There isn't a chance for me to become a Federal Leaguer. I have been with Charley Somers too long and he has treated me royally all the time. I would be ungrateful if I would ever listen to a proposition from the Feds, to say nothing of accepting it. I have signed with the Naps for next year and I will do my utmost to help Manager Birmingham land the Naps higher up in the race than last season."[3] A month later, Lajoie reiterated his stance. "The American League made high salaries possible, and I am going to stick,"[4] he said. Joe Jackson, also a rumored target of the new league, was similarly indifferent, though he claimed that Stovall's agents offered him $20,000 a year to jump. "There is no use of their bothering me," he told a reporter for the *Plain Dealer*, "I am not going to go to them."[5]

After a third-place finish in 1913, Cleveland fans expected the Naps to challenge the Athletics, Senators, and Red Sox for the pennant, but the team suffered a setback in January of 1914 when pitcher Cy Falkenberg, the team's most consistent right-handed starter, jumped to the Federal League. Falkenberg was joined by fellow Naps pitchers George Kahler and Fred Blanding, and though the major leagues fought in the courts to force Federal League jumpers to return (as had the National League in 1901 and 1902), the absence of three important starters left the Naps, for once, with a shortage of right-handed pitchers. Bill Steen injured his pitching hand in a fight in February, while Vean Gregg, a three-time 20-game winner for the Naps, arrived at training camp in Athens, Georgia, in March complaining of a sore arm. Both Steen and Gregg were slow to round into form, weakening the Cleveland pitching staff, which had been one of the team's strengths in 1913.

Lajoie takes infield practice (National Baseball Hall of Fame Library, Cooperstown, New York).

Napoleon Lajoie was a week late in reporting to camp, though his absence was not the result of an injury or a contract dispute. Myrtle Lajoie had contracted diphtheria, and though she soon recovered from what could have been a life-threatening illness, the Lajoie house was put under quarantine for seven days in late February by the local health department. In addition, Myrtle's doctors injected Larry with a strong protective antitoxin, which forced the ballplayer to take to his bed for several days. Training camp in Georgia opened on February 28, but he was not allowed to leave home until the quarantine period had expired. On March 5, with Myrtle out of danger, he boarded a southbound train and arrived at camp the next day.

The injury bug had often bitten the Naps during their 14-year history, but a rash of physical maladies struck the team in Athens and interfered with workouts. One freakish spring training injury occurred when the team trainer gave outfielder Jack Graney an acid solution to treat a scrape wound on his foot. Graney applied the solution without diluting it first and woke up the next morning with severe burns on his toes. He was out for two weeks. A knee injury put outfielder Nemo Leibold on the sidelines for more than a month, while pitcher Lefty James fell ill with stomach problems and was unable to pitch until May. The most damaging blow was suffered by shortstop Ray Chapman, the linchpin of the Cleveland defense, who broke his right leg while sliding on March 11. Chapman was out for three months, and the Naps struggled to fill his place during his recovery.

The Naps began the season severely undermanned, especially after Joe Birmingham suffered a back injury in the final exhibition game on April 13. Starting their campaign on the road, they lost four games in a row at Chicago, then traveled to Detroit and lost three more to the Tigers before heading to League Park for their home opener on April 22. Despite their 0–7 record, the Naps drew more than 10,000 fans on a cold, rainy afternoon. They saw a poor exhibition of ball playing, as a rash of errors and weak hitting helped the visitors to an easy 7–0 win. Cleveland finally tasted victory the next day, defeating the White Sox 4–1 behind Willie Mitchell, and won their next two games against Chicago to offer a glimmer of hope. Still, the injuries mounted, with pitcher Bill Steen on the shelf with a broken finger and two catchers, Steve O'Neill and Josh Billings, driven to the sidelines with ankle and knee injuries. The Naps were already in last place by this time, and another seven-game skid in May dropped their record to 8–21 after one month of the 1914 season.

Lajoie, who had made a habit of hitting well during the early weeks of a season, slumped badly in April and May of 1914. He started the campaign in an 0-for-15 slump and did not get a hit until the eighth inning of the fifth game of the season. After ten games, he had only five safeties in 36 times at bat, though his only hit on April 25 was a game-winning single in the tenth inning that defeated Chicago by a 1–0 score. The White Sox had elected to walk Joe Jackson with one out to pitch to Lajoie, a move that would have been unthinkable only a few years before. On the following day, Lajoie belted three singles in another Cleveland win, though he suffered the embarrassment of being called out on the basepaths when Jack Graney's line drive hit him.

In early May, *Sporting Life's* first report of player averages, which listed all batters above the .200 mark, did not show Lajoie's name. Time was catching up to Larry Lajoie, who was, at age 39, the oldest starting player in the American League.[6] He hit a little better in May, but his average stayed below the .250 mark for most of the season, and his once-feared power was fading fast. His speed was now a memory, too, as he stole 14 bases that year but was thrown out 15 times. Joe Birmingham kept his veteran star in the cleanup spot for most of April, waiting for Lajoie to shake himself out of the worst prolonged slump of his career, but on April 29 the manager shifted Joe Jackson down one notch to the fourth slot and dropped Lajoie to fifth. Nothing helped, and seven losses on an eastern road swing in mid–May left the Naps a dozen games out of first place and, with the season barely a month old, virtually out of the pennant chase.

The Federal League continued to cause problems for the Naps. The Feds were still interested in placing a team in Cleveland, though neither of the two biggest Naps stars, Lajoie and Jackson, professed any interest. George Stovall, however, was a persistent man. After the Naps decided to send pitcher Nick Cullop to the minors for more experience, Cullop instead left Cleveland and signed with Stovall's circuit. With injuries mounting to the Cleveland pitching staff, the Naps had wanted Cullop available to return to the big club when needed, and though Fred Blanding came back from the Feds in May, Cullop's departure was another blow to the sinking ballclub.

The losses mounted in June, with the Naps winning only six of their 30 games during the month. Lajoie still struggled to top the .250 mark, while the Naps played sluggish, sloppy baseball in front of small crowds. The team's best hitter, Joe Jackson, smacked a home run against St. Louis on June 1, but also committed three errors in the outfield, two on one play when he dropped a fly ball and made a wild throw. "The smallest crowd of the year was present," said the *Plain Dealer* in its recap. "That is probably one point in favor of the club. The fewer witnesses to such an affair, the better for the financial end of baseball."[7] Jackson, hitting .386 at the beginning of the month, was the only Nap performing up to expectations, and shortly thereafter the first major injury of Shoeless Joe's career struck the Naps at the worst possible time. He suffered a leg contusion while sliding on June 11, and when the wound became infected, the slugger was driven to the sidelines for three weeks. Not until July 8 did he reappear in the outfield.

Fans and sportswriters had often called Napoleon Lajoie the "king of ballplayers" during his career, but on July 11, 1914, Lajoie got his first look at the man who would eventually earn almost unanimous acclaim as the greatest player of all time. On that Saturday afternoon in Boston, the Naps faced a 19-year-old rookie pitcher named George "Babe" Ruth, recently purchased from Baltimore of the International League. Ruth, a six-foot, two-inch left-hander, performed well in his major league debut, striking out one batter and allowing eight Cleveland hits before Duffy Lewis pinch-hit for him in the seventh inning of a 4–3 Boston win. Joe Jackson singled twice off the rookie, but Lajoie went hitless in four times at bat against Ruth and reliever Dutch Leonard. "Manager Joe Birmingham, after the game, appeared to think that Ruth would develop into a sensational twirler," said the *Plain Dealer* the next day.

With the Naps hopelessly mired in last place, Joe Birmingham's position as manager of the team appeared tenuous. In July, rumors hit the New York papers that Charles Somers, panicked over the poor performance of the club and the resultant rows of empty seats at League Park, would soon fire Birmingham and appoint the still-popular Lajoie as manager. Somers took the rumors so seriously that he issued a strongly-worded statement denying the claim. Said the Cleveland team owner,

> There isn't a chance for Lajoie, Olson, or any other Nap, or even an outsider, taking Birmingham's place at the head of the Naps. I am satisfied in my own mind that Birmy has had more than his share of the breaks in bad luck, and were it not for the sickness and accidents that befell his players he would now be battling for the lead instead of being down at the bottom of the heap. I have great confidence in Birmingham and think he will ultimately give Cleveland fans a pennant-winner. Such in my faith in him that I have signed him to a contract

covering 1914, 1915 and 1916, and what's more, the ten days' clause is out of the document. That makes it look as if he is slated to continue as manager of the Naps, doesn't it? Reports have come to me about there being cliques on the club, and if such is the case I will weed out the disgruntled players. If there is any man on the Cleveland payroll who is not giving the club his best services and who is not loyal to Birmingham, I will have him suspended without pay.

   If necessary, I will get rid of any number of men to bring order out of chaos. I have always made it a point to treat the Cleveland players with the greatest consideration, but I can prove as hard a task master as I have an easy one. If there is to be any change in the Cleveland Club you can rest assured it will not be in the managerial end. Birmingham has my backing from first to last, for I believe in him. That story about Lajoie succeeding Birmy as leader of the team and retiring from active service to manage from the bench is bunk pure and simple. Larry had his chance for five years as manager and seemed glad enough to retire back in 1909. I don't believe that Lajoie aspires to take Birmingham's job, but if so, he might as well know now that there isn't a chance for him to land.[8]

The reports to which Somers alluded were true. Due to the constant losing, many of the Naps had lost all faith in their field leader, and the team divided into pro–Birmingham and anti–Birmingham factions. Larry Lajoie had never forgiven the manager for benching him in 1913 and was not shy about hiding his feelings for the man and his "rah-rah college" style of leadership. The animus was not displayed on the field where the fans could see it, but the clubhouse and the team hotel bristled with tension. By the end of July, a month that saw the Naps compile a 7–17 record, reports of open hostility among the Naps filled the local papers, with Lajoie, pitcher Vean Gregg, infielder Ivy Olson, and first baseman Doc Johnston identified as the main participants in the opposition to Birmingham.

   With the season already lost, Charles Somers came down firmly on the side of Birmingham. After extending the manager's contract for two more years, he gave "Birmy" the green light to bench, sell, or trade the malcontents, including the biggest star of all. On June 27, 1914, a rookie named Larry Pezold, fresh from a stint at Ironton in the Ohio State League, arrived in Cleveland and was inserted into the lineup at third base. Birmingham then shifted Terry Turner from third to second and moved Larry Lajoie, hitting .221 at the time, to the bench. The next day, Birmingham announced that he had traded Vean Gregg, the sore-armed former 20-game winner, to the Boston Red Sox for three younger players. Olson and Johnston remained with the team for the rest of the season, but both were sent packing before the start of the 1915 campaign. For better or worse, the last-place Naps now belonged to Joe Birmingham.

   Lajoie spent the next two and a half weeks on the bench, with only a few pinch-hitting appearances breaking the monotony of losing. Birmingham turned the season into a virtual tryout camp for young players, with Pezold, infielder Bill Wambsganss, outfielder Elmer Smith, and catcher Johnny Bassler among the many new Naps who saw their first major league action during the last two months of the 1914 season. Lajoie, who fought to keep his average above .220 and hit almost nothing but singles when he connected, could hardly complain about riding the bench, so he watched the younger men and pondered his future. "Napoleon Lajoie's baseball star is setting," proclaimed *The Sporting News*. "The records indicate Larry is slowing up. His age is against him. A younger man will have to be developed. Larry knows it and doubtless will help develop that young man."[9] Lajoie's National League counterpart, Honus Wagner, was in no better shape in Pittsburgh, where he lost his starting job and, like Lajoie, watched his teammates from an unaccustomed spot on the bench. During the month of August, while news of the coming world war filled the front

Lajoie at bat in 1913 or 1914 (Library of Congress).

pages of the nation's newspapers, the sporting sections proclaimed the imminent retirement of baseball's two greatest stars.

Lajoie's dispute with Birmingham cast a shadow over what most people expected to be his last days in a Cleveland uniform, and when Charles Somers revealed that he had asked for waivers on Lajoie in early August, a wave of sympathy for the 19-year veteran hit the papers. Washington manager Clark Griffith, a long-time admirer who would have likely added Larry to his Senators if not for the $9,000 price tag, made a plea on the Cleveland star's behalf.

> Napoleon Lajoie must not pass out of Cleveland baseball under a cloud. Lajoie has done too much for baseball in Cleveland and the game in general to be permitted to pass out of the sport except in a blaze of glory. I don't care if Lajoie and Manager Birmingham have not always agreed. Larry is too big a man to pass out of the game with a blot on his record simply because of a difference he may have had with another man. If another club cares to take over Larry's contract, and Larry consents to be transferred to that club, he should be permitted to go, but I think Lajoie should be permitted to end his major league playing days with the Cleveland club.[10]

Perhaps Birmingham and Somers listened to Griffith and others, and perhaps the empty seats at League Park prompted another lineup change on August 12 at Chicago. Whatever the reason, the manager shuffled his personnel again, putting Pezold on the bench, moving Turner back to third base, and shifting Lajoie to first, with the rookie Wambsganss at second and a healthy Ray Chapman at short. Lajoie, who had not played an inning in the field since July 26, remained at first base for the rest of August and most of September. He started hitting, with seven safeties in his first five games back, and moved his average steadily upward until he crossed the .250 mark in late September. It mattered little, as the Naps were already more than 40 games out of first place, but at least he could finish the season, and most likely his Cleveland career, on a positive note.

There remained one more goal for Lajoie to accomplish in a Cleveland uniform. He entered the 1914 campaign needing 108 hits to reach the 3,000 mark for his career, a level previously attained only by Cap Anson in 1897 and Honus Wagner in June of 1914. No one expected Lajoie to perform so poorly in 1914, and many feared that the Cleveland star would finish the season shy of the mark. Because his contract had two more years to run, Lajoie was assured of eventually reaching the exalted level, but with his Cleveland tenure coming to a close, it looked as if he would not do so with the team that was named for him.

Fortunately, Lajoie remained healthy enough in 1914 to play in 121 games, and accumulated enough plate appearances to make the mathematics of the situation work in his favor. On Sunday, September 27, in the first game of a doubleheader against the Yankees in Cleveland, Lajoie belted a double against right-hander Marty McHale for the 3,000th hit of his 19-year major league career. In a show of respect for the veteran, the Yankees stopped the game, retrieved the ball, and gave it to Lajoie at second base as the Cleveland fans rose in applause. It was one of the few positive things that happened all year for the Naps, who won the first contest that day but then, with Lajoie on the bench, lost the second game for their 100th setback of the season.

Afterward, Lajoie put a brave face on his performance. "I expect to remain in major company for several more years," he said, "and before I quit I expect to register at least another thousand hits."[11] However, there were five games remaining on Cleveland's schedule, and Lajoie did not play in four of them. His only appearance during the last week of the season came against the White Sox in Cleveland on September 30, in which he pinch-hit unsuccessfully in the 12th inning against Joe Benz. This was his final game in a Cleveland uniform. The Naps traveled to Detroit for a two-game, season-ending set against the Tigers, but Lajoie stayed home in Cleveland while Joe Birmingham auditioned prospects from the minor leagues. No one would say so on the record, but Napoleon Lajoie's 13-year career in Cleveland was finished.

The 1914 season was catastrophic for the Cleveland Naps, on the field and off. Never had Cleveland's American League ballclub finished in last place, and never had it crossed the century mark in losses. Pitcher Guy Morton set a record with 13 consecutive losses before he finally won his first major league game on the same day that Lajoie stroked his 3,000th hit. The Naps played 22 games against each of the other seven league teams and managed to break even with Washington, but won only three from the Athletics and six each from the Tigers and Red Sox. They lost 26 games by five runs or more. The fans responded to the losing and poor play by staying home. The total attendance at League Park was 185,000, the team's lowest since 1901 and barely a third of the turnstile count of the year before. This sharp drop in patronage severely damaged the team's balance sheet and put Charles Somers, whose coal business had suffered greatly due to a nationwide economic recession, on the edge of financial insolvency.

At season's end, Somers announced that despite the worst season in Cleveland's American League history, he intended to retain Joe Birmingham as manager. The Cleveland owner also confirmed that Napoleon Lajoie would no longer be a regular, but would serve as a pinch-hitter and occasional substitute in 1915. This statement was, in essence, an invitation for Lajoie to leave. There was no room for a 40-year-old, injury-prone .258 hitter on a team that needed a major rebuilding job. The club could not simply release Lajoie, as his guaranteed contract, signed in January of 1913, had two more years to run at a salary of $9,000 per year. However, if any other team was interested in acquiring the 19-year veteran, the Cleveland ballclub let it be known that it would listen to any reasonable offer.

24

Back to Philadelphia

I have my own ideas of how to develop players. That we have had success is due, I think, to the fact that we handle them differently. I want youngsters with the qualifications, and, when I see them, I will bring them out myself. This is really the happiest period of my life. I am broke financially, but full of ambition. It is like starting all over again for me, and I love base ball and love to build up teams. I have done it once and will do it again.—Connie Mack, 1915[1]

Connie Mack was Napoleon Lajoie's favorite manager, while Mack's admiration for the man who had batted .426 for him 14 years before had never waned. Accordingly, when no other major league club showed interest in taking on a high-salaried former star on the downside of his career, Mack and his Philadelphia Athletics threw both Lajoie and the Cleveland ballclub a lifeline. Lajoie wished to continue his career on a team with a chance to win a pennant, and the Athletics (called the A's after the large script capital A on the front of their uniform shirts) had played in four of the previous five World Series, winning three. The financially-stressed Cleveland club needed relief from Lajoie's large contract, and had no appetite for a third consecutive year of conflict between the aging second baseman and manager Joe Birmingham. Mack traveled to Cleveland to confer with his friend Charles Somers during the first week of 1915, and on January 5, Mack sent a telegram to the main Philadelphia newspapers that read, "Athletics have purchased release of Lajoie of the Cleveland club."[2]

The "purchase" to which Mack referred was apparently one in which no money changed hands, because the Philadelphia team's accounting books, which survive to this day, show no transfer of funds to Cleveland. Mack merely agreed to relieve Charles Somers of Lajoie's two-year, $9,000 contract, an arrangement that suited the purposes of all concerned.

Lajoie's return to Philadelphia after an absence of 13 seasons was received enthusiastically by the local baseball writers, who made the veteran star their guest of honor at their annual banquet in February. Meanwhile, his former ballclub, perhaps a bit hastily, moved to find a new nickname now that its namesake had found employment with an American League rival. Rather than allow a local paper to conduct a poll of fans, similar to the one the *Cleveland Press* conducted in 1903, Charles Somers solicited opinions from the Cleveland writing corps and, on January 17, 1915, announced that the club would henceforth be known as the Indians. "The nickname is but temporarily bestowed," asserted the *Cleveland Plain Dealer*, "as the club may so conduct itself during the present season as to earn some other cognomen which may be more appropriate. The choice of a name that would be significant just now was rather difficult with the club itself anchored in last place."[3] The Cleveland Naps, like the Spiders of the 1890s, faded into history, while the "temporarily bestowed" nickname Indians has lasted into the twenty-first century.

Connie Mack expressed optimism that Lajoie would regain his form after his poor 1914 season.

> Larry will play better ball for me than he has with the Cleveland club. You can bet all you have that Larry's ambition will be to "show up" the Nap owners. He wants to convince them and convince the public that he is just as good as ever.
>
> Now don't imagine that I infer that Larry did not give his best to the Cleveland club. On the contrary, I don't think there ever was a person who would accuse him of "laying down." But it's no secret that there was a lack of harmony in the Naps. He did not feel in harmony with his surroundings. No man under such conditions could do himself justice. On our club he will be working in new scenery, where everything is harmonious, where everyone is working for a definite purpose. Besides Larry believes as I believe, that he will have a chance to get into a world's series with our club and it is his greatest ambition to be a member of a championship club before he quits baseball.[4]

The Athletics were the defending American League champs, and if Lajoie had joined them a year before, he might have realized his ambition to play in a World Series. However, despite their pennant-winning performance in 1914, the Athletics lost a reported $50,000 due to weak attendance and high salaries. Perhaps the Philadelphia fans had become jaded by the team's success, and maybe a national economic recession that year had something to do with the lack of fan support. At any rate, Mack was convinced that the team had to be substantially remade. He also could not compete with the wads of cash being waved about by agents of the Federal League, which had survived its maiden season and was ready for another round of player raids on the two established leagues. Mack's stable of stars, winners of four pennants and three World Series during the previous five seasons, was a prime target for the upstart circuit.

Mack knew that the Feds had made offers to many of his players during the 1914 season, and their interference caused much friction between Mack and his charges. The veteran manager had not liked the atmosphere around the club even before losing the fall classic in four straight games, and even if the A's had won the Series, major changes would have been forthcoming. "In previous years," recalled Mack years later, "at the end of the season or the World's Series, there were always hearty partings between players and manager ... [but] no compliments were exchanged at the end of the World's Series of 1914. It was a most chilling and mournful parting."[5]

On November 1, three weeks after the Athletics lost the Series to George Stallings and the Boston Braves, Mack dropped a bombshell when he put pitchers Eddie Plank, Jack Coombs, and Charles "Chief" Bender on waivers. These three men had won a total of 592 games for the Athletics, providing the backbone of Philadelphia's championship teams. Plank, the last remaining player (besides part-timer Harry Davis) from the first edition of the Athletics in 1901, was 39 years old and had threatened to retire for several years. Still, Plank had attempted to use his offers from the Federal League as a lever to pry more money from Mack, and the Philadelphia manager decided to part with his longtime ace rather than overpay him. Bender, only 30 years old, was fragile despite his 17–3 record in 1914, while Coombs, a 31-game winner in 1910, was hobbled with a sore arm. Bender and Plank signed on with Federal League clubs, while Mack decided to use his shrinking bankroll to develop new pitchers, betting on youngsters Joe Bush, Bob Shawkey, Rube Bressler, and Herb Pennock, all of whom performed well in 1914, to form the nucleus of a new pennant-winning rotation.

Mack was not finished remaking his team. Fearing that second baseman Eddie Collins, the 1914 Chalmers Award winner as the league's Most Valuable Player, would bolt for the Federal League, Mack sold his contract for $50,000 to the Chicago White Sox. The sale also relieved the Athletics of Collins' $15,000 salary, the highest on the club. Collins' departure spelled the end of Mack's "$100,000 infield," and before long third sacker Frank "Home Run" Baker, distressed by the exodus of talent and Mack's hardnosed attitude during salary negotiations, quit the team and joined an independent club in his native Maryland. Perhaps no pennant-winning club in baseball history, with the possible exception of the 1997 Florida Marlins, has ever dissolved itself so completely before the start of the following season.

Larry Lajoie, installed as the starting second baseman for the defending American League champion Athletics, could not hope to fill the place of Eddie Collins, no matter what rosy pronouncements Mack made to the local reporters. Collins, at age 27, was in the prime of his Hall of Fame career and had no peer among American League infielders. Only Ty Cobb of the Tigers and Tris Speaker of the Red Sox rivaled Collins as all-around performers, and there were those who believed that Collins was, in fact, a more valuable talent than both Cobb and Speaker. Lajoie was 40 (though most sources gave his age as 39), injury-prone, and covered less ground in the field with each passing year. At spring training in Jacksonville, Florida, Lajoie joked that he wore a bigger glove to make up for his reduced range. However, he had two fine fielders next to him in Jack (Stuffy) McInnis at first and Jack Barry at short (the "Larry and Barry" keystone combo, the papers said) to cover some of Larry's lost ground.

The 40-year-old former star hit and fielded passably well during spring camp, but whatever speed he had in his younger days was long gone. The 1915 season was his 20th in the major leagues, and the end of his career was fast approaching, as the Cleveland club had realized. Connie Mack was his biggest booster, but the former Cleveland superstar was now merely the most prominent name in Mack's collection of untried prospects and veteran castoffs.

Lajoie uncharacteristically suffered through several embarrassing misplays in the field during the early stages of the new season. On April 14, Opening Day at Shibe Park for the Athletics, Herb Pennock took the mound for the A's against the Boston Red Sox. On a chilly, raw afternoon, Pennock held the Sox without a hit through eight and two-thirds innings, and with two out in the bottom of the ninth only Harry Hooper stood between Pennock and a no-hitter. Hooper, fooled on a pitch, tapped a slow roller to the right side of the mound. Pennock could have picked it up easily, but heard Lajoie's footsteps as the second baseman charged in after the dribbling baseball. The 21-year-old Pennock deferred to the veteran star and stood aside. Lajoie grabbed at the ball, missed it, and could only watch helplessly as Hooper crossed first base with a single to break up the no-hit bid. Pennock retired the next batter to complete a shutout, but the victory was bittersweet for all concerned.[6]

On April 22, the Athletics faced the Red Sox in Boston's home opener at Fenway Park. This game was played on a cold and windy afternoon, with fielding misplays aplenty, but Lajoie made headlines by committing five errors, tying a twentieth-century major league record for second basemen. Despite the worst fielding performance of Lajoie's career, the

Athletics entered the bottom of the ninth with a 6–5 lead. After Boston put two men on with two out, third baseman Danny Murphy dropped a wind-blown popup that allowed both runners to score and gave the Red Sox a 7–6 win. At least the contest provided Lajoie with a story to tell in later years. "I trudged into the dressing room after the game, berating myself something awful," said Larry many years later. "Connie Mack just let me sit for a few moments, not saying anything. Then he came over to me grim-like. 'Stick with it long enough and you'll get one,' Mack told me."[7]

Lajoie was happy to return to the city in which he began his major league career, but the bitterness he felt over his departure from Cleveland still simmered in his mind. That bitterness was never far from the surface, and in an interview with F. C. Lane of *Baseball Magazine*, he let his feelings pour out:

> I wouldn't have minded going from Cleveland so much if I had gone in an ordinary way. Not that I wished to leave the city under any circumstances, for the best years of my life have been spent there and I have made it my home. Still, for the best interests of all concerned, I would have said nothing. But to leave as if you were a second-story man is different. My trouble with manager Birmingham is no secret to anyone. For a time after he was appointed all went well. We had a good club and things were progressing smoothly. But Birmingham had to begin to show his authority, and from that time the success of the club was a thing of the past.
>
> I have no objection in the world to working under a competent manager, I believe I have showed that. I voluntarily resigned the management myself, which should indicate I think, that I wasn't crazy for the job and I worked willingly enough for several managers who followed. I worked for a time under Birmingham, but when a bush league player like him, tries to tell a club of old veterans how to play ball, it is ridiculous. There he was, trying to tell me how to bat, me who was hitting three hundred when he was in primary school, and he was doing the same for Joe Jackson when Joe was hitting over four hundred. Birmingham never hit over .250 in his life and where he gets the license to pose as a teacher would be hard to explain. That is only a sample.
>
> There is much more that I might say but what's the use? Somers chose to stand by Birmingham, and it's his funeral. It looks a good deal like a funeral, too, the way the club is shot to pieces. And I guess he feels as if he had been to a funeral.
>
> Now that I have left Cleveland I am working for a manager who knows his business. He can tell a man what he wants him to do without speaking to him as if he were a dog. My contract has still two more years to run, so I have no cause to kick. But money isn't everything. It's worth a good wad of cash to have to sit on the same bench with Birmingham.[8]

The still-festering acrimony caused by Lajoie's departure from Cleveland surprised many observers. Lajoie had almost always suffered his frustrations in silence, rarely spouting off to the newspapers with complaints about management. Now, with his career coming to a close, it appeared that the Frenchman had become another old ballplayer who refused to age gracefully. Joe Birmingham remained aloof from the controversy, but in the same article, Charles Somers fired off a response:

> Lajoie was a wonderful player and in his prime I doubt if he had an equal. He came to my club when he was at his best and I will give him credit, he made the club. But when he began to age and I appointed a younger manager to lead the team, I made a fatal mistake in signing Lajoie to a long time contract. Such a situation is almost certain to create friction and you cannot rightly blame either man. The manager is manager and as such he is to be obeyed. On the other hand, a veteran of Lajoie's age, experience, extraordinary ability, and remarkable career was bound to chafe under the restrictions of a much younger man. The situation was almost certain to cause discontent.

Yes, Lajoie made the club and he nearly wrecked it again. For where one prominent member of a club is at outs with the management it is certain to create a clique, for every prominent player has followers. And such cliques are apt to disrupt the club. In this case I stood by the manager. Where it comes to a show down of whether the manager or the players are going to run the club, back the manager. Birmingham has faults, he would be the quickest to admit it, but after all he was my manager, my representative on the club, and he had made me more money than I ever made before. I backed Birmingham to the finish.

Now that Lajoie has gone to another club, where there will be no such friction, I would not be in the least surprised to see him bat well over three hundred. He is a marvelous hitter and on the ground that he can cover, an equally marvelous fielder. He cannot range so far as some younger and fleeter men, but the ball that comes within Larry's reach is as certain to be caught as it is by any other fielder in the game.[9]

With Lajoie gone, the newly-named Cleveland Indians continued to deteriorate. Lajoie's former team, still fighting to stay out of last place during the first two months of the new season, made a number of questionable moves, one of which involved the shift of Shoeless Joe Jackson from the outfield to first base. Reportedly, this change was dictated by Charles Somers and strenuously opposed by Joe Birmingham, and when Jackson took to the bench with a sore arm, perhaps caused by the shorter, snappier throws required at his new position, Birmingham and Somers began sniping at each other. Because Birmingham lost the confidence of the owner and was unable to lift the team above seventh place, Somers fired him in late May of 1915 and replaced him with coach Lee Fohl. A reporter asked Lajoie, who never forgave his former manager for his troubles in Cleveland, if he was surprised by the news. "Not a bit," replied Lajoie. "Birmy was a pretty chesty boy in 1914 and he had Charley Somers persuaded that all the rest of us who knew anything about baseball weren't working for him. Somers finally woke up."[10]

The Athletics fell to the bottom of the league before a month of the season had passed, and the Philadelphia fans stayed away from Shibe Park. The club had led the American League in attendance just five years earlier, with more than 8,000 per game cheering the A's to their third pennant and first World Series victory in 1910. Now, with almost all the familiar faces playing for other teams, the Athletics drew less than 2,000 per contest, the fewest in the circuit. To make matters worse for Mack, the crosstown Phillies, mired in mediocrity for most of the first decade and a half of the twentieth century, fought an exciting battle for the National League pennant and grabbed the lion's share of local newspaper headlines and fan enthusiasm. The Phillies had dethroned the A's as the kings of Philadelphia baseball, and not even the presence of Napoleon Lajoie, who starred for both teams so long ago, made much of a difference for the struggling Athletics and their cash-poor management.

In an uncharacteristic display of poor judg-

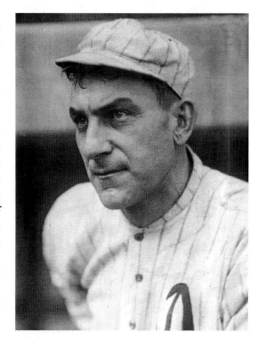

Lajoie with the A's in 1915 (National Baseball Hall of Fame Library, Cooperstown, New York).

ment, Mack lost his temper in May and committed what he later called the greatest mistake of his career. Herb Pennock, the left-hander who won 14 games for Mack in 1914 at the age of 20, did not pitch well after losing his no-hit bid on Opening Day. On May 19, he made a wild throw in the eighth inning against the White Sox, leading to a five-run Chicago rally and a loss that left the A's with a 9–19 record and dropped the team into last place for the first time in its 15-year history. Four days later, in his next start against Detroit, Pennock gave up two hits and two walks in the first inning. The mild-mannered pitcher's diffident attitude angered Mack, who decided that Pennock "lacked ambition" and would never succeed on the major league level. Mack yanked Pennock from the game, ignored him on the bench for a couple of weeks, and then stunned the league by putting the youngster on waivers. The Red Sox, who remembered how Pennock dominated them in his near no-hitter two months before, scooped him up and started him on a path that led to the Hall of Fame.

If Larry Lajoie wondered how the Cleveland fans felt about him, he received his answer on another "Lajoie Day" at League Park on May 9. The visiting A's made their first visit to Cleveland that day, and when Lajoie stepped to the plate for the first time that Sunday afternoon, more than 10,000 fans roared out a welcome. As local sportswriter Ed Bang described the scene, "It seemed that a 42-centimetre gun had been turned loose. Every human in the big enclosure stood and cheered and applauded the idol for several minutes. It was a demonstration never seen here before and one that will probably never be equaled in the days to come. Surely it will never be surpassed.... They were there to pay homage to 'The King,' who is regarded as a Cleveland base ball landmark by practically every fan in the Sixth City."[11] Lajoie went hitless that day in a 3–0 loss to his former teammates.

Lajoie's reception stood in stark contrast to the unpopularity of the newly named Indians. After suffering through a last-place finish in 1914, Cleveland fans saw little improvement in the 1915 edition of the team. Lajoie, the fan favorite, was gone, Joe Jackson was injured, and fan interest dissipated almost as quickly in Cleveland as it had for the A's in Philadelphia. Falling attendance and Federal League competition put the former Naps in severe financial trouble, and later that year the hard-pressed Charles Somers was forced to deal Jackson to the White Sox for four players and a large amount of cash. Somers, whose coal business suffered greatly during the 1914 economic recession, was at the end of his financial rope, and at season's end, his creditors forced him to sell the Cleveland ballclub to a new group of owners. Somers eventually recouped much of his fortune, but the man who was hailed as the "financial angel" of the American League in its early days never returned to the game.

Lajoie suffered what was, for him, an unprecedented embarrassment at bat on July 24 in the second game of a doubleheader at Cleveland. In the top of the ninth, with the A's losing to the Indians by a 12–4 count, Lajoie came to the plate with no one out and two runners, Lew Malone and Wally Schang, at second and first respectively. Lajoie belted a hard smash down the third base line, but Cleveland's Walter Barbare made a sensational catch for the first out of the inning. Barbare then threw to second baseman Bill Wambsganss to double off Malone. Wambsganss threw to first sacker Jay Kirke to catch Schang off base for a game-ending triple play, the only one Lajoie hit into during his career.

The A's fell to the bottom half of the league in May and never again rose higher than sixth place in 1915. Mack, increasingly desperate for cash to operate his failing team, sold off more veterans, sending Danny Murphy to the White Sox and Jack Barry to the Red Sox, breaking up the "Larry and Barry" infield tandem. He netted $21,500 but deprived his club of much-needed experience and talent. He also sold pitcher Bob Shawkey to the Yankees for another $3,500 infusion of cash. After completing these deals, the Athletics dropped to last place and stayed there. The infield was a disaster, with only first baseman Stuffy McInnis remaining from the vaunted "$100,000 infield" of yore. Fourteen different men, including catcher Wally Schang and Lajoie himself for two games, tried and failed to fill the void at third base, while rookie Larry Kopf struggled to replace Jack Barry at short. The aged Lajoie manned the second sack and led the team in runs batted in with 61, but his decreasing range in the field drew attention to his lack of speed and resulted in more grounders skipping past him into the outfield. Never fast to begin with, Lajoie played in 129 games and scored only 40 runs.

Lajoie was old and slow, but was by no means the worst performer on the team. He was still a capable hitter, though his power was only a memory, and could still help the team on offense. The A's could also count on a few holdovers from Mack's championship teams of the previous few seasons, including first baseman Stuffy McInnis, one of the best in the league at his position. Two other veterans, right fielder Amos Strunk and catcher Wally Schang, were still dependable, solid players. The team's main weakness lay in its pitching, as Mack trotted out an endless procession of young hurlers who could not get the ball over the plate. On June 23, Bruno Haas made his major league debut and allowed 11 hits while walking 16 batters in a 15–7 loss to the Red Sox. His 16 walks set a major league record for a nine-inning game that stands to this day. Several other starters pitched games in which they reached double figures in walks allowed. By season's end, the A's had surrendered 827 free passes, the highest team total of all time. They also gave up more runs and more hits than any team in the league.

In all, 56 players, 27 of them pitchers, saw action for the Athletics in 1915 as the season devolved into a never-ending tryout camp. On many mornings when the Athletics played at home, Mack would assemble a gaggle of prospects at Shibe Park and divide them into two teams, with Lajoie serving as captain of one squad and catcher Ira Thomas directing the other. With Mack watching, Lajoie and Thomas put the hopefuls through their paces in a simulated game, after which the manager kept the promising players and dismissed the others. They did not find many keepers, as the Federal League had absorbed much of the available young talent. Of the 56 men who wore an A's uniform in 1915, seven played in only one contest, while 21 took the field in fewer than five games.

Though his .280 average was the third-best on the team, Lajoie was clearly coming to the end, barely hanging onto what was left of his legendary career with the worst team in baseball. He could no more replace Eddie Collins in the Philadelphia lineup than Weldon Wyckoff (7–22) and Joe Bush (5–15) could replace Chief Bender and Eddie Plank on the mound. Despite Mack's brave predictions of the spring, the Athletics finished the year buried in last place with a 43–109 record, 58½ games behind the pennant-winning Red Sox. Only the 1904 Senators, who lost 113 games, and the 1908 Senators, who lost 109, had dropped more contests in an American League season up to that time, though the A's set a new league record for games behind at the finish of a campaign.

Because Connie Mack had built pennant-winning teams from the ground up before, many writers were willing to give him the benefit of the doubt even after his club's last-place finish in 1915. As the *New York Journal* opined, "There is something majestic in the quiet, unostentatious way [Mack] goes about building up his newest machine."[12] Heywood Broun of the *New York Tribune* also trusted the Philadelphia manager. "If there are any Collinses or Bakers or Barrys out there, Connie Mack will find them," wrote Broun. "Into classroom, mine, or ploughed field, his scouts will carry the search."[13] Unfortunately for

Napoleon Lajoie, the talent-challenged Athletics could not be expected to land a World Series berth in the near future. The team had to hit bottom before it began to recover, and it was clear that by the time the A's were ready to challenge for a pennant with its next assemblage of stars, Lajoie would be long retired. In 1916, he could do nothing but play his best and help out whenever he could, knowing all along that his dream of playing in a World Series was destined to remain unfulfilled.

Financial and attendance woes continued into the 1916 season, and by summer Mack's coffers were so empty that he proposed paying his players a percentage of the gate receipts in lieu of their salaries. None of the players showed the slightest bit of enthusiasm for that idea, and the proposal died quietly. The losses mounted as Mack continued to bring in new squadrons of young players, giving them playing time on the major league level, and dismissing the ones who failed to show promise. Through it all Napoleon Lajoie continued to hold down second base and bat in the fifth spot in the lineup, though his average remained beneath the .250 mark and his range in the infield appeared to deteriorate by the week. Lajoie was 41 years old and long past his prime, and though he might have remained useful as an occasional pinch-hitter, his $9,000 salary was the highest on the ballclub, so he played. He also remained in the lineup because he was still the best second baseman on the roster, which speaks volumes about the talent level on the team.

Though the Athletics were short on talent, two pitchers acquitted themselves well. Elmer Myers, a 22-year-old right-hander from York Springs, Pennsylvania, was signed by Mack after winning 29 games in the North Carolina State League the year before. In 1916 he won 14 games and lost 23 for the A's, but posted a decent 3.66 earned run average and completed 31 of his 35 starts. The other was "Bullet Joe" Bush, who had gone 17–13 for the 1914 champions at the age of 21. Bush, who compiled a 15–24 record for Mack in 1916, led the league in losses despite an excellent 2.57 earned run average. Though Myers and Bush were plagued by wildness — they finished first and second, respectively, in the league in bases on balls — they gave their team a chance to win when they pitched, and accounted for all but seven of the team's 36 victories in 1916.

The rest of the pitching staff was hopeless. The other two main starters, Jack Nabors and Tom Sheehan, finished the year with a combined total of two wins and 36 losses. Sheehan (1–16) finished only eight of his 17 starts, while Nabors (1–20) lost his first game of the season, won his second, then closed the year by losing his final 19 decisions. His .048 winning percentage is the worst ever compiled by any pitcher with at least 20 starts, and his streak of 19 consecutive losses tied the major league record set by Bob Groom seven years before, and has never been surpassed in one season. The A's had almost no chance on days that someone other than Bush and Myers took the mound, because the other 17 men who pitched for the Athletics that year won seven games and lost 70. Philadelphia pitchers led the league by a wide margin in walks allowed and gave up more than five runs per game, while every other American League team surrendered fewer than four.

Perhaps the most famous story about the hapless 1916 A's concerns a game Nabors pitched against the Red Sox. As his roommate Tom Sheehan related the tale,

> Once we go to Boston for a series. I pitch the opener and give up one hit, by Doc Hoblitzell. But it happens to follow a walk and an error by Witt and I lose, 1–0. Now Nabors pitches the second game and he is leading, 1–0, going into the ninth. He gets the first man. Witt boots one and the next guy walks. Hooper is up next, I think, and he singles to left and the guy on second tries to score. Well, Schang has a good arm and he throws one in that had the runner cold by fifteen feet. But we have one of those green catchers. I'll never forget his

Larry taking batting practice, 1915 (National Baseball Hall of Fame Library, Cooperstown, New York).

name, Mike Murphy. The ball bounces out of his glove, the run scores, the other runner takes third, and it is 1–1.

Nabors winds up and throws the next pitch 20 feet over the hitter's head into the grandstand, the man on third scores, and we lose another, 2–1. Later I asked Nabors why he threw that one away. "Look," he said, "I know those guys wouldn't get me another run, and if you think I'm going to throw nine more innings on a hot day like this, you're crazy."[14]

Larry Lajoie almost certainly never expected to find himself playing out the string on what many historians call the worst team in baseball history, one that suffered through a

2–41 skid from June 27 to August 8. He had always dreamed of playing for a pennant winner, a dream that had gone unrealized during his 21 seasons in the major leagues. He had been forced to leave the A's in 1902 when the courts declared his contract with Connie Mack invalid, after which he joined Cleveland and could only watch as Mack's club won the league title without him. He returned to the Athletics after the 1914 season, only to see the defending American League champs sell their stars to other teams and sink to the bottom of the league. Now, while his other former Philadelphia team, the Phillies, basked in the glow of their first National League flag, he played his final season in front of thousands of empty seats. In later years, Lajoie called his failure to play for a pennant winner "the greatest disappointment of my baseball life."[15]

One of the rare highlights of the 1916 season occurred on August 26, when Joe Bush, who had pitched so poorly earlier in the month that Mack yanked him out of the rotation, took the mound against the Indians and threw a no-hitter. Jack Graney, who walked to lead off the game, was the only Cleveland batter to reach base as Bush completed a 5–0 win. The pitcher so dominated the Indians that Lajoie, the second baseman, handled only one ball all afternoon. He threw out one runner at first and, because there were no runners on base besides Graney, was not required to make any putouts. Though he lost 24 games that year, Bush was clearly the best pitcher on the staff, as his no-hitter was one of eight shutouts he pitched for the A's that season. Only Babe Ruth of the Red Sox, with nine shutouts, topped Bush in that category among American League hurlers. His 15–24 record that year would certainly had been reversed with a good team behind him, and his later work with pennant-winning clubs in Boston and New York proved his worth. At least Connie Mack could boast that one of the many pitchers he brought to Philadelphia made good.

Bush's no-hitter marked a milestone in baseball history for another reason. It proved to be Napoleon Lajoie's final major league game. Lajoie walloped a liner that sailed over center fielder Tris Speaker's head and rolled to the scoreboard in the sixth inning, but, slowed by leg injuries and advancing age, he barely made it to third. The younger Lajoie would have scored standing up. The next batter, Charlie Pick, smacked what should have been a run-scoring single just past second base, but Lajoie hesitated, then stumbled on his way home. Speaker threw him out easily, and after hitting a weak fly to right in his final plate appearance of the day, Lajoie took to the sidelines for the rest of the season. Though his admiration for Connie Mack continued unabated, he was ready to leave Philadelphia. "I'm afraid I wasn't much use by then, hitting .280 in 1915 and .246 in 1916," he once said. "I was more of a coach than a player."[16] Lajoie watched from the bench as the Athletics stumbled through September and finished the season with 38 wins and a league-record 117 losses.

At season's end, his contract fulfilled, Napoleon Lajoie left the Athletics. He had compiled his third consecutive sub-.300 season, and at the age of 42, he was old, slow, and injury-prone. Norman Macht, Connie Mack's biographer, called the aged second baseman "an overpriced, over-the-hill liability,"[17] and Mack's never-ending talent search left no room on the roster for a faded superstar, even at a sharply reduced salary. Mack gave Lajoie, now a free agent, permission to make his own deal, but not one of the other 15 major league teams showed any interest in the man who had compiled a lifetime batting average of .338, stroked 3,242 hits, and belted a record 657 doubles. After 21 seasons, Lajoie's major league career was finished.

Lajoie was not the only star of note to depart the major league scene at the end of the

1916 campaign. Christy Mathewson, winner of 372 games for the New York Giants, was traded to the Cincinnati Reds in mid-season and installed as manager. On September 4 he pitched his only game for the Reds, defeating the Cubs for his last major league victory, then retired. Mathewson's opponent in his final game was Mordecai "Three Finger" Brown, another all-time great who also made his last appearance that day. A fourth major star to announce his retirement in the fall of 1916 was Honus Wagner, who decided to hang up his glove after 20 seasons in the National League. Wagner, unlike Brown, Mathewson, and Lajoie, later changed his mind and played in 74 games for the Pirates in 1917, adding to his hit total but batting an un–Wagnerian .265 before joining the others on the sidelines for good.[18]

Though he was finished with the American League, Lajoie was not yet ready to leave the game. For two seasons, he had studied his favorite manager, Connie Mack, and absorbed all the lessons that baseball's most experienced field leader had to offer. Though he was no longer young enough, nor agile enough, to play major league ball, he was ready to take another shot at a managing job. He applied for several positions in the top minor leagues, including open slots with Columbus of the American Association and Toronto of the International League. Columbus, the capital of Ohio, was closer to his home near Cleveland, but Toronto won out. On January 15, 1917, news hit the papers that Lajoie would not only manage the Toronto Maple Leafs during the upcoming season, but play for them as well.

25

A Pennant at Last

[I] have had many differences with Mr. Lajoie as to matters of discipline and deportment of the Cleveland team, but I want to say that his own personal record is spotless. Naturally a man who has played so much baseball has had his disagreements with umpires, but this big fellow carried his troubles off the field and I never had occasion to severely censure him. That, in my opinion, was due to his good sense and judgment. I am proud and happy to say that now, as he is leaving us, his relations with the American League are most pleasant, and I desire to thank him for his loyal service. — Ban Johnson[1]

Ed Barrow, the autocratic president of the International League, was a visionary. He had started his baseball career during the mid–1890s as part-owner of the Paterson club of the Atlantic League, where he discovered Honus Wagner and sold his contract to Louisville of the National League. After a brief stint as manager of the Detroit Tigers, he resigned in July of 1904 and spent the next three seasons managing minor league clubs in Indianapolis, Montreal, and Toronto. He quit the game at one point and spent a few years managing a hotel in Toronto, but in 1911 he was named president of the Eastern League, which featured two teams in Canada (Montreal and Toronto) and six in the United States, including the former major league cities of Buffalo, Baltimore, and Providence. The circuit was one of three Double-A, or top-level, minor leagues, and because it spanned two countries, the Eastern League changed its name in 1912 and became the International League at Barrow's suggestion.

Barrow guided the International League through turbulent times. All of the minor leagues suffered during the 1910s due to a national economic downturn, coupled with the emergence of the Federal League, a would-be third major circuit, in 1914. More than a dozen minor leagues went out of business between 1914 and 1916, but the International League plowed on, despite Canada's entry into World War One (two and a half years before the United States joined the conflict) and the war's effect on the Montreal and Toronto teams. Though the Federal League collapsed after two seasons, Barrow believed that the baseball world had room for a third major league, and dreamed of forming his own Union League by merging his circuit's four strongest teams (Newark, Toronto, Buffalo, and Baltimore) with four from the American Association (Toledo, Columbus, Indianapolis, and Louisville). That possibility, as appealing as it sounded, would have to wait until after the end of the world war.

232

Always looking to strengthen his circuit, Barrow was thrilled to learn that Napoleon Lajoie was interested in a minor league managing job. Barrow contacted the owners of the Providence Grays, figuring that Lajoie, a native of nearby Woonsocket, would be a perfect fit in the capital city of his home state. The Providence group never responded, probably because the team was undergoing a reorganization at the time, so Barrow shifted his attention to Toronto, which also had a managerial opening. Charles "Chief" Bender, the recently retired pitching star of the Athletics, had been the front-runner for the Toronto position, but when Lajoie entered the picture, Bender's candidacy was over. James A. McCaffrey, Toronto's principal owner, opened negotiations with Lajoie, who asked for a partial stake in the team as part of the deal. McCaffrey was not interested in giving Lajoie a piece of the ballclub, but Lajoie signed on anyway, at a salary of $3,500 per year.

Toronto, the most populous English-speaking city in Canada, boasted a long history in baseball. The Maple Leafs had joined the Eastern League, predecessor to the International, in 1895 and had won several pennants, employing well-known managers such as Arthur Irwin, Joe Kelley, and Ed Barrow. Though the war was a drag on attendance, Toronto was one of the most stable franchises in the circuit, and during this time the American League had seriously considered shifting the struggling Washington Senators to the Canadian city. Napoleon Lajoie, who traveled to Toronto in early February to assess the roster and make plans for spring training, liked what he saw in Toronto, though he and Myrtle decided to maintain their residence outside of Cleveland. Lajoie may also have enjoyed the fact that the Maple Leafs had finished in the second division in 1916 under the leadership of Joe Birmingham, his least favorite Cleveland manager. Birmingham's dismissal at the end of 1916 opened the position for him, and no doubt provided the new field leader with all the incentive he needed to succeed.

Lajoie and his new boss, James McCaffrey, announced plans to hold a two-week training camp in Petersburg, Virginia, starting on March 29. The new manager also decided to plant himself at first base. "Of course," he says, "I may be compelled to go back to second, but first base is the position I intend to play. I guess I will make an outfielder out of [Dawson] Graham, who has played first for Toronto two seasons."[2] Graham, who had played briefly for Cincinnati in 1914, was one of the team's best hitters, but because Lajoie could no longer cover much ground in the middle of the infield, Graham had to move. With several members of the 1916 Maple Leafs headed for major league clubs, Lajoie looked far and wide for talent to fill the holes in the Toronto roster. As spring camp approached, the Leafs were short at least two pitchers, two outfielders, and a reliable catcher.

Lajoie and McCaffrey worked hard to find players, but their task was complicated by the war. The United States officially entered the conflict when Congress declared war on Germany on April 6, 1917, 11 days before the start of the International League season, and though it would take a while for the government to institute a military draft, all teams knew that many of their players might be sent overseas before long. Canada, on the other hand, had been at war for two and a half years; as part of the British Commonwealth, it had taken up arms in September of 1914. The country's attention was focused on the war, and baseball paled in importance to Canadians, even with one of baseball's biggest names taking the reins as manager of the Maple Leafs. Now, with the United States joining the Allied effort, some observers wondered aloud if baseball leagues, both major and minor, would be allowed to complete their schedules in 1917.

The Leafs, along with all other major and minor league teams, also faced a threat from the Players Fraternity, an embryonic players' union headed by Dave Fultz, who had been a

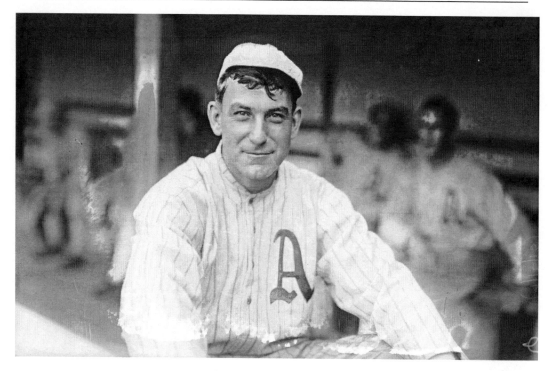

Lajoie in 1916. At age 41, he was the oldest regular player in the American League that year (author's collection).

teammate of Lajoie's on the 1901 Philadelphia Athletics. Fultz, who formed the Fraternity in 1912 and convinced hundreds of players to sign up, believed that the minor league draft was unfair to the players and called for a strike over the issue. Fultz requested that Fraternity members in both the major and minor leagues refrain from signing their contracts for 1917, but while a few players acquiesced, the strike threat went nowhere. "The Players' Union will receive no consideration from the International League," said McCaffery, "and if they choose to go ahead with their strike proposition we will simply suspend operations for the season."[3]

Larry Lajoie, a Fraternity member, criticized Fultz for his stand and soon resigned from the organization. "Fultz is ill-advised," said the new Toronto manager. "Major league, Double-A and Single-A players have no kick coming. We've been getting everything we asked for. No set of salaried men has ever been better treated than we have been by the magnates." Citing the shrinking number of jobs for minor leaguers, Lajoie opined that the magnates were making little, if any, money. "Every Tom, Dick, and Harry is a stockholder and they're assessed each year. This is no time for Mr. Fultz to impose additional hardships."[4] Lajoie, at age 42, was now a company man through and through, though his analysis was most likely an astute one. Due not only to the war, but also to competition from movies and vaudeville, baseball was struggling, merely trying to survive until peacetime. The Fraternity, which had gained a few concessions from the magnates during the Federal League years, could not achieve its stated goals in a time of financial hardship. The organization was widely ignored, and faded away before the end of the decade.

Spring camp opened on March 29 as scheduled, but to the new manager's surprise, only six players were present and ready to work. Dawson Graham, the former first baseman who Lajoie hoped would get enough work in the outfield to be comfortable at the position, did not arrive until April 4, while Bunny Hearn, a key left-handed pitcher, did not show up at all. He was busy coaching the team at the University of North Carolina in Chapel Hill, and would not be available until the second week of the season. With a skeleton crew in tow, Lajoie put his players through their drills and played a series of contests against the Petersburg club, winning three and losing none.

The Maple Leafs roster was in a state of disarray, and though the Toronto club was slated to open the season after its final exhibition game, a 10–0 win over Norfolk, Lajoie was forced to make several moves. Desperately short of pitching, he begged Chicago Cubs manager Fred Mitchell to return Bill McTigue, who had won 16 games for Toronto in 1916, to the Maple Leafs, but Mitchell, who was impressed by the pitcher in spring training but had no room for him in Chicago, instead sent McTigue to Providence. Lajoie and McCaffrey then made a trade with the Baltimore Orioles, sending second baseman Frank Truesdale, one of the team's key performers the year before, to the Orioles for pitcher Dan Tipple. This trade forced Lajoie to move back to second base and allowed him to keep Dawson Graham, who showed little enthusiasm for the outfield, on first. Thus fortified, the Leafs traveled to Baltimore to open the season on April 17.

The Maple Leafs began the season slowly, hovering around the .500 mark during the first few weeks, but Lajoie's star power gave the entire league a much-needed boost. Lajoie drew extra fans in each International League city, all of which held a "Lajoie Day" at some point during the season. He was plied with gifts in almost every ballpark, although the Montreal Royals hosted a celebration that was long on speeches but gave nothing tangible to baseball's most prominent French-Canadian star. Other cities, however, were happy to celebrate one of baseball's greatest players, and he received trophies, gold coins, and other items from friends and admirers all season long. Perhaps the best celebration came at Providence, in his home state of Rhode Island, on June 19. Friends from Woonsocket and Fall River stopped the game before he came to bat in the first inning and presented their hero with a baseball made of sterling silver. Lajoie then stepped in and belted a single, leading the Maple Leafs to a 5–1 win that day.

Lajoie, who had last played minor league ball in 1896, found the International League in general, and Toronto in particular, full of challenges. The Maple Leafs played their home games at the cavernous Hanlan's Point grounds, a 19,000-seat edifice which was situated next to an amusement park on an island in the Toronto River and was only accessible by ferry boat. Given Lajoie's well-known antipathy for travel over water, merely getting to and from the park each day must have been a chore for the Toronto manager. He also had to deal with the weather in Canada, which was particularly cold and rainy during the spring of 1917. As late as Victoria Day, a holiday celebrated on May 24 throughout the British Commonwealth, a doubleheader in Montreal was cancelled because of freezing temperatures. In Toronto, where the Leafs were slated to play a twin bill against Buffalo that day, the morning game was called off due to the cold. The teams completed the afternoon contest, though players and fans had to move around constantly to stay warm.

The Maple Leafs bounced between first and fourth place as May turned into June, but hit a losing streak and fell briefly to fifth with four consecutive losses at Newark on a weekend in mid–June. The Bears scored two one-run victories against Lajoie's team on Friday and Saturday, then swept a Sunday doubleheader by scores of 7–0 and 15–2. Lajoie, despite the roster limitations that were part and parcel of managing a minor league team, shuffled his lineup, moving Joe Schultz from center field to third base, shifting Merwin

Jacobson from the bench to center, and signing Jack Warhop, a former major leaguer who had pitched with the Yankees for eight seasons. Warhop could not only play multiple positions, but at age 33 was also safe from the military draft.[5] These moves put some life into the Maple Leafs and put them back on the right track, at least for a while. Toronto also received stellar starting pitching from Bunny Hearn, who won 23 games that year, and Harry Thompson, a 25-game winner. Both men were left-handers, a luxury that Lajoie never enjoyed in Cleveland.

Lajoie, who had adopted a hands-off managing style in Cleveland, grappled with a few troublemakers on his roster and, though it went against his nature, found the need to deal firmly with them. Jimmy Smith, an infielder, asked for a few days off to go home to Pennsylvania and deal with a family matter. Lajoie agreed, but Smith stayed away for 17 days and was angry when Lajoie fined and suspended him upon his return. Smith filed a complaint against the Leafs with the National Commission, which ruled in the team's favor. Pitcher George Zabel, who went 10–5 for the Leafs but abandoned the team in July (took "French leave," as the local papers put it) and joined an independent club in Wisconsin, left the team short-handed on the mound. Perhaps Lajoie's biggest problem child was Dawson Graham, who took an instant dislike to the manager when ordered to move to the outfield during spring training. Graham's behavior and attitude deteriorated so badly that Lajoie suspended him without pay in early July and signed a recent college player from Harvard, Dan Costello, to play first.

The Toronto club stayed in the pennant chase despite its need to, in the words of *The Sporting News*, "weed out the disaffected players."[6] The biggest reason for the Leafs' success, at least offensively, was manager Lajoie. The Toronto cleanup batter, he compiled a 21-game hitting streak in May and kept his average near the .400 mark into the late summer months. With his 43rd birthday fast approaching, he was the most dangerous hitter in the International League, though people still remarked about his penchant for swinging at bad balls. He belted 30 hits in 69 trips to the plate during one early-season stretch, and though he hit only five home runs, he pounded out singles and doubles at an impressive clip. After batting below the .300 mark during his last three seasons in the American League, Lajoie appeared to have rediscovered his batting eye. Major league teams sent their scouts to search the minors for infield help, but, as a Providence newspaper reported, "After a thorough combing of the brush, the wise men brought back the reports that there were no hard hitters in the minor league second base ranks with the exception of a youngster named Lajoie of the Toronto club."[7]

Not all was perfect with Lajoie's play, however. He was deathly slow, stealing only four bases all year and covering little ground at second base. He also reverted to form in his treatment of the International League umpires. With the responsibility for the Maple Leafs resting on his shoulders, his arguments with the arbiters became so heated that league president Ed Barrow suspended him twice, once in May and again in June, for what *The Sporting News* called "umpire baiting" and "law-bumping." This second suspension was cut short when Barrow reinstated Lajoie in time to play in a doubleheader in Toronto on Dominion Day, Canada's most important national holiday. The Leafs defeated Rochester twice in that July 1 twin bill, ending the day in third place, within striking distance of the league-leading Baltimore Orioles.

By this time, the pennant chase had boiled down to four teams, all tightly bunched at the top of the International League. Toronto slumped in mid–June, but soon righted the ship and resumed their fight for the lead with Baltimore, Providence, and Newark. Baltimore, owned and managed by onetime big league pitcher Jack Dunn, boasted plenty of future major league talent and held first place through June. Providence, managed by former umpire Jack Egan, and Tom Needham's Newark club jockeyed for position with Toronto and Baltimore, making the 1917 International League race one of the closest and hardest-fought in minor league history.

Lajoie's outstanding performance with the Maple Leafs impressed many in the baseball world, and several major league clubs, including the Washington Senators and the Chicago Cubs, inquired about his availability. In June Clark Griffith, manager and part-owner of the weak-hitting Senators, told the Washington papers that he would be happy to sign Lajoie as a pinch-hitter and occasional starter at first base. According to a report in the *Washington Times*, Griffith was already negotiating with the Maple Leafs and expected to acquire Lajoie within a few days. The Washington manager was obliged to disavow this report soon after, perhaps because Lajoie was not interested in playing for the Senators. The Cubs also suffered from a poor hitting attack and viewed Lajoie as a remedy for their offensive woes, though he made it clear that he was unwilling to return to the National League after a 17-year absence. He had a job to do in Toronto, and he knew that he could lead the Maple Leafs to the flag if things proceeded as expected.

The 42-year-old Lajoie appealed to major league clubs, at least in part, because he was not likely to be called away for military service any time soon. Several big leaguers had already donned the uniform, but Lajoie, due to his age, was not affected, at least not yet. On June 5, 1917, the United States government ordered the conscription of all men between the ages of 21 and 31, and because all the players on Toronto's roster were Americans, all but the oldest were covered by the edict. This ruling made Lajoie's job, and that of all major and minor league managers, more complicated, as players left their teams in mid-season to enter the military or take jobs in factories and shipyards. Lajoie, the International League's leading hitter, did not have to worry about being sent to fight in France. Not until September 12, 1918, when the Selective Service required all men up to the age of 45 to appear before their local draft boards, would Larry Lajoie be obliged to fill out a registration form.

Lajoie continued to tinker with his lineup, playing pitcher Jack Warhop at shortstop and putting ace hurler Harry Thompson in the outfield when needed, but in July he finally stabilized the right side of his infield. Due to Dawson Graham's suspension and Dan Costello's inability to hit, Lajoie moved back to first base, the position he had planned to play all along. To fill the hole at second, the Leafs made a trade with the Orioles and retrieved Frank Truesdale, whom the Toronto club had traded away a few months before. Reinstalled at second base, Truesdale not only hit well, but took some of the defensive pressure off the aging Lajoie. He also allowed Lajoie to release the troublesome Dawson Graham. Truesdale's return and Graham's dismissal bolstered the Leafs, who zoomed past Baltimore, Newark, and Providence to grab first place in early August.

The unpredictable Toronto weather helped Lajoie's men win one game. On August 20, Leafs pitcher Bunny Hearn held a 5–0 margin over the Newark Bears after six innings at Hanlan's Point, but the Bears scored three times in the seventh to threaten Toronto's lead. Just then, a sudden, unexpected squall hit the Toronto ballpark with full force. The wind, which may actually have been a tornado, ripped the roof off the grandstands, knocked the scoreboard flat, and spewed debris around the park while fans and players scurried onto the field to escape the mayhem. The center field flagpole, "which was flying the Union Jack and Old Glory, was doubled up like a pack-knife without the least regard for the colors of the two great powers which it carried," said *The Sporting News*, which captioned its article about the game, "Larry Calls Elements To Aid Pennant Fight."[8] Fortunately, no one was hurt, but the game was called, with Toronto declared the winner.

The 1917 season was an interesting one for the Maple Leafs. On June 28, a Richmond batter hit a grounder that rolled up third baseman George Whiteman's sleeve. Whiteman, the best hitter on the team after Lajoie, could not free the ball from his clothing, and the Richmond player legged out a home run, though the Leafs won the game that day. On August 30, a pitching duel between Toronto's Harry Thompson and Baltimore's Rube Parnham ended when Red Shannon of Baltimore stole home in the ninth inning for a 1–0 win. Parnham had pitched and won both ends of a doubleheader, 24 innings in all, against Rochester six days before. Toronto's longest day occurred on August 29, when the Maple Leafs defeated the Richmond club a 16-inning contest, then played six frames of an exhibition game against the visiting Washington Senators before darkness fell. The Maple Leafs defeated two Senators pitchers, Bert Gallia and Walter Johnson, taking a 3–1 win over the major leaguers.

On the last day of August, Lajoie smacked three hits as the Leafs defeated Baltimore and ended the month only .013 behind first-place Providence. The last two weeks of the season turned into a dogfight among the four contenders, but none of the other teams had a hitter like Napoleon Lajoie in the cleanup spot. He led his men by example, going 6-for-8 as the Maple Leafs swept a twin bill against Buffalo on September 7 to edge past Providence into first place. Three days later, after splitting another twin bill with the Bisons and losing another doubleheader to foul weather, they battled at Montreal in weather so cold that the players had trouble handling the ball. It was a wild game, in which three men from each team, including Lajoie, belted homers in the first inning. He walloped his second homer of the day as Toronto scored six runs in the second, and the Leafs enjoyed a 15–9 lead before the Royals scored six times in the ninth to send the game into extra innings. Toronto put the game away with three runs in the 12th off 18-year-old rookie right-hander Waite Hoyt and escaped with a 19–16 win, leaving the Maple Leafs in first by mere percentage points with six games left to play.

After closing their home schedule with five wins in three days against Montreal, Lajoie's men traveled to Rochester for two season-ending twin bills. On Friday, September 14, the Leafs split with the Hustlers as Lajoie, with his first pennant since Fall River 21 years before in his sights, belted six hits in eight trips to the plate. This doubleheader split left Toronto, at 91–61, in first with a .598 percentage, .004 ahead of Providence at 88–60. The Grays had three games left, and would take the flag if they won all of them and Toronto lost once against Rochester. If Toronto won both of their games, they would win the pennant no matter what Providence did.

Larry Lajoie and his Maple Leafs took the decision out of their competitors' hands. They won the first game on Saturday by a 1–0 count as Harry Thompson pitched a three-hit shutout. In Game 2, after five scoreless frames, Toronto grabbed the lead in the sixth when Frank Truesdale and George Whitman singled, and Lajoie doubled both men home. Rochester scored on an error by Lajoie, who missed a throw at first from pitcher Bunny Hearn, but the Leafs held fast and entered the ninth with a 5–1 lead. With two out, the Rochester batter grounded to shortstop Billy Murray, who threw to Lajoie at first to end the game. "A broad grin overspread Lajoie's features when he took the throw from Murray for the 27th out," reported the local paper, the *Globe*, the next day. Lajoie was thrilled with his first pennant as a manager. "If my error, which gave Rochester a run in that second game, had lost the game and the pennant," he said after the game, "I don't believe I could

1, Hearne; 2, Leake; 3, Schultz; 4, A. A. Irwin, Bus. Mgr.; 5, Jacobson; 6, Kelly; 7, Lalonge; 8, Gould; 9, Warhop; 10, Whiteman; 11, Lajoie, Mgr.; 12, J. J. McCaffery, Pres.; 13, Blackburn; 14, Murray; 15, Thompson; 16, Truesdale; 17, Carroll, Trainer.

TORONTO TEAM—CHAMPIONS INTERNATIONAL LEAGUE.

The 1917 Toronto Maple Leafs (author's collection).

have gone to the clubhouse and faced the boys."[9] The *Toronto Star* pointed out that the Leafs had won the title despite carrying only 15 men, one fewer than the International League limit. However, the paper said that the smaller roster made little difference, because "Larry Lajoie was himself worth four ordinary players."[10]

The International League champion Maple Leafs spent the next week playing exhibition games against semipro teams in small Ontario cities, then agreed to meet the Indianapolis Indians, winners of the American Association, in a seven-game set for the unofficial minor league championship of North America. Indianapolis swept the series in five games, with Lajoie, perhaps exhausted from the hard pennant fight, stroking only three hits in 18 times at bat. The payday was worth the trouble however, as each Maple Leaf took home $304 for his efforts.

Lajoie, who had suffered greatly from injuries during his final few American League campaigns, proved remarkably durable for the Maple Leafs, playing in all but three of Toronto's 154 games. He led the circuit with a .380 average, 221 hits, and 39 doubles, and if the league had given a Most Valuable Player award at the time, he would almost certainly have won it. He also drew thousands of fans to ballparks in every league city. *The Sporting News* paid tribute to the Toronto field leader.

> Not only has Nap been a great manager, but he is one of the leading hitters of the International circuit. And yet they told us a year ago that he was done, that he had lost his spirit as well as his physical qualifications. Give heed, therefore, to those who have always believed in Lajoie. List[en] while they rise up to tell you that what he has done in Toronto he might have done with Cleveland, had he been given the cooperation and support without which no manager can make a showing.[11]

Lajoie had finally proven himself as a manager, and looked forward to another season with the Maple Leafs. However, the baseball world was already feeling the effects of the war in both the United States and Canada, and with an increasing number of young men headed for service in Europe, the very existence of professional baseball in 1918 was cast into doubt. Attendance in two International League cities, Richmond and Montreal, was so poor in 1917 that those teams hovered on the brink of bankruptcy, and with the war intensifying, many feared that entire leagues might be forced to suspend operations until peacetime. How long that would be, with the Allies and Central Powers fighting to a deadly stalemate in Europe, was anybody's guess and boded ill for the immediate future of baseball, especially of the minor league variety.

International League president Ed Barrow foresaw the troubles that faced his league in 1918, but his proposed course of action angered the league magnates. Barrow recommended that the International League suspend play for one year, but the team owners rebelled, showing their displeasure by cutting the president's salary from $7,500 per year to $2,500. This was an invitation to resign, which Barrow did at a stormy league meeting on December 17, 1917. The always feisty Barrow, who nearly traded punches with some of his former bosses on his way out of the meeting, was offered the manager's post with the Boston Red Sox soon afterward. Barrow, after more than a decade away from the major leagues, led the Red Sox to the 1918 pennant and a World Series victory.

In truth, the International League magnates forced Barrow out for daring to state the obvious. With the military draft in full swing in both the United States and Canada, the survival of every minor and major league was by no means assured as the 1918 season dawned. Many players had joined the armed services in 1917, and many more had left baseball behind and taken what the War Department called "essential labor" in factories, farms, and shipyards. As late as March, with less than a month to go before the presumed start of the season, International League officials were not sure if their circuit would operate at all in 1918. Several team owners, led by those in the failing franchises of Montreal and Richmond, pushed to suspend play until the end of the war.

The uncertain future of the International League left Napoleon Lajoie in a quandary. He liked his situation in Toronto, but if he simply waited for the league to decide if it wanted to operate at all in 1918, he might be left without a position in an ever-shrinking pool of managerial jobs. To complicate matters, several major league teams were anxious to hire Lajoie as a player. He gave mixed signals about returning to the majors. In September 1917, the *Washington Times* claimed that Lajoie "has remarked to several friends that he'd like to take a crack at the first base job in the big show for just one more season."[12] On the other hand, he had tasted success as a manager, and did not appear anxious to return to a big league roster as a player only.

The Boston Red Sox needed a new manager after their 1917 skipper, Jack Barry, resigned to enter the navy, but the team bypassed Lajoie, a native New Englander, and hired Ed Barrow. The New York Yankees fired Wild Bill Donovan and hired Miller Huggins away from the Cardinals, leaving an opening in St. Louis, but that team selected Jack Hendricks to fill that spot. Lajoie may have been interested in returning to Cleveland, but the Indians were happy with their leadership tandem of manager Lee Fohl and captain Tris Speaker. The Pittsburgh Pirates did not even have a baseball man running their team, having given the job to Hugo Bezdek, the head football coach at Oregon (and later Penn State), who knew little about baseball but much about leading men. By early 1918 all the managerial jobs in the major leagues were filled. If Lajoie harbored a desire to return to the big leagues, he would have to wait a while longer.

26

The Final Season

Old Nap Lajoie was the only man I ever observed who could chew scrap tobacco in such a way as to give a jaunty refinement to a habit vulgar and untidy in so many others. — A fan of Lajoie's as quoted by sportswriter Tom Meany, 1950[1]

Napoleon Lajoie wanted to return to the Toronto Maple Leafs, the scene of his spectacularly successful 1917 campaign, but the survival of the International League was an open question during the early months of the following year. In mid–March, with the start of the new season only a few weeks away, the league magnates had not yet decided if the circuit would play at all in 1918. Some of the team owners were ready to play ball, while others called for a suspension of play for the duration of the world war.

Lajoie was not a man who allowed others to determine his future. He had impressed many with his performance as a hitter and a manager in 1917, and though all the major league managerial posts were filled, several minor league teams made inquiries about hiring him. One such team was the Indianapolis club of the American Association, the club that Lajoie and the Maple Leafs had faced in a post-season tilt the previous October. The Indianapolis Indians, managed by Jack Hendricks, had won that series, but Hendricks had been hired away by the St. Louis Cardinals, leaving the Indianapolis managerial post open. While the International League dithered, McGill decided to hire Lajoie as his field leader for 1918. In January of that year, McGill met with Lajoie (though the meeting probably met the definition of tampering) and offered him the post at a salary of $7,000 a year, which was more than most major league skippers were making at the time. Lajoie, who was as impressed with McGill as McGill was with him, agreed to lead the Indians should Toronto disband or otherwise fail to start the season.

In the meantime, the International League hit upon a scheme to rid itself of some of its weaker teams. Its leaders met in March and voted to disband, then immediately reformed as the "new International League," eliminating the Montreal, Richmond, and Providence franchises in so doing. This new organization replaced its three former members with new teams in Jersey City (New Jersey), Binghamton (New York), and Syracuse, reconstituting itself into what the magnates hoped would be a stronger circuit. This series of moves was ethically questionable, to say the least, and drew criticism from sportswriters in both the United States and Canada. It also angered the National Commission, baseball's ruling body, which withheld recognition of the new league and threatened to cast the circuit into "outlaw" status. All the while, the "new International League" still publicly hemmed and hawed on the question of when, or if, it would open its 1918 campaign.

In late January, news of Lajoie's tentative deal with the Indianapolis club hit the papers, though James McCaffrey downplayed such talk. "If they are in the market for the big fellow," said the Toronto team owner, "I am the man to approach. Lajoie belongs to the Toronto club, and before anybody can do business with him they must see me first."[2] However, the veteran ballplayer had soured on the Maple Leafs, no doubt in part because the Indianapolis club was willing to double his base salary. Moreover, Lajoie was upset with the news that McCaffrey had offered to sell his manager and star hitter to any major league club for $3,000 (though some reports put the amount at $3,500). Lajoie believed that he deserved more consideration from Toronto management after winning the pennant and the batting title. He would not be sold like a side of beef, and after 22 years in professional ball, Lajoie believed that he had earned the right to decide for himself where he would play and manage.

In addition, the uncertain status of the International League grated on Lajoie's nerves. He did not want to cling to what appeared to be a sinking ship, and because the American Association had stated unequivocally that it would operate in 1918 as usual, he was eager to quit Toronto and lead the Indians. However, he was still the property of the Maple Leafs, and with James McGill spending most of February and March on a long vacation in California and Florida, he could do nothing but wait for the situation to sort itself out. The Indians gathered for spring training in Hattiesburg, Mississippi, with third baseman Herman Bronkie, a former Cleveland teammate of Lajoie's, serving as acting manager.

As the weeks rolled on, Lajoie and McCaffrey continued to snipe at each other. McCaffrey believed that Lajoie's services were his to use or dispose of as he saw fit, while Lajoie demanded the right to decide for himself where he would play and manage in 1918. Lajoie wanted no part of a weakened or suspended International League, and when McCaffrey suggested that the Toronto club might continue to play as an independent or semipro outfit, Lajoie's distaste for the situation deepened. In an attempt to free himself from Toronto, Lajoie told the papers that McCaffrey had given him a $1,000 bonus for winning the pennant but had not included the amount in his contract, a technical violation of baseball law. On March 20, though the future of the league was still undecided, McCaffrey told the papers that he had no intention of allowing his star to go to Indianapolis, calling the request "absurd." A day later, the Toronto owner announced that Lajoie would not play for the Maple Leafs in 1918 after all. McCaffrey had sold the veteran player and manager to the Brooklyn Dodgers for $3,000.

Lajoie was stunned by the news and vowed to appeal the sale to the National Commission. The Dodgers intended to use the 43-year-old as an occasional first baseman and pinch-hitter, and Lajoie made it clear that he was not interested in a return to the National League. After tasting success as a manager, he would not accept a post as a mere bench player. "I might not have objected to a berth in Brooklyn had I been consulted," said Lajoie. "But I do not propose to be bandied about like a 'busher.' Very fortunately for me, I have laid by enough money for the proverbial rainy day, so that I do not have to worry whether I play ball or not. Certainly I do not have to go anywhere against my wishes."[3]

On its face, Lajoie's transfer to Brooklyn seemed legal according to the rules of organized baseball, but the International League's machinations complicated the matter. When the circuit dissolved and reassembled itself into a "new International League," the National Commission withheld recognition, making the new organization an outlaw league, at least for the time being. Without that recognition, all International League players could be considered free agents so far as organized baseball was concerned. Lajoie intended to argue that point, along with the claim that McCaffrey's promised bonus for winning the pennant had not been included in his 1917 contract.

The National Commission heard the Lajoie case on April 13, less than three weeks before the start of the American Association season, and after reviewing the testimony of Lajoie, McCaffrey, and others, the three-member panel (consisting of league presidents Ban Johnson and John Tener and Cincinnati Reds president Garry Herrmann) ruled in the ballplayer's favor. Because baseball law required that all financial agreements between team management and its employees be written and not merely verbal, the absence of the pennant bonus from Larry's contract was the lever that Lajoie used to gain his free agency. Wrote the Commission:

> Every player before signing a minor league contract should carefully scrutinize the same to ascertain whether all of the conditions agreed upon between the player and the club president, or its authorized agent, have been incorporated therein, and if any have been omitted the player should insist upon having all the terms, conditions, promises and agreements inserted in the contract before he signs the same.

This phrase brought to mind the battle that Lajoie had waged with the Phillies 17 years before. Lajoie had claimed that he signed his contract for the 1900 season without reading it, and did not realize that the reserve clause and the ten-day notice clause were contained therein. Now Lajoie insisted that McCaffrey's offer of $1,000 for winning the pennant was nowhere to be found in his 1917 agreement with the Maple Leafs. McCaffrey admitted to the Commission that he had indeed paid the bonus to his manager, and that verbal commitment gave the Commission a pretext for releasing Lajoie from his contract. The Commission further stated:

> If at any time, as a result of an official investigation, it is ascertained that an agreement of any kind between a minor league club president and a player is not fully set forth in the player's regular contract or made a part thereof, then a penalty shall be inflicted against the club and manager violating this provision according to classification, the same to be paid into the treasury of the league of which the contracting club is a member, and the said contract shall be null and void and the player unconditionally released.
>
> The compensation of the party of the second part (Lajoie) as stipulated in his Toronto contract is $3,500 for his 1917 services. It is contended by the player and practically conceded by President McCaffrey that the total compensation of the complainant last season was $4,500 as agreed between the parties, $3,500 of which was salary and $1,000 contingent on the Toronto Club's winning the championship of its season last year. A settlement has been made on this basis for 1917.
>
> The Commission, therefore, rules the reservation right of the Toronto club to the player under its illegal contract with Player Lajoie null and void; annuls his transfer to the Brooklyn Club; and declares him a free agent.[4]

Spring training was over by the time the National Commission handed down its decision, so Lajoie hurried to Indianapolis to join his new team. The Indianapolis Indians had won the American Association pennant the year before under Jack Hendricks, but some of the stars of the 1917 club were gone, either to the major leagues or to the military. Lajoie surveyed the roster and found two former Cleveland Naps, pitcher Cy Falkenberg and third baseman Herman Bronkie, ready to play key roles. Two other pitchers, Dana Fillingim and Jack Northrop, were spitball specialists who had won 20 games apiece for the 1917 edition of the team. However, both men needed to find new ways to get batters out, as the Association had recently banned the wet pitch. Pitcher Jack Nabors, who had posted a 1–20 record for the Athletics two years earlier, was also in camp, though he complained of soreness in his pitching arm. While Lajoie directed the club in an exhibition contest against his old team, the Cleveland Indians, James McGill traveled to St. Louis in an attempt to pry a few players loose from the Browns and Cardinals. McGill failed to land any new men, and the "Indianaps," as the papers called them, began their season short-handed at several positions, especially pitching.

The American Association, like the International League, was a top-level (Class AA) minor league. Based in the Midwest, it featured teams in four former National League cities (Indianapolis, Milwaukee, Kansas City, and Louisville) as well as Toledo, Columbus, Minneapolis, and St. Paul. It was a haven for former major league players and managers, with future Hall of Famers Lajoie, Joe Tinker of Columbus, and Roger Bresnahan of Toledo holding managerial posts. Joe Cantillon, the former umpire and promoter who took Lajoie and the "All-American" team on a post-season tour of California 17 years before, managed the Minneapolis Millers, while another ex-arbiter, Jack Egan, directed the Milwaukee Brewers. Most experts predicted that Louisville, managed by Bill Clymer, and John Ganzel's Kansas City team would provide the Indianapolis club with its strongest competition for the 1918 pennant.

The aging veteran had little time to prepare for the season. He had missed all of spring training while waiting for his status to be resolved, and he was not in his usual excellent physical condition. "I haven't had a ball in my hands since last season," he told the papers. "All I did all winter was shovel snow."[5] He would have to round into shape quickly, a tall task for one of the oldest active players in all of professional baseball.

Lajoie's men started the season on the road at Columbus on May 1, and after the usual Opening Day parade, a flag-raising ceremony, and a Liberty Loan drive, the Indians defeated Joe Tinker's Senators by a 9–0 score. Jack Northrop threw a shutout, Lajoie belted two singles, and Herman Bronkie pounded out four hits. The Senators won the next two games, after which the Indians traveled to Toledo to face Roger Bresnahan's Iron Men (they had dropped the familiar Mud Hens moniker temporarily). Indianapolis won their first two games against the weakest team in the Association, and lost the third despite two singles and a double off the bat of Lajoie. The club then returned to Indianapolis for its home opener.

On May 8, Lajoie made his debut before the home fans, but despite the presence of one of the game's most popular stars, only about 2,500 turned out to see the Indians defeat Columbus by a 10–7 score. Attendance was down in every American Association city, and even the major leagues had a hard time drawing fans to their ballparks in 1918. The conflict in Europe dominated the headlines, and Americans were more interested in the war than in sports and entertainment.

The military draft played havoc with all major and minor league teams during the early part of the season, and Lajoie's Indianapolis club felt the effects of the war before the campaign was a week old. The club had signed the veteran Olaf Hendrickson, formerly of the Red Sox, to solidify its outfield, but Hendrickson elected to find work in a shipyard instead (where he could avoid the draft and play baseball on the weekends). A promising young catcher, Butch Henline, was called away by the Army and left the team so short-handed that Lajoie added trainer Windy Lotshaw to the playing roster on a temporary basis. Only four Indians were over the draft age (including Lajoie), so keeping a team together promised to be a difficult task. Later that season, Lajoie sent a telegram to an old friend, Washington manager Clark Griffith, asking for a spare pitcher. "Larry," replied Griffith, "if I had a pitcher who could stand in the box, I would hug him."[6]

There were other headaches as well. Dana Fillingim could not get anyone out without his spitball, so the Indians traded him to the Boston Braves for pitcher Cal Crum and first baseman Sam (Tex) Covington. Covington could only play first base, so his arrival pushed Lajoie to the second sack. The sore-armed Jack Nabors pitched on May 3 against Columbus, lasted only six innings, and took the loss. After the game, Indianapolis sent him to the Western League. Jack Northrop pitched well, but left the team in early June due to his wife's illness. Shortstop Jack Lewis, who had been classified as 1-A by his local draft board, quit the club and joined a shipyard league, but Lajoie was able to acquire a major league veteran, Bruno Betzel, from the St. Louis Cardinals to fill in. Unfortunately, the Cardinals called Betzel back after only two weeks, forcing Lajoie to shuffle the Indianapolis infield once again.

All the while, the Indians floated along near the .500 mark, bouncing from fourth place to sixth in the eight-team league. Lajoie hit for a good average, ranking in the top five in the league, though the extra-base power he showed in Toronto appeared to be gone. He was beginning to play like a 43-year-old, though the strain of managing a constantly changing cast of characters would have taxed the very best managers in the game. He had to prepare for the unexpected, as illustrated on Decoration Day when outfielder Gus Williams, one of the Indians' top hitting threats, failed to appear at the park for the game. Several days later, Lajoie received word that Williams had returned to his native Pittsburgh to take a job in a steel mill. Williams' defection prompted James McGill to tell the papers that many teams in the Association, including his own, might not be able to put nine men in the field by September.

Lajoie hit only two homers in 1918. The first was a three-run shot that came against a future major leaguer, Milwaukee's Dickie Kerr, on May 25, and the second was one of the strangest of his long career. On June 12, in a home contest against Milwaukee, he whacked a long fly ball to left. Austin McHenry of the Brewers caught up to it, but the ball hit his glove, rolled up his arm, and fell over the fence for a four-bagger. In that same game, Jack Northrop rejoined the team and won his fifth decision in a row. Northrop's arrival was a blessing, as the Indians were down to four healthy pitchers before his return. The day before, Tex Covington and pitcher Gene Dale were drafted into the Army, so Lajoie returned to first base, the position he had intended to play all along.

An odd play cost the Indians a game against the St. Paul Saints on June 16. The Saints had a runner on third when the hitter, Artie Butler, swung mightily and let go of his bat, which came to rest in foul territory to the left of third base. Herman Bronkie, the Indianapolis third sacker, helpfully retrieved the bat but neglected to call time, so the St. Paul baserunner set out for home and scored the go-ahead run. Lajoie and his teammates put up a heated argument, but the run counted, and the Saints withstood a ninth-inning Indians rally to win the game by a 12–11 score. Another spirited dispute had occurred a few days before, when St. Paul outfielder Red Corriden caught a fly ball by Lajoie and threw out an Indianapolis runner at home on a close play. This decision touched off an argument that grew so intense that the umpire asked for police protection when he left the field at game's end. The outfielder was the same Corriden who had played a deep position at third base on the last day of the 1910 season and nearly boosted Lajoie to the batting title.

The Indians held fifth place on July 1, but caught fire and began to climb in the standings. Their improvement was largely due to the fine pitching of Jake Northrop (who went 13–3 that year) and 38-year-old Cy Falkenberg (10–10), though Lajoie's skill at filling holes in his lineup on the fly played a part in the Indianapolis revival. The Indians put together a 10–1–1 streak and reached second place on July 20 despite a batting slump by Lajoie, who suffered through a string of hitless games and saw his average fall below the .300 mark. He was finally showing his age, possibly because his lack of conditioning during the spring took a toll in the heat of the summer. Most of his best hitting performances, including a win over Columbus in which he drove in five runs, had come early in the season. Now, he looked like just another old player.

Though the Indians were playing fine ball, few in Indianapolis and other cities appeared to notice. Americans were too busy concentrating on the war effort to pay attention to the pennant races, and many circuits (including the Pacific Coast League and the Texas League) had already packed it in, choosing to cancel the rest of their scheduled games rather than continue to operate in an increasingly difficult environment. The public was not only indifferent to baseball, but growing actively hostile as well; with thousands of young Americans heading to Europe to fight the Germans, the public saw no reason for healthy men of draft age to be playing a game. Many editorial writers denounced athletes who were not in uniform, and it appeared to be only a matter of time before professional baseball shut down for the duration of the war.

Some players, despite the mood of the country, tried to keep their careers going. Eddie Ainsmith, a catcher for the Washington Senators, was ordered to report for Army induction in June of 1918, but he and his manager, Clark Griffith, appealed the order, with Griffith protesting that baseball, as a business, would be hurt irreparably if it lost its players to the military. Also, claimed Griffith on Ainsmith's behalf, baseball was an entertainment that provided much-needed relief for those involved in the war effort, and because actors had already gained exemption from the draft, baseball players should be accorded the same courtesy.

On July 19, Newton D. Baker, the Secretary of War in President Woodrow Wilson's cabinet, issued his decision on the Ainsmith matter. "The times are not normal," ruled the Secretary, "[and] the demands of the army and of the country are such that we must all make sacrifices, and the non-productive employment of able-bodied persons useful in the national defense, either as military men or in the industry and commerce of our country cannot be justified."[7] This ruling expanded the definition of "non-essential" work to include actors and entertainers as well as athletes, and rejected Griffith's notion that sporting events were important enough to warrant exemption from the sacrifices other industries were then making. Baker, who declared that the American people would surely be "resourceful enough" to find other sources of entertainment, sent an unmistakable message. All able-bodied young men, ballplayers included, between the ages of 18 and 35 were now required either to join the armed forces or to find "essential" work in factories, farms, and elsewhere.

This ruling brought a premature end to the 1918 baseball season. Although the two major leagues were allowed to play until Labor Day and hold a World Series in early September, the minor circuits received no such extension. Most of them had already shut down by the time Secretary Baker issued his order, and on Sunday, July 21, the American Association followed suit. League president Thomas J. Hickey cancelled the remaining two months of the season, closing the campaign with the contests played on that date.

The Indianapolis Indians played their final two games in Columbus on that Sunday afternoon, winning the opener, 8–2, behind Cy Falkenberg and losing the nightcap to a four-hitter by the Senators' Clyde Barfoot. Lajoie whacked a single in the first game and went hitless in the second, closing his 23rd professional baseball season with a .282 average. He avoided injury all year and played in all of the Indians' 78 contests, though only 16 of his 82 hits (12 doubles, two triples, and two homers) went for extra bases. Had the season continued, the Indians, who won 13 of their final 16 games, might have fought their way to the pennant, but the campaign closed with Indianapolis in third position, three games behind the champion Kansas City Blues and one behind the second-place Columbus squad.

Lajoie remained in Indianapolis for a few days to settle the team's affairs before returning to his farm in South Euclid. Several major league clubs contacted him, hoping to get the aged veteran in uniform as a pinch-hitter and occasional first baseman for the final few weeks of the major league season, but he was not interested in being a short-time player. Though John McGraw, who had pursued Lajoie so ardently during the war between the leagues in 1902 and 1903, made noises about taking on the former Cleveland star, nothing developed between the aging ballplayer and the New York manager. It would have mattered little anyway, as the Giants suffered through a losing skid and lost their chance to catch the eventual champion Chicago Cubs in the National League pennant race. Besides, the season had only a few more weeks to run. Instead, Lajoie settled in at home, registered for the draft (because men up to the age of 45 were now required to do so)[8] and watched the passing scene.

The war ended in November, but Larry Lajoie had already started planning for life after baseball. He had been hired as a salesman by a local tire company, a position that appeared more suitable for a 44-year-old man than a spot on a playing roster. Lajoie had accomplished all he wanted in the sport, so in late December, he decided to retire from the game. He told the papers a few days after Christmas:

> I have been a professional ball player for twenty-three seasons. That is the skidoo number and it fits my case exactly. Twenty-three years is a fairly long time to stick to the old game. I guess I could get in pretty good shape to play once more, but there is no use of me saying that I could come back and be as good as I used to be, for I can't. And I am tired of getting in shape and I think it about time I should settle down in Cleveland for the entire year instead of merely the winter time. Mrs. Lajoie wants me to quit. She has wanted me to do so for several years, and now she finds me of the same opinion.[9]

27

"The Past Is All a Dream"

I guess you know what I think about: Frank Dwyer and the chewing tobacco and Colonel Rogers and his $400 and that ball that Dode Criss hit that just landed fair and 1,009 silver dollars tied around some roses — the things we talked about. Yes, it's been a long ride for the hack driver from Woonsocket. — Napoleon Lajoie in *The Sporting News*, 1953

After directing the Indianapolis club to a third-place finish during the abbreviated 1918 campaign, Napoleon Lajoie decided that he was finished with baseball. He was satisfied with his accomplishments, and had nothing left to prove to the game or to himself. He had finally won a pennant as a manager and might have won a second if the 1918 season had lasted a week or two longer. For Lajoie, that was enough. He did not want to grow old in the game; instead, he preferred to spend his evenings at home with Myrtle all year round, not only during the winter months. Though he agreed to serve as the commissioner of a semipro circuit, the Ohio-Pennsylvania League, in 1919, the job seems to have been merely ceremonial in nature. During the last four decades of his life, Lajoie held no official position in organized ball, a state of affairs that suited the former "King of Ballplayers" just fine.

Instead, Lajoie took a job with the Miller Rubber Company of Cleveland as a tire salesman. He worked for that firm, and later for the Searles Rubber Company, for several years. While selling tires and tending to his farm in South Euclid, Lajoie stayed in the public eye as a member of the Cleveland Boxing Commission during the 1920s, and made an unsuccessful foray into politics as a Republican candidate for sheriff of Cuyahoga County in Ohio. Having managed his money well, he could work because he wanted to, not because he had to.

He was a welcome, if infrequent, visitor to League Park (which was called Dunn Field after the new majority owner of the club, James Dunn) during this time. In 1920 he celebrated with the rest of the city as his old team, the newly-named Indians, finally won the first pennant in Cleveland baseball history, then defeated the Brooklyn Dodgers in the World Series that October. Lajoie attended only one Series game, the fourth, in which Stanley Coveleski pitched a five-hitter and paced the Indians to a 5–1 win. Five years earlier, Coveleski had given up the final hit of Lajoie's career. Larry, whose Naps had come so painfully close to the championship in 1908, could only watch as Cleveland center fielder and manager Tris Speaker accomplished the feat that he had tried, and failed, to achieve.

Lajoie also made the occasional appearance on the field in uniform. On June 29, 1921, the Indians staged an old-timers game at Dunn Field to celebrate the 125th anniversary of the city's founding. With Lajoie serving as captain, a group of old ballplayers that included Cy Young, Bill Bradley, Terry Turner, Harry Bay, Elmer Flick, and other Cleveland heroes of the past took on a hand-picked team of local amateurs. Lajoie, who never lost his competitive streak, looked forward to the contest. "Give us a few days to get into practice and develop our winds," he said, "and we won't make any alibis."[1] The 54-year-old Young pitched the first two innings, while Bradley and Lajoie played the entire game, with Bradley whacking three hits and Lajoie two. Experience trumped youth on this day, as Lajoie's band of old-timers defeated their much younger opponents by a score of 11 to 8.

Lajoie turned 50 in September of 1924, and it was at this time that he and Myrtle grew tired of the cold, snowy Cleveland winters. They had visited Florida, liked what they saw there, and decided to spend the winter months in the state. He retired from his sales career in 1925, and thereafter he and Myrtle split their time between their home in the Cleveland area and a rented house in Lake Worth, a small city in Palm Beach County on the Atlantic coast. The mild Florida climate allowed Larry to pursue his new passion, golf, and he played the sport with gusto on a year-round basis. He was a no-nonsense golfer who stroked his putts with a minimum of preparation. "Why fool around?" he said. "There's the ball, there's the hole. What else is there but to tap it in?"[2] He shot in the low 80s (and sometimes the high 70s) and though he was obliged to wear glasses as he aged, he had the same graceful, powerful swing that had brought him success on the diamond.

For the next 20 years or so, the Lajoies led a predictable lifestyle. They traveled from Ohio to Florida in the fall, stayed in the south until May, then returned to Cleveland to spend the summer in the north. In most years, they took a midsummer trip to Woonsocket to visit his surviving brothers and sisters and a growing brood of nieces and nephews, not to mention grand-nieces and grand-nephews. He went to a few Indians games each year, but not many, though he could be counted on to attend important ceremonies. On July 31, 1932, when the new home of the Indians, the 80,000-seat Municipal Stadium, opened its doors for the first time, Lajoie was an honored guest, as were Cy Young, Elmer Flick, Tris Speaker, and other giants of Cleveland baseball history. When Lajoie played for the Naps in the original League Park, it took only 9,000 people to fill all the seats. He and the other old-timers must have marveled at the sight of the packed Municipal Stadium, as the Indians and Philadelphia Athletics played before 80,234 people, the largest crowd in baseball history up to that time.

Other old stars of the Indians and Naps such as Speaker, Young, and Flick, who all lived in or near Cleveland, were regular visitors to Municipal Stadium (and to League Park, where the Indians continued to play weekday games until 1946), but Lajoie's visits were few and far between. Still, he followed the game, and listened to his old Naps teammate Jack Graney, the scatter-armed rookie pitcher who once knocked him unconscious with a fastball, call the games on the radio. When teenaged pitching sensation Bob Feller made headlines during the late 1930s, Lajoie made it a point to see the newest Cleveland star. "Pretty fast, that Feller," said Lajoie in 1940. "Almost as fast as [Walter] Johnson, I would say. Everybody asks me about that.... The night I saw Feller, he had it. Fast and a dandy curve. I sat behind home plate and there were times when you could just about see the whole bleacher section between ball and bat, the hitters were missin' that far."[3]

One of Lajoie's rare forays to League Park demonstrated that the competitive nature of old ballplayers had not dimmed much with the passage of time. On September 30, 1934, the 60-year-old Lajoie suited up to play in an old-timers game with other retired standouts such as Walter Johnson (who managed the Indians that season) and Cy Young, who at the age of 67 still pitched in exhibition games every now and then. Young's "Antiques" played Johnson's "Has-Beens" between games of a season-ending doubleheader between the White Sox and Indians, and in the second and final inning, Young attempted to pick Lajoie off second base. The umpire, a local politician, called Lajoie safe, and the heated argument that ensued made the crowd so excited and unruly that the police were called in to escort the umpire off the field for his own safety. Such an on-field dispute would have been a regular occurrence in baseball four decades earlier, and the scene, while unfortunate, gave the fans a glimpse of the game as it was when Lajoie and the others were younger men.

Lajoie returned to public attention during the 1930s, after a group of businessmen in Cooperstown, New York, hit upon a scheme to bring tourist traffic to their struggling community. Because a highly improbable but widely believed legend held that the sport of baseball was invented in their town in 1839, the city fathers decided to build a museum to honor the sport. Eventually, the idea of a Baseball Hall of Fame to honor the game's greatest players gained favor with the public, and though the country was barely beginning to emerge from the worst economic depression in American history, plans for the Hall of Fame moved forward. The building itself was scheduled for completion in 1939, the 100th anniversary of the game's alleged founding, and baseball fans around the nation eagerly debated which stars of the past deserved to be included in the new Hall of Fame.

The Baseball Writers Association of America, having been entrusted with the responsibility of choosing deserving players for the Hall of Fame, held its first election in early 1936 and released the results of the balloting to the press on February 2 of that year. Ty Cobb led the poll with 222 votes from the 226 participating writers, while Babe Ruth and Honus Wagner tied for second place with 215 apiece. Two legendary pitchers, Christy Mathewson (205) and Walter Johnson (189) finished in fourth and fifth place. All these men received more than the required 75 percent of the ballots cast and gained election to the Hall of Fame.

Napoleon Lajoie, in sixth place with 146 tallies, fell short of election by only 24 votes, with such stars as Cy Young, Tris Speaker, and Rogers Hornsby trailing behind. The long-retired Lajoie expressed no disappointment about the outcome, at least not publicly, though with Cobb, Ruth, Wagner, Mathewson, and Johnson off the ballot, most observers expected the former Cleveland star to gain the honor in the next go-round. On January 19, 1937, the BBWAA announced the results of its second election, and Lajoie, predictably, finished on top with 169 votes from the 202 electors, topping the 75 percent standard with 17 votes to spare. Joining Lajoie in the Hall were Tris Speaker (165) and his former Naps teammate Cy Young (153).

A reporter from the Associated Press contacted the retired second baseman in Lake Worth, Florida, where Lajoie and his wife made their winter home. Lajoie was pleased with his election, and responded to the news with humility. "It's a wonderful game," he said, "but you have to have the luck and the breaks to make the most of it. I took chances. I tried to figure out the pitcher, watch him throw and then steal a base. Because I got away with it successfully everything was fine. But if I hadn't, they would have called me a bum instead."[4]

Asked to name the greatest players of past and present, Lajoie did not hesitate. "It's easy," he said. "Nothing to it. For the past, you may say Ty Cobb. There is the player who gave the most to the game.... As for today's outstanding players, I select Lou Gehrig, the scintillating first baseman of the Yankees. He has a record of 12 years of consistent baseball, every game a consecutive game. That takes good playing, along with the breaks and luck."[5]

Larry with other stars of the past at League Park in 1921. Lajoie is to the right of the man in the suit and tie, while Cy Young is on the man's other side (author's collection).

Despite his self-imposed absence from the major league scene, Lajoie was happy to travel to upstate New York and attend the Hall of Fame induction ceremony on June 12, 1939. Before the festivities began, Lajoie posed for one of baseball's most iconic photographs with Babe Ruth, Connie Mack, Cy Young, and all the other living honorees save one. Ty Cobb arrived too late to be included in the famous photograph of baseball immortals; Cobb claimed travel difficulties, but some suspected that the old Tiger, ever the prima donna, purposely delayed his arrival due to long-simmering resentment of Judge Landis in particular and the baseball establishment in general.

Lajoie, however, was all smiles that day. His induction speech, one of the shortest on record, was only two sentences long. "Ladies and gentlemen," said the 64-year-old second baseman, "I'm very glad to be here today and to meet all the old-timers that you probably watched play baseball and some of the greatest men that ever walked on the ball field, and I am glad to have the honor to be here today and join with them, and I hope everybody enjoys it as I do because I'm certainly having a great day. Thank you."[6] He happily signed hundreds of autographs, and showed his humility when he signed a card for a child, then pointed out Ty Cobb and Honus Wagner standing a short distance away. "Now," said the old Cleveland star, "go get the cream of the crop, son."[7]

After the ceremony, veteran American League umpire Tommy Connolly congratulated Lajoie and fellow inductees Eddie Collins and Tris Speaker on their speeches with the remark, "I must say you fellows' language has improved a lot since I was umpiring behind you."[8] The entire group then adjourned to nearby Doubleday Field, where Collins, Ruth, Wagner, and Walter Johnson donned their old uniforms and took part in an all-star game. Lajoie chose to remain on the sidelines, saving himself the embarrassment of the Babe, who popped up in his only plate appearance. Ruth had retired from the game only four years before, but his batting eye was long gone. "I can't hit the floor with my hat,"[9] he complained good-naturedly.

Lajoie enjoyed his stay in Cooperstown, but never returned to the Hall of Fame. Base-ball was no longer the focus of his life, and while he cherished the memories of his 23-year career, he was more interested in playing golf and enjoying his retirement with Myrtle. "You get enough of it," he told an interviewer in 1949. "You get filled up."[10] In 1940, he spoke to John Carmichael of the *Chicago Daily News* and revealed the real reason he retired from the game. "I guess I could have played a few more years," he said. "But all of a sudden I got so sick of trains, of bats, of fences ... tired of everything ... that I quit. Somehow, now, the past is all a dream and I'd like to keep it that way."[11]

Sometime during the 1920s, Larry and Myrtle moved from their farm in South Euclid to a smaller house in Mentor, a town in Lake County about 20 miles east of Cleveland. They spent their summers there and their winters in Florida for several years, but in 1943 they moved to Florida permanently, eventually buying a house in Holly Hill outside of Daytona Beach on the Atlantic coast. There Larry spent his days playing golf and working on his car. He also visited old baseball friends, including Shoeless Joe Jackson, who had returned to his home state of South Carolina after his banishment from baseball and opened a restaurant and, later, a liquor store in his home town of Greenville. In July of 1942 Lajoie

Induction Day at the Baseball Hall of Fame, June 12, 1939. Front row: Eddie Collins, Babe Ruth, Connie Mack, Cy Young. Back row: Honus Wagner, Grover Alexander, Tris Speaker, Napoleon Lajoie, George Sisler, Walter Johnson (National Baseball Hall of Fame Library, Cooperstown, New York).

passed through Greenville and stopped by the Jackson house to wish his former teammate a happy 54th birthday. Jackson, who had been expelled from the game in disgrace two decades before, was thrilled to see his old teammate, and told a local reporter that Lajoie, who batted behind him in the Cleveland lineup, was the best hit-and-run man in baseball. "And that ball always was hit so hard," said Shoeless Joe, "it sounded like a bullet whizzing by."[12]

Myrtle Lajoie, who had been in poor health for several years, died on November 4, 1954, at the age of 78. Larry was alone now, but not for long. The old ballplayer needed someone to care for him, so a niece from Woonsocket named Lillian Lamoureux and her husband Dolor decided to sell their furniture business in Rhode Island and move into the Lajoie house in Holly Hill. Lillian, along with another niece named Ella Adam, had helped care for Myrtle during the last few months of her life, and it seemed fitting that Lillian would help her favorite uncle as well. Larry was 80 years old and still fairly healthy, but needed some companionship, which Dolor (called Del), a baseball fan, was happy to provide. "They're worth their weight in gold," said Lajoie of his younger relatives. "They take care of me like they would a baby. I'm mighty lucky to have them with me."[13]

By this time, Larry had retreated from the public eye, though he received one more "Lajoie Day" celebration from his old team, the Cleveland Indians. The Indians had constructed a minor league training camp called Indianville in Daytona Beach with multiple baseball diamonds, one of which was called "Nap Lajoie Field" after the man who starred for and managed the team more than half a century before. In April of 1957, the Indians recognized their long-retired star with a day in his honor. Lajoie threw out the first ball before an exhibition game between the Indians and the New York Giants, then attended a round of parties and presentations that lasted until late in the evening. "When we got home that night," said his niece Lillian, "he was tired — but so happy! We talked about that game and the parties for weeks afterward."[14]

In his 80s, Lajoie spent much of his time watching major league baseball on television with Del Lamoureux and going to Little League games in the area. He loved to watch the youngsters play, and was always gracious enough to sign autographs for them, though his reign as "King of Ballplayers" had ended long before the kids, and most of their parents, were born. Sportswriters visited him in search of quotes for their stories, and old teammates and rivals (including Ty Cobb on one memorable afternoon in 1957) stopped by to chat, but Lajoie was now content to let others stand in the spotlight. In May of 1958, when Stan Musial of the St. Louis Cardinals joined Lajoie, Cobb, and six other men in the 3,000 hit club, Lajoie was invited to the celebration, but sent his regrets. He admired Musial ("A great fellow, quiet, attends to his work and minds his own business. He's a credit to the game,"[15] said Lajoie of the Cardinals star), but was not up to the trip.

With each passing year, fewer players of Lajoie's generation remained. Ty Cobb, though in declining health, was still around, and Elmer Flick still lived in the Cleveland area, but Connie Mack, Lajoie's favorite manager, had died in 1956 at the age of 93. Joe Jackson, Tris Speaker, Honus Wagner, Cy Young, and many other old teammates and competitors passed on during the 1950s, leaving Lajoie as one of the oldest of old ballplayers. He and Flick had started their playing careers during the nineteenth century, and now, more than halfway through the twentieth, they were two of the few survivors of the era. Their time was running out, and though Flick lived on for more than a decade (he died in 1971 at age 95), Larry Lajoie was rounding third and heading for home.

His health began to fail early in 1958. In February, the 83-year-old tripped over one of his dogs at home and broke his arm, necessitating a stay in a Daytona Beach hospital. Discharged after a few days, he returned to his Holly Hill home, where he smoked his pipe, read the sports pages, and followed the game on television. He had slowed down noticeably, though he showed some of his old spirit in October. During the 1958 World Series, as he watched several Milwaukee Braves fail to deliver a game-winning hit, he asked his niece Lillian to get one of his bats out of his bedroom closet. "I guess I'll have to pinch-hit,"[16] he said.

In January of 1959, Lajoie fell ill with pneumonia and was admitted once again to the hospital. He remained for several weeks, and showed enough improvement that by the first week of February his doctors decided that the old ballplayer had recovered enough to go home. His discharge was in the works when, on Thursday, February 5, he suddenly suffered a relapse. He sank quickly and quietly, and on the morning of February 7, 1959, Napoleon "Larry" Lajoie died peacefully at the age of 84. His funeral, which featured a clutch of Little League ballplayers as honorary pallbearers, was held on the following Monday at St. Paul's Catholic Church in Daytona Beach. He was buried in Cedar Hill Cemetery, and as a nephew, Lionel Lajoie, later remarked, "They made sure the funeral didn't go by a ball park because he'd get out to play."[17]

Napoleon Lajoie never played in a World Series, but left a legacy that few players in the history of baseball have surpassed. He not only compiled an enviable record as a hitter and as a second baseman, but played a major, and perhaps decisive, role in the survival and eventual success of the American League. Baseball in Cleveland was on the ropes when he joined the team in 1902, and it is fair to say that the franchise itself, which was called the Naps in his honor for more than a decade, would have failed without him.

He was a good man, but by no means a perfect one. He let his temper get the better of him at times on the field, and his many conflicts with umpires, and even a few of his managers, spiraled out of control at inopportune moments. However, Lajoie matured with the passing years and became one of the most popular players in the game, as shown in 1910 when most of the baseball world rooted for him to defeat Ty Cobb for the batting title and the Chalmers automobile that went with it. Lajoie was a proud man, but not an arrogant one, and, unlike Cobb, could play hard, competitive baseball without arousing the ire of his opponents. It speaks well for Lajoie that he not only performed at a high level on the baseball field, but managed his money well, enjoyed a happy marriage, and made friendships in the game that lasted until the end of his life.

From the late 1890s to the end of the following decade, Napoleon Lajoie was widely hailed as the "King of Ballplayers" and as the greatest player of all time. He no longer holds that distinction, but when he was at the peak of his stardom, no one could match him as a hitter or as a second baseman. Though he left the game nearly a century ago, he deserves to be remembered as one of baseball's immortals.

Appendix A:
Lajoie's Career Statistics

Batting Record

Year	Team	G	AB	R	H	2B	3B	HR	RBI	AVG	BB	SO	SB
1896	PHI N	39	175	36	57	12	7	4	42	.326	1	11	7
1897	PHI N	127	545	107	197	40	23	9	127	.361	15	25	20
1898	PHI N	147	608	113	197	43	11	6	127	.324	21	23	25
1899	PHI N	77	312	70	118	19	9	6	70	.378	12	7	13
1900	PHI N	102	451	95	152	33	12	7	92	.337	10	8	22
1901	PHI A	131	544	145	232	48	14	14	125	.426	24	9	27
1902	PHI A	1	4	0	1	0	0	0	1	.250	0	7	1
1902	CLE A	86	348	81	132	35	5	7	64	.379	19	0	19
	Total	*87*	*352*	*81*	*133*	*35*	*5*	*7*	*65*	*.378*	*19*	*7*	*20*
1903	CLE A	125	485	90	167	41	11	7	93	.344	24	26	21
1904	CLE A	140	553	92	208	49	15	5	102	.376	27	19	29
1905	CLE A	65	249	29	82	12	2	2	41	.329	17	8	11
1906	CLE A	152	602	88	214	48	9	0	91	.355	30	19	20
1907	CLE A	137	509	53	152	30	6	2	63	.299	30	27	24
1908	CLE A	157	581	77	168	32	6	2	74	.289	47	20	15
1909	CLE A	128	469	56	152	33	7	1	47	.324	35	19	13
1910	CLE A	159	591	94	227	51	7	4	76	.384	60	18	26
1911	CLE A	90	315	36	115	20	1	2	60	.365	26	15	13
1912	CLE A	117	448	66	165	34	4	0	90	.368	28	11	18
1913	CLE A	137	465	66	156	25	2	1	68	.335	33	17	17
1914	CLE A	121	419	37	108	14	3	0	50	.258	32	15	14
1915	PHI A	129	490	40	137	24	5	1	61	.280	11	16	10
1916	PHI A	113	426	33	105	14	4	2	35	.246	14	26	15
	Total	2480	9589	1504	3242	657	163	82	1599	.338	516	346	380

Managerial Record

Year	Team	G	W	L	PCT	Position
1905	CLE A	114	56	57	.496	5
1906	CLE A	157	89	64	.582	3
1907	CLE A	158	85	67	.559	4
1908	CLE A	157	90	64	.584	2
1909	CLE A	114	57	57	.500	4
	Total	700	377	309	.550	

The information used here was obtained free of charge from and is copyrighted by Retrosheet. Interested parties may contact Retrosheet at http://www.retrosheet.org.

Retrosheet does not have Lajoie's strikeout totals for most of his career, but Baseball Reference (http://www.Baseball-Reference.com) does. That site says that Lajoie struck out 346 times during his career.

Appendix B:
Lajoie's Nine
Commandments of Hitting

Napoleon Lajoie's commandments of hitting, as recounted by *The Sporting News* where they appeared on August 23, 1950, p. 14:

1. Select a bat consistent with your size and weight. The biggest man with the biggest bat does not make the heaviest hitter.
2. Go up to the plate determined to hit the ball. Determination is "half the battle."
3. Imagine that all pitchers look alike to you. Most pitchers are afraid of you.
4. Never allow a pitcher to tease you out of your position at the plate, either by driving you back or making you lunge toward the ball.
5. Try to judge the pitcher. Keep your eye on him and the ball.
6. Observe the positions the fielders have taken for you and try to place the ball in open territory.
7. Be calm and collected. Let the pitcher do the worrying.
8. Keep your mind on your task. Do not allow yourself to be distracted by talk from the catcher. The umpire can see the ball better than you can.
9. Practice, and practice some more. Take every opportunity to learn how to judge a pitcher by plenty of practice.

Chapter Notes

Chapter 1

1. Alfred H. Spink, *The National Game* (St. Louis: The National Game, 1910), p. 202.
2. *Washington Post*, July 29, 1906. In this article, Jeremie Lajoie is quoted as saying that Prospere was "Dick," but Prospere was 10 or 11 years older than Napoleon. He was already an adult when Napoleon was ten, so David, only three years older, was the more likely candidate to be sneaking out of the house to play ball with Napoleon.
3. F. C. Lane, "The Inside Facts of the Great Lajoie Deal," *Baseball Magazine*, June 1915, pp. 61–62.
4. *Cleveland Plain Dealer*, February 8, 1959.
5. *Los Angeles Times*, November 5, 1912.
6. *The Sporting News*, November 4, 1953, p. 13.
7. Lane, p. 53.
8. J. M. Murphy, "Napoleon Lajoie: Modern Baseball's First Superstar," *The National Pastime*, Spring 1988, p. 11.
9. *Reading Eagle*, May 5, 1907.
10. Murphy, p. 12.
11. *The Sporting News*, November 4, 1953, p. 13.
12. *The Sporting News*, November 4, 1953, p. 13.
13. *Reading Eagle*, May 5, 1907.

Chapter 2

1. *Boston Globe*, April 19, 1896, p. 82.
2. *Boston Globe*, June 3, 1896.
3. Tim Murnane, *How to Play Base Ball* (New York: American Sports, 1905), p. 15.
4. *The Sporting News*, November 4, 1953, p. 14.
5. *Boston Globe*, July 15, 1896.
6. *Boston Globe*, July 5, 1896, p. 7.
7. *Daily Kennebec* (Maine) *Journal*, July 9, 1896, p. 2.
8. Jerrold Casway, *Ed Delahanty in the Emerald Age of Baseball* (Notre Dame, IN: University of Notre Dame Press, 2004), pp. 118–119.
9. *Boston Globe*, August 4, 1896, p. 13.
10. *Boston Globe*, August 30, 1896, p. 4.
11. *The Sporting News*, August 8, 1896, p. 5.

Chapter 3

1. James M. Murphy, who wrote the entire Spring 1988 issue of the Society for American Baseball Research (SABR) publication *The National Pastime*, an issue dedicated to Lajoie, obtained a copy of Lajoie's baptismal certificate in the public records section of the Woonsocket, Rhode Island, city hall. Murphy proved conclusively that Lajoie was born in 1874.
2. *Cleveland Plain Dealer*, December 26, 1941, p. 14.
3. Robert Smith, *Baseball* (New York: Simon & Schuster, 1947), p. 156.
4. *Boston Globe*, October 8, 1893.
5. Roger Connor, who played mostly for the New York Giants, was the major league career leader in home runs during the 19th century, but some of his homers were hit in the Players League in 1890. Thompson hit all of his home runs in National League play.
6. In a 1953 interview, Lajoie reported that the name Larry came from pitcher "Bollicky Bill" Taylor, "a pitcher from Staten Island who was with me on the Phillies." Bollicky Bill's National League career had ended nearly a decade before, and it seems that Lajoie confused him with "Brewery Jack" Taylor, who pitched for the Phillies when Lajoie joined the club and had grown up on Staten Island. *The Sporting News*, November 4, 1953, p. 13.
7. *Boston Globe*, June 13, 1898.
8. David Nemec, *Major League Baseball Profiles 1871–1900 Volume 1* (Lincoln: University of Nebraska Press, 2011), p. 225. Clements was the most successful left-handed catcher, by far, in baseball history.
9. *Philadelphia Record*, August 13, 1896.
10. *Sporting Life*, August 22, 1896, p. 6.
11. *Sporting Life*, September 26, 1896, p. 6.
12. *Sporting Life*, October 31, 1896, p. 8.
13. *Sporting Life*, September 12, 1896, p. 4.

Chapter 4

1. *Sporting Life*, March 26, 1898, p. 7.
2. Tom Meany, "The Miracle Man," *Baseball Digest*, July 1949, p. 71. This article was an excerpt from

Meany's book, *Baseball's Greatest Teams* (New York: A.S. Barnes, 1949).

3. Jerrold Casway, *Ed Delahanty in the Emerald Age of Baseball* (Notre Dame, IN: University of Notre Dame Press, 2004), pp. 119–120; the quote is found in *Sporting Life*, December 12, 1896, p. 8. *Sporting Life* ran a retraction on February 6, 1897, p. 9.

4. The first Boston Marathon was also run on that day.

5. *Sporting Life*, May 1, 1897, p. 8.
6. *Sporting Life*, May 29, 1897, p. 7.
7. *Sporting Life*, May 29, 1897, p. 10.
8. Meany, p. 71.
9. *Sporting Life*, May 29, 1897, p. 10.
10. *The Sporting News*, July 3, 1897, p. 5.
11. Casway, p. 136.
12. Casway, p. 132.
13. *Sporting Life*, August 21, 1897, p. 4.
14. *Sporting Life*, April 3, 1897, p. 6.
15. *Sporting Life*, September 4, 1897, p. 13.

Chapter 5

1. *Sporting Life*, September 17, 1898, p. 4.
2. *Collier's*, October 31, 1914, p. 15.
3. Harold Kaese, *The Boston Braves* (New York: G. P. Putnam's Sons, 1948), p. 139.
4. *Sporting Life*, March 26, 1898, p. 7.
5. *Sporting Life*, April 2, 1898, p. 4.
6. Fred Lieb and Stan Baumgartner, *The Philadelphia Phillies* (New York: G. P. Putnam's Sons, 1948), p. 53.
7. *The Sporting News*, June 25, 1898, p. 7.
8. Martin Kohout, "George Stallings," biography on the SABR BioProject website (http://bioproj.sabr.org).
9. *Sporting Life*, July 9, 1899, p. 6.
10. David Jones and Stephen Constantelos, "Napoleon Lajoie," biography on the SABR BioProject website (http://bioproj.sabr.org).
11. *Sporting Life*, August 6, 1898, p. 6.
12. *Sporting Life*, August 6, 1898, p. 6.
13. *Baseball Digest*, May 1959, p. 28. The story was related by Ossie Bluege, longtime Washington Senators player and close friend of Griffith, to Burton Hawkins of the *Washington Star*.
14. John Phillips, *The 1898 Cleveland Spiders* (Cabin John, MD: Capital, 1997), p. 108.
15. *Sporting Life*, August 6, 1898, p. 6.
16. *Sporting Life*, October 8, 1898, p. 8.
17. *Sporting Life*, October 8, 1898, p. 8.
18. *Sporting Life*, September 17, 1898, p. 4.

Chapter 6

1. *Sporting Life*, December 2, 1899, p. 7.
2. Lee Allen, *The National League Story* (New York: Hill and Wang, 1961), p. 79.
3. *Sporting Life*, May 20, 1899, p. 1.
4. *Sporting Life*, May 20, 1899, p. 6.
5. *Cincinnati Enquirer*, June 21, 1899.
6. *The Sporting News*, May 20, 1899, p. 5.
7. *Sporting Life*, May 27, 1899, p. 5.
8. *Cincinnati Enquirer*, June 20, 1899.

9. *Cincinnati Enquirer*, June 21, 1899.
10. *Cincinnati Enquirer*, June 21, 1899.
11. *Sporting Life*, June 17, 1899, p. 8.
12. *Richmond* (Virginia) *Times*, July 27, 1899, p. 2.
13. Ibid.
14. *Sporting Life*, September 23, 1899, p. 5.
15. John Phillips, *The '99 Spiders* (Cabin John, MD: Capital, 1988), September 9 entry.

Chapter 7

1. *Sporting Life*, April 28, 1900, p. 3.
2. Jerrold Casway, *Ed Delahanty in the Emerald Age of Baseball* (Notre Dame, IN: University of Notre Dame Press, 2004), p. 171.
3. *Philadelphia Record*, April 16, 1900.
4. *Brooklyn Eagle*, April 2, 1900.
5. *Philadelphia Press*, April 13, 1900.
6. Casway, p. 178.
7. *Chicago Tribune*, April 18, 1900.
8. *Philadelphia Record*, April 18, 1900.
9. *Sporting Life*, April 28, 1900, p. 3.
10. *Cleveland Plain Dealer*, December 27, 1941, p. 14.
11. *Brooklyn Eagle*, June 10, 1900.
12. *Sporting Life*, May 20, 1899, p. 1.
13. *Sporting Life*, June 6, 1900, p. 3.
14. *Sporting Life*, September 30, 1900, p. 6.
15. Ibid.
16. Casway, p. 194. Oddly enough, Elmer Flick hit better on the road (.374) than at home (.323) in 1899, and enjoyed only a slight home advantage (.388 to .363) in 1900.
17. *Sporting Life*, September 30, 1900, p. 6.
18. Casway, p. 193.
19. Casway, p. 195.
20. *The Sporting News*, November 4, 1953, p. 14.

Chapter 8

1. *Sporting Life*, July 15, 1899, p. 5. Charley Ferguson was a highly talented young Philadelphia pitcher and outfielder whose death due to typhoid fever in 1888 cut short a promising career.
2. Warren Wilbert, *The Arrival of the American League* (Jefferson, NC: McFarland, 2011), p. 13.
3. Norman Macht, *Connie Mack and the Early Years of Baseball* (Lincoln: University of Nebraska Press, 2007), p. 224.
4. Macht, p. 223.
5. *Sporting Life*, April 27, 1901, p. 7. The author has elected to use *Sporting Life*, the Philadelphia-based weekly newspaper, as the source for the quoted testimony that appears in these pages. Other contemporary sources may have reported the quotes differently, though only slightly.
6. *Sporting Life*, April 27, 1901, p. 6.
7. Ibid.
8. *Sporting Life*, April 27, 1901, pp. 6–7.
9. *Sporting Life*, April 27, 1901, p. 7.
10. A summary of the case appeared in an article by attorney C. Paul Rogers III, "Napoleon Lajoie, Breach of Contract and the Great Baseball War,"

Southern Methodist University Law Review, Winter 2002 (55), p. 325.

11. In 2007, researcher Trent McCotter discovered an intentional bases-loaded walk in the National League during the 1881 season. According to the August 3, 1881, issue of the *Chicago Tribune*, "In the eighth the bases were filled, and nobody out, on successive hits by [Fred] Goldsmith, [Silver] Flint, and [Joe] Quest, and [Buffalo pitcher Jack] Lynch was so afraid of [Chicago batter Abner] Dalrymple that he gave him his base on balls and brought Goldsmith in with the gift." Lynch was required to throw seven balls wide of the plate to walk Dalrymple, in keeping with the rules of the time.

12. *Sporting Life*, June 1, 1901, p. 7.

13. Gordon Edes, "Maddon's walk into the record books," Yahoo Sports (http://sports.yahoo.com), August 18, 2008.

14. Macht, p. 255.

Chapter 9

1. J. M. Murphy, "Napoleon Lajoie: Modern Baseball's First Superstar," *The National Pastime*, Spring 1988, p. 22.

2. *Sporting Life*, February 1, 1902, p. 1.

3. *Cleveland Plain Dealer*, February 8, 1959.

4. *New York Evening World*, April 4, 1902, p. 8.

5. *The Sporting News*, February 8, 1902, p. 2.

6. *Washington Times*, April 23, 1902, p. 3.

7. *Washington Times*, April 23, 1902, p. 3.

8. *Sporting Life*, April 26, 1902, pp. 1 and 4. The text can also be found in the *Washington Times*, April 23, 1902, p. 3.

9. *Sporting Life*, April 26, 1902, p. 4.

10. *Washington Times*, April 22, 1902, p. 4.

11. *Sporting Life*, April 26, 1902, p. 4.

12. Norman Macht, *Connie Mack and the Early Years of Baseball* (Lincoln: University of Nebraska Press, 2007), p. 265.

13. *Washington Times*, April 29, 1902.

14. Macht, p. 271.

15. *Sporting Life*, May 24, 1902, p. 5.

16. *Philadelphia Public Ledger*, May 28, 1902.

17. John Phillips, *When Lajoie Came to Town: The Story of the Cleveland Blues of 1902* (Cabin John, MD: Capital, 1988), May 26 entry.

Chapter 10

1. *Sporting Life*, July 5, 1902, p. 11.

2. Mike Attiyeh, "John Gochnaur: Worst Player of All Time." This article, written in 2003, was retrieved at the Baseball Fever website, http://www.baseball-fever.com/archive.

3. John Phillips, *When Lajoie Came to Town: The Story of the Cleveland Blues of 1902* (Cabin John, MD: Capital, 1988), June 4 entry.

4. *Cleveland Leader*, June 5, 1902.

5. *Cleveland Plain Dealer*, June 5, 1902.

6. *Philadelphia North American*, July 10, 1902.

7. *Cleveland Plain Dealer*, December 25, 1941, p. 36.

8. Phillips, July 20 entry.

9. *Sporting Life*, July 5, 1902, p. 2.

10. The Baseball Reference website, http://www.baseball-reference.com, upon which this book relies for its statistics, lists Lajoie as the 1902 batting champion.

11. *Sporting Life*, October 18, 1902, p. 7.

12. G. W. Axelson, *Commy: The Life Story of Charles A. Comiskey* (Chicago: Reilly and Lee, 1919), pp. 234–235.

Chapter 11

1. Lawrence Ritter, *The Glory of Their Times, Enlarged Edition* (New York: William Morrow, 1984), pp. 32–33.

2. *Youngstown Vindicator*, January 4, 1903.

3. Franklin Lewis, in *The Cleveland Indians* (New York: G. P. Putnam's Sons, 1949), stated that the players chose the name Bronchos.

4. *Cleveland Press*, April 4, 1903.

5. *Cleveland Press*, April 6, 1903.

6. *The Sporting News*, November 4, 1953, p. 13.

7. *Cleveland Plain Dealer*, December 27, 1941.

8. John Phillips, *The 1903 Naps* (Cabin John, MD: Capital, 1989), May 9 entry.

9. *Sporting Life*, May 23, 1903, p. 17.

10. *Philadelphia Record*, June 12, 1903.

11. *Sporting Life*, February 17, 1906, p. 9.

12. *The Sporting News*, November 4, 1953, p. 14.

13. J. M. Murphy, "Napoleon Lajoie: Modern Baseball's First Superstar," *The National Pastime*, Spring 1988, p. 26.

14. *Sporting Life*, October 24, 1903, p. 10.

15. *Sporting Life*, December 19, 1903, p. 10.

16. Phillips, July 4 entry.

17. *Sporting Life*, October 24, 1903, p. 10.

Chapter 12

1. *Milwaukee Journal*, August 5, 1916.

2. Lajoie is often identified as the only player with the word "graceful" on his plaque, but the plaques of Carl Yastrzemski (elected in 1989) and Vic Willis (1995) also contain that word.

3. Tim Murnane, *How to Play Base Ball* (New York: American Sports, 1905), pp. 15–17.

4. F. C. Lane, *Batting: One Thousand Opinions on Every Conceivable Angle of Batting Science* (New York: Baseball Magazine Company, 1925), p. 185.

5. Murnane, pp. 15–17.

6. *Sporting Life*, August 8, 1896, p. 7.

7. John Phillips, *The '99 Spiders* (Cabin John, MD: Capital, 1988), May 25 entry.

8. *Sporting Life*, September 12, 1896, p. 4.

9. Roberto Clemente (621 walks), Lou Brock (761) and Tony Gwynn (790) are the only members of the 3,000 hit club with fewer than 963 walks. Rickey Henderson, by contrast, received 2,190 free passes, more than four times as many as Lajoie.

10. Murnane, pp. 15–17.

11. Lane, p. 135.

12. *The Sporting News*, August 23, 1950, p. 13.

13. *Washington Post*, October 12, 1910

14. *The Sporting News*, June 8, 1901, p. 5.

15. Arthur Daley, *Times at Bat: A Half Century of Baseball* (New York: Random House, 1950), p. 31.

16. *Sporting Life*, May 9, 1914, p. 2.

17. Murnane, pp. 15–17.

18. *Sporting Life*, January 23, 1915, p. 5.

19. Murnane, pp. 15–17.

20. *Salt Lake City* (Utah) *Herald*, September 27, 1903.

21. Murnane, pp. 15–17.

22. Bill James, *The New Bill James Historical Baseball Abstract* (New York: Free Press, 2001), p. 489.

23. Murnane, pp. 15–17.

Chapter 13

1. *Sporting Life*, June 11, 1904, p. 3.

2. Scott Turner, "Terry Turner," biography on the SABR BioProject website (http://bioproj.sabr.org).

3. *St. Louis Republic*, April 19, 1904, p. 7.

4. *The Sporting News*, November 4, 1953, p. 14.

5. *The Sporting News*, June 11, 1904, p. 11.

6. The Sporting News, November 4, 1953, p. 14.

7. Steve Constantelos, "George Stovall," biography on the SABR BioProject website (http://bioproj.sabr.org).

8. *Washington Times*, June 26, 1904, p. 10.

9. *St. Louis Republic*, September 9, 1904.

10. *Sporting Life*, October 1, 1904, p. 11.

11. David Jones and Steve Constantelos, "Nap Lajoie," biography on the SABR BioProject website (http://bioproj.sabr.org).

12. *Pittsburgh Press*, September 10, 1904.

13. *Cleveland Press*, October 4, 1904, p. 10.

14. *Sporting Life*, December 31, 1904, p. 2.

15. *Sporting Life*, December 10, 1904, p. 5.

Chapter 14

1. *Sporting Life*, November 26, 1904, p. 5.

2. *Sporting Life*, April 15, 1905, p. 12.

3. *Sporting Life*, April 15, 1905, p. 12.

4. *Sporting Life*, March 25, 1905, p. 9.

5. *Salt Lake Tribune*, April 16, 1905, p. 2.

6. *Washington Times*, May 13, 1905, p. 8.

7. *The Sporting News*, June 10, 1905, p. 4.

8. The Washington club was officially called the Nationals beginning in 1905, but the terms Nationals and Senators were often used interchangeably.

9. *Washington Times*, June 20, 1905, p. 8.

10. *The Sporting News*, June 17, 1905, p. 4.

11. *Wall Street Journal*, April 21, 2009.

12. *Boston Globe*, July 20, 1905.

13. *Boston Globe*, July 28, 1905.

14. *Sporting Life*, August 19, 1905, p. 7.

15. *Boston Globe*, October 5, 1905.

16. *St. Louis Globe-Democrat*, September 6, 1905.

17. *Sporting Life*, November 25, 1905, p. 5.

Chapter 15

1. *Sporting Life*, August 25, 1906, p. 11. The article was titled "Lajoie a Croesus."

2. Grantland Rice, *The Tumult and the Shouting* (New York: Barnes, 1954), p. 34.

3. *Sporting Life*, August 25, 1906, p. 11.

4. Franklin Lewis, *The Cleveland Indians* (New York: G. P. Putnam's Sons, 1949), p. 47.

5. Napoleon Lajoie and M. A. Bobrick, eds., *Napoleon Lajoie's Official Base Ball Guide* (Cleveland: American League Publishing, 1906), preface.

6. *Sporting Life*, April 7, 1906, p. 12.

7. Stephen Constantelos, "Bill Bradley," biography on the SABR BioProject website (http://bioproj.sabr.org).

8. *Sporting Life*, September 15, 1906, p. 1.

9. Myrtle's given name is often recorded as "Everturf" because writer Lee Allen interviewed Lajoie for *The Sporting News* in 1953 and wrote it that way. It appears that Allen either misunderstood Lajoie or made a mistake in transcribing his notes, somehow turning "Ivy Smith" into "Everturf."

10. *Sporting Life*, October 20, 1906, p. 17.

11. Ibid.

12. A fine analysis of Cleveland's failure to win the flag in 1906 can be found in an article by Rod Caborn and Dave Larson, "1906 Cleveland Naps: Deadball Era Underachiever," *Baseball Research Journal*, Spring 2012, pp. 78–85.

13. *Sporting Life*, July 21, 1906, p. 9.

14. *Sporting Life*, November 24, 1906, p. 4.

Chapter 16

1. Lee Allen, *The American League Story* (New York: Hill and Wang, 1962), p. 13.

2. Jack Coombs, *Spokane Spokesman-Review*, October 2, 1910.

3. *Detroit Free Press*, June 25, 2002.

4. Franklin Lewis, *The Cleveland Indians* (New York: G. P. Putnam's Sons, 1949), p. 52.

5. *Sporting Life*, February 9, 1907, p. 3.

6. *Sporting Life*, May 11, 1907, p. 11.

7. Angelo Louisa, "Elmer Flick," biography on the SABR BioProject website (http://bioproj.sabr.org). The quote appeared in the July 22, 1907, issue of the *Cleveland Press*.

8. F. C. Lane, "George Stovall the Hero of 1911," *Baseball Magazine*, September 1912, p. 64.

9. *The Sporting News*, November 11, 1953, p. 11.

10. *The Sporting News*, November 11, 1953, p. 11.

11. *Sporting Life*, August 10, 1907, p. 7. The article is subtitled "Manager Lajoie Shining as Disciplinarian."

12. *Pittsburgh Press*, August 6, 1907.

13. *Cleveland Plain Dealer*, February 8, 1959.

14. Steve Constantelos, "George Stovall," biography on the SABR BioProject website (http://bioproj.sabr.org).

15. Lewis, p. 65.

16. *Cleveland Plain Dealer*, January 6, 1942, p. 17.

17. Tom Meany, *Baseball's Greatest Hitters* (New York: A. S. Barnes, 1950), p. 115.

18. *Sporting Life*, August 24, 1907, p. 11.

19. *Sporting Life*, September 21, 1907, p. 13.

20. *Sporting Life*, September 28, 1907, p. 11.

21. *Washington Times*, September 14, 1907, p. 8.

Chapter 17

1. *Sporting Life*, October 3, 1908, p. 1.
2. Lawrence Ritter, *The Glory of Their Times, enlarged edition* (New York: William Morrow, 1984), p. 56.
3. *Sporting Life*, April 4, 1908, p. 7.
4. *Cleveland Plain Dealer*, January 3, 1942, p. 16.
5. Ibid.
6. Russell Schneider, *The Cleveland Indians Encyclopedia, 3rd edition* (Champaign, IL: Sports Publishing, 2004), p. 175.
7. Angelo Louisa, "Elmer Flick," biography on the SABR BioProject website (http://bioproj.sabr.org). This quote appeared in the July 22, 1907, issue of the *Cleveland Press*.
8. John Phillips, *Bill Hinchman's Boner and the 1908 Naps* (Cabin John, MD: Capital, 1991), August 26 entry.
9. *Sporting Life*, October 3, 1908, p. 1.
10. Hugh Daily (1883) and Cy Young (1897) had thrown no-hitters for Cleveland in the National League.
11. Alex Semchuck, "Addie Joss," biography on the SABR BioProject website (http://bioproj.sabr.org).
12. *Cleveland Plain Dealer*, October 3, 1908.
13. Ibid.
14. *Pittsburgh Press*, January 10, 1945. The article was written by Ed Walsh and Francis J. Powers, and also appeared in the March 1945 issue of *Baseball Digest*.
15. Ibid.
16. *The Sporting News*, November 11, 1953, p. 11.
17. *Sporting Life*, October 17, 1908, p. 2.

Chapter 18

1. *Baseball Magazine*, June 1925, p. 291.
2. *Sporting Life*, April 10, 1909, p. 3.
3. Tom Meany, *Baseball's Greatest Hitters* (New York: A. S. Barnes, 1950), pp. 114–115.
4. *Sporting Life*, May 15, 1909, p. 20.
5. *Sporting Life*, May 22, 1909, p. 3.
6. *Sporting Life*, July 24, 1909, p. 5.
7. *Cleveland Plain Dealer*, July 18, 2009. This article was written by Kathia Miller, the grand-niece of Neal Ball, and appeared on the 100th anniversary of the famous play.
8. Franklin Lewis, *The Cleveland Indians* (New York: G. P. Putnam's Sons, 1949), p. 64.
9. *Cleveland Press*, August 18, 1909.
10. *Cleveland Press*, August 18, 1909.
11. *The Sporting News*, November 11, 1953, p. 11.
12. *Cleveland Press*, August 22, 1909.
13. *Cleveland Press*, August 22, 1909.
14. *Cleveland Plain Dealer*, January 3, 1942, p. 16.
15. Pete Rose, the last major league playing manager as of the end of the 2012 season, did not win a pennant either, and compiled a winning percentage of .518 in six seasons at the helm of the Cincinnati Reds.
16. *Cleveland Press*, September 1, 1909.

Chapter 19

1. F. C. Lane, "George Stovall the Hero of 1911," *Baseball Magazine*, September 1912, pp. 58–59.
2. *Sporting Life*, February 12, 1910, p. 6.
3. *Sporting Life*, April 30, 1910, p. 9.
4. *Sporting Life*, June 25, 1910, p. 7.
5. L. Jon Wertheim, "The Amazing Race," *Sports Illustrated*, September 20, 2010.
6. David Southwick, "Cy Young," biography on the SABR BioProject website (http://bioproj.sabr.org).
7. Norman Macht, *Connie Mack and the Early Years of Baseball* (Lincoln: University of Nebraska Press, 2007), p. 453.
8. Lawrence Ritter, *The Glory of Their Times, enlarged edition* (New York: William Morrow, 1984), pp. 32–33.
9. *Cleveland Plain Dealer*, October 9, 1910.
10. *Chicago Tribune*, October 13, 1910.
11. *Cleveland Plain Dealer*, October 10, 1910.
12. Ibid.
13. *Washington Post*, October 11, 1910.
14. *Washington Post*, October 12, 1910
15. *Cleveland Plain Dealer*, October 11, 1910.
16. Wertheim.
17. *Washington Post*, October 11, 1910.
18. *The New York Times*, October 16, 1910.
19. Paul MacFarlane, "Lajoie Beats Out Cobb," *The Sporting News*, April 18, 1981, pp. 10–11.
20. *Chicago Tribune*, October 16, 1910.
21. Ibid.
22. David Jones and Stephen Constantelos, "Nap Lajoie," biography on the SABR BioProject website (http://bioproj.sabr.org).
23. *The Sporting News*, November 11, 1953, p. 11.
24. MacFarlane, pp. 10–11.

Chapter 20

1. *The Sporting News*, August 23, 1950, p. 13.
2. *Sporting Life*, April 30, 1898, p. 6.
3. *Sporting Life*, May 20, 1905, p. 17.
4. *The Sporting News*, November 4, 1953, p. 14. Further statistical corrections leave Lajoie's 1901 totals at 232 hits, 544 at bats, and a .426 average, according to the Retrosheet and Baseball Reference websites.
5. *Sporting Life*, April 15, 1911, p. 11.
6. Scott Longert, *Addie Joss: King of the Pitchers* (Cleveland: Society for American Baseball Research, 1998), p. 113.
7. *Cleveland Plain Dealer*, April 14, 1911.
8. David Jones, ed. *Deadball Stars of the American League* (Dulles, VA: Potomac Books, 2006), p. 663. The chapter on George Stovall was written by Steve Constantelos.
9. Jones, p. 663.
10. *Sporting Life*, January 6, 1912, p. 3.
11. Jones, p. 663.

Chapter 21

1. "Cleveland Notes: Pennant Prospects in the Forest City," *Baseball Magazine*, March 1912, p. 98.
2. *Sporting Life*, January 6, 1912, p. 3.
3. *Cleveland Plain Dealer*, March 3, 1912.
4. *The Sporting News*, March 21, 1912, p. 7.
5. *The Sporting News*, March 28, 1912, p. 4.
6. *The Sporting News*, March 7, 1912, p. 2.

7. *Cleveland Plain Dealer*, March 20, 1912.

8. Brian Stevens, "Ivy Olson," biography on the SABR BioProject website (http://bioproj.sabr.org).

9. *Cleveland News*, April 4, 1912.

10. *The Sporting News*, November 11, 1953, p. 11.

11. *Cleveland Plain Dealer*, July 16, 1912.

12. *Ogden City* (Utah) *Evening Standard*, June 8, 1912, p. 2.

13. *Spokane* (Washington) *Spokesman-Review*, December 14, 1913, p. 3.

Chapter 22

1. "Failure as a Factor in the National Game," *Baseball Magazine*, August 1913, p. 102.

2. *El Paso Herald*, March 9, 1913.

3. *Washington Times*, April 21, 1913, p. 11.

4. *Sporting Life*, January 25, 1913, p. 13.

5. *Sporting Life*, January 25, 1913, p. 11.

6. *San Francisco Call*, February 23, 1913, p. 75.

7. *The Sporting News*, April 24, 1913, p. 3.

8. *Sporting Life*, May 17, 1913, p. 6.

9. *Sporting Life*, June 21, 1913, p. 5.

10. *Milwaukee Journal*, June 25, 1913.

11. *Sporting Life*, July 5, 1913, p. 6.

12. *Cleveland Plain Dealer*, June 28, 1913.

13. *Cleveland Plain Dealer*, June 28, 1913.

14. *Washington Times*, June 29, 1913.

15. *The Sporting News*, July 3, 1913, p. 3.

16. *Washington Times*, June 30, 1913.

17. *Cleveland Plain Dealer*, June 28, 1913.

18. Norman Macht, *Connie Mack and the Early Years of Baseball* (Lincoln: University of Nebraska Press, 2007), p. 582.

19. *Pittsburgh Press*, October 1, 1913.

Chapter 23

1. F. C. Lane, *Batting* (New York: Baseball Magazine Company, 1925), p. 190.

2. Lawrence Ritter, *The Glory of Their Times, Enlarged Edition* (New York: William Morrow, 1984), p. 85.

3. *Sporting Life*, December 13, 1913, p. 9.

4. *Sporting Life*, January 24, 1914, p. 14.

5. *Cleveland Plain Dealer*, March 24, 1914.

6. Bobby Wallace of the Browns, Harry Davis of the Athletics, and Clark Griffith of the Senators were all older than Lajoie and still active in 1914, but none were regulars.

7. *Cleveland Plain Dealer*, June 2, 1914.

8. *Sporting Life*, July 18, 1914, p. 10.

9. *The Sporting News*, July 26, 1914.

10. *Washington Herald*, August 16, 1914, p. 33.

11. *Sporting Life*, October 3, 1914, p. 14.

Chapter 24

1. *Sporting Life*, July 10, 1915, p. 6.

2. Norman Macht, *Connie Mack: The Turbulent and Triumphant Years, 1915–1931* (Lincoln: University of Nebraska Press, 2012), p. 10.

3. *Cleveland Plain Dealer*, January 17, 1915.

4. *Meriden* (Connecticut) *Daily Journal*, January 12, 1915.

5. Norman Macht, *Connie Mack and the Early Years of Baseball* (Lincoln: University of Nebraska Press, 2007), p. 649.

6. Pennock missed out on becoming the first pitcher to throw a no-hitter on Opening Day. That honor went to Bob Feller, who performed the feat in 1940.

7. *The Sporting News*, November 11, 1953, p. 11.

8. F. C. Lane, "The Inside Facts of the Great Lajoie Deal," *Baseball Magazine*, June 1915, pp. 58–59.

9. Lane, p. 59.

10. *Pittsburgh Press*, May 28, 1914, p. 36.

11. *Sporting Life*, May 22, 1915, p. 9.

12. *Sporting Life*, September 2, 1916, p. 3.

13. Macht, p. 59.

14. Charles Einstein, *The Second Fireside Book of Baseball* (New York: Simon & Schuster, 1958), pp. 274–275. This story was included in an article titled "The Worst Team of All: The 1916 A's," by Jack Orr.

15. *The Sporting News*, November 11, 1953, p. 12.

16. Ibid.

17. Macht, p. 10.

18. Another future Hall of Famer, Joe Tinker, also played his final major league game in 1916, while Eddie Plank, Sam Crawford, and Honus Wagner, all of whom made it to Cooperstown, played their last in 1917.

Chapter 25

1. *Reach Official American League Base Ball Guide 1919* (Philadelphia: A. J. Reach, 1919), p. 265.

2. *Sporting Life*, February 24, 1917, p. 8.

3. *Sporting Life*, February 10, 1917, p. 8.

4. J. M. Murphy, "Napoleon Lajoie: Modern Baseball's First Superstar," *The National Pastime*, Spring 1988, p. 59.

5. Warhop is best remembered today as the pitcher who gave up Babe Ruth's first major league home run in 1915.

6. *The Sporting News*, August 2, 1917, p. 7.

7. *Providence Tribune*, September 16, 1917, p. 15.

8. *The Sporting News*, August 30, 1917, p. 7.

9. Murphy, p. 62.

10. *Toronto Star*, September 17, 1917.

11. *The Sporting News*, September 20, 1917, p. 2.

12. *Washington Times*, September 23, 1917.

Chapter 26

1. Tom Meany, *Baseball's Greatest Hitters* (New York: A. S. Barnes, 1950), p. 111.

2. *Ogden Standard*, January 29, 1918, p. 6.

3. *New York Tribune*, March 28, 1918.

4. *The Sporting News*, April 18, 1918, p. 3.

5. J. M. Murphy, "Napoleon Lajoie: Modern Baseball's First Superstar," *The National Pastime*, Spring 1988, p. 64.

6. Murphy, p. 64.

7. *The New York Times*, July 20, 1918.

8. An image of Lajoie's draft registration card can be found on the Ancestry.com (http://www.ancestry.com) website. Though he had always given 1875 as his year of birth, the card shows his correct birth date of September 5, 1874.

9. *Philadelphia Evening Public Ledger*, December 28, 1918, p. 6.

Chapter 27

1. *Ellensburg* (Washington) *Daily Record*, June 27, 1921, p. 7.

2. *The New York Times*, February 8, 1959.

3. *The Sporting News*, February 29, 1940, p. 2.

4. Associated Press, January 27, 1937.

5. Ibid.

6. Napoleon Lajoie page, Baseball Hall of Fame website (http://baseballhall.org).

7. Ken Smith, *Baseball's Hall of Fame* (New York: Grosset and Dunlap, 1970), p. 20.

8. Ibid.

9. Dennis Corcoran, *Induction Day at Cooperstown: A History of the Baseball Hall of Fame Ceremony* (Jefferson, NC: McFarland, 2011), p. 38.

10. *Chicago Tribune*, April 18, 1949.

11. *The Sporting News*, February 29, 1940, p. 2.

12. *The Sporting News*, September 24, 1942, p. 8.

13. J. M. Murphy, "Napoleon Lajoie: Modern Baseball's First Superstar," *The National Pastime*, Spring 1988, p. 70.

14. Murphy, p. 68.

15. *Sarasota Herald Tribune*, May 11, 1958, p. 78.

16. Murphy, p. 70.

17. This quote was taken from an interview by Joe Kuras with Lionel Lajoie, the ballplayer's nephew, posted on the website of the Buffalo Head Society (http://webpages.charter.net/joekuras/blckstne.htm).

Bibliography

Books

Allen, Lee. *The American League Story*. New York: Hill and Wang, 1962.

_____. *The National League Story*. New York: Hill and Wang, 1961.

Appel, Marty, and Burt Goldblatt. *Baseball's Best: The Hall of Fame Gallery*. New York: McGraw-Hill, 1980.

Axelson, G. W. *Commy: The Life Story of Charles A. Comiskey*. Chicago: Reilly and Lee, 1919.

Casway, Jerrold. *Ed Delahanty in the Emerald Age of Baseball*. Notre Dame, IN: University of Notre Dame Press, 2004.

Corcoran, Dennis. *Induction Day at Cooperstown: A History of the Baseball Hall of Fame Ceremony*. Jefferson, NC: McFarland, 2011.

Daley, Arthur. *Times at Bat: A Half Century of Baseball*. New York: Random House, 1950.

Danzig, Allison, and Joe Reichler. *The History of Baseball*. Englewood Cliffs, NJ: Prentice-Hall, 1959.

Einstein, Charles. *The Second Fireside Book of Baseball*. New York: Simon & Schuster, 1958.

Faber, Charles F. *Baseball Ratings: The All-Time Best Players at Each Position*. Jefferson, NC: McFarland, 1985. (A third edition was published in 2008.)

Grayson, Harry. *They Played the Game*. New York: A. S. Barnes, 1944.

Ivor-Campbell, Frederick, and Robert L. Tiemann, eds. *Baseball's First Stars*. Cleveland: Society for American Baseball Research, 1996.

James, Bill. *The Bill James Historical Baseball Abstract*. New York: Villard Books, 1986.

_____. *The New Bill James Historical Baseball Abstract*. New York: Free Press, 2001.

Jones, David, ed. *Deadball Stars of the American League*. Dulles, VA: Potomac Books, 2006.

Kaese, Harold. *The Boston Braves*. New York: G. P. Putnam's Sons, 1948.

Lajoie, Napoleon, and M. A. Bobrick, eds. *Napoleon Lajoie's Official Base Ball Guide*. Cleveland: American League, 1906.

Lane, F. C. *Batting*. New York: Baseball Magazine Company, 1925.

Lewis, Franklin. *The Cleveland Indians*, reprint edition. Kent, OH: Kent State University Press, 2006. Original edition published in 1949 by G. P. Putnam's Sons, New York.

Lieb, Fred, and Stan Baumgartner. *The Philadelphia Phillies*. New York: G. P. Putnam's Sons, 1948.

Light, Jonathan Taylor. *The Cultural Encyclopedia of Baseball*, 2nd edition. Jefferson, NC: McFarland, 2005.

Longert, Scott. *Addie Joss: King of the Pitchers*. Cleveland: Society for American Baseball Research, 1998.

Macht, Norman. *Connie Mack and the Early Years of Baseball*. Lincoln: University of Nebraska Press, 2007.

_____. *Connie Mack: The Turbulent and Triumphant Years, 1915–1931*. Lincoln: University of Nebraska Press, 2012.

Meany, Tom. *Baseball's Greatest Hitters*. New York: A. S. Barnes, 1950.

Murnane, Tim. *How to Play Base Ball*. New York: American Sports, 1905.

Nemec, David. *The Great Encyclopedia of 19th-Century Major League Baseball*. New York: Donald I. Fine Books, 1997.

Nemec, David, ed. *Major League Baseball Profiles 1871–1900*, volumes 1 and 2. Lincoln: University of Nebraska Press, 2011.

Phillips, John. *Bill Hinchman's Boner and the 1908 Naps*. Cabin John, MD: Capital, 1990.

_____. *Chief Sockalexis and the 1897 Cleveland Indians*. Cabin John, MD: Capital, 1991.

_____. *The 1898 Cleveland Spiders*. Cabin John, MD: Capital, 1997.

_____. *The 1903 Naps*. Cabin John, MD: Capital, 1989.

_____. *The '99 Spiders*. Cabin John, MD: Capital, 1988.

_____. *When Lajoie Came to Town: The Story of the Cleveland Blues of 1902*. Cabin John, MD: Capital, 1988.

Reach Official American League Base Ball Guide 1919. Philadelphia: A. J. Reach, 1919.

Rice, Grantland. *The Tumult and the Shouting*. New York: Barnes, 1954.

Ritter, Lawrence. *The Glory of Their Times*, enlarged edition. New York: William Morrow, 1984.

Schneider, Russell. *The Cleveland Indians Encyclopedia*, 3rd edition. Champaign, IL: Sports Publishing, 2004.

Smith, Ken. *Baseball's Hall of Fame*. New York: Grosset and Dunlap, 1970.

Smith, Robert. *Baseball*. New York: Simon & Schuster, 1947.

Spink, Alfred H. *The National Game: A History of Baseball, America's Leading Out-Door Sport*. St. Louis: The National Game, 1910.

Thorn, John, and Pete Palmer, eds. *Total Baseball: The Official Encyclopedia of Major League Baseball*, 2nd edition. New York: Warner Books, 1991.

Wilbert, Warren. *The Arrival of the American League*. Jefferson, NC: McFarland, 2011.

Newspapers

Boston Globe
Brooklyn Eagle
Chicago Tribune
Cincinnati Enquirer
Cleveland Leader
Cleveland News
Cleveland Plain Dealer
Cleveland Press
Los Angeles Times
New York Evening World

The New York Times
Philadelphia North American
Philadelphia Press
Philadelphia Public Ledger
Philadelphia Record
Philadelphia Inquirer
Pittsburgh Press
Providence Tribune
Reading Eagle
Richmond (Virginia) *Times*

St. Louis Globe-Democrat
St. Louis Republic
Salt Lake Tribune
Toledo Blade
Toronto Star
Toronto World
Washington Post
Washington Times
Youngstown Vindicator

Magazines

Baseball Digest
Baseball Magazine
Baseball Research Journal
The National Pastime
Sporting Life
The Sporting News
Sports Illustrated

Internet

Baseball Almanac (http://www.baseball-almanac.com)
Baseball Page (http://www.thebaseballpage.com)
Baseball Prospectus (http://www.baseballprospectus.com)
Baseball Reference (http://www.baseball-reference.com)
Major League Baseball (http://www.mlb.com)
National Baseball Hall of Fame and Museum (http://baseballhall.org)
Retrosheet (http://www.retrosheet.org)
SABR (Society of American Baseball Research) BioProject (http://bioproj.sabr.org)
Yahoo Sports (http://sports.yahoo.com)

Index

269